DISRUPTING THE SCHOOL-TO-PRISON PIPELINE

DISRUPTING THE SCHOOL-TO-PRISON PIPELINE

EDITED BY

SOFÍA BAHENA
NORTH COOC
RACHEL CURRIE-RUBIN
PAUL KUTTNER
MONICA NG

HARVARD EDUCATIONAL REVIEW
CAMBRIDGE, MASSACHUSETTS

Library of Congress Control Number 2012941014

Paperback ISBN 978-0-916690-54-0
Library Edition ISBN 978-0-916690-55-7

Published by Harvard Educational Review,
an imprint of the Harvard Education Publishing Group

Harvard Educational Review
8 Story Street
Cambridge, MA 02138

Cover Design: Joel Gendron
Cover Photo: Hal Bergman Photography/Flickr/Getty Images

The typefaces used in this book are New Baskerville for text and
Futura Condensed for display.

CONTENTS

ACKNOWLEDGMENTS

The editors acknowledge those individuals who have been instrumental in working with some of the authors in this volume in order to bring their words to our pages: Douglas W. Price, Gordon Bernell Charter School; Gillian Knapp and Andrew Nurkin, Princeton University; Tom Bolema, Literacy Program, San Quentin; Anisa Onofre, Writers in Communities.

The editors also acknowledge the members of our Editorial Advisory Committee, all former HER editors, for their invaluable role in reviewing anonymized versions of submitted essays: Candice Bocala, Gretchen Brion-Meisels, Kristy Cooper, Raygine DiAquoi, Christina Dobbs, Chantal Francois, Liliana Garces, Julia Hayden, Jay Huguley, Irene Liefshitz, Rebecca Miller, Soojin Oh, Carla Shalaby, and Mara Tieken.

INTRODUCTION

DISRUPTING THE SCHOOL-TO-PRISON PIPELINE

■

THE EDITORS

In the United States, the public education and penal systems have long been related. Both developed, in part, as ways of controlling and disciplining populations, drawing on similar institutional models (Noguera, 1995). And both have progressive, reformist roots as well—efforts towards empowerment and rehabilitation rather than control and punishment (Hayes, 2006; Sullivan, 1990). But in the United States during the last few decades, this relationship has taken on new and disturbing forms. For young people across the country— particularly youth of color, low-income youth, and students with disabilities— the lines between the education system and the justice system are becoming increasingly blurred. The practices and discourses of the justice system have made their way into many schools, leading to the criminalization of behaviors previously dealt with through school discipline (Kupchik, 2010; Nolan, 2011). Meanwhile, as funding for prisons far outpaces funding for education, and as neoliberal economic policies lead to increasing inequality, students poorly served or pushed out of schools are less likely to find work and more likely to find themselves caught in the justice system (Meiners, 2011).

A new term has emerged to describe this "disturbing national trend" whereby "children are funneled out of public schools and into the juvenile and criminal justice systems": the *school-to-prison pipeline* (American Civil Liberties Union, n.d., para. 1).[1] The term, and the complex phenomenon it describes, has increasingly appeared in the education reform discourse over the past few years as academics, educators, parents, students, advocates, and organizers across the country have responded to this shocking trend.

In reality, the school-to-prison pipeline is an amalgamation of a number of different trends—from the overrepresentation of students of color in special education to the rise of zero tolerance school discipline policies; from an increased fear related to school safety to perverse incentives from test-based accountability systems to push out low-performing students. The pipeline functions on multiple levels, from one-on-one interactions between students and police officers, to policies that drain resources from schools, to societal discourses of racial inferiority and punishment. But the pipeline metaphor offers

1

a powerful lens through which one can see the interconnections between these issues, too often treated as separate, and creates holistic solutions. And people are working on solutions from many angles—changing laws, creating alternative disciplinary processes, improving equity in schools, developing arts-based youth programming, increasing youth voice in education, and much more.

As editors of the *Harvard Educational Review* (*HER*), each of us has come to care deeply about this issue, whether through teaching in prisons and juvenile detention centers, working with special education students, or simply attempting to understand the everyday challenges of the public education system. When the opportunity arose to put together an edited volume, we agreed on the value and timeliness of a publication about the school-to-prison pipeline. It was important to us that it not be simply another description of the problems our schools face, but, rather, that it feature the work that educators, students, organizers, scholars, and many more are doing on the ground to disrupt, reverse, and redirect the pipeline. We also saw a need for a volume that brings together voices from multiple disciplines, from both practice and research, and from both inside and outside the justice system. After all, it will take collaboration across disciplines, fields, ages, and institutions in order to fully understand—and disrupt—this tragic phenomenon.

In this volume we gather together voices of established and emerging scholars as well as those of educators, students, and community activists. Some of the articles are reprinted from the pages of *HER*, included here because of their power and continued relevance. Others are new pieces that speak to topics on which *HER* has yet to publish. Alongside these authors we situate the voices of those most affected: youth and adults who have been incarcerated or whose lives have been shaped by the school-to-prison pipeline. Through stories, essays, and poems, these individuals share their insights into how our education and justice systems function and offer visions of what might be.

We begin, as is fitting, in our public school system. Part 1, "Discipline and Justice in Schools," opens with a classic article from Pedro A. Noguera in which he turns his critical eye toward the disciplinary response to school violence in the United States and the important roles that class and race play. Situating his discussion in a history of U.S. schools as institutions of social control, Noguera calls on us to move from controlling to humanizing educational environments. Next, in this reprinted *HER* gem, Peter Sipe brings the realities of the "prison-like schools" critiqued by Noguera to life through a thoughtful comparison between his first year as a middle school teacher and the experience of a first-year prison guard. Following this, Daniel J. Losen brings a civil rights law perspective to one of the central contentious issues in school discipline: out-of-school suspension. He lays out a case for racial and gender disparities in discipline as a form of "disparate impact" discrimination and offers a set of policy recommendations that can help in addressing these disparities. Finally, we get an in-depth look at restorative justice—a promising alternative disciplinary strategy that moves away from control and punishment toward healing and reconciliation—through an edited transcript of a roundtable discussion among students, educators, and a community activist practicing restorative justice in Boston schools. In this section Alejandro G. Vera offers a poem recounting his experience of being criminalized in school; Robert Wilson shares the struggles of supporting a son in school while incarcerated; Seth G. Cooper tells a story of his brother dealing with frequent suspensions and his own education in a detention center; and Elizabeth A. Reid shares how school can be a place of fear and of transformation.

Part 2, "Education in Detention," moves us outside of the regular public schools and into the alternative schools, juvenile detention centers, and prisons, where too many of our young people are sent. We start this section with an article by Joseph Cambone, who paints a portrait of the day-to-day challenges of teaching and learning in a school for young boys with emotional and behavioral problems who have been removed from traditional schools. In the midst of these struggles, Cambone offers a vision of teaching as "an act of love," while at the same time complicating the notion that the lives of these boys can be altered through an individual teacher's devotion alone. Following this, Joanne Karger, David H. Rose, and Kathleen B. Boundy outline serious deficits in the education offered to youth in juvenile corrections facilities, despite their right to quality education and the necessity of such education for any successful reintegration after detention. The authors offer Universal Design for Learning as a framework that could help to rethink and redesign formal education in these facilities. Next, Sabina E. Vaught shares a piece of her ethnographic research into a school inside one juvenile corrections facility. Combining critical race theory and psychoanalytic theory, she reconceptualizes the racism that infiltrates the school as *institutionalized racist melancholia*— an unresolved, structural form of grief. Last, in another classic *HER* article, Kathy Boudin, writing from prison, deftly analyzes the ways that education in prison can serve as a mechanism of control. But at the same time, as her own story of running creative writing workshops demonstrates, when done right it can be a form of liberation as well. Along the way, part 2 includes stories from Douglas W. Price, a teacher in a charter school located in a prison; Bobby Dean Evans Jr., who traces his road to prison starting with early exclusionary special education practices; Michael Satterfield, who found hope through educational opportunities while in detention and became a teacher aide to share this hope with others; and Christopher Dankovich, who found himself becoming an educator and mentor for a younger inmate.

The third part, "Transforming the Pipeline," takes a step back to look at what it will take to transform the school-to-prison pipeline in a broad-based way. First, Kavitha Mediratta looks behind recent developments at the national level to address discipline and the pipeline, showing how this change has been driven by a growing grassroots movement for reform, led in large part by students and their parents seeking to transform practices at the local and state level. She argues that if we hope to disrupt the pipeline, our energy

3

must go to supporting, researching, and raising awareness about the work of these youth and adult organizers to change zero tolerance discipline. Next, Jane Hereth, Mariame Kaba, Erica R. Meiners, and Lewis Wallace draw on their experiences as restorative justice practitioners and researchers in Chicago to begin to assess the potential and the challenges of implementing these practices across a school district. They argue that to truly engage with the pipeline—and the broader prison-industrial complex of which it is a part—we need to move from restorative to *transformative justice*, a practice that also includes addressing larger systems of control in our society. The section also offers a short piece by Starcia Ague, recounting her own fight for education while incarcerated as a youth, and a final poem by Derek R. Russel, offering an image of love, hope, and freedom.

Because one book could never cover all aspects of the school-to-prison pipeline, we end with an epilogue of sorts: Paul Kuttner's review of five books on the topic published in the last couple of years. This review draws out lessons learned and delineates the multiple faces of the pipeline and the multiple avenues for effecting change.

NOTE

1. Other related terms include the *schools-to-prisons pipeline* (Hartnett, 2011) and the *schoolhouse to jailhouse track* (Advancement Project, 2005).

REFERENCES

Advancement Project. (2005). *Education on lockdown: The schoolhouse to jailhouse track*. Washington, DC: Author.

American Civil Liberties Union. (n.d.). School-to-prison pipeline. Retrieved from https://www.aclu.org/racial-justice/school-prison-pipeline

Hartnett, S. J. (2011). *Challenging the prison-industrial complex: Activism, arts, and educational alternatives*. Urbana: University of Illinois Press.

Hayes, W. (2006). *The progressive education movement: Is it still a factor in today's schools?* Lanham, MD: Rowman & Littlefield.

Kupchik, A. (2010). *Homeroom security: School discipline in an age of fear*. New York: New York University Press.

Meiners, E. R. (2011). Building an abolition democracy; or, The fight against public fear, private benefits, and prison expansion. In S. J. Hartnett, *Challenging the prison-industrial complex: Activism, arts, and educational alternatives*. Urbana: University of Illinois Press.

Noguera, P. A. (1995). Preventing and producing violence: A critical analysis of responses to school violence. *Harvard Educational Review, 65*(2), 189–212.

Nolan, K. (2011). *Police in the hallways: Discipline in an urban high school*. Minneapolis: University of Minnesota Press.

Sullivan, L. E. (1990). *The prison reform movement: Forlorn hope*. Boston: Twayne.

The editors thank Laura Clos for her steadfast support of this book and the ongoing work of the *Harvard Educational Review*. We would not have been able to produce this volume without her.

PART I

■

DISCIPLINE AND JUSTICE IN SCHOOLS

PREVENTING AND PRODUCING VIOLENCE

A CRITICAL ANALYSIS OF RESPONSES TO SCHOOL VIOLENCE

■

PEDRO A. NOGUERA

Do the strategies that schools adopt in response to "disciplinary problems," including vio-lence, actually perpetuate violence? In this thoughtful article, Pedro Noguera traces the history of institutional disciplinary measures, showing that the underlying philosophi-cal orientation toward social control exacts a heavy toll on students, teachers, and the entire school community by producing prison-like schools that remain unsafe. Noguera maintains that a "get-tough" approach fails to create a safe environment because the use of coercive strategies interrupts learning and ultimately produces an environment of mistrust and resistance. He offers alternative strategies for humanizing school environ-ments, encouraging a sense of community and collective responsibility.

The problem of violence in schools, which is part of the overall problem of violence in society, has become one of the most pressing educational issues in the United States. In many school districts, concerns about violence have even surpassed academic achievement—traditionally the most persistent theme on the nation's education agenda—as the highest priority for reform and inter-vention.[1] Public clamorings over the need to do something about violence in schools has brought the issue to a critical juncture; if schools fail to respond decisively to this problem, popular support for public education may be endangered. The escalation of violent incidents and the apparent inadequacy of traditional methods to curtail them has led to a search for new strategies to ensure the safety and security of children and teachers in schools.[2]

Accepting the fact that it may not be realistic to expect that schools can ever be completely immune from the violence that plagues our society, this article seeks to understand why schools may be especially vulnerable to its occurrence. Current efforts aimed at combating violence may, in fact, have the opposite effect, particularly given the weakening of the moral authority schools once enjoyed. Following a brief critique of popular strategies used to curtail school violence, my analysis begins by examining how the early preoccupation with social control influenced the design and operation of schools at the turn of the century. From there I consider the practical and symbolic effects of the ways in which discipline is typically exercised in school, and analyze the race and class dynamics among the population that is most frequently targeted for punishment. Finally, I discuss alternative approaches to addressing the problem of violence and strategies that have been shown to be effective alternative routes to school safety.

The search for solutions to the problem of violence in schools has generated a package of remedies that closely resembles those used to combat the threat of violence and crime in U. S. society.[3] Some of the more popular measures include: the installation of metal detectors at school entrances to prevent students from bringing weapons onto school grounds;[4] the enactment of "zero tolerance" policies that guarantee the automatic removal of students (through either suspension, expulsion, or transfer) who perpetrate acts of violence;[5] and the use of police officers and security guards to patrol and monitor student behavior while school is in session. Accompanying such measures has been an increased tendency of school officials to treat violent incidents (and sometimes nonviolent incidents) involving students as criminal offenses to be handled by law enforcement officials and the courts, rather than by school personnel. In their desire to demonstrate toughness and reassure the public that they are in control, school officials have become increasingly rigid and inflexible when meting out punishment upon students who violate school rules, even when the infractions are not of a violent nature.[6]

Other, less punitive approaches have been introduced to reduce the incidence of violence in schools. Conflict resolution programs have been promoted as a way of teaching children to settle disputes nonviolently. Mentoring programs that pair students with adult role models have also become popular in school districts across the country, serving to reduce violence by providing students perceived to be at risk with the attention, support, and counseling of an adult.[7] Teachers have been encouraged to design curricula that teach children how to avoid violent situations and to explore in their classrooms the ethical and moral issues related to violent behavior.[8] Finally, a variety of counseling programs have been implemented by establishing partnerships between schools and social service agencies to provide direct services to students.[9]

Though some of these less coercive strategies for reducing violence have proven relatively successful in particular schools, the overall momentum of school policy has been biased in favor of the "get-tough" approach. In response to the pervasive fear of violence among parents and students, politicians and school officials have pledged to quell the tide of violence by converting schools into prison-like, "lock-down" facilities, and by increasing the penalties incurred for committing violent acts. Yet despite the tough talk, the track record of these methods provides little reason for optimism. For example, in California, law enforcement officials have attempted to reduce gang activity by increasing penalties against juvenile felons who are alleged to be gang members. While such measures have contributed to a sharp increase in the prison population, there has been no reduction in gang activity in targeted communities. Additionally, gang activity has become such a major problem in the state's prisons that gang affiliation must now be considered when convicts are being assigned to correctional facilities.[10]

Relatively speaking, young people may in fact be far safer in school than they are in their neighborhoods or, for that matter, at the park, the roller rink, or even in their homes.[11] For many parents and students, the fact that schools are "relatively safe" provides little solace, given the expectation that schools should be absolutely safe and therefore should not be judged by the same standard that we use to gauge security in other public, or even private, places. Schools are controlled institutions, public spaces where individuals sacrifice a measure of individual liberty in exchange for the opportunity to learn. In such a setting, the threat of violence constitutes more than just a threat to personal safety. It represents a fundamental violation of the social contract between school and community, an abrogation that could easily hasten the collapse of popular support for public education.[12]

To address the problem of violence in schools effectively, I believe we must begin by asking ourselves why schools are vulnerable to the occurrence of violence. What is there about the *structure* and *culture* of schools that has, in recent times, increased the likelihood that acts of violence will be perpetrated within them? In the following pages I will demonstrate why I believe that many of the popular strategies for disciplining students and curtailing violence in schools are ineffective. I will focus on urban schools, where violence tends to occur more frequently, because I believe that social and economic conditions in urban areas add considerably to the extent and degree of the problem.[13] I believe that it is in the context of fulfilling goals that have traditionally prioritized maintaining order and control over students, as opposed to creating humane environments for learning, that schools have become increasingly susceptible to violence. As an alternative approach, I will argue that schools must seek ways to create more humane learning environments, both to counter escalating violence and to transform social relationships within schools, so that those who spend their time there feel less alienated, threatened, and repressed. As I argue for this alternative, I will also consider the ways in which issues related to the symbolic representation of violence, and the fight against it, influence interaction between adults and children within school, paying particular attention to the ways in which race and class inscribe these images.

This article draws heavily from my years of working directly with schools in the San Francisco Bay Area in a variety of capacities: as a classroom teacher, a school board member, a university-based researcher, and a consultant. My experience leads me to avoid offering specific remedies or to claim that I know what should be done to address a problem that is so complex and multidimensional. Still, it is my hope that suggesting new ways of approaching the question "What is to be done about violence in schools?" will enable educators to open the door to new strategies, based on a different conceptual framework, for dealing with the issue of violence in schools throughout this country.

WAGING THE FIGHT AGAINST VIOLENCE

The phrase "fighting violence" might seem to be an oxymoron. For those concerned with finding ways to prevent or reduce the occurrence of violence, "fighting" it might seem to be the wrong way to describe or to engage in the effort to address the problem. The choice of terms, however, is not accidental. The prevailing wisdom among policymakers and school officials is that you must counter violence with force;[14] that schools can be made safe by converting them into prison-like facilities;[15] and that the best way to curtail violence is to identify, apprehend, and exclude students who have the potential for committing acts of violence from the rest of the population.[16] Therefore, it is important to examine the ideological stance held toward violence when critiquing the methods used to fight it, for without doing so it is not possible to understand why failed strategies remain popular.[17]

In the campaign against school violence, school officials often point to statistics on the number of weapons confiscated, and to the number of students suspended, expelled, or arrested for violent reasons as evidence that something is being done about the problem. The number of reported violent incidents is also used to demonstrate that while valiant efforts are being made to reduce violence, the problem persists, and therefore the fight against violence must continue.[18] The compilation of such data plays an important role in rationalizing the expenditure of resources on security-related services—resource allocations that often result in the elimination of other educational programs and services. Such data is also instrumental in framing the public discourse about violence, for as long as it can be shown that quantifiable results are obtained as a result of the fight against violence, combatants in the war can be assured of continued financial backing.[19]

For parents and students who live with the reality of violence and who must contend with the threat of physical harm on a daily basis, data on how many students have been arrested, expelled, or suspended does little to allay their fears. When engaging in once ordinary activities such as walking to school or playing in a park evokes such extreme anxiety so as to no longer seem feasible, news that arrests or suspensions have increased provides little reassurance.

In my capacity as a consultant to a local school district, I recently attended a meeting with school officials from an urban school district on the West Coast, at which we were discussing the problem of violence and what could be done about it. While reviewing data from the past year on the incidence of violence, I remarked sardonically, "Here's some good news; homicides are down 100 percent from last year." To my amazement, an administrator replied, "Yes, the news isn't all bad. Some of our efforts are beginning to pay off." What surprised me about the comment was his apparent belief that since there had been no murders at any of the schools in the district at the midpoint of the school year, compared to the two that occurred the previous academic year, there was reason for hope and optimism. I found it hard to believe that district administrators, who generally have little contact with school sites on a regular basis, could accept a statistical analysis as evidence that the schools had in fact become safer. And even if data on crime shows that homicides are down, statistics don't tell us whether or not teachers or students *feel* any safer.

Within the context of the fight against violence, symbols such as crime statistics take on great significance, although they have little bearing upon how people actually feel about the occurrence of violence.[20] Pressed to demonstrate to the public that the efforts to reduce violence are effective, school districts often pursue one of two strategies: either they present statistics quantifying the results of their efforts, or they go to great lengths to suppress information altogether, hoping that the community will perceive no news as good news.[21] Metal detectors, barbed wire fences, armed guards and policemen, and principals wielding baseball bats as they patrol the halls are all symbols of tough action. And while most students that I have spoken to during my visits to schools realize that a student who wants to bring a weapon to school can get it into a building without being discovered by a metal detector, or that it is highly unlikely that any principal will hit a student with a baseball bat, the symbols persist, masking the truth that those responsible for school safety really don't have a clue about what to do to stem the tide of violence. Rather than looking to solve this problem through increased security or improved technology, school administrators must begin to ask more fundamental questions as to why these institutions have become so vulnerable to violence. I believe that this is a question that must be answered in the context of the purpose and social function that schools have historically performed.

THE SCHOOL AS AN AGENT OF CONTROL

To understand why violence has become rampant and how a climate of fear and intimidation gradually came to be the norm in so many schools, we must examine the influences that guided the creation of public schools and consider the social role that they were expected to perform. When public schools were being developed in northeastern cities during the latter part of the nineteenth century, their architecture, organization, and operation was profoundly influenced by the prevailing conception of the asylum.[22] Whether designed to house the indigent, the insane, the sick, or the criminally inclined, the asylum served as the model for human service institutions. While the client base of the early prisons, almshouses, and mental hospitals differed, those who developed and administered the institutions shared a common preoccupation with the need to control those held in custody. The custodial function of the institution should not be confused with rehabilitating or reforming, for in post-colonial America, crime, immorality, hunger, and poverty were seen as inherent to society. David Rothman writes:

> Although eighteenth century Americans were apprehensive about deviant behavior and adopted elaborate procedures to control it, they did not interpret its presence as symptomatic of a basic flaw in community structure, nor did they expect to eliminate it.[23]

The role of the asylum was to regiment, control, and discipline the social outcasts who were housed there. These goals were accomplished through the routinization of every aspect of life within the asylum, and through the imposition of a set of rules and regulations that were rigidly enforced.[24] A military tone characterized life in the asylum, as did a focus upon sanitation, orderliness, punctuality, and discipline. Since the goal of these institutions was not to prepare the inmate for readmission to society but to eliminate the threat they posed to the safety and security of others, the managers of the institutions believed that this could best be done by enforcing rigid discipline and by removing undesirables indefinitely from the community.

Although schools were designed with a different purpose in mind, Rothman suggests that it was logical for the architects of the first large urban schools to turn to the asylum as the blueprint for these new public institutions.[25] Though schools were never envisioned as asylums for the young, the need for them to serve as a vehicle for controlling the minds and bodies of youth helped to convince many of those who questioned the merits of public education that it was an enterprise worth supporting.[26] Educational historian Lawrence Cremin identifies three dominant and distinct agendas among the many influences shaping public education at the turn of the century that were pursued in relation to the public schools: 1) the need to provide a custodial function for children and thereby serve as an agent of social control; 2) the need to acculturate and "Americanize" large numbers of children born of European immigrants; 3) the need to prepare future workers for U.S. industry. At times overlapping and at other times conflicting, these goals influenced the content of school curriculum, the training of teachers, and most importantly for the purposes of this analysis, the way in which the schools were to be administered.

Though the goals of education tended to be framed in humanitarian terms, the need to regiment and control the behavior of students dominated the educational mission.[27] Motivated by a combination of benevolence related to child welfare, and fear related to the perceived threat of crime and delinquency, schools were called upon to assume greater responsibility for the rearing of urban children. Defining the problem in moral terms, reformers felt that "raised amid intemperance, indulgence, and neglect, the lower class urban child began life predisposed to criminality and unprepared for honest work."[28] Educators such as G. Stanley Hall called for the creation of *pedocentric* schools, which were to be designed so that the school's central mission was to treat the social and psychological needs of children.[29] Though child-rearing was seen primarily as a responsibility of the family, social reformers feared that many poor and immigrant parents were unfit to raise their children properly.[30] For this reason, public schools were seen as the vehicle through which poor children could be "saved." Regarding this point, Cremin writes:

> It was to the school that progressives turned as the institution that would at least complement familial education and in many instances correct it and compensate for its shortcomings. The school would rear the children of ordinary families, it would provide refuge for the children of exploitative families, and it would acculturate the children of immigrant families. . . . The school would deliver whatever services children needed to develop into healthy, happy and well-instructed citizens—it would provide meals for the poorly fed, medical treatment for the unhealthy, and guidance for the emotionally disturbed. . . . Though progressives asserted the primacy of familial education, they advanced the pre-eminence of schooling.[31]

To carry out these social goals, reformers promoted efficiency in the organization and operation of schools. These reformers borrowed from the writings of Frederick Taylor, an engineer who championed the idea that industrial production could be made more efficient through the application of scientific techniques. His ideas were later applied to the operation of schools, where the need for order and efficiency were perceived as essential to effective management.[32] Supported enthusiastically by many of the businessmen who served on local school boards, efficiency and routinization of school activities were emphasized as ways to bring order to city schools. The combination of rising enrollments—due to the steady influx of immigrant and rural children into eastern cities—and inadequate facilities had gradually transformed urban schools into little more than warehouses for children. Cremin's descriptions of schools during this period is helpful in understanding why a focus on order might have seemed warranted:

> Whatever the high-minded philosophies that justified them, the schools of the 1890s were a depressing study in contrasts. . . . In the cities, problems of skyrocketing enrollments were compounded by a host of other issues . . . school buildings were badly lighted, poorly heated, unsanitary, and bursting at the seams; young immigrants from a dozen different countries swelled the tide of newly arriving farm children. Superintendents spoke hopefully of reducing class size to sixty per teacher, but the hope was most often a pious one. Little wonder that a desire for efficiency reigned supreme.[33]

Acting under mandates issued by authorities who were almost always far removed from the direct management of schools, superintendents and principals employed a variety of strategies to control the students and teachers in their charge. In many school districts, teachers and students were tested on a regular basis "to see if the program was being followed."[34] Specific instructions were given to teachers that addressed not only curriculum and methods, but ways to discipline and control the bodies of their students as well.[35]

Describing this preoccupation with disciplining the body, one observer wrote that students were required to comply with the following set of instructions when asked to recite memorized text: "Stand on the line, perfectly motionless, bodies erect, knees and feet together, the tips of shoes touching the edge of a board in the floor."[36]

To ensure that students were trained appropriately for the kinds of work they would perform after graduation, specialized high schools were created in several cities. Vocational high schools were set up to cater to lower-class immigrant youth, and academic high schools were established to prepare middle-class students for higher education and professional careers. At the vocational schools, the curriculum was designed to provide the skills and training needed to obtain industrial employment upon graduation. In this respect, David Tyack's comment that "urban education in the nineteenth century did more to industrialize humanity than to humanize industry" is helpful in understanding how the relationship between education and the economy influenced the character of schools.[37] Though many of the newly created urban secondary schools sought to provide vocational training, what the expanding industrial sector primarily required was an ample supply of low-skilled, cheap labor. Schools helped to meet this demand by emphasizing citizenship training for the children of newly arrived immigrants, and offering a curriculum that placed greater weight on punctuality and obedience than on the acquisition of technical skills.[38]

While students were sorted and educated differently to satisfy the needs of industry, educators still wanted them to undergo a common socialization process to prevent fragmentation and to insure that "American" values would remain dominant and undiluted. Fearing that the arrival of this "illiterate, docile mass" would "dilute tremendously our national stock, and corrupt our civic life," educators were called upon "to assimilate and amalgamate these people as part of our American race, and implant in their children, so far as can be done, the Anglo-Saxon conception of righteousness, law and order, and popular government."[39] An important part of the assimilation process included conforming to an assortment of rules governing student behavior and to values promoting the virtues of hard work, punctuality, and obedience.[40]

While there is some evidence that schools were challenged in their attempts to fulfill their role as the keepers of children, in most cases it seems they succeeded in producing "docile bodies"; students who could be "subjected, used, transformed, and improved."[41]

DISCIPLINE AS AN EXERCISE OF POWER

With concerns about order, efficiency, and control dominating the thinking that guided the early development of schools in the United States, we must ask ourselves how this legacy has influenced the current character of public schools. As the demographics of cities began to change in the 1950s and 1960s with the arrival of new immigrants (e.g., West Indians, Puerto Ricans, and other Latinos) and the migration of Blacks from the South,[42] and as social and economic conditions within urban areas began to deteriorate,[43] the character and condition of schools also began to change. However this shift did not produce immediate changes, for while the student population changed, in many cases the teachers remained the same, with most still relying on methods of control that had proven successful in the past.[44] Writing about the conditions of schools in what he described as "slum areas," James Conant spoke of the need to impose a harsher standard of discipline to insure that discipline and order prevailed:

> Many educators would doubtless be shocked by the practice of on-the-spot demotion of one full academic year, with no questions asked, for all participants in fights. In one junior high school I know of, a very able principal found so intolerable a situation that he established that very rule. As a consequence, there are fewer fights in his school among boys, many of whom at one time or another have been in trouble with the police. The school must attempt to bring some kind of order to their chaotic lives. . . . This formal atmosphere appears to work. School spirit has developed. . . . Children must stay in school till they are sixteen or till graduation to prevent unemployed, out-of-school youth from roaming the streets.[45]

By the mid 1960s, however, the situation had changed. Students' insubordination and aggression toward teachers was becoming increasingly common, and violence within schools, especially among students, was widely seen as the norm.[46] Some educators made the connection between the difficulty schools were having in maintaining control over students, to the political turmoil that accompanied the civil rights movement, and the riots that took place in many cities across the country.[47] Describing the political dimension of this problem and advising teachers about how to respond to it, Allan Ornstein wrote:

> Some Negro children have newly gained confidence, as expressed in the social revolution sweeping across the country. Some see themselves as leaders, and not helpless, inferior youngsters. This new pride is evidenced by their tendency to challenge authority. The teacher should expect, encourage and channel this energy toward constructive goals.[48]

With control and compliance increasingly difficult to obtain, many urban schools lowered their expectations with respect to student behavior.[49] The preoccupation with enforcing rules was gradually replaced with a desire to maintain average daily attendance, since this was the key funding formula for schools. As teachers have come to realize that they cannot elicit obedience through the "terror of degradation,"[50] concerns about safety have led more of them to think twice about how to reprimand a student, lest their attempt at chastisement be taken as a challenge for a physical confrontation, for which most are unprepared.[51]

Still, schools have not given up entirely on the goal of exercising control over students: though the task may be far more difficult now than it ever was, schools are still expected to maintain some form of order. Beyond being a threat to the personal safety of students and teachers, violence in schools challenges the authority and power of school officials. In carrying out their duties as caretakers of youth, school officials serve as both legal and symbolic representatives of state authority. With the power vested in their position, they are expected to control the behavior of those in their charge. When violence occurs with impunity, a loss of authority is exposed. Therefore, the issue of violence is seldom discussed in isolation from other control issues. More often, violence is equated with insubordination, student misconduct, and the general problem of maintaining order in school. The way the issues become melded together is indicative of how schools perceive their role in relation to the social control function that schools have historically performed in the United States.

The Disciplining Event

The exercise of discipline in schools takes on great importance because it serves as the primary means through which symbols of power and authority are perpetuated. In analyzing the symbolic issues associated with discipline and violence in schools, it is helpful to consider the work of Michel Foucault. Writing about the role of punishment meted out upon criminal offenders in France during the nineteenth century, Foucault describes what he calls the "juridico-political" function of the act:

> The ceremony of punishment is an act of terror. . . . The practice of torture was not an economy of example . . . but a policy of terror: to make everyone aware, through the body of the criminal, of the unrestrained presence of the sovereign. The public execution did not re-establish justice; it reactivated power. . . . Its ruthlessness, its spectacle, its physical violence, its unbalanced play of forces, its meticulous ceremonial, its entire apparatus were inscribed in the political functioning of the penal system.[52]

While the kinds of public executions and tortures carried out in France during the nineteenth century may seem far removed from the forms of discipline carried out in schools today, Foucault's focus on the relationship between the disciplining act and the "reactivation" of power is relevant to understanding the symbolic role of discipline. The disciplining event, whether it occurs in public or private, serves as one of the primary means through which school officials "send a message" to perpetrators of violence, and to the community generally, that the authority vested in them by the state is still secure. Particularly within the current political climate created by the fight against violence, the disciplining event provides an opportunity for school authorities to use those accused of committing acts of violence as an example to others.

From a symbolic standpoint, within the context of the school, the student expulsion hearing is perhaps the most important spectacle at which the meting out of punishment upon those accused of violence can be used for larger political purposes. As a quasi-judicial ceremony, the formality of an expulsion hearing often contains all of the drama and suspense associated with a courtroom trial. Though the event itself is closed to the public, news of the decision rendered by the school board or hearing officers often travels quickly, particularly when the student is charged with committing an act of violence.

I had the opportunity to attend an expulsion hearing at an urban school district for which I was working as a consultant. I describe what happened because I think it helps to illuminate important dynamics of power and knowledge embedded within the disciplining event. The accused in this case was charged with bringing a loaded gun to school. The education code in this particular state called for automatic expulsion hearings whenever students were apprehended for bringing weapons to school. When asked to explain why he had brought the weapon to school, the student informed the board members that his father and mother had recently separated, and that his father, who was distraught over the separation, mentioned that he was thinking of killing himself. He instructed his son to remove his 9-mm handgun from the house so that he wouldn't harm himself or anyone else.

The boy informed the board that during the summer, his grandmother had attempted to commit suicide by slashing her wrists, and that he and his father had to apply pressure to her bloodied arms in order to prevent her from bleeding to death while they waited for an ambulance. With vivid memories of that traumatic event in his head, and fearing that his father might follow through on his threat to take his own life, the boy placed the gun in his backpack and took it with him to school. He explained that he later showed it to a friend at school because he wanted to talk to someone about what was going on, but that he had not shown the weapon to anyone else, nor had he brought the gun back to school after that day.

In questioning the student about his actions, one board member noted that the student possessed an exemplary academic record, and that all of his teachers spoke highly of him, referring to him as "respectful, honest, hard working, etc." He was then asked whether in retrospect he would have handled the situation differently. The student explained that he still wasn't sure what he should have done, but thought that maybe he could have hidden the gun in the bushes near his house instead of bringing it with him to school. Upon hearing this, one of the board members proceeded to lecture the student and his father who had accompanied him to the hearing about the danger of guns. One board member commented that the student didn't seem to have learned a lesson from this serious error in judgement. Exasperated by their doubts, the student claimed he had learned a lesson and promised to never bring a weapon to school again. A board member then asked what punishment the school principal recommended, and was told that the principal wanted to see the student expelled so that "we send a clear message that guns on campus will not be tolerated." After deliberating for several minutes, the board responded with a unanimous vote for expulsion.

As an observer of this event, I was struck by several aspects of what took place. First, all five board members judging this student, as well as the principal who presented the evidence against him, were White and middle class, while the student was Black and from a low-income family.[53] From the questions they asked and the lectures that they directed at the student and his father, it seemed evident that they were unable to identify with the student and the situation that he was in. While I felt uncomfortable hearing the student and his father divulge the problems they were having in their personal lives, there was no apparent consternation among board members over the imbalance of the situation, and no attempts were made to communicate that they could empathize with the anguish and pressure that either the student or his father must have been experiencing. After hearing one board member ask the student if he would have handled the situation differently in retrospect, I wanted to ask how she would have handled it, or if she or any of the others had ever experienced anything similar. The gulf in experience between the board members and the student seemed to be compounded by the obvious differences of race, class, and age. However, I sensed no indication that the board regarded this as a problem, nor did I sense any effort on their part to understand the student's actions from his point of view.

Second, despite evidence that this incident represented an aberration from this student's "normal" behavior in school, and despite the fact that no one at the school was actually threatened by the presence of the gun, the board members and principal seemed primarily concerned with using the case to communicate a message about guns in school. No effort was made to try to figure out an appropriate way of responding to this student's particular situation. In this respect, the hearing provided an occasion through which the district's power could be communicated. By ignoring the circumstances of the offense, and focusing exclusively on the issue of the gun, the board could demonstrate its toughness and intolerance for those who threatened the security of others. While there was no evidence that the punishment of this individual student would have any influence on the behavior of others, his expulsion reinforced the institutional authority of the district leadership by serving as an example of their prerogative and power to punish. In a setting where most perpetrators of violence are not apprehended, and where most efforts to ensure the safety of students and teachers are ineffective, the act of punishment becomes an important exercise for showing who has control.

Finally, the disciplining moment also reveals the way in which the adult professionals, and to a lesser extent the student and his father, were constrained by the "discipline" embedded in the roles each party occupies within the institution. To the extent that the board members and the principal have power or authority, it is derived from their relation to an institutional structure—a structure whose history is rooted in nineteenth-century preoccupations with social control. In their roles as prosecutor and judge, their sense of how to discipline this youngster is profoundly influenced by a body of knowledge or "discipline" that is rooted in the power relations that exist between the state and the school as a social institution. This power/knowledge limits the ability of the board and administrators to identify with the student on a human level, for to do so would open up the possibility that there might be other ways to understand his actions.[54] To recognize that there might be another way of viewing this behavior that goes beyond a focus on crime, violence, and misconduct might lead to a different type of intervention. However, school board members and administrators typically see their job as protecting the institution and the staff, students, and teachers in their charge. The state provides explicit guidelines on how this is to be done, but there are also implicit guidelines pertaining to notions of how schools are supposed to operate and function, and how students are supposed to behave. To explore alternative ways of responding to violent, or potentially violent, behavior would necessarily require a fundamental change in how the institution and the provision of educational services were conceptualized by those in authority, a prospect that at the disciplining moment often seems unimaginable.

Though a less sympathetic case could have been selected for analysis, I chose this one because I feel it demonstrates how the act of violation is in many ways irrelevant to the form of discipline that is employed. Beyond their real-life effects, violence and discipline take on a symbolic life of their own, symbols that play heavily on interactions within schools and that ultimately influence how schools and violence are perceived by others. In the pages ahead, I will pursue further how a preoccupation with control limits the ability of administrators to respond creatively to the crisis created by the increase in violence in schools.

RACE, CLASS, AND THE POLITICS OF DISCIPLINE

In many school districts across the country, considerable controversy has been generated over the disproportionate number of African American and, in some cases, Latino students who are subjected to various forms of school discipline.[55] In California, legislation has been proposed to limit the ability of school districts to use suspensions and expulsions as a form of punishment, in response to the imbalance in the number of Black and Latino students subjected to these sorts of penalties.[56] Although the legislation has little chance of being approved by the state legislature, the fact that it was proposed indicates the depth of feeling in many Black communities that Black children are being treated unfairly. In Cincinnati, Ohio, the disproportionate number of Black students who are suspended and expelled in public schools prompted a judge to call for teachers and administrators to be held accountable for "student behavior management" as part of a court order monitoring desegregation in the district's schools.[57]

Although there is evidence that schools that serve White middle-class students in the suburbs also have problems with violence, this is downplayed in the public media.[58] Just as the threat of violent crime in society is characterized largely as a problem created by Black perpetrators, violence in schools is also equated with Black, and in some cases, Latino, students.[59] While the correlation between race and who gets arrested, suspended, or expelled in schools is so consistent that it is impossible to deny that a linkage exists, the issue tends to be avoided in public discussions, due to the controversy and tensions surrounding racial issues in U.S. society. To avoid the charge of racism, many school officials argue that the connection between race and punishment disguises what is really more an issue of class than an issue of race, since most of those receiving discipline come from lower-class families.[60] While this may be true, the correlation between race and class is also high in many school districts, and so the three variables—race, class, and violence—tend to be associated.

The unwillingness to confront the implications of these kinds of correlations is replicated in the general refusal of most policymakers and school officials to place the problem of violence within the broader context of race and education. Not only is school punishment consistently correlated with race, it is also highly correlated with academic grouping and high school graduation rates. Those most likely to receive punishment in school are also more likely to have been placed in classes for Educationally Mentally Retarded (EMR) or Trainable Mentally Retarded (TMR) students.[61] The consistency of these trends is more than mere coincidence. Such patterns point to what some have described as a "second-generation discrimination effect":

> In every case where policy reflects positively on a student, black students are under-represented. In every case where policy reflects negatively on a student, black students are over-represented. . . . That a pattern similar to the one revealed here could occur without some discrimination is virtually impossible to believe.[62]

The Role of Teachers

While police officers, security guards, and administrators generally assume primary responsibility for managing and enforcing school discipline, in most cases teachers make the first referral in the discipline process, and therefore have tremendous influence in determining who receives discipline and why. In my work with urban schools, the most frequent concern I hear from teachers is that they have trouble disciplining and controlling their students. This has been especially true in schools at which the majority of students are Black and the majority of teachers are White. Having taught in urban public schools, I am familiar with what teachers are up against, and recognize that some semblance of order and safety is essential if teaching and learning are to take place. However, whenever I conduct workshops in schools, I generally try to shift the focus of talk about discipline to discussions about what teachers know about their students. I do this because I have generally found that teachers who lack familiarity with their students are more likely to misunderstand and fear them.

Two years ago, I had the opportunity to conduct a workshop on student discipline for a multiracial group of teachers at an urban middle school located in an economically depressed community. Before addressing what I knew to be their primary concern—a recipe for controlling student behavior in the classroom—I wanted to impress upon the teachers the importance of knowing the students with whom they worked. These teachers, like many in urban school districts, did not live in the community where they worked and knew little about the neighborhood in which the school was located. From our discussions at the workshop, it was clear that most of the teachers also knew little about the lives of the children they taught, and most assumed that the majority of children came from deprived, dysfunctional, and impoverished families.

In an effort to increase the awareness of the group about the importance of knowing the community in which they worked, a community with which I was familiar, I presented them with a hypothetical situation: If you were invited to teach in a foreign country, what kind of information would you want to know before leaving? The teachers responded by generating a long list of what they felt was relevant information that would assist them in teaching in a land that they did not know. The list included information about politics, culture, the economy, history, and geography. After discussing why they felt this information was important, I asked how much of this information they knew about the community in which they worked.

Two of the teachers said that they didn't need to know this sort of information in order to teach effectively because the school was located within the United States, and therefore was part of familiar territory. Most of the others, however, recognized the inconsistency in this perspective, particularly after being primed by the previous discussion, and acknowledged that a lack of knowledge might pose a problem for them in their work with students.

I suggested that we visit some of the housing projects and neighborhoods where their students lived, the stores where families shopped, the health clinics, libraries, parks, and some of the noteworthy historic landmarks in the community. I pointed out that a brief tour of the community would provide them only limited useful information, but that it could be a start at becoming better acquainted with their students.

They agreed to go, and the following day we piled into my van for a four-hour tour. Interestingly, after the tour nearly all of the teachers told me that they resented me for taking them on this excursion because it made them feel like tourists. "Didn't you see the people staring at us?" one teacher commented. "They were probably wondering why we were there." Only one teacher disagreed with the group's reaction and expressed appreciation for being exposed to the community in this way. As it turned out, this teacher had lived in this community when she was a child, and the trip had served as a reminder to her that most of the residents in the area were working-class homeowners. The winos and crack addicts who were visible on certain street corners, and who many other teachers believed were typical of a majority of the residents, actually constituted a small minority. However, the other teachers took up the position espoused by two of their colleagues earlier, insisting that they did not need to know the community in order to teach effectively. One asserted that "A good teacher can work with any child. I don't have to become an anthropologist to teach." I responded by asking if it was possible to be an effective teacher if you did not know your students, but by this point most of the teachers were unwilling to pursue this line of inquiry.

For me, this experience illustrated, in a profound way, the gulf in experience between teacher and student, which is typical in many urban schools. The pretense operating in many schools is that teachers should treat all students the same, although numerous studies on teacher expectations have shown that race, class, and gender have considerable influence over the assumptions, conscious and unconscious, that teachers hold toward students.[63] Although multicultural education and student diversity have become popular topics of discussion among teachers, understanding how the politics of difference influences teacher-student interactions generally remains largely unexplored, except at the most superficial level.[64]

When teachers and administrators remain unfamiliar with the places and the ways in which their students live their lives outside of the school walls, they often fill the knowledge void with stereotypes based upon what they read or see in the media, or what they pick up indirectly from stories told to them by children. Many teachers, like others who live outside of poor urban communities, tend to hold negative views toward these areas, views that are rooted in a fear of violence and in media representations of the people who reside in the inner city as less than civilized. This fear invariably influences the interaction between teachers and administrators and their students. In the eyes of these teachers and administrators, who are "foreigners" to the school's community, the students often seem to embody the traits and exhibit the behavior of the hoodlums and thugs they have heard about or seen from afar. Many of the teachers with whom I have worked in urban schools seem to fear the children that they teach; more often than not, where the students are aware of it, they may attempt to use the teacher's fear to their advantage.

This is not to say that violence in schools is an imagined problem. I do believe, however, that it is a problem exacerbated by fear. A teacher who fears the student that she or he teaches is more likely to resort to some form of discipline when challenged, or to ignore the challenge in the hope that she or he will be left alone. Rather than handling a classroom disruption on their own, they are also more likely to request assistance from the central office.

My work with teachers and students at a number of urban schools has shown me that students often know when their teachers fear them. In many cases, I have seen students use a teacher's fear to assert their control over the class-room and, if possible, the entire school. I have visited schools where children openly gamble and play dice in the hallways, and where the presence of an adult is insufficient reason to put out a cigarette or a joint. When adults are frightened or intimidated, disorder prevails, and acts of crime and violence become the norm. Moreover, when fear is at the center of student-teacher interactions, teaching becomes almost impossible, and concerns about safety and control take precedence over concerns about teaching.

From speaking to students and teachers at such schools, I have found that they typically share a common characteristic: the adults don't really know who their students are. Their sense of what the children's lives are like outside of school is either distorted by images of pathological and dysfunctional families, or simply shrouded in ignorance. School personnel who hold such views may make little effort to increase parental participation in school because they can't see any benefits that might be gained through parents' involvement. School staff and faculty may also be reluctant to reach out to the community to establish partnerships with community-based organizations and churches that are interested in providing services to youth, because all they can see in the neighborhood are problems that are best kept out of the school. Fear and ignorance can serve as a barrier greater than any fence, and can be more insu-lating than any security system.

In many schools, differences in age and life experience make it difficult for students and teachers to communicate and understand one another. When such differences are compounded by race and class differences, a huge gap can be created that can easily be filled by fear and suspicion. Anonymity and ignorance create shields that protect the identities of those who perpetrate acts of violence and crime. In such an atmosphere, adults and students may welcome armed guards, metal detectors, and barbed-wire fences because they can't envision another way to ensure their safety. Even if they come to find the prison-like conditions depressing and oppressive, they are likely to cling to such measures because chaos is worse, and no other alternative seems imaginable.

HUMANIZING THE ENVIRONMENT: ALTERNATIVE APPROACHES TO VIOLENCE PREVENTION IN SCHOOLS

In critiquing the approach to discipline that is most widely practiced in the United States today, I in no way want to belittle the fact that many teachers and students have been victims of violence and deserve the right to work at and attend safe schools. In many schools, violence is real, and the fear that it produces is understandable. Still, I am struck by the fact that even when I visit schools with a notorious reputation for the prevalence of violence, I can find at least one classroom where teachers are working effectively with their stu-dents, and where fear is not an obstacle to dialogue or even friendship. While other teachers in the school may be preoccupied with managing their student's behavior, an endeavor at which they are seldom successful, I have seen the same students enter other classrooms willing to learn and comply with their teacher's instructions.

Many of these "exceptional" teachers have to "cross borders" and negotiate differences of race, class, or experience in order to establish rapport with their students.[65] When I have asked students in interviews what makes a particular teacher "special" and worthy of respect, the students consistently cite three characteristics: firmness, compassion, and an interesting, engaging, and challenging teaching style.[66] Of course, even a teacher who is perceived as exceptional by students can be a victim of violence, particularly because of its increasingly random occurrence. I have, however, witnessed such teachers confront students in situations that others would not dare to engage, boldly breaking up fights or dice games, or confronting a rude and disrespectful student, without showing the slightest bit of apprehension or fear.

What is there about the structure and culture of the institution that propagates and reproduces the destructive interpersonal dynamics evident in so many schools? The vast majority of teachers that I meet seem genuinely concerned about their students, and sincerely desire to be effective at what they do. Even those who have become cynical and bitter as a result of enduring years of unrewarded work in under-funded schools generally strike me as people who would prefer more humane interactions with their students.[67]

What stands in the way of better relations between teachers and students, and why do fear and distrust characterize those relations, rather than compassion and respect?

My answer to these questions focuses on the legacy of social control that continues to dominate the educational agenda, and that profoundly influences the structure and culture of schools. The pervasive dysfunction that characterizes social relations in urban public schools is not accidental, but is due to the severity of social and economic conditions in the inner city. However, it is also not unavoidable. There are a few important exceptions to this norm, schools where teachers and students support each other in pursuit of higher personal and collective goals.[68] Such schools, however, are not typical or common. Rather, the average urban high school tends to be large, impersonal, and foreboding, a place where bells and security guards attempt to govern the movements of students, and where students more often than not have lost sight of the fact that education and personal growth are ostensibly the reasons why they are required to attend this anonymous institution five days a week.

I have visited urban schools that have found ways to address effectively the problem of violence, ways that do not rely upon coercion or excessive forms of control. At one such school, rather than hiring security guards, a grandmother from the surrounding community was hired to monitor students. Instead of using physical intimidation to carry out her duties, this woman greets children with hugs, and when some form of punishment is needed, she admonishes them to behave themselves, saying that she expects better behavior from them.[69] I have also visited a continuation high school,[70] where the principal was able to close the campus, not permitting the students to leave at lunch time, without installing a fence or some other security apparatus, but simply by communicating with students about other alternatives for purchasing food so that they no longer felt it necessary to leave for meals.[71] Now the students operate a campus store that both teachers and students patronize. Such measures are effective because they make it possible for children and adults to relate to one another as human beings, rather than as anonymous actors playing out roles.

I believe that there are a variety of ways in which to humanize school environments, and thereby reduce the potential for violence. Improving the aesthetic character of schools by including art in the design of schools, or by making space available within schools for students to create gardens or greenhouses, can make schools more pleasant and attractive. Similarly, by overcoming the divide that separates urban schools from the communities in which schools are located, the lack of adults who have authority and respect in the eyes of children can be addressed. Adults who live within the community can be encouraged to volunteer or, if possible, be paid to tutor, teach, mentor, coach, perform, or just plain help out with a variety of school activities. The above examples are meant to begin a discussion of alternative practices for building humane school communities. There are undoubtedly a variety of ways this can be done, and while such efforts may not eliminate the threat of random violence, they can help to make schools safer, less impersonal, and better able to provide students with a sense of stability in their lives.

The goal of maintaining social control through the use of force and discipline has persisted for too long. While past generations could be made to accept the passivity and constraint such practices engender, present generations will not. Most urban youth today are neither passive nor compliant. The rewards dangled before them of a decent job and material wealth for those who do well in school are seen by too many as either undesirable or unattainable. New strategies for providing an education that is perceived as meaningful, and relevant, and that begins to tap into the intrinsic desire of all individuals to obtain greater personal fulfillment, must be devised and supported. Anything short of this will leave us mired in a situation that grows increasingly depressing and dangerous every day.

The urban schools that I know that feel safe to those who spend their time there don't have metal detectors or armed security guards, and their principals don't carry baseball bats. What these schools do have is a strong sense of community and collective responsibility. Such schools are seen by students as sacred territory, too special to be spoiled by crime and violence, and too important to risk one's being excluded. Such schools are few, but their existence serves as tangible proof that there are alternatives to chaotic schools plagued by violence, and controlled institutions that aim at producing docile bodies.

NOTES

1. Several educational organizations have designated violence prevention their highest priority. For example, the Association of California School Administrators made efforts to reduce violence in schools their top priority for the 1993–1994 school year. For a discussion of national education priorities since 1980, see Beatrice Gross and Ronald Gross, eds., *The Great School Debate* (New York: Touchstone Books, 1985).

2. Evidence that there has been an escalation in the number of violent incidents occurring in schools is provided in an analysis of trends in Jackson Toby, "Everyday School Violence: How Disorder Fuels It," *American Educator,* Winter (1993/1994), 4–6.

3. Numerous bills for curtailing violent crimes are presently under consideration in the Senate and House of Representatives. For a critical discussion of the Clinton administration's crime bill, see Elliott Currie, "What's Wrong With the Crime Bill?" *The Nation,* January 31, 1994, 4–5.

4. In New York City, over $28 million was spent on metal detectors during the 1980s. See Pat Kemper, "Disarming Youth," *California School Boards Journal,* Fall (1993), 25–33.

5. Kemper, "Disarming Youth," p. 27.

6. A recent example of such an approach can be seen in Denver, where Assistant Principal Ruben Perez at the Horace Mann Middle School suspended ninety-seven students in a three-day period for a variety of nonviolent infractions. In defense of his action, Perez argued that "the troublemakers weren't doing us any good. They were just interrupting the educational process for good students who come to school every day." See Florangela Davila, "Denver Debates School Ousters," *Washington Post,* January 20, 1995, p. 18. There is also the case of Dejundra Caldwell, who was sentenced to three years in prison for stealing $20 worth of ice cream from the school cafeteria at a high school in Birmingham, Alabama. See Kenneth Freed, "Youth Receives Three Years for Stealing Ice Cream," *Los Angeles Times,* September 30, 1994, p. 23. See also Harold Foster, *Ribbin' Jivin' and Playin' the Dozens: The Unrecognized Dilemma of Innercity Schools* (Cambridge, MA: Ballinger, 1974). Foster hypothesizes that Black males are suspended and expelled more often than Whites because they exhibit certain "cool" behaviors, which teachers and administrators perceive as rude, arrogant, intimidating, sexually provocative, and threatening.

7. For a discussion of the success of mentoring in addressing the needs of "at-risk" students, see James McPartland and Saundra Murray Nettles, "Using Community Adults as Advocates or Mentors for At-Risk Middle School Students: A Two Year Evaluation of Project RAISE," *American Journal of Education, 99,* No. 4 (1991), 568–586.

8. For a discussion on how to address violence through the curriculum, see Tim Daux, "Fostering Self-Discipline," *Rethinking Schools, 4,* No. 3 (1990), 6–7.

9. For a discussion of this approach and others being used by urban school districts to improve the delivery of social services to students and their families, see Jeannie Oakes, *Improving Inner-City Schools: Current Directions in Urban District Reform* (Madison, WI: Center for Policy Research in Education Joint Note Series, 1987).

10. See Erin Hallisey, "Gang Activity in State's Prisons on the Increase," *San Francisco Chronicle,* May 17, 1994, p. 14.

11. For example, during 1992, in the city of Oakland, California, the number of violent crimes committed by juveniles while on school property was substantially less than the number of violent crimes committed away from school property. See Oakland Police Department, "Oakland Police Department Report on Crime in the City of Oakland," September 1992.

12. According to a recent national poll on attitudes toward public education conducted by Public Agenda, a national organization that conducts research on educational issues, the need for safety in schools was identified as the most important issue of public concern. For a summary and discussion of the survey, see Jean Johnson and John Immer-

wahr, "What Americans Expect from the Public Schools," *American Educator,* Winter (1994/1995), 4–13.

13. A 1989 survey by the Justice Department reported that incidents of violence in urban schools occurred with twice the frequency as such incidents in suburban schools, and nearly four times the frequency of incidents in rural schools. See Sara Rimer, "Violence Isn't Just in Cities, Suburban and Rural Schools Find," *New York Times,* April 21, 1993, p. A16.

14. An example of the "get-tough" approach can be seen in the policies advocated by the American Federation of Teachers (AFT). Citing figures that indicate a dramatic rise in violence in public schools throughout the country, the AFT compiled a list of the tough actions being taken by school districts and new policies adopted by state legislatures to curtail the problem. The AFT also recommended that its local affiliates include violence reduction strategies in collective bargaining agreements. See Priscilla Nemeth, "Caught in the Crossfire," *American Teacher,* 77, No. 2, 6–7. Also see an editorial by AFT President Albert Shanker, "Privileging Violence: Too Much Focus on the Needs and Rights of Disruptive Students," *American Educator,* Winter (1994/1995), 8.

15. During a recent visit to an urban high school, I commented to a school administrator that I was impressed by the lack of graffiti on school walls. The administrator laughed and told me, "This is a lock-down facility. They can't even get out of their classrooms while class is in session without being picked up. We run this place like San Quentin."

16. Such an approach has been advocated in a number of newspaper editorials (see, for example, "Time To Get Tough On School Violence," Editorial, *Oakland Tribune,* November 21, 1991, p. 13, and "Cracking Down on Violence in Schools," Editorial, *San Francisco Chronicle,* November 21, 1991, p. 24), and in several school districts. See Celeste Hunter, "Jail Threat Effective in Truancy Program," *Los Angeles Times,* January 9, 1994, p. 16.

17. A clear example of how traditional approaches to fighting school violence have failed can be seen in Richmond, California. Despite making a substantial increase in funding for metal detectors and other security measures, several schools in the district have reported an increase in violence. In fact, two students were shot recently at Richmond High School, even though metal detectors were installed at the school entrances two years ago. See Rob Shea, "High School Kids Want Security Program Junked," *West County Times,* April 21, 1994, p. 14.

18. Statistics frequently cited as evidence of the problem include: the number of students who report bringing weapons to school (13%), the number of teachers (one in ten) and students (one in four) who report that they have been victims of violence at school (Associated Press report on a Metropolitan Life Survey sponsored by *American Teacher,* December 17, 1993); and the perception of students, teachers, and administrators regarding the degree to which violence is a problem. See John McDermot, *Violent Schools – Safe Schools* (Washington, DC: National Institute of Education, 1978).

19. In Richmond, California, although the school district was still in the process of repaying a $30 million loan to the state after declaring bankruptcy in 1989, it set aside $50,000 in 1993 to pay for the installation of metal detectors. One teacher remarked: "They're spending money on this and we still need paper in our classrooms." In defense of the expenditure, a school administrator responded, "The overall program of the district is to provide a safe environment regardless of the cost. It's something we have to do." Ikimulisa Sockwell, "Detecting Weapon-free Schools," *West Contra Costa Times,* December 8, 1993, p. 13.

20. A recent opinion poll conducted by the *Los Angeles Times* found that concerns about safety remain high, despite a 12 percent decrease in the number of violent crimes committed in the state. See Belinda Lawson, "Fear of Crime Remains High Despite Reduction in Crime Rate," *Los Angeles Times,* October 22, 1994, p. 17.

21. According to the American Federation of Teachers (AFT), several school districts do not accurately report the number of violent incidents that occur in the schools because they fear negative publicity. See Nemeth, "Caught in the Crossfire," pp. 6–7. The *New York Times* claimed that similar attempts are made to downplay the frequency of violent incidents in New York City schools, in "Controlling School Violence," Editorial, *New York Times,* May 3, 1993, p. A24.

22. For a discussion on how the conception of the asylum influenced the design and operation of public schools, see David Rothman, *Discovery of the Asylum* (Boston: Little, Brown, 1971), pp. 83–84. Also see David Tyack, *The One Best System* (Cambridge, MA: Harvard University Press, 1974), pp. 51–58.

23. Rothman, *Discovery,* p. 15.

24. Rothman, *Discovery,* p. 235.

25. Rothman, *Discovery,* pp. 137–139.

26. Lawrence Cremin, *American Education: The Metropolitan Experience 1876–1980* (New York: Harper & Row, 1988), p. 118.

27. The progressive intentions of educators and social reformers is documented in Cremin, *American Education,* pp. 164–179.

28. Michael Katz, *Reconstructing American Education* (Cambridge, MA: Harvard University Press, 1987), p. 17.

29. G. Stanley Hall, *Adolescence: Its Psychology and Its Relations to Physiology, Sex, Crime, Religion, and Education,* 2 vols. (New York: D. Appleton, 1904).

30. Cremin, *American Education,* p. 195.

31. Cremin, *American Education,* p. 295.

32. Jeanie Oakes, *Keeping Track: How Schools Structure Inequality* (New Haven: Yale University Press, 1985), p. 28; Martin Carnoy and Henry Levin, *Schooling and Work in the Democratic State* (Stanford, CA: Stanford University Press, 1985), p. 95.

33. Cremin, *American Education,* p. 21.

34. Tyack, *The One Best,* p. 82.

35. Tyack, *The One Best,* pp. 91–97.

36. The observer was Edward Joseph Rice, a pediatrician who visited thirty-six schools in 1892 to prepare a series of articles on the condition of urban schools. Focusing again on the body, Rice observed one teacher scold her students by asking, "How can you learn anything with your knees and toes out of order?" From Edward J. Rice, *The Public School System of the United States* (New York: Century Press, 1893), p. 98.

37. Tyack, *The One Best,* p. 74.

38. Norton Grubb, "The Old Problem of 'New Students': Purpose, Content, and Pedagogy," in *Changing Populations, Changing Schools,* ed. Irwin Flexnard and Harry Passow (New York: Teachers College Press, 1995), pp. 3–5.

39. Lawrence Cremin, *The Transformation of the School* (New York: Vintage Books, 1961), p. 68.

40. Oakes, *Keeping Track,* pp. 32–33.

41. Writing about disciplinary practices used in the military and in prisons in eighteenth-century France, Michel Foucault describes a preoccupation with the production of "docile bodies" in which "power is dissociated from the body, and aptitude is turned into a capacity which it seeks to increase. . . . If economic exploitation separates the force and the product of labour, let us say that disciplinary coercion establishes in the body the constricting link between an increased aptitude and an increased domination." Michel Foucault, *Discipline and Punish* (New York: Vintage Books, 1979), p. 138.

42. For a discussion of how changes brought about by migration and immigration changed the character of eastern U.S. cities, see Daniel P. Moynihan and Nathan Glazer, *Beyond the Melting Pot* (Cambridge, MA: Joint Center for Urban Studies, 1963), pp. vii–xxi.

43. The factors leading to the deterioration of urban areas is well described in William Julius Wilson, *The Truly Disadvantaged* (Chicago: University of Chicago Press, 1987).

44. James Conant, *Slums and Suburbs* (New York: McGraw Hill, 1961).

45. Conant, *Slums and Suburbs,* p. 22.

46. Describing the loss of school control as a "crisis in authority," Mary Haywood Metz analyzes how school districts attempted to respond to this situation in *Classrooms and Corridors: The Crisis of Authority in Desegregated Secondary Schools* (Berkeley: University of California Press, 1978).

47. Allan Ornstein, "Discipline: A Major Function in Teaching the Disadvantaged," in *Urban Education,* ed. Richard Heidenreich (Arlington, VA: College Readings, 1972).

48. Ornstein, "Discipline," p. 2.

49. In a study on the changes in school culture that accompanied desegregation, Metz describes how many schools experienced a crisis of authority, much of which she attributes to fundamental miscommunications between White teachers and Black students. See Metz, *Classrooms and Corridors.*

50. Tyack, *The One Best,* p. 54.

51. In response to the rise in attacks on teachers, the American Federation of Teachers has developed a victim support program. For a discussion of the program and the problems responsible for its creation, see Nemeth "Caught in the Crossfire," pp. 6–7.

52. Foucault, *Discipline,* p. 54.

53. During the hearing, the father mentioned that he had recently lost his job and that the financial problems created by his unemployment had added to the problems he was having with his wife.

54. In describing how power-knowledge relations constrain the ability of those designated to exercise authority to use their own judgement, Foucault writes: "Power-knowledge relations are to be analyzed not on the basis of a subject of knowledge who is or is not free in relation to the power system, but, on the contrary the subject who knows, the objects to be known and the modalities of knowledge must be regarded as so many effects of these fundamental implications of power-knowledge and their historical transformations." Foucault, *Discipline,* pp. 27–28.

55. A national study carried out by the U.S. Office of Civil Rights reports that Black students are 74 to 86 percent more likely than White students to receive corporal punishment; 54 to 88 percent more likely to be suspended; and 3 to 8 times as likely to be expelled. See Kenneth Meier, Joseph Stewart, and Robert England, *Race, Class and Education: The Politics of Second Generation Discrimination* (Madison: University of Wisconsin Press, 1989), pp. 84–86.

56. In 1991, Assembly Bill #2140 was proposed by Barbara Lee, D-Oakland, to insure that the removal of students from school was viewed as a last resort and "not to eliminate from the classroom students who are difficult to teach." See "Assembly Bill Would Alter School Suspension Policy," *Oakland Tribune,* November 27, 1991, p. B1.

57. Black parents and community members in Cincinnati also worked to defeat the approval of a school facilities bond measure that would have raised $348 million to finance repairs to deteriorating schools because of their anger over the treatment of Black students. See Adrian King, "Student Rights vs. School Safety: School Districts Grapple with the Racial Implications of New Security Measures," *Education Week,* January 19, 1994, p. 8.

58. A study conducted at Xavier University and cited by the *New York Times* supports the idea that violence is not solely an urban issue. The study found that 54 percent of the 294 suburban schools and 43 percent of the 344 small town schools surveyed reported an increase in the number of violent incidents. See Daniel Goldman, "Hope Seen for Curbing Youth Violence," *New York Times,* April 21, 1993, p. A12.

59. For a discussion of how the equation of Blacks with crime has become central to public discourse about violence and crime, see Amos Wilson, *Black-on-Black Violence* (New York: Afrikan World Infosystems, 1990), pp. 1–34. Also see Richard Majors and Janet Billson,

Cool Pose (New York: Touchtone, 1992), pp. 33–35, for a discussion on perceptions of Black male violence.

60. This argument is made in Jackson Toby, "Everyday School Violence: How Disorder Fuels It," *American Educator,* Winter (1993/1994), pp. 4-13; and in Daniel Patrick Moynihan, "Defining Deviancy Down," *American Educator,* Winter (1993/1994), 16.

61. Meier et al., *Race, Class, and Education,* pp. 81–84.

62. Meier et al., *Race, Class, and Education,* p. 89.

63. Wilbur Brookover and Edsel Erickson, *The Sociology of Education* (Homewood, IL: Dorsey Press, 1975); Nancy St. John, *School Desegregation Outcomes for Children* (New York: John Wiley, 1975); Good Thomas and Harris Cooper, *Pygmalion Grows Up* (New York: Longman, 1983); Jerome Dusek and Gail Joseph, "The Bases of Teacher Expectancies: A Meta-Analysis," *Journal of Educational Psychology, 75,* (1983), 327–346; Rhona Weinstein and Charles Soule, "Expectations and High School Change: Teacher-Researcher Collaboration to Prevent School Failure," *American Journal of Community Psychology, 19,* No. 3 (1991).

64. For a discussion on the various forms of multicultural education and the discourses associated with it, see Christine Sleeter, *Empowerment Through Multicultural Education* (Albany: State University of New York Press, 1991), pp. 1–23.

65. "Border crossing" is a phrase coined by Henry Giroux to describe the personal transformation experienced by teachers and students engaged in critical discourse and pedagogy. He writes: "Critical educators take up culture as a vital source for developing a politics of identity, community and pedagogy. Culture is not monolithic or unchanging, but is a site of multiple and heterogeneous borders where different histories, languages, experiences, and voices intermingle amidst diverse relations of power and privilege. Within this pedagogical borderland known as school, subordinate cultures push against and permeate the alleged unproblematic and homogeneous borders of the dominant cultural forms and practices. . . . Radical educators must provide conditions for students to speak so that their narratives can be affirmed." Henry Giroux, *Border Crossings* (New York: Routledge, 1992), p. 169.

66. These interviews were part of a survey that I conducted with 125 students at an urban continuation high school in northern California in 1990–991.

67. My impression of the attitudes and intentions of many urban teachers is supported by Carl Grant, who cites research on teacher attitudes in his "Urban Teachers: Their New Colleagues and Curriculum," *Transforming Urban Education* (Boston: Allyn & Bacon, 1994), pp. 315–321, and by Pamela Boltin Joseph and Gale E. Burnaford, whose study on teachers' self-images challenges many of the prevailing notions about teachers' incompetence and indifference. See Pamela Boltin Joseph and Gale E. Burnaford, eds., *Images of Schoolteachers in Twentieth Century America* (New York: St. Martin's Press, 1994).

68. Several exceptionally good high schools are described and analyzed in detail in Sara Lawrence Lightfoot, *The Good High School* (New York: Basic Books, 1983).

69. This school was also the only junior high school in the district where no weapons were confiscated from students. See "Selected School Characteristics," Office of the Superintendent, Oakland Unified School District, December, 1993.

70. Continuation high schools are set up for students who have either been forced or who have volunteered to leave a regular high school. Many students at continuation schools have a record of poor attendance and/or poor behavior in school. Some students are required to attend continuation school as a condition of juvenile probation.

71. Efforts to close a campus for security reasons have often met with resistance from students. In Richmond, California, the district's attempt to close high school campuses at lunch time led to protests and walkouts from school. See Sockwell, "Detecting Weapon-free Schools," p. 13.

BROWN THREAT 2 SOCIETY

ALEJANDRO G. VERA

A menace to society and a vago from the hood
And porque my skin is brown
People assume I'm up to no good
They don't feel safe when I'm around
They look down on me cuando hablo Espanglish
A bloodthirsty descendant of the Aztecs
Porque I don't speak the "proper" language
I speak what's known as Tex-Mex
Because I come from the Deep South
And have aggressive attitude towards people
But in my life, there's been nothing to smile about
It's full of sin, struggles, and evil
All they show is resentment and fear
But if you look closely into my eyes
You'll see the pain from all those troubled years
I disguise it with black shades in daylight
And at night wash it away with a case of beers
But still at times in the still of the night
Alone in the dark I fight away tears
Pero no me entiendes, you can't understand
When the odds are against you, how can you prosper?
When during childhood you become a man
And after that derange into a monster
This is for all my misunderstood brothers
Who won't settle for minimum wages
Who are a danger to themselves and others
For all the carnales confined up in cages

This poem is reprinted from the Push and Pull *poetry anthology by residents of the Cyndi Taylor Krier Juvenile Correctional Treatment Center in San Antonio, TX, in partnership with Gemini Ink, Readers and Writers Today and Tomorrow, writer-in-residence Gregg Barrios.*

NEWJACK

TEACHING IN A FAILING MIDDLE SCHOOL

■

PETER SIPE

In this article, Peter Sipe compares his first year as a middle school teacher in Brooklyn, New York, to that of a rookie corrections officer at Sing Sing prison. Sipe explores what he considers to be disturbing similarities in these experiences, namely, a preoccupation with control, immersion in an adversarial social dynamic, and the prevalence of stress. Most ominously, Sipe suggests that both institutions share a legacy of failure. He posits that, just as prisons do not live up to their titles as "correctional facilities," his middle school does not produce educated children.

> "Raise Our Expectations to Cross the Bridge to Success"
> — *Our school's motto*

Last year, before I had even thought of becoming a teacher in New York, I read the book *Newjack: Guarding Sing Sing,* by journalist Ted Conover (2001). Having been refused a request to shadow a prison officer recruit for a writing piece, Conover applied to the New York State Corrections Academy and became a recruit himself. The book is an account of the year he spent as a guard in the famous New York prison. In candid and compassionate terms, Conover describes the training and daily life of a first-year corrections officer working in a facility renowned both for its history and its unruliness. The book description on the back cover of the paperback reads:

> Through his insights into the harsh culture of prison, the grueling and demeaning working conditions of the officers, and the unexpected ways the job encroaches on his own family life, we begin to see how our burgeoning prison system brutalizes everyone connected with it.

In June 2003, I finished my first year as a middle school teacher in New York City. I am part of the New York City Teaching Fellows, an alternative certification program that seeks to fill teacher shortages by training professionals and college graduates from other fields to be educators. Fellows receive three months of intensive summer training and then begin teaching in "hard-

Harvard Educational Review   Vol. 74   No. 3   Fall 2004

to-staff" schools, many of whose credentials are in jeopardy due to low test scores. I teach sixth grade at a public middle school in Bushwick, a neighborhood in Brooklyn. My year has been tough, and filled with many of the complaints shared by my colleagues in the program—poor student behavior and academic performance, insufficient administrative support, and sheer exhaustion. One reaction, however, has been completely unexpected. I have been both intrigued and appalled by how often I have thought of *Newjack* since beginning my job. Many of my own experiences led me to recall Conover's memoir, comparing my first year as a New York Department of Education teacher to his as a Department of Correctional Services officer. I have concluded that my school shares many—too many—similarities with the prison where Conover spent twelve months. From their physical structures to the human relations within, to the legacy of failure in both institutions, the parallels between Sing Sing and our school are clear and ominous.

I will discuss these parallels, using Conover's book as a foundation. My aim is not to say that our school is just like a prison. Rather, I hope to make clear that, because the school replicates many of the elements and dynamics of a prison, it makes its motto, "Raise Our Expectations to Cross the Bridge to Success," all the more unlikely to be fulfilled.

THE PHYSICAL ENVIRONMENT

I started at the school on a hot July day, the first day of summer school. Having received my assignment at the district office, I walked the ten blocks from there to the school. The school, which is in a neighborhood that is visibly poor but relatively well kept, appears stately at first glance. Its rectangular, yellow brick structure reminded me of my high school in Boston, also built in the early twentieth century. A fence encircles the grounds, and there is even a bit of enclosed greenery in the front, although a sheet of asphalt covers the back. To enter, you must sign in with the unarmed school safety officer (one of four on duty) and proceed upstairs to the main hallway. My immediate impression of the school's interior was that it was a dreary place, not at all the warm, inviting place that a school should be. There is no natural light in the corridors, and their hard, dull surfaces give the place an institutional feel. The light that does enter the building is heavily filtered by the sturdy metal grates that cover each window. These metal grates, as well as the cage-like structures that "fallproof" the stairwells, were what first caused me to think of a prison. Walking through the halls, peering into different rooms, I saw that some were orderly and some were in varying stages of disrepair—several were strewn with trash, and one room appeared to have been flooded. Few rooms were air conditioned, and the oppressive summer heat did not make the prospect of student teaching summer school any more appealing. As I walked to my assigned room, I considered the fact that I would spend the next two years of my life working in this building, and the thought did not cheer me.

THE SOCIAL ENVIRONMENT

In his book *The Tipping Point*, Malcolm Gladwell (2000) discusses what he calls "the power of context." Reviewing various experiments on the circumstances in which schoolchildren cheat on tests (as well as the famous Stanford Prison Experiment where students took the roles of jailers and prisoners), Gladwell concludes that environmental conditions such as order, chaos, tranquility, or disrepair significantly determine how people behave. For example, turnstile jumping is more common in a dirty, dangerous subway station than a clean, safe one. Children who misbehave in a rowdy classroom are less likely to do so in a well-managed one. This means that "children are powerfully shaped by their external environment, [and] that the features of our immediate social and physical world . . . play a huge role in shaping who we are and how we act" (p. 168). In other words, physical and social environments that promote good behavior are more likely to result in good behavior. Gladwell explains, "In ways that we don't necessarily appreciate, our inner states are the result of our outer circumstances" (p. 152).

As indicated above, our school's physical environment bears resemblance to a prison-like structure, and the social behavior inside all too often reflects that similarity. Below I will focus on how the social environment of my school, namely, interactions between staff and students, affects the behavior of both and reinforces the similarity to the interpersonal dynamics found in Conover's prison.

CONTROL

In order to occupy a position of authority, one must assume that authority. Just as Conover (2001) learned that wearing a uniform and a badge does not necessarily engender respect and obedience, I also quickly found that holding the position of teacher in a classroom does not automatically earn me respect. Both the corrections officer and the teacher must assume their authority; in other words, they must make clear that they are in charge through word and deed. Conover describes the importance of control in this process: "Many judged themselves and their peers by the degree of control they were able to maintain over inmates" (p. 31). "Officers critiqued the permissiveness they perceived in each other more than any other quality" (p. 90). The same circumstances exist among the faculty of our school. Those who can control their classes are accorded the most respect. Ms. X and Ms. Y are lauded for their superior control, and many—myself included—have spoken of their skills in wistful terms as we wonder just how they do it. However, teachers who have no control are viewed with either pity or scorn. Control is viewed as the *sine qua non* of teaching at our school, to the extent that even a teacher who is unsuccessful as an educator can be valued solely for his or her ability to make students comply with instructions. For example, the teacher of one of the most notorious classes, a group of eighth graders with academic and behavior problems, failed a state teacher exam, but she was nevertheless viewed as an essential teacher because the consensus was that she was the only one who could control those students.

One quickly learns that the school, for the most part, leaves the issue of control to the teachers. Discipline, except for the most egregious violations (e.g., assaults that cause injury), is mainly the classroom teacher's province. While school discipline guidelines do exist, these are followed inconsistently. Conover speaks of the effort expended to "become savvy as to which rules were commonly ignored" (2001, p. 107), an unsanctioned but necessary part of fitting into the culture of the institution. I remember that I spent a lot of time during my first months trying to discipline students for infractions of these guidelines—being out of uniform, using bad language—that in retrospect seem inconsequential to the point of being comic. I gradually learned to conserve my disciplinary ammunition for the "big stuff," like fighting or other serious disruptions.

US VS. THEM

While there are as many routes to achieving control as there are teachers, some prevalent themes are apparent. Conover observes that prison "is actually a world of two sides . . . the 'us' and the 'them'" (2001, p. 18). This separation creates a palpable adversarial dynamic in which each side expresses contempt for the other. He recalls officers who dehumanize their charges, referring to them in derogatory terms. Conover reasons that regarding inmates as savages is a coping mechanism for the officers: "If a savage dissed you, what did it matter? And if a savage got hurt (particularly due to an error on your part), who cared?" (p. 87). Like Conover, I remember being repulsed by colleagues who referred to their students as "bitches," "assholes," and "animals," to name but a few epithets. But given the oppositional atmosphere of our school, this same dehumanization strategy is perhaps a natural, if extremely distressing, reaction to the circumstances: If a disruptive student insults you, what does it matter? After all, he or she is just an "asshole." And if your students do not learn, well, it is because they are "animals." This logic does not make the place any more pleasant and it wreaks havoc on the educational mission, but for some it makes the job more bearable.

The "us vs. them" dynamic frequently manifests itself on a quotidian level. Every challenge by a student is a test for the teacher, who must constantly reassert authority in order to maintain control. Conover recounts a seemingly minor dispute with an inmate over a radio antenna that erupted into a fierce exchange, which echoes the daily arguments I have with students over such trivial matters as borrowing pencils, where to sit, or going to the bathroom: "In prison, unlike the outside world, power and authority were at stake in nearly every transaction" (2001, p. 98). Unfortunately, our school seems to be "unlike the outside world" as well. Challenges to authority are frequent, as are refusals to comply.

Conover writes of the fear of a confrontation in which an inmate refuses to back down from a relatively minor infraction: "But what were you to do in such a situation? Write the inmate a ticket for disobeying a direct order? Walk away and lose face?" (2001, p. 58). I too am afraid of confrontation. Rather than subsiding as I gained more experience, this fear grew over the course of my first year, because it became clear to me that little in the way of substantive consequences exist for all but the most disruptive behavior. Writing tickets, or in our school "referrals," is futile, and I largely stopped issuing them. Discipline, apart from a short-lived and anemic lunch detention program for tardy students, seems reserved for infractions that would be better termed felonies. The suspensions that I am aware of are due to injurious physical assaults on teachers and students, several of whom have gone to the hospital for treatment. By way of comparison, what would be considered suspension-worthy in many other schools—for instance, loudly telling the principal to "shut the fuck up" on the first day of school—tends to conclude with the loss of face, not for the offender but for the victim. In this case, the principal shook his head, told the student not to speak to him like that, and walked away. In order to avoid the potential loss of face, many teachers resort to bluster and verbal aggression, as if to overpower and suppress any resistance from their students. Some teachers seek to develop the "command" voices favored by law enforcement to obtain immediate compliance; others simply yell at the top of their lungs. This very much unnerved me when I began teaching; now I barely pause when I hear the savage adult bellowing that constantly echoes down the halls. While screaming is of dubious pedagogical value, many of its practitioners would agree with the corrections officer who, referring to his preference for using profanity, allowed that "it's the fastest way to get the job done" (Conover, 2001, p. 69).

STRESS

Conover notes that prison changed his natural disposition from one of calm to one of stress. He writes of the physical response he felt as he entered the prison: "Your stomach lets you know, just before the shift starts, what it thinks of this job" (2001, p. 5). I felt a comparable response in my inability to sleep on Sunday nights. I would lie awake, dreading the uninterrupted stress of the next five days. The stress comes from many places: the inevitable exhaustion that the next day will bring, the knowledge that my students (almost all of whom perform below grade level) are not sufficiently progressing, fear of being involved in one of the frequent physical altercations that take place in the halls, fear of unexpected censure from an assistant principal for any one of countless possible "adminis-trivial" infractions, fear of having to cover an unknown class for an absent teacher, fear of not being able to hack it . . . the list goes on. In short, one feels caught between upward and downward forces. The students—who don't enjoy being there—present academic and management challenges from below. The administrators, responding to strong demands to raise test scores, put intense pressure on teachers to adhere to strict instructional models and curriculum pacing schedules, despite the school's chaotic state. Although Conover deals with different anxieties, I recognize and sympathize with his situation:

> It was an experience of living with fear—fear of inmates, as individuals and as a mob, and fear of our own capacity to fuck up. We were sandwiched between two groups: Make a mistake around the white-shirts [supervisors] and you would get in trouble; make a mistake around the inmates and you might get hurt. (2001, p. 95)

The teachers are not the only ones who suffer from stress. The disorder that prevails within school walls creates a stressful environment for students as well, which is certainly a determining factor in their poor academic performance and their frequent aggression. Lack of order and discipline go hand in hand with student dissatisfaction and misbehavior, a phenomenon similar to what Conover noticed in Sing Sing. Inmates preferred order, rules, and facilities with strict discipline. High staff turnover and new officers "irritated inmates in much the same way that substitute teachers irritate schoolchildren" (2001, p. 99). Conover concludes that, to some extent, prisoner aggression "had its roots in Sing Sing's frequent changes of officers" (p. 99).

As noted above, coverage, or the practice of using teachers who have a planning period to substitute teach for absent teachers (our school has enormous difficulty hiring substitutes, due to a lack of interested candidates), is one of the most unpleasant experiences of the job. You walk into a classroom of unknown students who immediately sense your disorientation and take it as license to act as they wish. Given the students' preference for consistency and tendency toward aggravation at the sight of a new face, you can imagine the effects of the high staff absenteeism rate at our school. One teacher called in sick more than thirty (!) days, and there were several "emergency" days, when ten to fifteen teachers (nearly a quarter of the staff) were out. I took each sick day I earned, one per month.

GET OUT OR GO UNDER

Unsurprisingly, and not unlike the officers Conover met in Sing Sing, many of my colleagues and I talk of moving on. Forty percent of teachers at our school—about the same average for other city schools—have spent fewer than two years there (NYC Department of Education, 2002). Just as Sing Sing has a reputation for greater indiscipline and disorder than the more tightly run facilities upstate, many NYC public schools, mine included, appear more difficult and unappealing than their suburban counterparts. I have frequently received the same counsel from experienced colleagues: "Do your two years [the length of the Teaching Fellows' contractual commitment] and then go teach in the suburbs."

In all likelihood, I will take their advice to leave—not necessarily to "the suburbs," but to a school that won't cause me sleepless nights. I want to work in a "normal" school, where students and teachers don't scream at each other, you don't find urine in the stairwells, and I don't need a supervisor's signature to make photocopies. I especially want a school where education isn't understood simply in terms of how well one scores on a citywide exam in April. I know such schools exist, because I've traveled to them for classes and meetings. They are clean and orderly, student work hangs undamaged in the hallways, kids go up the "up" stairways and down the "down" stairways, and the fire alarm isn't pulled every hour. Our school is far from the worst in the system, but I know there are a lot better schools out there, and I want to work in one of them.

I already see the negative effects of our school's atmosphere on my own behavior and perspective. Conover writes of how the prison's oppressive environment ate away at his previously held compassion and tolerance, such as when he took comfort in the story of officers abusing an inmate who had hurt a colleague. I noticed a similar coarsening of my spirit during my year teaching. I longed for my more disruptive students to be absent and felt my spirits fall when they entered the room. Despite campaigning to get my students to be more respectful, I felt a mixture of envy and delight when children directly insulted administrators that I didn't respect. I found myself doing things for which I used to criticize my colleagues; for example, one day in a private discussion with a fellow teacher, I dismissed a particularly difficult student with an expletive. Although I caught myself, I felt a shiver of dread. "Oh no, I'm becoming Mr. Z" [a teacher particularly scornful of his students], I joked, but I felt no mirth. I have observed my colleagues, and I have come to the conclusion that remaining at our school results in one of three phenomena: 1) you cope by falling prey to the inhumanity of the "us vs. them" mentality and act accordingly; 2) you insulate yourself by refusing to care and bide your time until you can transfer or retire; or 3) the stress gets to you and your mental health suffers. None of those choices appeals to me, so next year I will update my resume and begin checking the classifieds. I suppose there is a fourth possibility, in which one could work to improve the culture of the school from inside the classroom, but this strikes me as being as daunting a task as a corrections officer changing a prison's culture from his/her assigned post. My own efforts to this end, such as making it a point to always be civil to my students, never to raise my voice to them, and to smile a lot, seem nice but pathetically feeble in the context of our school's dysfunction. As I compare the inadequacy of my response to the magnitude of the problem, my preference is to abandon ship.

CROSSING THE BRIDGE TO FAILURE?

In his study of why the tiny African country of Lesotho has not developed economically, political scientist James Ferguson (1990) makes an interesting comparison. The scores of aid agencies that make up the development industry in the country—Lesotho has received no small amount of development assistance from wealthy countries—labor incessantly in pursuit of their goal of development. Despite this considerable attention, however, Lesotho remains one of the poorest countries in the world, belying the efforts and money expended. Nevertheless, the development industry continues to pursue development, apparently heedless of its continued lack of success. This diligent but fruitless devotion to a desired objective, Ferguson argues, bears much in common with the way prisons work. Both fail to the extent that their failure eclipses any successes achieved, but this does not dim their ardor.

Citing philosopher Michel Foucault's (1977) study of prisons, Ferguson (1990) notes that, while prisons are envisioned as "correctional" institutions, they produce the opposite effect. Instead of reforming criminals, their operation is such that they reinforce a criminal's delinquency. While at first this might appear to be a failure, Foucault argues that it is, in fact, a success. "The prison, apparently 'failing,' does not miss its target" (1977, p. 276). The goal of the prison is not reform, he maintains:

> For the observation that the prison fails to eliminate crime, one should perhaps substitute the hypothesis that prison has succeeded extremely well in producing delinquency . . . in an apparently marginal, but centrally supervised milieu. . . . So successful has the prison been that, after a century and a half of "failures," the prison still exists, producing the same results, and there is the greatest reluctance to dispense with it. (p. 277)

When one examines the dismal academic performance of our school, with only 14 percent of students meeting state standards in language arts, and 75 percent below standards in math (NYC Department of Education, 2002), one begins to wonder if the nature of our school is failure to educate its students. How can such a profound failure be tolerated, let alone allowed to continue? Despite the No Child Left Behind legislation and our status as a "corrective action" school for language arts, failure is indeed allowed to flourish. The administration strives to meet required targets by nibbling at the margins, by trying to push students who are approaching standards to cross the line. Those who fall far below standards—no small portion of the student population—are essentially cut loose and allowed to languish. In correctional facilities, rehabilitation occurs so infrequently that it is considered the exception rather than the norm. In our school, it seems that education is a similarly exceptional outcome. Three out of four students graduate unable to do math sufficiently, and four out of five are unable to read or write acceptably.

A 2002 decision by a state appeals court provides a useful perspective on why this failure exists and continues. The court overturned a previous ruling that New York City public schools were underfunded, a ruling that would have obligated the state to increase its financing of city schools. In rejecting that ruling, the appeals court demonstrated a shockingly callous logic. The *New York Times* summarized the court's conclusion that

> the state was obliged to provide no more than a middle school education, and to prepare students for nothing more than the lowest-level job. . . . Even if students were not properly educated . . . that did not mean that the state had failed its obligation. "The proper standard is that the state must offer all children the opportunity of a sound basic education, not ensure that they actually receive it."
> (Pérez-Peña, 2002, p. 1)

The court's definition of a "sound basic education" exposes the failure in their logic. Rejecting evidence that New York's public schools offer a substandard education, the court ruled that "teachers with poor qualifications, overcrowded schools, poor physical conditions, and schools that do not have libraries, did not mean that the essentials were not being provided" (Pérez-Peña, 2002, p. 1). One would like to believe that, in twenty-first century America, such a school would hardly be seen as providing "the essentials." In all likelihood, such a school would not be where the ruling judges choose to send their children.[1]

Last winter, I stopped to take a look at the bulletin board outside the guidance office. Three flyers were posted; two advertised for local public high schools, each with academic records even more wretched than those at our school, and one highlighted a training program run by a local pharmacy chain. This program offered teens certification in retail sales, and promised those who completed training preferential candidacy for entry-level vacancies. As I walked away, I wondered how the bulletin board outside the guidance office of a suburban middle school must look. There would be brochures for preparatory high schools, as well as for summer programs in art, music, science, and sports. Students would be encouraged to become doctors, lawyers, artists, and executives; at our school, a lone flyer exhorts students to work cash registers.

Does this mean our school is a failure? Following Foucault's (1977) logic, one could conclude that, rather than failing, it is succeeding. As the appeals court decided by allowing to continue operation of a school where most children do not learn to read, write, or do math, we "educate" them for the world of minimum-wage, unskilled work. We don't need to concern ourselves with providing a better education for our students; there are plenty of schools that will do that for other children. We have already taught our children—at least those who do manage to find employment, for some will no doubt become the charges of Conover's erstwhile colleagues—on which side of the till they belong.

NOTE

1. This decision has since been reversed, offering the prospect of much needed hope—and cash (Schrag, 2003).

REFERENCES

Conover, T. (2001). *Newjack: Guarding Sing Sing.* New York: Vintage Books.

Ferguson, J. (1990). *The anti-politics machine: "Development," depoliticization and bureaucratic power in Lesotho.* New York: Cambridge University Press.

Foucault, M. (1977). *Discipline and punish: The birth of the prison.* New York: Vintage Books.

Gladwell, M. (2000). *The tipping point: How little things can make a big difference.* New York: Little, Brown.

New York City Department of Education. (2002). *2001–2002 annual school report, IS 162.* Retrieved May 3, 2003 from http://www.nycboe.net

Pérez-Peña, R. (2002, June 26). Court reverses finance ruling on city schools. *New York Times.* Retrieved May 3, 2003 from http://www.nytimes.com

Schrag, P. (2003, June 28). Adequacy in education: Why is clear. But how? *New York Times,* p. A15.

AGAINST THE PIPELINE

■

ROBERT WILSON

My son was arrested at school last year. I was on house arrest at the time and couldn't even pick him up from the police station. The remorse I suffered knowing I had been a bad influence was worse than the guilt I felt over my whole criminal history. I wanted the ground to open up and swallow me. I was arrested my sophomore year of high school with lasting consequences. Malcolm was only in the eighth grade.

After his suspension, I attended a conference at my son's middle school. This was where I met his teachers for the first time. I came prepared—I'd read up on attention deficit disorder and prepared a list of "Learning Strategies for the Global Thinker." I had begun to tame disorder with order by setting up a quiet study area at home free from distracting media and gadgets. Helping Malcolm with his homework was a good way for us to spend more time together. My son needed a better father. I was committed to becoming one. When we entered the room, the teachers and school guidance counselor were assembled in formation around a table—a panel of judges.

Nothing would improve without all of us working together. Hardest of all, for me, was admitting I needed help and asking for it. Yet, I was there to ask for help. The teachers looked at each other before answering me, giving bland replies to my suggestions. After a few attempts to engage them in meaningful discussion, I realized they were only prepared to give each family fifteen minutes. We weren't there to communicate; we were there to plead our case. Malcolm had arrived at the off-ramp where school turns toward prison, merging seamlessly with the highway to hell.

In order to end Malcolm's suspension and avoid further punishment, we would have to sign a contract, promising his attendance and grades would improve. "We can't control him," they were saying. "He's failing." Looking into their eyes, I felt we were not quite finished on the subject of failure. "Why is my kid so bored in your classes?" I asked. I wanted to know what additional attention they were willing to commit to. Since we were signing a contract, why would I not try to negotiate a better deal?

What we got out of this meeting was the Gradebook Wizard. With this automated system, teachers can alert parents, via e-mail, of missing classes and incomplete assignments—in theory, it's a way to maintain ongoing and helpful communication. When I responded to these e-mails, I received curt confirmations or no reply at all. An excused absence could generate twenty or more automated messages. The Wizard seemed like one-way communication, the educational equivalent of spam, a tool to limit contact with parents. There could have been a peer group, a mentoring program—they could have offered to educate *me*, at the very least.

Malcolm's public defender warned us about the possibility of us being charged with "obstructing the educational process," a fourth-degree felony added on to any offense committed in school. This is often the first step before permanent expulsion. Schools often find it expedient to lock troublemakers into the legal system, handing them over to an adversarial juvenile justice system only interested in keeping them off of the streets. Charter schools and home schooling serve as an alternative, but getting into one can mean setbacks as students adjust to a new environment.

Everyone is self-educated. A teacher may present material, set a syllabus, and even be clever enough to throw that spark that starts a discussion, but anyone who attends classes, pays attention, and completes assignments is, in a sense, self-taught. Knowledge germinates in the prepared mind, the one that has decided to learn. We do that or not on our own initiative.

Today, my son and I are both in high school. He made it through a program for juvenile offenders and into the high school I should have graduated from. I'm writing from the Gordon Bernell Charter School in county jail. This school offers help with parenting, career planning, and college preparation. At Gordon Bernell we can also receive counseling to help with substance abuse, relapse prevention, and anger management. Here, adults can receive basic education, advancing at their own pace in pursuit of a high school diploma. I'm in charge of my education; my experience in public schools didn't foster this kind of independent thinking. The legal system is giving me an opportunity to remake myself into a better role model.

I've heard some parents ask why kids aren't learning. Actually, they are. They know all the words to the songs on their iPods. They know the legal negotiations involving their sports heroes—financial and criminal. They know how to label people according to the finest nuance of dress or speech. If they find a subject of interest to them, they exhaust it and move on to something else. They know how to get along with each other and get around parents—and what *not* to say to the school safety officer. They are preparing themselves for the dangerous, competitive world they are building.

It isn't our children who fail us, but the other way around. Their job is to grow and learn. The more I became involved in his life, the more I learned Malcolm was doing what he wanted and going to school on top of it. His varied interests and complex relationships were an overlooked masterpiece of multitasking. Once I invested the time and attention necessary to earn his trust, he showed me just how big his world was. I became his student.

The problem was that some of the things my son wanted were bad for him. It was difficult to accept that, as close as I wanted us to be, my guidance wasn't enough. Peer counseling and mentorship, which he received in the juvenile justice system, would have worked better in school, where it wasn't offered. He really responded to some of the programs he was court-ordered to attend. He was able to connect with good influences. Even his probation officer was positive and encouraging. His attitude changed completely. Although helpful, this background has resulted in him being stigmatized by his record and isolated by teachers. Malcolm began high school with a bad reputation and a criminal record. No child deserves that.

I'm working on my own reputation. The Gordon Bernell Charter School and the Honor Pod, in which program participants reside, focus on basic education and socialization. There is the sense that this pilot program is all an experiment and that it can all be taken away if it fails, as important as it is to us. Like my son, I have benefited from special programs trying to disrupt the "school-to-prison" pipeline, yet when I consider the ease with which potential employers may review my criminal history, it seems like too little too late.

A chart from a local community college has a list of careers, each marked red, yellow, or green. Red careers are discouraged for felons, yellow are "pursue at your own risk," and green says, "No foreseeable barriers to employment." There are invisible signs everywhere telling us we aren't wanted. Some of the men in here have legacies like mine going back generations. Once you're in the system, it isn't your crimes that keep you down, it's your record. The responsibility of the educational system is to create an environment that fosters a desire for learning and encourages the foresight to avoid criminal behavior.

Public schools need to be more accountable and less insular. More class time should be devoted to critical and analytical thinking. Businesses and communities should sponsor mentoring and recreational programs, opening clear paths to desirable careers. All kids are "at risk." Americans, as a people, need to let children know we need them.

I'm willing to accept I will never do all the things I once wanted to in life. Lately, I've been letting go of dreams simply because I'm thinking of more noble things. My future may include nothing more exciting than college courses in prison. I don't know what the future holds. It seems like the whole world turns against you when you start looking for a way back. What I do know is that there is no sacrifice too great to make this cycle end with me.

SOUND DISCIPLINE POLICY FOR SUCCESSFUL SCHOOLS

HOW REDRESSING RACIAL DISPARITIES CAN MAKE
A POSITIVE IMPACT FOR ALL

■

DANIEL J. LOSEN

There is a national phenomenon which shows that young students of color, particularly males, are disproportionately suspended and disciplined more harshly than their White peers. In this essay, Daniel J. Losen analyzes the school-to-prison pipeline and the frequent use of out-of-school suspensions using disparate impact theory, *which asks three central questions: Do suspension policies and practices impact students of color disproportionately? Is the use of these exclusionary measures educationally necessary and justifiable? And are there better alternatives? Losen reviews state and federal data and the research literature on effective school discipline to respond to these questions and concludes with three policy recommendations, which include increased data collection and reporting, the inclusion of systemwide triggers for intervention, and alignment between academic assessment and discipline policy. These remedies, designed to prevent racial injustice, would also help ensure that school discipline policy and practice more effectively serve an educational mission for all students.*

In March of 2010, Secretary of Education Arne Duncan (2010) stood on the Edmund Pettis Bridge in Selma, Alabama, highlighting the racial disparities in the use of suspension and expulsion and speaking on the importance of strengthening civil rights enforcement in education. The secretary suggested that students with disabilities and Black students, especially males, were suspended far more often than their White peers and often punished more severely for similar misdeeds. Subsequently, U.S. Attorney General Eric Holder and Secretary Duncan addressed a conference of civil rights lawyers in Washington, DC, and affirmed their departments' commitment to remedying these disparities (Zehr, 2010). As part of their promised efforts, they indicated that new guidelines would be released to help states and districts determine whether their discipline policies may have an unlawful "disparate impact" under the U.S. Department of Education's Title VI regulations, which are enforced by its Office for Civil Rights (OCR).[1] The guidance is still forthcoming, but a simple application of the Title VI regulations to school discipline would read as follows:

> Under the "disparate impact" theory, a method of discipline that is racially neutral on its face but has a discriminatory effect may be found unlawful absent sufficient justification such as educational necessity. Even if a school's action is justified, it still may be unlawful if equally effective, less discriminatory alternatives are available. (Kim, Losen, & Hewitt, 2010, p. 39)

The disparate impact approach does not ask whether similarly situated students were disciplined differently along racial lines. Instead, a policy or practice may be found in violation of Title VI if it has a more adverse impact on a protected minority group. In addition, the policy is only a violation of the law if either there is no educational necessity or if the necessity exists but there is an equally effective alternative with a less adverse impact available.

Ideally, policy and program reforms are those that have been proven effective. Further, principles of efficiency demand that we improve policies and practices so that as we strive for safe and effective school environments, we continuously improve outcomes and diminish any unintended costs. These goals, shared by all educators, are at the core of the argument in favor of applying disparate impact analysis. Even when a complainant makes a disparate impact claim against a district, the outcome would now be determined solely as a matter of administrative law by the U.S. Department of Education. The remedies in disparate impact cases are limited to forms of injunctive relief. There are no money or punitive damages to be gained and no jobs in jeopardy. The vast majority of complaints that are resolved for the complainant do not even wind up before an administrative judge but lead to a "resolution agreement" negotiated between the district and the Department of Education and/or the complainant(s). The purpose of filing a disparate impact administrative complaint is to move school districts to adopt more effective discipline practices and policies that serve the goal of creating safe and orderly school environments but in a manner that has less of an adverse impact on students of color, or no adverse impact at all. Disparate impact legal analysis requires the examination of three prongs: (1) Does the race neutral policy or practice have a racially disparate negative impact? (2) Is the policy educationally necessary? (3) If justified by necessity, is there an equally effective less discriminatory alternative?

Although every district is unique, the data presented here suggests that the first prong would often be met.[2] In many districts, one or more minority racial groups appear to be suspended frequently and at far higher rates than White students. There is no question about the *intended* benefits of out-of-school suspensions; safer and more productive educational environments are critically important to achieving the educational mission of our public schools. Equally obvious are the direct costs, such as the loss of instructional time and the stigma experienced by the punished student. More recently, research has pointed to large indirect costs from frequent suspensions, including increased risk for all of the following: low achievement, dropping out, delinquency and gang affiliation, and involvement in the juvenile justice system. It is now well established that there are high costs incurred by those students who are suspended out of school, costs that can last a lifetime. Out-of-school suspensions also impose costs on the community that stem from the heightened risk that suspended students will drop out, commit crimes, wind up in the juvenile justice system, and be less likely to succeed in school or the workforce. The increased risk for low productivity, crime, juvenile justice involvement, and incarceration translates into higher costs to the taxpayer.

Prong two of the disparate impact analysis asks whether the policy or practice of *frequently* suspending children is educationally necessary. While most would agree that a suspension out of school, especially for an older student who poses a danger to himself or others, might be necessary in some circumstances, this essay focuses on the high frequency with which minority youth are suspended for minor and mostly nonviolent offenses, not just the disparity. The research discussed herein did not examine whether the use of out-of-school suspension was ever, or could ever be, a sound practice.

Finally, in accord with the third prong of the legal framework, the research presented suggests that there may be equally effective and less discriminatory alternatives to the frequent reliance on out-of-school suspensions. Questions of Title VI regulatory compliance aside, the research presented suggests that as a matter of policy, all school districts with high out-of-school suspension rates, and large racial disparities in those rates, should be encouraged to explore viable alternatives to ensuring safe and effective educational environments. This article concludes by documenting how, as policy makers come to understand the costs of frequent disciplinary exclusion from school, there is growing interest in reforming federal and state policy to reduce out-of-school suspensions in favor of alternative ways of improving behavior, including systemic approaches that look at improving instruction and more effective school leadership.

DOES THE FREQUENT RELIANCE ON OUT-OF-SCHOOL SUSPENSION HAVE AN ADVERSE IMPACT ON STUDENTS OF COLOR?

Policies that result in out-of-school suspensions and expulsions are described as "exclusionary" because they remove students from school. The emphasis of the analysis here is placed on out-of-school suspensions, rather than expulsions, in part because schools expel rather than suspend the most serious offenders, such as students who pose a real danger to others. Further, the use of out-of-school suspensions dwarfs expulsions by about thirty-two to one. According to the U.S. Department of Education's 2006 Civil Rights Data Collection (CRDC), more than 3.25 million students, approximately 7 percent of all students enrolled in K–12, are estimated to have been suspended at least once (U.S. Department of Education, 2006) This means that, on average, for each day public schools are in session in the United States, a new group of approximately 18,000 public school students is suspended out of school for at least a day. In contrast, on average, nationally there are about 560 expulsions each day.

Increases in Suspension Rates Since the Early 1970s

Since 1968 the federal government has been collecting data on out-of-school suspension and expulsion (Hawley & Ready, 2003). OCR administers a biennial survey, which typically includes one-third to one-half of U.S. public schools and districts. In 2000 it conducted a nearly universal survey, and another universal survey is scheduled for 2011–2012. Schools are instructed to count each suspended student only once, even if the student received several suspensions. This head-count data can be used alongside enrollment data to determine what percentage of a given subgroup was suspended (see figure 1). Researchers point out, however, that the unduplicated data yield a conservative estimate of students' time out of school because the data do not capture repeat suspensions or the length of the suspensions (Losen & Skiba, 2010).

An analysis of OCR data describing the number of students (not incidents) shows a large increase in K–12 suspension rates for all groups since the early 1970s, more than doubling since the early 1970s for all non-Whites but not for Whites (Losen & Skiba, 2010). Concurrently, the Black/White gap more than tripled in size, increasing from a difference of three percentage points in the 1970s to over ten percentage points in 2006. According to an analysis of the publicly released data, the most recent survey sample of approximately half the nation's school districts for 2009–2010 produced rates for Whites, Hispanics, Asian/Pacific Islanders, and Native Americans that were within a percentage point of their estimated rates for 2006. Black estimated rates, however, may have risen by more than 2 percentage points (Losen & Gillespie, 2012).[3] However, a number of minor differences between current and prior data collection and reporting requirements, and slight differences in the formulas used to calculate the national estimates, means that no firm conclusions should be drawn about whether suspension rates across the nation have actually risen or fallen since the 2006–2007 school year.[4] This means that approximately one out of every six Black students enrolled in 2009–2010 was suspended at least once compared to about one out of every twenty White students.

Higher Rates in Many States and Districts

Further analysis of the 2009–2010 data demonstrates that there is a high variation in suspension rates from state to state and district to district. For example, based on the totals of the sampled districts from Illinois, it is estimated that 25.3 percent of all enrolled Black K–12 students were suspended out of school at least once, compared with just 3.9 percent of all enrolled White students.

FIGURE 1   Racial impact of the rising use of suspension
Percent of enrollment by race suspended out of school one day or more

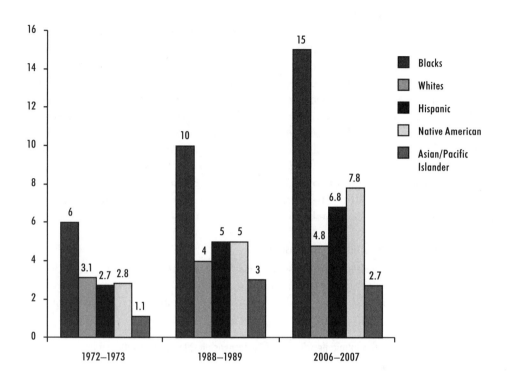

Source: Losen & Skiba (2010). Copyright © The Civil Rights Project at UCLA 2012. Adapted with permission. http://civilrightsproject.ucla.edu/

Similarly, in Michigan it is estimated that Black students were suspended at much higher rates than White students (22.1% versus just 6.2%). However, in Montana, which had relatively low rates across the board, the estimates show almost no racial disparity in the suspension rates among Hispanic (3.9%), White (3.8%), and Black students (3.4%).

The most dramatic racial disparities are found at the district level. According to the same OCR survey, in 2009–2010 Fort Wayne, Indiana,[5] suspended 55.7 percent of all Black students, 14.4 percent of all Hispanic students, 27.3 percent of all American Indian students, 19.1 percent of all White students, and 4.1 percent of all Asian American students. This district reported alarmingly high rates for most groups, but the high rates for Blacks and the 36.6 percentage point difference between Black and White students put this district among the top fifty districts in the nation for both the suspension rates for Black students and for the percentage point divide between Black and White suspension rates. It should be noted that some of the districts with high rates according to the survey data from 2009–2010 may have implemented changes in the last two years to reduce their high rates.

Disparities in Middle School by Race and Gender

The 2010 report *Suspended Education: Urban Middle Schools in Crisis* revealed profound racial and gender disparities at the middle school level, showing much higher rates than appear when aggregate K–12 data are analyzed (Losen & Skiba, 2010). For example, based on OCR data from every state, 28 percent of Black males in middle school were suspended, compared to just 10 percent of White males in middle school nationally. Moreover, 18 percent of Black females were suspended, compared to just 4 percent of White females. The report's further analysis of data for eighteen of the nation's largest districts found that in fifteen of them, at least 30 percent of all enrolled middle school Black males were suspended one or more times. Across these eighteen urban districts, hundreds of individual middle schools had extraordinarily high suspension rates—50 percent or higher for Black males (see figure 2).

Racial Disparities Among Students with Disabilities

Racial disparities in discipline also appear within the subgroup of students with disabilities (see table 1). In ten states in 2007–2008, more than one in five Black students with disabilities were suspended for at least one day. Three states

FIGURE 2   Racial disparities in middle school student suspension rates by race with gender

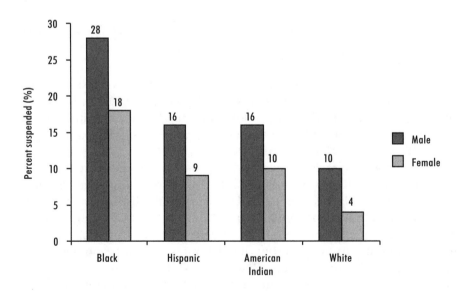

Source: Losen & Skiba (2010). Copyright © The Civil Rights Project at UCLA 2012. Adapted with permission. http://civilrightsproject.ucla.edu/

TABLE 1   National comparison of students with disabilities and risk for suspension by race

	American Indian	Asian (combined)	Hispanic	Black	White	Total
Students with disabilities	11.1	3.4	12.2	24.8	8.9	13.0
Students without disabilities	7.7	2.1	6.7	16.0	4.1	6.7
Combined all students	8.2	2.2	7.3	17.2	4.7	7.4

Source of raw data: OCR (2009–2010). These data were analyzed using the data collected in the OCR sample without further statistical adjustments. From *Opportunities Suspended: The Disparate Impact of Disciplinary Exclusion from School,* by Daniel J. Losen and Jonathan Gillespie (August, 2012), published by The Center for Civil Rights Remedies at The Civil Rights Project of UCLA.

Copyright © The Civil Rights Project at UCLA 2012. Adapted with permission. http://civilrightsproject.ucla.edu/

(Nebraska, Wisconsin, and Nevada) suspended over 30 percent of all Black students with disabilities, with Nebraska reporting the highest rate (37%). In contrast, in those same states, White students with disabilities were suspended at half to one-fifth the rate of Blacks, with White rates never exceeding 12 percent (DAC, 2007–2008). Newer data from the 2009–2010 collection reveal that nationally, for every racial group, students with disabilities are suspended out of school at about twice the rate of their nondisabled peers.

IS THE FREQUENT USE OF SUSPENSION EDUCATIONALLY NECESSARY AND JUSTIFIABLE?

The data clearly demonstrate that some student subgroups receive a disproportionate number of exclusionary punishments. In light of these data, the question often arises whether Black children are treated differently because of their race, while others may wonder if Black children are simply misbehaving more. Importantly, the disparate impact approach does not center on the question of "different treatment," and therefore it does not require an investigation into whether some groups of children misbehave more than others. Even though disparate impact analysis focuses on whether unintended harmful consequences are justifiable or avoidable, it is useful to address the oft-heard defense that disparities in punishment simply reflect disparities in misbehavior.

One problem with answering this question is that without neutral observers in classrooms, there is no objective baseline for comparison. One can imagine that a teacher's snap judgment to refer a student for suspension may be influenced by a multitude of additional subjective considerations, including the relationship the teacher has with the student and with the child's parents. Both cultural and class differences may influence these relationships and judgments. Based on research suggesting that unconscious negative racial bias toward Black students is pervasive, though varied in degree, one would expect that teachers in the aggregate would have a greater tendency to perceive behavior of Black students in a negative light and to more quickly conclude that they were misbehaving or in need of punishment. If true, even a very subtle perceptual tendency would be expected to show up in a higher number of punishments meted out to Black students for offenses that involve more subjective judgment (e.g., insubordination, disruption, disrespect).

So when considering the evidence, it is important to understand that *unconscious* bias against Black students would not be expected to manifest itself as blatant and easily observable different treatment in discipline. Blacks would not *always* or *almost always* get punished more harshly. Instead, one would expect to see such unconscious bias reflected in disparities in rates of discipline for certain racial groups over the course of a year or more. While the disparities would be expected for large numbers of teachers in the aggregate, the degree of the disparity would be expected to differ considerably by individual teacher, school, and district.

Ultimately, looking only for proof of intentional different treatment, and asserting as a defense that a higher frequency of misbehavior explains stark racial disparities in suspensions, skirts the central question under disparate impact: whether frequently suspending students out of school is a sound educational policy response to the wide range of misbehaviors at issue. Yet, as a practical matter, it is also likely that if research revealed at least some evidence suggesting "different treatment," it may help persuade those on the fence about unconscious bias, as well as those who hesitate to support a disparate impact approach for fear of overreaching in school policy. It is worth noting that although the large disparities described thus far suggest that intentional "different treatment" may be a factor in some districts, the CRDC data neither include the reasons for suspension nor otherwise enable an observer to compare "similarly situated" students. However, the following section explores the evidence of different treatment from a variety of other sources.

Greater Suspension Rates Are Not Clearly Linked to More Frequent or More Serious Misbehavior

Research on student behavior, race, and discipline has found no evidence that Black overrepresentation in school suspension is due to higher rates of misbehavior (Kelly, 2010; McCarthy & Hoge, 1987). Strikingly, the Council of State Governments report found that Black students were more likely to be disciplined for less serious "discretionary" offenses and that when poverty and other factors were controlled for, higher percentages of White students were disciplined on more serious nondiscretionary grounds, such as possessing drugs or carrying a weapon (Fabelo et al., 2011). This robust study controlled for eighty-three variables that made it possible to isolate race and compare otherwise similarly situated students. The researchers concluded that among similar students, a student's race was predictive of the risk for being punished.

Further, a 2010 study, led by Johns Hopkins researcher Catherine Bradshaw (2010b) and based on twenty-one schools, found that even when controlling for teacher ratings of student misbehavior, Black students were more likely to be sent to the office for disciplinary reasons. These and numerous other empirical studies (Skiba, Michael, Nardo, & Peterson, 2002; Skiba et al., 2011) suggest that Black students are being unfairly singled out when it comes to prosecuting misbehavior that requires a more subjective evaluation.

Similar conclusions are suggested by an analysis of recent data from North Carolina concerning first-time offenders with no prior offenses. As figure 3 illustrates, Black first-time offenders in North Carolina were far more likely than White first-time offenders to be suspended for minor offenses, including cell phone use, disruptive behavior, and public displays of affection.[6]

Data on first-time offenders, disaggregated by race and type of offense, is not generally accessible or reported to the public but was obtained by lawyers who filed an OCR complaint against the Wake County School District. The district data, like the state data charted in figure 3, demonstrated that for the

FIGURE 3   North Carolina Black/White suspension rates, 2008–2009

Racial disparities in use of suspension for first-time offenders by type of offense

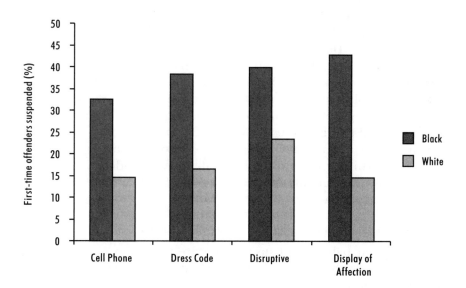

Source: Losen (2011a). Copyright © National Education Policy Center. Adapted with permission. http://nepc.colorado.edu

This figure is excerpted from data provided by Benita Jones and Elizabeth Haddix, based on data received by Jason Langberg, Equal Justice Works Fellow and staff attorney for Advocates for Children, Inc. The data were obtained pursuant to a Freedom of Information Act request to the state of North Carolina. Advocates for Children assisted in the discipline data analysis used by attorney Elizabeth Haddix in the filing of the administrative OCR complaint. Note that being a first-time offender means that those who were not suspended out of school the first time received another less severe punishment, such as in-school suspension, or no punishment at all.

same category of offense, far higher percentages of Black first-time offenders received out-of-school suspensions than White first-time offenders (Hui & Locke, 2010; UNC Center for Civil Rights, 2010). However, it should be noted that the "first-time" designation was based solely on behavior reported for the 2008–2009 school year and did not permit a consideration of prior years.

Other research also suggests that suspension rates are significantly influenced by factors other than differences in student misbehavior. For example, a statewide study of Indiana that controlled for race and poverty concluded that the attitude of a school's principal toward the use of suspension correlated highly with its actual use (Rausch & Skiba, 2005). Principals who believed frequent punishments helped improve behavior and who blamed behavioral problems on poor parenting and poverty also tended to suspend more students than those principals who strongly believed in enforcing school rules yet regarded suspension as a measure to be used sparingly. This evidence raises the possibility that schools with high levels of poverty and racial isolation are more likely to embrace the kind of harsh discipline policy and school leadership embodied by the iconic bat-and-bullhorn principal Joe Clark. According to *TIME* magazine, "On a single day in his first year, he threw out 300 students for being tardy or absent and, he said, for disrupting the school. 'Leeches and parasites,' he calls such pupils. Over the next five years he tossed out hundreds more" (Bowen, 1988).

The methods used by Clark, who was portrayed by Morgan Freeman in the popular movie *Lean on Me*, can be summarized as kicking out the *bad kids* so the *good kids* can learn. Despite the common-sense appeal, and the near-heroic status that Clark achieved, there is no evidence that Clark's approach worked to improve the education of well-behaved students, let alone those students removed from school (Biama & Moses, 1989). To the contrary, the schools run by the low-suspending principals in Indiana had higher test scores after controlling for race and poverty (Rausch & Skiba, 2005).

Still, many believe a heavy reliance on out-of-school suspension is necessary to protect the learning environment for well-behaved students. Misperceptions about the use and benefits of suspending students may contribute to the public embrace of the practice.

Three Common Misperceptions Used to Justify Frequent Use of Suspension

Contrary to popular belief, most suspensions are for minor and nonviolent offenses, not for guns, drugs, or serious violent acts. Rausch and Skiba (2006) reported that 95 percent of suspensions fell into two categories: *disruptive behavior* and *other*. Only 5 percent of all out-of-school suspensions in the state they studied were issued for disciplinary incidents typically considered serious or dangerous, such as possession of weapons or drugs. Similarly, the Texas study from the Council of State Governments demonstrated that 97 percent of the disciplinary actions were discretionary, meted out for violations of schools' conduct codes (Fabelo et al., 2011). Accordingly, the high rates of suspension for minor offenses raise questions about their justification, questions we might hesitate to pursue if they were responses to dangerous or criminal misbehavior.

Three reasons appear to account for the common use of out-of-school suspension or expulsion for nonviolent or repeated school code violations:

- To improve the student's behavior in the future by getting the parents' attention and active involvement
- To deter other students from misbehaving
- To ensure that the school environment is conducive to teaching and learning.

These speak to the second "educational necessity" prong of the disparate impact analysis.

Suspension to Get Parental Attention

Ideally, if suspensions heightened parental awareness, they would foster a more effective collaborative home and school effort to teach appropriate behavior. In turn, disruptive behavior would decrease, which would then improve the learning environment. In reality, to the extent that a child's persistent misbehavior is a signal of weaknesses in parenting or problems in the home environment, there is little reason to believe that removing a child from school to spend more time at home will improve behavior. Certainly, less extreme approaches, such as calling for a parent conference, can get parents to pay attention.

Moreover, the American Academy of Pediatrics Committee on School Health (2003), which studied the impact of suspensions and expulsions, pointed out the following related issues:

> Children with single parents are between 2 and 4 times as likely to be suspended or expelled from school as are children with both parents at home, even when controlling for other social and demographic factors . . . For students with major home-life stresses, academic suspension in turn provides yet another life stress that, when compounded with what is already occurring in their lives, may predispose them to even higher risks of behavioral problems. (p. 1207)

In addition, poor and single parents may feel that they must leave a child home unsupervised or risk losing their employment. Thus, there seems little reason to accept the claim that exclusion is an effective way to secure the kind of productive parental support that will improve the behavior of those children most likely to be excluded from schools. If out-of-school suspensions did serve this objective well, one would expect to see few students suspended repeatedly and marked improvements in behavior and academic outcomes. The opposite appears to the case.

Out-of-School Suspensions as Deterrence

If frequent use of suspensions deters future misbehavior, we would expect to see a positive cycle, with high levels of suspension one year leading to improved behavior in subsequent years. Yet, according to the American Psychological Association Zero Tolerance Task Force's (2008) published review of the literature, there is no evidence that zero tolerance disciplinary policies, as applied to mundane and nonviolent misbehavior, improve school safety or student behavior. Longitudinal studies have shown that students suspended in sixth grade are *more* likely to receive office referrals or suspensions by eighth grade, prompting some researchers to conclude that suspension may *reinforce* rather than punish inappropriate behavior (Sprague, Sugai, & Walker, 1998). Certainly, there are some struggling students who hate school and might therefore regard a suspension as more reward than punishment. Another longitudinal study of students from 150 schools in Florida's Pinellas County found a strong relationship, for both Black and White students, between the number of sixth-grade suspensions students received and the number of suspensions they subsequently received as seventh- and eighth-graders (Raffaele Mendez, 2003). In sum, research offers no support for the theory that suspensions deter future misbehavior.

Out-of-School Suspension to Improve the Teaching and Learning Environment

Certainly, suspending disruptive children might improve teaching conditions by relieving some of the teachers' burden and stress. Clearly, when teachers seek to remove a seriously disruptive student, the teacher feels that removal will help her be more effective with the students who remain. Along these lines, the American Federation of Teachers (AFT, 2009) in West Virginia recently launched a successful lobbying campaign called Discipline Without Delay and passed legislation to put more teeth in a 1995 act that gave teachers and bus drivers more authority to exclude "disruptive students."[7] The AFT has highlighted this campaign in its national literature as a model example of how the union can change policy to benefit teachers. But the stress-reduction argument assumes that just a few difficult students are the source of all the behavior problems. However, as Pedro Noguera (2001) observed, when a school in Oakland experimented with allowing teachers to remove disruptive students to a separate class, many teachers soon reported that in the wake of their departure "other children who had not been particularly disruptive had emerged as major behavior problems" (pp. 204–205).

Moreover, the question posed by the data is not as simple as how to respond to a few difficult students generating most of the behavior problems. Rather, the observed "unduplicated" rates of suspension are on average 28 percent of the enrollment of Black males attending middle school. While some students undoubtedly need a more restrictive educational setting, the need for such interventions on a case-by-case basis does not justify rates of suspension of this magnitude. If suspending large numbers of disruptive students, with no guarantee of adult supervision, helped improve instruction and the learning environment, better academic results would be expected. But the research indicates that this is not the case. Research on the frequent use of school suspension has indicated that, after controlling for race and poverty, higher rates of out-of-school suspension correlate with lower achievement scores (Skiba & Rausch, 2006) or showed no academic benefits as measured by test scores and were predictors of higher dropout rates (Fabelo et al., 2011).

Moreover, qualitative researchers have documented how the same student can behave very differently in different classrooms (Harry & Klingner, 2006). Disruptions tend to increase or decrease with the skill of the teacher in providing engaging instruction and in managing the classroom. As engagement goes up, misbehavior and suspensions tend to go down (Osher, Bear, Sprague, & Doyle, 2010).

Many teachers say they would like help improving their classroom management skills (Kratochwill, 2009). Researchers also find a strong connection between effective classroom management and improved educational outcomes. And these skills can be learned and developed (Green, 2010). According to the American Psychological Association, "When applied correctly, effective classroom management principles can work across all subject areas and all developmental levels . . . They can be expected to promote students' self-regulation, reduce the incidence of misbehavior, and increase student productivity" (Kratochwill, 2009, p. 5).

Negative Impact on Students Who Are Removed from School

Since children are not expendable, we must be concerned about how disciplinary removal affects the suspended students, and not just those who remain in class. One review of research exploring why students drop out found that "several studies . . . have demonstrated how schools contribute to students' involuntary departure by systematically excluding and discharging troublemakers and other problematic students" (Rumberger, 2004, pp. 143–144). Responding to this sort of evidence, states and districts are increasingly treating suspensions and other indicators of poor behavior as early-warning indications of dropout risk (Vaznis, 2010).

Further, and as noted earlier, the exclusion of these students presents immediate risks to their success and well-being. In the words of the American Academy of Pediatrics Committee on School Health (2003):

> Without the services of trained professionals (such as pediatricians, mental health professionals, and school counselors) and without a parent at home during the day, students with out-of-school suspensions and expulsions are far more likely to commit crimes. A Centers for Diseases Control and Prevention study found that when youth are not in school, they are more likely to become involved in a physical fight and to carry a weapon . . . The lack of professional assistance at the time of exclusion from school, a time when a student most needs it, increases the risk of permanent school drop-out. (p. 1207.)

In fact, many in law enforcement have echoed these concerns about the repercussions of having high numbers of unsupervised suspended students (Fight Crime: Invest in Kids, 2009).

As the Council of State Governments *Breaking Schools' Rules* study definitively demonstrated by tracking over one million middle school students for six years, there are strong links between suspensions and dropping out and heightened risks of juvenile justice involvement (Fabelo et al., 2011). These increased risks raise serious questions about the justification for suspending children, especially for relatively minor violations. This strong evidence of heightened risk stands in stark contrast to the total lack of evidence to suggest there are any long-term benefits.

ARE LESS DISCRIMINATORY ALTERNATIVES AVAILABLE?

Evidence does suggest the viability of alternatives to frequent disciplinary exclusion. In Baltimore public schools, for example, recent reforms put in place by Superintendent Andres Alonso illustrate one such alternative policy. As reported in the *New York Times* (Tavernise, 2010):

> Alonso took on the culture of the schools, which relied heavily on suspensions for discipline, a practice Dr. Alonso strongly opposed. "Kids come as is," he likes to say, "and it's our job to engage them" . . . Now school administrators have to get his deputy's signature for any suspension longer than five days. This year, suspensions fell below 10,000, far fewer than the 26,000 the system gave out in 2004 . . . Instead, schools handled discipline problems more through mediation, counseling and parent-teacher conferences, and offered incentives like sports and clubs. Mental health professionals were placed in every school with middle grades. (p. A19)

During this period of declining suspension rates, graduation rates in Baltimore rose. The Baltimore example suggests that alternatives to out-of-school suspensions may prove more effective in creating school communities that are more productive and inclusive. Moreover, there is research evidence that suggests there are many effective alternatives that promote safe and orderly schools and reduce delinquency—while keeping students in school (Dwyer, Osher & Warger, 1998; Gagnon & Leone, 2001; Gottfredson, 1997). Some of those alternatives are described briefly below.

Systemwide Positive Behavior Interventions and Supports

Systemwide Positive Behavioral Interventions and Supports (PBIS) is a well-established systemic and data-driven approach to improving school learning environments. Its emphasis is on changing underlying attitudes and policies concerning how behavior is addressed (Sugai & Horner, 2002). Several prominent civil rights organizations have been seeking greater federal support for PBIS, and several child advocacy groups point to successful PBIS-based interventions (Dignity in Schools Campaign, 2010; Advocates for Children and Youth, 2006).

PBIS consists of three different levels of intervention. The schoolwide level affects every member of the school community. Its goal is to ensure a safe and effective learning environment by emphasizing appropriate student behavior and simultaneously working to reduce punitive disciplinary measures. At this level, PBIS entails frequent monitoring of office referrals for discipline and setting schoolwide goals for reducing these referrals. The system of interventions and supports is designed to shift the focus from the individual student as the primary problem to the "collective behaviors, working structures, and routines of educators" and to "the whole school as the unit of analysis" (Culos et al., 2006). Numerous studies have found positive results with schoolwide PBIS (Bradshaw, Mitchell, & Leaf, 2010a; Horner et al., 2009; Lassen, Steele, & Sailor, 2006; Metzler, Biglan, Rusby, & Sprague, 2001; Muscott, Mann, & Lebrun, 2008).

The second and third levels of intervention provide additional supports and services for smaller numbers of students who exhibit challenging behavior. These include interventions conducted in individual classrooms and more focus on specialized instruction of school expectations, skills training for students, or other strategies tailored to specific behaviors.

One study of PBIS, however, demonstrated that, after a year of implementation, Black and Latino students received more severe punishment for the category *minor misbehavior* and concluded that one cannot assume that interventions intended to improve behavior while reducing reliance on punishments will be equally effective for all groups (Skiba et al., 2011). The researchers suggested that PBIS would benefit from using data disaggregated by race and that a more race, gender, and disability conscious and culturally responsive PBIS approach is possible. PBIS systems do, in fact, enable users to disaggregate and analyze discipline by race, ethnicity, gender, and disability. Although underutilized, the use of such disaggregated data by districts implementing PBIS appears to be rising (Vincent, 2008).

Support and Training for Teachers and Leaders

A wealth of research links effective classroom management with improved educational outcomes (Brophy, 1986). The significantly higher rates of suspensions as students move from elementary to middle school suggest that classroom management issues become greater as young children become adolescents and are more likely to challenge authority figures. Teachers serving adolescents may need more specialized training and greater understanding of adolescent development. Large racial differences in suspension rates also raise questions about whether training to bolster classroom management skills might be even more useful if it included components of multicultural sensitivity to make teachers aware that implicit bias may affect how they discipline their students. Likewise, the data suggest that teachers might benefit from increased support and training in working with students with disabilities, who are increasingly mainstreamed in general education classrooms.

Leadership training might also generate improvements. As noted earlier, variations in a leader's approach to school discipline can make a profound difference in attendance and educational outcomes. Therefore, significant gains might be made toward both reducing school exclusion and improving academic progress if we replaced the attitude of kick-out proponents, like Joe Clark, with the attitude embraced by Baltimore's superintendent, Alonso: "Kids come as is, and it's our job to engage them" (Tavernise, 2010).

In addition to PBIS and professional development strategies, other methods include ecological approaches to classroom management and social emotional learning. An ecological classroom management approach "deals with school discipline by increasing the strength and quality of classroom activities" (Osher et al., 2010, p. 49). Well-planned lessons, varied methods of instruction, clear and developmentally appropriate behavioral expectations, careful monitoring of student engagement with effective empathetic responses designed to reengage students and avoid conflict escalation are some of its defining characteristics.

Social emotional learning is perhaps best described as "the process through which we learn to recognize and manage emotions, care about others, make good decisions, behave ethically and responsibly, develop positive relationships, and avoid negative behaviors" (Zins, Bloodworth, Weissberg, & Walberg, 2004, p. 4). Social and emotional strategies aim at developing student assets that foster self-discipline (Osher et al., 2010). Researcher David Osher suggests that "if classroom activities lack holding power, it is unlikely that school-wide discipline approaches [positive behavioral supports and social emotional learning] will make up for this deficiency" (Osher et al., 2010, pp. 49–50). Therefore social emotional and ecological management approaches are likely most effective if implemented in combination with schoolwide PBIS (Osher et al., 2010).

DISCUSSION: IMPLICATIONS FOR CHANGES TO FEDERAL AND STATE POLICY AND PRACTICE

What is clear from the research at this point is that a discipline policy that relies on frequent out-of-school suspensions as response to minor school code violations would be hard to justify if viewed through the lens of disparate impact. Under a disparate impact standard, educators at the district level would always strive to replace ineffective policies and practices that also had an adverse impact.

This discussion has intentionally focused on the frequent use of out-of-school suspensions because of the growing multitudes of students—especially students of color and students with disabilities—suspended each year. One simple policy change, adopted as law by the state of Connecticut, would severely limit the use of suspension to those instances of severe misconduct, such as when a student poses a danger to himself or others (Losen, 2011b).

A great deal of progress could be made if more states followed Connecticut's example and enacted legislation or promulgated regulations to ensure that out-of-school suspensions were only used as measures of last resort and that explicit efforts were made to eliminate racial disparities. While frequent reliance on in-school suspensions is a less adverse alternative, it may not be the least discriminatory alternative available, and it certainly does little to get at the root cause of the behavior.

There is a wide range of policy changes that federal and state policy makers may use to ensure that the least discriminatory alternatives to the frequent use of out-of-school suspension are pursued at the school and district levels.[8] The following three policy approaches have been enacted or are gaining traction at both state and federal levels:

1. Require annual collection and public reporting of a wide range of school discipline data, at the school, district, and state levels that is disaggregated by race, ethnicity, gender, disability status, English learner status, and socioeconomic status.
2. Create response systems that are triggered by high and disparate rates of suspension.
3. Include discipline rates among the multiple indicators of performance that state or federal law will use evaluate schools and districts.

The current status of the federal government's collection and reporting of discipline data looks like a patchwork quilt with some detailed squares and several holes.[9] Legislation requiring the collection and public reporting of school discipline data should convey the following kinds of information in annual, or more frequent, reports to the public, down to the district level:

- The types of disciplinary exclusion, including in-school suspension, out-of-school suspension, long-term suspensions (longer than ten days), expulsion, and the removal to alternative disciplinary school or programs
- Clear definitions of each term
- The frequency of each type of suspension used by a school, district, and state
- The total number of days of missed instruction that result from disciplinary exclusion
- The number of disciplinary exclusions, by categories of offense (e.g., possession of a weapon or unlawful substance, fighting, disruption, tardiness, and truancy)
- All the above information disaggregated by race/ethnicity, gender, disability status, English learner status, and socioeconomic status, with numbers and percentages for each group and the capacity to calculate rates for combined categories (such as cross-tabulation to facilitate, for example, an analysis of Black males)

- A calculation of the percentage (risk) of each group's membership disciplined at least once (the so-called "unduplicated count") on the basis of each group's enrollment
- The number of students suspended more than once during a school year (also unduplicated)
- A calculation of the incidence rate, which provides the average number of suspensions for each subgroup member[10]
- A disaggregation of the disciplinary actions taken for first-time offense by category of rule violation, such as that collected by the state of North Carolina

The requirements of the Individuals with Disabilities Education Act (IDEA) comprise the most comprehensive annual collection of discipline data of any federal statute. Discipline data independently required by the U.S. Department of Education pursuant to regulatory authority and antidiscrimination law enables the collection of data elements not included by IDEA. The CRDC, implemented by the OCR (and also known as OCR data),[11] is a biennial survey that requires districts to report discipline data by race with gender for both students with disabilities and their nondisabled peers, including the unduplicated numbers of students repeatedly suspended, information the IDEA does not explicitly require. Title IV of the Elementary and Secondary Education Act (ESEA, 2002) also has data collection and reporting requirements (known as the Safe and Drug Free Schools and Communities Act), including some data on the number of suspensions and expulsions for specific serious offenses, data not included by the IDEA or the CRDC. However, each federal data requirement is missing at least one essential element. The CRDC data are not collected or reported annually, nor does the CRDC provide information about the offense categories or loss of instructional time. Title IV does require some data on the numbers of suspensions, by category of offense, but does not require information about students by race or other subgroup categories. The IDEA data often only require state-level reporting and with no explicit reporting requirement for the majority of students who are not eligible for special education (see table 2).

Despite some serious shortcomings, the IDEA contains comprehensive requirements for disaggregated discipline data collection and reporting and is the only federal statute that requires *annual* collection from every district. However, only public reporting at the state level and to the U.S. secretary of education is included among the IDEA's core data requirements. The most straightforward legislative improvement would amend federal legislation to ensure that the IDEA's comprehensive data collection and reporting applies to all students, not simply those eligible for services under the IDEA. The current statutory requirements of the IDEA could be leveraged to gain improvements in data collection and reporting at both the federal and state levels.

If the ESEA contained corollary requirements to the IDEA's requirements, the nation's discipline data collection and reporting requirements would be significantly stronger and would be consistent for all students. No change to

TABLE 2   Required data for annual public reports on school discipline

	CO	FL	KY	MD	MN	NC	TX*	WI
Race & ethnicity	X	X	X	X	X	X	X	X
Gender	X	X	X	X	X	X	X	X
Disability status	X	X**		X	X	X	X	X
Number of students	X	X	X	X	X	X	X	X
Number of incidents	X	X	X	X	X	X	X	X
Type of offense/reason	X	X	X	X	X	X	X	X
Grade level			X	X	X	X	Ad hoc	X
Named districts	X	X	X	X		X	X	X

Source: 2006 Civil Rights Data Collection (CRDC). Copyright © The Civil Rights Project at UCLA.

Note: This table was compiled by the author to demonstrate that several states collect and publicly report more extensive discipline data than what is collected and reported under federal requirements. A complete, 50 state review is being conducted by the Center for Civil Rights Remedies.

the IDEA would be required. In legislative language, the IDEA requirements could be incorporated by reference. The new reporting language would fit naturally into the ESEA's annual Title I reporting on achievement and other data, which is required at the state, district, and school levels. Further, in order to analyze whether a policy or practice continues to have a disparate impact, policy makers and researchers must have access to this level of baseline data. Perhaps an even better solution would be to bolster the existing Title IV of the ESEA.

It is worth noting that Senate Bill 919, sponsored by Health, Education, Labor, and Pensions (HELP) committee chair Tom Harkin (D-IA) and minority leader Michael Enzi (R-WY) in 2011, as a revision to Title IV of the ESEA, contains quite comprehensive discipline reporting requirements that would apply to every state which accepts the federal funding.[12] If this proposal becomes law, many of the disciplinary provisions recommended here and in the legislative brief *Good Discipline: Legislation for Education Reform* (Losen, 2011b) would be required of Title IV grant recipients under federal law. One especially strong component of these data reporting requirements is that they would be annually reported to the public down to the district level. The proposed legislation is not explicit as to whether unduplicated student data must also be collected and reported. However, the proposal makes reference to making this discipline data collection, "to the extent possible, part of the State's statewide longitudinal data system." The referenced system allows the state to track each individual student down to the district and school levels with a unique identifier and to follow each and every student's outcomes over time on a large number of factors. The unique identifier enables the state to track the progress of students within the state, even as they change schools and school districts. Currently, states typically use these systems to track achievement levels, attendance, and graduation rates. It was data of this high quality that enabled the Council of State Governments to track the impact of school discipline on every middle school student in Texas over the course of six years.

Discipline Triggers in Education Policy

The obvious shortcoming of legislation that only requires states to report discipline data is that there is no requirement for any more to happen. Ideally, frequent use of suspensions and large discipline disparities should, as a matter of policy, trigger schools and districts to initiate some sort of intervention designed to reduce high rates and large disparities.

After ten years of No Child Left Behind (NCLB), policy makers may be skittish about any federal system where data can drive consequences. However, a triggering mechanism need not be punitive or harsh. In fact, there are currently discipline triggers in both state and federal law, but, unlike those found in NCLB, they have received little attention. Specifically, pursuant to the IDEA, school districts found to have significant racial disproportionality amounting to overrepresentation in special education identification, placement, or discipline must use 15 percent of their Part B IDEA funds for coordinated early intervening services, which may include professional development, behavioral evaluations, services, and supports for students. One theoretical strength of this statutory framework is that, like disparate impact, by shifting a percentage of federal funds to prevention activities, it suggests that there are actions the school or district can take to reduce the disparities, actions that will likely yield lower levels of racial disparity. Although beyond the scope of this essay, there have also been serious obstacles to meaningful implementation of these requirements. One reason may lie in the fact that although the identified district receives no fewer dollars, it also receives no extra dollars when interventions are required. Instead, 15 percent of the federal funds shift from special education to general education. Many special educators have complained that they and students with disabilities are punished when funds are shifted. With a sufficient pool of federal funds, those identified districts might instead be encouraged to more actively seek a remedy.

For example, originally passed in 2004, a Maryland law requires that if suspensions reach 10 percent of an elementary school's enrollment, the elementary school must engage in a PBIS program.[13] Although the triggers are based on aggregate rates and not subgroups, the requirements of the Maryland law present an excellent example of legislation that creates a data-driven trigger mechanism to support the districts most in need. A similar measure, applying a 25 percent trigger to all schools and disaggregated by race/ethnicity, was recently proposed in the California state legislature and may become law before the end of 2012. "Commencing with the 2014–15 school year, the bill

64

would decrease by 2% each year the percentage of enrollment or significant subgroup of enrollment required to trigger this requirement until it is 15%" (SB 1235).[14]

Those seeking to propose legislation should consider the California proposal, or replicating Maryland's law, adding similar triggers for middle schools and high schools and including specific attention to subgroups. Further, advocates should seek to amend state laws by infusing suspension rates into school and district academic accountability regimes, as most states will continue to have their own accountability system (Sunderman, Kim, & Orfield, 2005).

Aligning Discipline Policy with Academic Achievement Goals and Addressing Significant Discipline Disparities

Properly constructed, federal and state legislation might go much further than raising awareness through better discipline data reporting or driving remedies for just those districts with the highest suspension rates or largest racial discipline disparities. More widespread federal policy changes have the potential to do more to ensure that schools and districts use suspensions sparingly and more equally but to also think about school discipline policy as a central component of the educational system.

There is an emerging consensus that an evaluation of public education should include multiple measures, not simply test results. Proposed indicators of effectiveness and improvement include an increased percentage of students earning a high school diploma, reductions in chronic absenteeism and grade retention, and an increasing number of students taking and passing advanced-level courses. Typically, however, the frequency of disciplinary exclusion is considered only an indicator of school order and safety—as if student discipline had little connection to overarching educational goals.[15]

It is also necessary to acknowledge that current discipline trends are not occurring in a vacuum. Federal policy now provides an incentive for school leaders to remove low-achieving students from the cohort of students used to evaluate school performance. These lower achievers are more likely to be disruptive (Kelly, 2010). NCLB has imposed accountability measures for schools based primarily on student test results—but only for the test scores of students who attend a school for a full academic year. There is, in fact, research supporting the possibility that frequent suspensions are used to avoid accountability for the test scores of lower achievers (Figlio, 2006), and civil rights advocates have expressed concern that test-driven accountability for schools encourages frequent suspension for minor offenses—the "push-out" of low-achieving students, especially students of color (Advancement Project, 2010). Does the near-exclusive emphasis on test-driven accountability have a disparate impact on students of color? Although beyond the scope of this discussion, many have argued that disparate impact analysis should also be used to evaluate school accountability policies and practices, not to mention policies governing education resource distribution (Losen, 2004).

While some may argue that the antidote to the heavy-handed federal accountability provisions of NCLB is to remove the federal government from any involvement, most policy makers realize that many of the NCLB requirements criticized for being too heavy-handed were modeled closely after Texas's test-driven school accountability system. In other words, when left alone, state policy makers have created their own imperfect accountability systems. Instead of rejecting all forms of federally designed school accountability systems, many policy makers believe that they can create a better-balanced federal accountability system that is far more constructive than punitive.

It is in the spirit of finding a more balanced approach that Senators Harkin and Enzi were able to cobble together a bipartisan proposal to reauthorize the ESEA, which was reported favorably out of their committee in the fall of 2011. Many civil rights activists, however, voiced disapproval over the degree to which the accountability requirements were dismantled (LCCR, 2011), while other politicians on both the Left and Right argued that the proposal did not go far enough.

What is most noteworthy about the Harkin-Enzi proposed language with regard to school discipline policy—besides the aforementioned inclusion of the discipline reporting requirements—is that there are a number of provisions where efforts to improve overall achievement require the entity receiving the federal grant to pursue the reduction of the use of suspensions. In other words, reducing suspensions is beginning to show up in federal policy proposals as directly tied to efforts to improve educational outcomes. Even before the prospective grantee is awarded funding, the jointly proposed law requires applicants for "turn around" funding to provide a needs analysis and capacity assessment. The applicants' needs assessments must include "suspension rates" to be eligible to apply to receive funds. Further, applying districts must also examine several data indicators for the middle schools feeding into the "dropout factories," including "annual rates of expulsions, suspensions, school violence" (Elementary and Secondary Education Reauthorization Act of 2011, 2011, p. 184).

CONCLUSION

The fact that the Harkin-Enzi federal bipartisan policy proposal frames reducing high suspension rates as an important goal next to improving achievement and graduation rates and that it requires grant recipients to embrace such an objective as one of several funding preconditions suggests that, as a matter of policy, the frequent use of out-of-school suspensions is not regarded as sound educational policy or practice. There are additional signs that a broad spectrum of educators is listening to what the research says and now rejecting, or at least doubting, the heavy use of suspensions. These include Chester Finn, the secretary of education under Ronald Regan, who recently stated on *PBS News Hour* (2012) that it was ludicrous to suspend kids out of school for merely mouthing off at the teacher. If more policy makers with doubts about out-of-school suspensions reviewed the current data describing how one out of every six Black students was suspended at least once out of school, and then thought about current federal policy using a disparate impact lens, they might observe that nothing in our federal laws even remotely discourages the overuse of out-of-school suspensions.

While the U.S. Department of Education's enforcement arm has brought much-needed attention to the issue, explicitly stating that these high and disparate rates may constitute violations of Title VI, along with a renewed commitment to disparate impact enforcement, policy makers need not wait for either an act of Congress or until OCR or civil rights and community groups file disparate impact complaints. State- and district-level educators don't even need to wait for their state legislatures to act. They can follow the example set recently by the Maryland State Board of Education (2012), which on its own initiative recently proposed regulations to limit the use of out-of-school suspensions with a goal of eliminating racial disparities in three years.

NOTES

This paper is an updated and modified version of the following: D. J. Losen, *Discipline Policies, Successful Schools, and Racial Justice* (Boulder, CO: National Education Policy Center, 2011); and D. J. Losen, *Good Discipline: Legislation for Education Reform* (Boulder, CO: National Education Policy Center, 2011). *HER* is grateful to the original publisher, National Education Policy Center, http://nepc.colorado.edu, for their permission to adapt the material. For an in-depth discussion of the data and data sources, please see the original research papers.

The analysis of data on suspensions for 2009–2010 school year as reported in this essay originates in Losen and Gillespie (2012), a national report published by The Center for Civil Rights Remedies at The Civil Rights Project at UCLA. The Civil Rights Project at UCLA retains copyright to all information and analysis pertaining to this report and expressly permits *Harvard Educational Review* to publish this analysis.

1. In the context of a desegregation case, disparate impact evidence is often considered relevant to the question of whether a district is maintaining a dual system, and some federal districts courts may consider the statistical disparity as a proxy for intent regarding the disparity as a vestige of the prior intentional discrimination. For a fuller discussion, see Losen and Edley (2001).
2. For an in-depth discussion of the data and data sources, see Losen (2011a, 2011b).
3. It is important to note that the estimated national data from the prior years was a projected estimate based on the OCR sample but with additional statistical weights applied by OCR. The data presented here as a national estimate did not have access to OCR's statistical weights, and none was applied.
4. Further, although estimates based on OCR's data for 2009–2010 are based on a highly similar data collection as the prior years, only the more recent survey allows for combining the out-of-school suspensions of students with disabilities with those of students without disabilities.
5. No district or state was contacted by the author to verify the data. However, this analysis is based on data that is publicly reported by the U.S. Department of Education. Each district was asked to officially certify the data it submitted. All the raw data used in this

analysis are available at http://ocrdata.ed.gov. On this Web site the U.S. Department of Education provides notice in cases when the data has to be corrected. The descriptions of the state-level data describe only the aggregation of the districts in the sample and should not be confused with weighted estimates. Statewide projections using statistical weights will be provided by the U.S. Department of Education.

6. The data was provided by Jason Langford, Equal Justice Works Fellow and staff attorney for Advocates for Children, Inc., Wake County, who received the data from the state of North Carolina pursuant to a legal request. The analysis was performed by Daniel Losen and presented at the conference "Safe Schools, Fair Schools: A Community Dialogue about School Suspensions in North Carolina," November 18, 2010, Wake County (NC) Community College.

7. It should be noted that, despite highlighting this example of lobbying success, one cannot assume that the AFT, as a national organization, currently supports this approach over systemic interventions that provide teachers with better training and help improve behavior with fewer exclusions.

8. For extensive details and specific recommendations, see Losen (2011a).

9. For a comprehensive review of federal discipline data collection and reporting requirements, see Losen (2011b).

10. Additional data are useful and important but could be difficult to require as a matter of legislation. For example, office referral rates and first-time offender data are very helpful to have whenever discrimination is at issue. Such data would increase the capacity to compare the use of discipline for subgroups of students. Racial disaggregation of the disciplinary data for first-time offenders, as well as by numbers of students who were referred for possible action (known as "office disciplinary referrals") yet not subjected to disciplinary removal from school or the classroom, can help reveal whether students of different groups were treated differently for similar misbehavior. Ideally, states and districts that keep individual student identifier records in digital form can track office referrals that do not result in in- or out-of-school suspensions. Increasingly, districts and schools are using systems of positive behavioral supports, and these systems do track office referrals. However, this level of information might not be kept or reported by schools and districts that have not implemented a PBIS system. Nor are office referrals and first-time offender data typically part of state-level reports. Considering the added value, but also the added costs, legislation drafters at the state level should seek to offer additional funding as an incentive to collect and report office referral and first-time offense data. Such funding is not realistic at the federal level, as of this writing.

11. Much of the information about OCR's data collection can be found at http://www.crdc2009.org/downloads/Definitions.pdf. A review of these changes was presented at the joint OCR/Department of Justice conference on September 27, 2010, and is found in the conference materials. See Fitch (2012) and CRDC (2009–2010).

12. Called the Successful, Safe, and Healthy Students Act, this substantial revision of Title IV includes most of the data requirements recommended in this brief. The bill was introduced on May 9, 2011. http://thomas.loc.gov/cgi-bin/query/z?c112:S.919:

13. For a more complete description, see Losen (2011b).

14. A copy of the bill as introduced to the legislature can be found at http://www.leginfo.ca.gov/pub/11-12/bill/sen/sb_1201-1250/sb_1235_bill_20120223_introduced.html

15. For example, the ESEA only addresses school discipline and behavior in the subpart of the act called the Safe and Drug Free Schools and Communities Act. The Safe and Drug Free Schools and Communities provisions of the ESEA (2002) requires that states provide information on a school-by-school basis on: truancy rates and the frequency, seriousness, and incidence of violence and drug-related offenses resulting in suspensions and expulsions in elementary schools and secondary schools in the state (Title IV, Part A § 4112 (c)(3)(ii)).

REFERENCES

Advancement Project. (2010). *How zero tolerance and high stakes testing funnel youth into the school-to-prison pipeline.* Retrieved from http://www.advancementproject.org/sites/default/files/publications/01-EducationReport-2009v8-HiRes.pdf

Advocates for Children and Youth. (2006, April). *School suspension: Effects and alternatives.* Retrieved from http://www.soros.org/sites/default/files/issuebrief_20060418.pdf

American Academy of Pediatrics Committee on School Health. (2003). Out-of-school suspension and expulsion. *Pediatrics, 112*(5), 1206–1209. Retrieved from http://aappolicy.aappublications.org/cgi/content/full/pediatircs;112/5/1206

American Federation of Teachers [AFT]. (2009). *Standing together.* Retrieved from http://www.aft.org/pdfs/americanteacher/AT_FEB09prot.pdf

American Psychological Association Zero Tolerance Task Force. (2008). Are zero tolerance policies effective in the schools? An evidentiary review and recommendations. *American Psychologist, 63*(9), 852–862.

Biama, D. V., & Moses, G. (1989, March 27). His pupils want someone to lean on, but Joe Clark may simply want out. *People.* Retrieved from http://www.people.com/people/archive/article/0,,20119876,00.html

Bowen, E. (1988, February). Education: Getting tough. *TIME.* Retrieved from http://www.time.com/time/magazine/article/0,9171,966577-2,00.html#ixzz17eDfRhsf

Bradshaw, C. P., Mitchell, M. M., & Leaf, P. J. (2010a). Examining the effects of school-wide positive behavioral interventions and supports on student outcomes: Results from a randomized controlled effectiveness trial in elementary schools. *Journal of Positive Behavior Interventions, 12*(3), 133–148.

Bradshaw, C. P., Mitchell, M. M., O'Brennan, L. M., & Leaf, P. J. (2010b). Multilevel exploration of factors contributing to the overrepresentation of Black students in office disciplinary referrals. *Journal of Educational Psychology, 102*(2), 508–520.

Brophy, J. (1986). Teacher influences on student achievement. *American Psychologist, 41*(10), 1069–1077.

Civil Rights Data Collection [CRDC]. (2009–2010). Retrieved from http://www2.ed.gov/about/offices/list/ocr/docs/crdc-2009-10-p1-p2.doc

Culos, C., Bohanon, H., Carney, K., Piggott, T., Hicks, K., Anderson-Harriss, S., et al. (2006). Schoolwide application of positive behavior support in an urban high school: A case study. *Journal of Positive Behavior Interventions, 8*(3), 131–145.

Data Accountability Center [DAC]. (2007—2008). Table 5–18: Calculated as a percentage of students with disabilities ages 3–21. Retrieved from www.ideadata.org

Dignity in Schools Campaign [DSC]. (2010). *Re: School climate, school discipline and the reauthorization of the Elementary and Secondary Education Act.* Retrieved from http://www.dignityinschools.org/files/Dignity_in_Schools_House_ESEA_Letter.pdf

Duncan, A. (2010, March 8). *Crossing the next bridge: Remarks of the U.S. Secretary of Education, Selma, Alabama.* U.S. Department of Education. Retrieved from http://www2.ed.gov/news/speeches/2010/03/03082010.html

Dwyer, K., Osher, D., & Warger, C. (1998). *Early warning, timely response: A guide to safe schools.* Washington, DC: U.S. Department of Education.

Elementary and Secondary Education Act [ESEA]. Pub L. No. 107–110, § 1111(b)(3)(C)(xi) (2002).

Elementary and Secondary Education Reauthorization Act of 2011. (2011). Retrieved from http://www.help.senate.gov/imo/media/doc/ROM117523.pdf

Fabelo, T., Thompson, M. D., Plotkin, M., Carmichael, D., Marchbanks, M. P., & Booth, E. A. (2011). *Breaking schools' rules: A statewide study of how school discipline relates to students' success and juvenile justice involvement.* New York: Council of State Governments Justice Center.

Fight Crime: Invest in Kids. (2009, November 10). Comments pursuant to notice of proposed information collection request [Letter]. New York.

Figlio, D. N. (2006). Testing, crime, and punishment. *Journal of Public Economics, 90*(4–5), 837–851.

Fitch, R. (2012, March). Using the civil rights data collection, 2009–10 CRDC discipline data. Paper presented at the Leadership Summit on School-Justice Partnerships: Keeping Kids in School and out of Court, New York. Retrieved from http://school-justicesummit.org/presentations/presentation_details.cfm?topicID=6

Gagnon, J. C., & Leone, P. E. (2001). Alternative strategies for youth violence prevention. In R. J. Skiba & G. G. Noam (Eds.), *New directions for youth development: Vol. 92. Zero tolerance: Can suspension and expulsion keep school safe?* pp. 101–125. San Francisco: Jossey-Bass.

Gottfredson, D. C. (1997). School-based crime prevention. In L. Sherman, D. Gottfredson, D. MacKenzie, J. Eck, P. Ruter, & S. Bushway (Eds.), *Preventing crime: What works, what doesn't, what's promising; A report to the United States Congress* (pp. 1–74). Washington, DC: U.S. Department of Justice, Office of Justice Programs.

Green, E. (2010, March 7). Can good teaching be learned? *The New York Times Magazine,* 30–46.

Harry, B., & Klingner, J. (2006). *Why are so many minority students in special education? Understanding race and disability in schools.* New York: Teachers College Press.

Hawley, W. D., & Ready, T. (Eds.). (2003). *Measuring access to learning opportunities.* Washington, DC: National Academies Press.

Horner, R. H., Sugai, G., Smolkowski, K., Eber, L., Nakasato, J., Todd, A. W., & Esperanza, J. (2009). A randomized, wait-list controlled effectiveness trial assessing school-wide positive behavior support in elementary schools. *Journal of Positive Behavior Interventions, 11*(3), 133–144.

Hui, T., & Locke, M. (2010). Federal civil rights complaint filed against Wake schools. *Urban Review, 34,* 317–342.

Kelly, S. (2010). A crisis in authority in predominantly black schools? *Teachers College Record, 112*(5), 1247–1274.

Kim, Y. K., Losen, D. J., & Hewitt, D. T. (2010). *The school-to-prison pipeline: Structuring legal reform* (1st ed.). New York: New York University Press.

Kratochwill, T. (2009). *Classroom management: Teachers modules.* American Psychological Association. Retrieved from http://wwwapa.org/education/k12/classroom-mgmt.aspx

Lassen, S. R., Steele, M. M., & Sailor, W. (2006). The relationship of school-wide positive behavior support to academic achievement in an urban middle school. *Psychology in the Schools, 43*(6), 701–712.

Leadership Conference on Civil Rights [LCCR]. (2011). More groups withhold support for ESEA proposal: Coalition leader to testify at Senate HELP Committee hearing. Retrieved from http://www.civilrights.org/press/2011/more-groups-withhold-support.html

Losen, D. J. (2004). Challenging racial disparities: The promise and pitfalls of the No Child Left Behind Act's race-conscious accountability. *Howard Law Journal, 47*(2), 243–298.

Losen, D. J. (2011a). *Discipline policies, successful schools, and racial justice.* Boulder, CO: National Education Policy Center

Losen, D. J. (2011b). *Good discipline: Legislation for education reform.* Boulder, CO: National Education Policy Center.

Losen, D. L., & Edley Jr., C. (2001). Why zero tolerance is a civil rights issue. In W. Ayers, R. Ayers, & B. Dohrn (Eds.), *Zero tolerance: Resisting the drive for punishment in our schools* (pp. 230–256). New York: New Press.

Losen, D. J., & Gillespie, J. (2012). *Opportunities suspended: The disparate impact of discisciplinary exclusion from school.* Los Angeles: The Center for Civil Rights Remedies at The Civil Rights Project at UCLA.

Losen, D. L., & Skiba, R. J. (2010, September). *Suspended education: Urban middle schools in crisis.* The Civil Rights Project at UCLA and the Southern Poverty Law Center. Retrieved from http://civilrightsproject.ucla.edu/research/k-12-education/school-discipline/suspended-education-urban-middle-schools-in-crisis/Suspended-Education_FINAL-2.pdf

Maryland State Board of Education. (2012). A safe school, successful students, and a fair and equitable disciplinary process go hand in hand: A study of school discipline practices and proposed regulatory changes. Retrieved from http://msde.state.md.us/School_Discipline_Report02272012.pdf

McCarthy, J. D., & Hoge, D. R. (1987). The social construction of school punishment: Racial disadvantage out of universalistic process. *Social Forces, 65,* 1101–1120.

Metzler, C. W., Biglan, A., Rusby, J. C., & Sprague, J. R. (2001). Evaluation of a comprehensive behavior management program to improve school-wide positive behavior support. *Education and Treatment of Children, 24,* 448–479.

Muscott, H. S., Mann, E. L., & Lebrun, M. R. (2008). Positive Behavioral Interventions and Supports in New Hampshire: Effects of large-scale implementation of schoolwide positive behavior support on student discipline and academic achievement. *Journal of Positive Behavior Interventions, 10*(3), 190–205.

No Child Left Behind [NCLB] Act of 2001, Pub. L. No. 107-110, § 115, Stat. 1425 (2002).

Noguera, P. A. (2001). Finding safety where we least expect it: The role of social capital in preventing school violence. In W. Ayers, R. Ayers, & B. Dohrn (Eds.), *Zero tolerance: Resisting the drive for punishment in our schools* (pp. 202–218). New York: New Press.

Osher, D., Bear, G. G., Sprague, J. R., & Doyle, W. (2010). How can we improve school discipline? *Educational Researcher, 39*(1), 48–58. Retrieved from http://er.aera.net

PBS News Hour. (2012, March). Report: Minority students face harsher discipline. Retrieved from http://www.pbs.org/newshour/bb/education/jan-june12/minority_03-06.html

Raffaele Mendez, L. M. (2003). Predictors of suspension and negative school outcomes: A longitudinal investigation. In J. Wald & D. L. Losen (Eds.), *Deconstructing the school to prison pipeline* (pp. 17–33). San Francisco: Jossey-Bass.

Rausch, M. K., & Skiba, R. J. (2005, April). *The academic cost of discipline: The contribution of school discipline to achievement.* Paper presented at the Annual Meeting of the American Educational Research Association, Montreal.

Rausch, M. K., & Skiba, R. J. (2006). *Discipline, disability, and race: Disproportionality in Indiana schools.* Bloomington, IN: Center for Evaluation and Education Policy.

Rumberger, R. W. (2004). Why students drop out of school. In G. Orfield (Ed.), *Dropouts in America: Confronting the graduation rate crisis* (pp. 143–144). Cambridge, MA: Harvard Education Press.

SB 1235. (2012). Retrieved from http://www.leginfo.ca.gov/pub/11-12/bill/sen/sb_1201-1250/sb_1235_bill_20120223_introduced.html

Skiba, R. J., Horner, R. H., Chung, C. G., Karega Rausch, M., May, S. L., & Tobin, T. (2011). Race is not neutral: A national investigation of African American and Latino disproportionality in school discipline. *School Psychology Review, 40*(1), 85.

Skiba, R. J., Michael, R. S., Nardo, A. C., & Peterson, R. L. (2002). The color of discipline: Sources of racial and gender disproportionality in school punishment. *The Urban Review, 34*(40, 317–342.

Skiba, R. J., & Rausch, M. K. (2006). Zero tolerance, suspension, and expulsion: Questions of equity and effectiveness. In C. M. Evertson & C. S. Weinstein (Eds.), *Handbook for classroom management: Research, practice, and contemporary issues* (pp. 1063–1089). Mahwah, NJ: Erlbaum.

Sprague, J., Sugai, G., & Walker, H. (1998). Antisocial behavior in schools. In S. Watson & F. Gresham (Eds.), *Child behavior therapy: Ecological considerations in assessment, treatment, and evaluation* (pp. 451-474). New York: Plenum Press.

Successful, Safe, and Healthy Students Act, S.919. (2011).

Sugai, G., & Horner, R. (2002). The evolution of discipline practices: School-wide positive behavior supports. *Child and Family Behavior Therapy, 24*(1/2), 23–50.

Sunderman, G. L., Kim, J. S., & Orfield, G. (2005). *NCLB meets school realities: Lessons from the field*. Thousand Oaks, CA: Corwin Press.

Tavernise, S. (2010, December 1). A mission to transform Baltimore's beaten schools. *The New York Times*. Retrieved from http://www.nytimes.com/2010/12/02/education/02baltimore.html?emc=eta1&pagewanted=print

UNC Center for Civil Rights. (2010). Retrieved from http://www.law.unc.edu/documents/civilrights/titlevicomplaintwcsb9242010final.pdf

U.S. Department of Education. (2006). National and state projections: Projects values for the nation based on a survey of over one third of the nation's districts at 3,328,754 students suspended at least one time. Retrieved from fhttp://ocrdata.ed.gov/Projections_2006.aspx

Vaznis, J. (2010, November 29). Thousands called dropout risks. *The Boston Globe*. Retrieved from http://www.bosoton.com/news/education/k_12/articles/2010/11/29/thousands_called_dropouts_risks/

Vincent, C. (2008). *Do schools using SWIS take advantage of the school ethnicity report?* Retrieved from http://www.pbis.org/evaluation/evaluation_briefs/nov_08_(1).aspx

Zehr, M. (2010, December). Obama administration targets "disparate impact" of school discipline. *Education Week*. Retrieved from http://www.edweek.org/login.html?source=http://www.edweek.org/ew/articles/2010/10/07/07disparate_

Zins, J. E., Bloodworth, M. R., Weissberg, R. P., & Walberg, H. J. (2004). The scientific base linking social and emotional learning to school succes. In J. E. Zins, R. P. Weissberg, M. C. Wang, & H. J. Walberg (Eds.), *Building academic success on social and emotional learning: What does the research say?* (pp. 3–22). New York: Teachers College Press. Retrieved from http://digilib.bc.edu/reserves/py633/mont/py63340.pdf

The author thanks his research assistants, Cheri Hodson and Jonathan Gillespie, for their assistance with this piece.

ONE MONTH
IN HIGH SCHOOL

■

SETH G. COOPER

On the morning of the first day of high school, my brother, some friends, and I walked instead of taking the bus. On our walk, before we crossed the overpass that connects one side of town to the other, we stopped to smoke some weed in a small patch of woods along the way. We then crossed the overpass, making it about halfway before we decided to be careful and spray ourselves down with Old Spice cologne from a bottle my friend carried with him. All of us did so, except my brother. For whatever reason, he refused, even becoming incensed when my friend attempted to spray him.

We all walked into the school building. All of us barely aware of where our classrooms were located. All of us stoned. All of us, minus my brother, wearing thick clouds of Old Spice. And, sure enough, all of us, minus my brother, reaching our respective home rooms without incident. My brother, however, was stopped by a teacher and questioned. (I should mention here that my brother is a white kid with dreadlocks and John Lennon–style glasses and vintage rock 'n' roll shirts.) He must have not held up under interrogation, either that or the clinging odor of marijuana was simply too strong, because the teacher alerted the school's single police officer, who then frisked my brother, discovering a flattened joint end in an obscure pocket in my brother's wallet. He was arrested and suspended. His suspension lasted two weeks; and, per school policy, if he wished to return after two weeks, he must test negative on a urine screening. No drugs showed up in his urine screen, and the school authorities allowed him to return. But not for long.

A few more weeks into school my brother faced another suspension, with me accompanying him. My brother had been back in school for a week or two and was doing well, or at least he wasn't doing badly. I, on the other hand, missed classes frequently. The truth is that I left school every day at 11:45 A.M. with the seniors, simply walking out of the front entrance. The vice principal called me to his office a few times to address this issue, with a general lack of success on his part. At that time it was the first or second week of October, and my brother and I were late for school, so my mom had to drive us there.

We walked in and were immediately stopped by a teacher who needed us to sign some ledger that records who the late students are and how late they've arrived. We signed in the appropriate slots. Then the teacher accused us of smelling like burnt marijuana. That morning we had not smoked, though I suppose it's possible that the smell lingered on our bodies or hair from the night before when we had last smoked, but that supposition always seemed to me tenuous at best. Naturally, I became indignant. How, I asked the teacher, do you know what burnt marijuana smells like? I meant my inflection to imply that there is only one way to be an authority on such things. The teacher ignored me, answering brusquely and in the way people desperate for small amounts of power answer when anyone without power asks an insubordinate question that challenges the very premise of their authority.

The teacher's answer was "I'm trained," and then the teacher called for backup. This time there wasn't a police officer, only the vice principal. They attempted to search us (we refused anything more than a pocket check), demanded that we provide urine samples immediately (we refused), and then called our mom. She arrived promptly and in a furious state. My mom has never been the delusional parent who refuses to acknowledge that her little angels are capable of even the slightest mistake, but this was the second time in the first month of the school year that the school authorities singled us out for smelling like "burnt marijuana." With a second suspension, my brother would have attended only two out of the first six weeks of school. How did they suppose we would learn anything if we were constantly being suspended? That was the argument my mom made, anyway.

She started to scream at the vice principal, a little white guy in his thirties whose face showed weakness and fear. I kind of felt sorry for him then, mainly because my mom was sticking her dark red face inches away from his as she berated him. I could see little droplets of saliva flying from her lips, and I knew that some stray droplets must have found their way onto one of his eyelids or pressed lips. I don't know if she grew momentarily rash as a consequence of her maternal belligerence or what, but after concluding her rant, my mom told the vice principal that if the school didn't want her sons there, she would home school us. She demanded that he provide us with all of our textbooks to take home, which he obliged. Then we left and never went back. (This was illegal on the part of the school, by the way. My mom was never required to officially document that she withdrew us from public school in order to home school us. I should also add that I am not a proponent of home schooling.) I was fourteen.

Those textbooks were never read, or even opened. My mom bought a home schooling program for our computer, but I never spent any time on it. Instead, my brothers (my oldest brother had already dropped out) and I stayed home and smoked weed while my mom went to work. That December, less than four months after I stopped going to school, I was arrested for possession of marijuana and placed on probation. I summarily violated a condition of probation.

In May I was arrested for several felonies, including more possession charges. That was the first time I was incarcerated by the state of New Jersey. Luckily, I had endeared myself to my public defender, and he got me off with three weeks in jail, time served.

In the detention center I went to school during the day, as was mandatory. The work seemed to be sixth-grade material. I got out, and a year later I was locked back up. Again, I was released after weeks. This time one of the teachers gave me the GED pretest to take. My scores were good, so she suggested that I take the real thing as soon as I got out. Weeks after I was released, I signed up and took the test. Shortly afterward the Department of Education, or whatever it's called, awarded me a GED. I never attended any pre-GED classes. I had spent maybe a month in high school (less if you consider that I only went for half the day). And I had been smoking weed every day since I was twelve years old. I can't say I wasn't a little proud of myself. I was sixteen years old.

As soon as I received my GED, I registered for community college and took the entrance exam. My test scores for English and math were below entrance levels, so I had to take prerequisite classes in those subjects. I turned seventeen halfway through my first semester. My grades for that term were a D in algebra, a D in English, and a B in sociology. At the beginning of the next semester I tested out of the prerequisite English, and I ended up passing the algebra class with a B this time. I enrolled into two other classes and dropped both. I didn't go back for a year after that. When I did go back, I registered for four classes, eventually dropping them all (I stayed in Western Civilization the longest).

My run-ins with the law had never stopped. One time the security guard at the college had to call me out of my computer class because the cops were there to arrest me on a warrant. They had come the day before and had the front desk print out my schedule, so they knew when to nab me. Weeks after I went to my history class for the last time, I was arrested for first-degree murder.

I waited to go to trial for over two years, spending all that time in the county jail, where no college classes are offered. Finally, I was sentenced and subsequently transferred to a state correctional facility, where I remain. I am now twenty-four.

"HOW CAN WE HOLD YOU?"

RESTORATIVE JUSTICE IN BOSTON SCHOOLS

■

A CONVERSATION WITH
CURTIS BANNER[1], LAURENT BENNETT, JANET CONNORS, SUNG-JOON PAI,
HILARY SHANAHAN, AND ANITA WADHWA

In this roundtable discussion, two educators, two youth, one community activist, and one scholar discuss the use of restorative justice in two Boston schools. The participants outline the ideas underpinning restorative justice, which has become a prominent alternative to the harsh and punitive disciplinary policies common across the United States. They then share their experiences implementing restorative justice practices in their schools and classrooms. The participants explore the power of restorative justice to build community, develop understanding among students and between students and teachers, and lead to healing and personal growth—while also sharing the challenges and limitations faced along the way.

Over the past few decades, zero tolerance discipline policies—which set punishments for a wide range of legal and school policy infractions regardless of circumstances—have become the norm in many U.S. schools (Gregory & Cornell, 2009). On its surface a response to fears about school violence, zero tolerance policies have shown to be ineffective at addressing school safety (Dignity in Schools, 2009; Gregory & Cornell, 2009; Martinez, 2009) and to disproportionately target working-class students and students of color (Jordan & Bulent, 2009; Wald & Losen, 2003). These and other punitive discipline strategies are a part of the school-to-prison pipeline—a set of processes by which young people are pushed out of schools and either directly or indirectly into the hands of the criminal justice system (Wald & Losen, 2003).

In response to these issues, a growing number of schools are moving away from punitive disciplinary strategies and implementing alternative models under the name *restorative justice*. As explained by the Center for Restorative Justice at Suffolk University (n.d.):

> Rather than privileging the law, professionals and the state, restorative resolutions engage those who are harmed, wrongdoers and their affected communities in search of solutions that promote repair, reconciliation and the rebuilding

of relationships. Restorative justice seeks to build partnerships to reestablish mutual responsibility for constructive responses to wrongdoing within our communities. (para. 3)

Rooted in the practices of indigenous cultures in the Americas, and more commonly used in connection with the criminal justice system (McCold, 2005), restorative justice is being brought into schools and adapted to supplement and, in some cases, replace more traditional approaches to discipline.

In order to explore how restorative justice looks on the ground in schools, the editors of this volume asked Anita Wadhwa, a doctoral student at the Harvard Graduate School of Education studying restorative justice, to gather together a group of practitioners from around Boston for a roundtable discussion. In addition to Anita, who led the discussion, participants included:

- Sung-Joon (Sunny) Pai, director of the Diploma Plus[2] small learning community at Charlestown High School, where restorative justice practices have been instituted across the program
- Laurent Bennett, a former student at Diploma Plus who took part in and eventually trained to facilitate restorative justice practices
- Hilary Shanahan, a former teacher at the Social Justice Academy[3] in Boston who used restorative justice in her Law and Justice class, which took on discipline cases from the school
- Curtis Banner, one of Hilary's former students who helped to facilitate restorative justice at Social Justice Academy
- Janet Connors, a community activist and restorative justice practitioner who has worked to support the efforts at both schools

The group gathered in Janet's Dorchester home for what grew into a two-and-a-half-hour animated discussion. What follows is an edited transcript of this discussion.

WHAT IS RESTORATIVE JUSTICE?

Anita: I'd like to start with the question, "What is restorative justice?" Janet, maybe you could start off since you are a restorative justice practitioner, and then others can chime in.

Janet: Restorative justice to me is not a program—it is a way of being. It is about transformation; it is about healing; it is about bringing things back into balance when things have gotten out of whack. It is about bringing parties together when an incident of harm has occurred, in order for those who caused the harm to accept responsibility and for those who were harmed to have a voice and say what it is that they need to make it right. Making it right doesn't necessarily mean it's going to be restored to the way it was before, but as best as possible. If you have an old cabinet and you restore it, it's not the same as it was before, but it's still now a good thing. So it's about needs and obligations—the needs of the people that were harmed and the obligations of the people who caused the harm to meet those needs.

Too often in school discipline now the primary focus becomes the person who caused the harm and the person who is harmed gets sort of shifted aside. So you want to make sure that the primary focus is about repairing the harm to the person who was hurt. However, it's also about the needs of the person who caused the harm, in terms of "What's going on for you?" Because all behavior comes from a need. I always say that my Lady Justice, she has a balance of support and accountability in her scales.

Curtis: I see restorative justice as a way to recycle the community. Let's say you have a bottle, you drink it, and it's trash. That's what we were doing before, we was polluting the planet, just throwing trash away, getting rid of it, doing whatever we could to make sure it wasn't with society anymore. That's how we are treating people in the school-to-prison pipeline, or in the streets, trying to put people in prison and not trying to let them back into society. But what we want to do now is recycle. We take a bottle that you were once going to throw away, but now we put it through a process and it comes out in the end as a clean bottle that you can use again. As the years go on we develop more skills to make the water bottles thinner, the plastic better, so the recycling becomes better. If we keep using restorative justice for years and years, we'll develop the skills for it and it will become better, and maybe this world won't be such a violent place anymore; we'll have a lot more peace.

Hilary: As a classroom teacher, restorative justice meant building relationships. It also allowed me to kind of level the playing field in my classroom and to share about myself in a way that the classroom teacher doesn't normally do. It allowed me to create a very safe space for students. And the model that we used at Social Justice Academy also gave kids power to have a voice in how discipline happens in our school.

Laurent: For me, restorative justice is a different way to communicate with other people. Growing up, I felt like I was never really listened to. People would hear me but they would never really listen. But if I'm in a restorative justice circle, I really feel at peace. You can use restorative to really address anything, issues in society, global issues; it can be about sports, it can be about relationships, it can be about the African American community—anything. It's a way to trust that people are gonna listen to you.

Sunny: I feel like Janet described it well. I've never heard you say it that way—as a way of being. Because last year we were using restorative justice to address conflicts that happened between students, but this year we haven't had any student-to-student conflict. However, there is this fundamental conflict, I think, between the students who arrive in our program and school. For most kids in our Diploma Plus program, they don't want to be in high school. Why would you want to be in high school if you had failed everything in middle school and they just moved you along? Most of our students, when they arrive to us, have a fundamental conflict with high school as an institution. So some of the healing, some of the restoring, is about recycling that relationship between the students and school, recycling the relationship between students and teachers. To us, restorative justice is about trying to create a different way of being both for the adults and for the students given that starting point.

COMING TO RESTORATIVE JUSTICE: JANET'S STORY

Janet Connors has been working for years facilitating restorative justice processes in Boston communities. She shared with the group the story of her son, which helped launch her into this work.

Janet: My son Joel was murdered eleven years ago. I've always worked with kids and families here in Dorchester, and I was somewhat familiar with restorative justice. So when my son was killed, I really laid it down. I didn't want anyone else to get hurt in Joel's name. He was killed in January, and we had these restorative justice gatherings in March with some of his friends. And the kids wanted to do them here in the house. They didn't want to do them in a hall or something like that. But so many kids came that we wound up being out in the backyard. So we scurried around the neighborhood and grabbed everybody's lawn stuff. And we asked the kids to make a commitment to keep the peace and not hurt anybody else.

And I've met with two of the young men who were responsible for my son's murder in Victim Offender Dialogue.[4] I met with each of them alone first with a dialogue facilitator, and then I met with them with their parents. And I asked them to make agreements to stay in Alcoholics Anonymous or Narcotics Anonymous and get a job and earn an honest living and to talk to other young people and just not cause any more harm to the community. The way that they would make amends to me was to make the best of their lives.

They are both keeping their agreements. One of them has been out for three years now. And one of them was released last year. I wanted my son's life and the taking of my son's life to matter enough to them that they could value their own precious life and value the fact that they still had it, and understand not only the impact of what their actions had on me and my family and certainly my son but also what the impact of their actions had on their own families and their own communities.

RESTORATIVE JUSTICE PRACTICE: THE CIRCLE

In both Charlestown High School and Social Justice Academy, the central restorative justice practice has been the "circle." The participants broke down what a circle looks like by describing what they call a "community circle," a circle that is done regularly as a way of building community and relationships, addressing ongoing issues, and preventing major conflict before it arises.

Laurent: Basically, the circle is a way to communicate with others. There's a talking piece, and whoever has the talking piece can say whatever they want. They can address whatever is on their mind. From there you pass the talking piece around the circle, and whoever has the talking piece you listen to them, you don't speak. For each circle you have a circle facilitator, and that person addresses what we're gonna talk about, what we're gonna discuss.

Janet: We usually call the person who holds or leads the circle a "keeper." The keeper's role is different from how we normally think about a facilitator. The keeper is an equal participant in the circle and is in a relationship of care for each and every member of the circle. The keeper models for the group the creation of a safe, sacred, collective space that allows people to openly reflect and share. The keeper uses influence rather than control and does not try to move the participants toward a particular outcome or point of view. The keeper prepares the space, organizes the logistics, and does an opening.

Curtis: Right. The opening of the circle is a quote or a poem or a statement that the keeper thinks would get everybody comfortable with the situation. It would pertain to the topic of the circle.

Anita: And the keeper runs a check-in and has planned the questions and the prompts for the circle.

Laurent: And when you're the keeper, there's a difference between asking a good question and asking the right question. You can always ask a good question; but when you ask the right question at the right time, people really think about it, because a lot of people think about things but they won't say them out loud because they think it might sound stupid or don't know how others will react to it.

Curtis: But somebody else thinks the same thing.

Laurent: Other people think the same thing. And once you're aware of that, the conversation blows up, and you're able to communicate.

Hilary: There is something magical about putting kids in a circle. I use them not just with restorative justice. When things are not going well in a class or things just get out of hand or whatever is happening, there are times when I would stop class just to be like, "We're going to circle up." And just getting them physically in a circle—whatever it is about a circle, it just would change the energy of the room and we would be able to get somewhere. Not always anywhere positive or great, but we would be able to get somewhere different.

RESTORATIVE JUSTICE IN ACTION: SOCIAL JUSTICE ACADEMY

Hilary and Curtis explained how restorative justice practices were carried out when they were at Social Justice Academy. They fleshed out the multiple types of circles they used—from community circles to healing circles, which address a particular conflict or discipline problem.

Hilary: I taught an elective course called Law and Justice. It was two-pronged. One part of it was learning about constitutional law as it applied to student rights. The other part was learning about restorative justice and holding circles in class. So in the beginning of the school year there would be a training process for the first term, and kids who were on the upper learning curve would take over leadership roles as keepers of the circle. We would start off in the beginning of the year sitting in a circle and learning what it meant to hold a talking piece. That part was very, very frustrating as a teacher, because having kids sit quietly in a classroom and listen to one another—the respect isn't always there in the beginning of the year. Janet had a big part in running those circles, discussing sacred space and what respect means to you.

Janet: The values.

Hilary: Right. We always did a values circle, with community agreements. Then kids would make value cards and they would become our centerpiece, to be put down at the beginning of every circle to remind us. Those value cards were really important because kids would constantly refer to them.

The second part of our restorative justice work was taking cases from the school, actual disciplinary issues. Fights were probably the biggest issues, and conflicts between students and teachers. Once teachers started getting onboard—and not every teacher was onboard—they were willing to sit in circles with students. It was pretty amazing sometimes that those teachers who were the most involved in that process were the teachers that I would have thought would have nixed it from the beginning. It was a learning curve for everybody.

Curtis: We had teacher-student/student-student conflict. The school police were involved in one of our situations. And we had conflict with other small schools in the building. Students from one school would get involved with students from another school and things would escalate. We did a lot with that and actually turned things around.

Hilary: Healing circles in my class were typically on Friday, because to me it was such a nice way to end the week. On an earlier day in the week, typically a Tuesday, we would get a case from the disciplinary people and we would plan our circle for Friday. Janet really pushed for this, and having a planning circle ended up being really important to the impact the healing circle ended up having. We went around, did a quick check-in, and then I would read the case.

In the beginning I was the facilitator of the planning circles. We would just go around with initial reactions.

Janet: Then we would talk about who we think was harmed and how, what was the impact of these actions, who do we think has the most responsibility, and what are some solutions.

Curtis: Before we actually started doing healing circles, we did *practice* healing circles. We would come up with situations that may have happened and we would pick out students that would act in a little skit about a conflict was between two students or a conflict between a teacher and a student. Once we started getting comfortable with doing those types of circles, we decided, "Okay, now we can fully do this disciplinary thing with the school." And the teachers in the school, they said, "Okay, we'll let you do this but we'll start you off with something small and see how it goes from there."

I facilitated one myself. It was between two female students that had got into a physical problem. But it was a total misunderstanding, and we got to the bottom of it. By the end of the circle, we got them both to agree—not to stay friends, but to not be involved with each other in a way that would be violent. That was the main goal of the circle.

Hilary: Also, on Friday we would have a community circle that was student led, with topics the students came up with. Sometimes it would be things that were happening in our classroom or things the kids were frustrated about. I was very open to kids being able to have full reign over that. There was a grading component. There were two different ways you could get points. One was by talking, and the other was by respecting the talking piece. I had to find a way to put some type of grade value to circles, which in a perfect world I wouldn't have to do. In a class situation I felt it was important to hold kids accountable that way. I made it so it was very possible for everybody to get full points if everybody participated.

Curtis: A lot of people didn't want to do the community circles but gradually, over time, got more comfortable hearing somebody talk about their life and what goes on behind the shades, what's going on after school. Before all the circle stuff we just seen each other at school, except for little posses that teenagers have. These circles allowed all those posses and everything to come together and become a community. That's why we call them "community circles."

RESTORATIVE JUSTICE IN ACTION: CHARLESTOWN HIGH SCHOOL

Sunny and Laurent shared their experiences with the schoolwide restorative model that they use at the Diploma Plus (DP) small school in Charlestown High School.

Sunny: The way we do restorative justice has evolved over the years. Currently we have an advisory that meets four times a week for the last hour of the day. We have one all-male advisory, one all-female advisory, and one that's mixed. Those advisories meet in circle almost all the time and have a curriculum that cycles through some different topics. One is around resolving conflict, one is around figuring out your future, college and career. One is around developing resilience for yourself. That's the preventative, baseline work where we are both teaching people how to be in the circle and also examining these restorative justice ways of being.

I wouldn't say it's 100 percent getting its job done yet. The critical mass of students who like advisory, to me, is not big enough to have momentum yet. And because it's the first time we're doing this curriculum, we're still working out these kinks. But there are a lot of great moments. There were two students in an advisory that had a conflict before. One of the students had come to our unit[5] because she had developed a reputation in her previous unit in Charlestown that she didn't like, that she was responsible for having created but wanted to get away from. Another student that was already in DP had been one of the people who was mad at her. And as often happens, those two individuals start to say, "Oh, I didn't know you like this before. Now I feel like I can really understand you. I know where you're coming from, I see you as a person." That stuff happens organically, but I think we need to get better and better at trying to have that happen more often.

Laurent: That happened to me so many times last year. I opened up one day in circle, and another student pulled me to the side after and was like, "I didn't know you thought that way. I didn't know you felt that way. I feel like I really know you now." And me and her just sat down and talked for two hours after that, and she's like my sister now. You can always hang out with somebody, go to dinner or to the movies. But if you see a movie, you're not focused on the person next to you; if you're out to dinner, you're focused on eating. But with circles, you're there to learn about somebody.

Sunny: So advisory has from ten to eighteen kids depending on what the attendance might be that day. And every other week there's what we call a "unit circle," which is everybody, somewhere from thirty to fifty kids. This year it's been completely student run, and Janet's been coaching the students who run them—mainly community-building circles.

We also started a peer justice system this year—the students named it the Justice League—which meets once a week after school. That's a circle with students who have been trained in restorative justice and adults from the community. There has to be at least an equal number of students as adults. One of our teachers was very adamant that if this is going to be a peer panel, it can't be more adults that kids. It needs to be students working with students, but having other adults there helps, I think, to create intergenerational conversation.

Students are referred to the Justice League, and the person who was called can also pull in a support person.

Anita: Who refers the students, and what are they referred for?

Sunny: Right now, students are referred by teachers, mainly for issues that would normally be handled through school discipline. The referring person has to fill out a form that talks to the student's strengths, talks to what happened, and provides some data about how the student is doing in school. We've had four rounds of this so far. The first situation was a senior who was being incredibly immature, driving his teachers and classmates crazy, and not getting any work done. The sparking incident was with our cell phone policy. The second one was a student who similarly is not doing well in school, has been very stubborn about basic rules, and has been failing for two years. His sparking incident was that his teachers kept complaining about how every day he has his hat on, every day they tell him to take it off, and every day he puts it back on. It was driving them nuts and it was bleeding into his work. In both cases it wasn't about the hat or the phone.

The third one was a student who brought drugs to school—OxyContin. He had been prescribed OxyContin for something he had, but he had specifically been told by the school nurse and his doctor not to bring it in to school, and it wasn't in a prescription bottles; it was in little baggies. So he normally would have been expelled. We got in touch with his middle school guidance counselor, and she came as his support person and they did a circle for him. Based on that circle, they met with the principal and the assistant principal and advocated for him not to be expelled. He actually had an expulsion hearing scheduled and then they canceled it based on the conversation they had. To me, that is the way restorative justice ideally can work. The last one was similar to the first two—a student not getting work done, not really seeking help, and becoming more and more defiant.

THE SUCCESSES AND CHALLENGES OF RESTORATIVE JUSTICE IN SCHOOLS

The rest of the conversation moved between personal stories about the successes and power of restorative justice in practice and some of the tensions or challenges that people faced in implementation. As the conversation came to a close, it ended where it had started—at the roots and values that undergird this difficult work.

Anita: Since we're talking about the school-to-prison pipeline, if someone asked you why we should use restorative justice, how does it disrupt this phenomenon, how would you answer that?

Hilary: For me, I feel like it is very simple. What it does in my classroom is it creates a safe space where kids can change their view on school. I love getting a group of kids that's not meshing well and watching them learn to trust each other and to trust me, and to learn each other's names. So because they trust me, then they want to succeed more in my classroom. I still have kids that struggle, but they know that with that struggle comes support and caring and love and understanding. And I think that that's what keeps me doing restorative justice.

I have a lot of those fears that teachers have: fear of not being respected, fear of not being in charge—all of those things. And I also have a huge attitude and a fiery personality. I can be that teacher who is, like, "Get out of my classroom!" But restorative justice helped teach me that there are different ways of dealing with things and that I don't have to let my fear get in the way of my relationships with kids. I think that that's how it's disrupted things for me.

I'm not a fan of watching my students be kicked out of school so much. And that's something that I see so often, over silly things. I hear people in the hallway saying, "I've seen him too many times in the hall today, just kick him out." And I know that's real and it's frustrating, and sometimes it's hard to figure out how to deal with it. But it's really painful to watch. You see the amount of absences that can be caused by suspensions and being kicked out just for part of the day and the amount of learning that they lose.

Sunny: Suspension and expulsion are for the convenience of the school, not for the education of the offender. And it's not for the benefit of the community either, because you have kids who are out now in the community during the day unsupervised.

And schools in general don't always make sense, right? Especially schools in urban systems where the structures were designed for suburban kids in the eighties. For example, schools are not set up for black boys to be successful. So you try to make schools make more sense for the particular students who are in your school. And restorative justice is a big piece of this picture. It's not the only piece if we're going to disrupt the pipeline completely, but it's something that makes really good sense. It's something that builds better relationships. It's something that opens up communication.

Anita: What are the difficulties with implementing something like circle practices?

Sunny: I think the hardest part is, logistically, how do you do this in school? Because if you're gonna have a proper healing circle, you don't want to have a start and end time, whereas in school we have a start and end time because the teachers have to go out and teach their class and they're only free at certain times.

Hilary: In our school, the accountability piece was the toughest. We had the circles down pat. But at the end of the healing circles, when people became responsible for remedies—whether that would be writing a letter, apologizing to somebody—there wasn't a lot of follow-through on that end. When that happened, the circles became a bit of a cop-out for some kids. They would be willing to sit in a circle because they wouldn't get punished in that traditional punitive way. It was hard to figure out who was responsible for following up. Is it the responsibility of the school discipline person? Is it my responsibility as the classroom teacher?

Curtis: But even though we did have those problems at the end of circles—students who wouldn't follow through with their remedies, or where no one would follow through making sure that they were doing them—we, like, started seeing a decrease in problems. The next year people weren't getting suspended as much. People weren't getting detentions as much. I don't think we had any expels.

Hilary: Yes, I think overall we definitely developed a culture of circles in our school. There was a language. I mean, kids in my classes, if there was a conflict, they would say, "We need to have a circle." That was a very normal thing to hear. But there were some things that weren't circle-able.

Janet: The other limitation is that, unfortunately, right now it seems as though there are more incidents than there is the time to deal with them restoratively. But over time, as the culture of a school shifts, then, as Curtis was saying, the amount of incidences will lessen too.

Anita: Similarly, I think a limitation of restorative justice, particularly for a researcher trying to document the outcomes, is that it takes time to have an effect.

Janet: That is the problem for me with all evidence-based outcome measures and that sort of stuff. In many arenas there is not necessarily a direct cause and effect. It's really an accumulation of things over time, and letting it grow inside of yourself into what you want it to be. That's why I hate all of this talk about outcome measures and evidence-based practice, because I feel like people are then going to try and work toward the outcomes just like they teach to the MCAS [Massachusetts Comprehensive Assessment System] test.

I also worry about restorative justice being professionalized. I believe restorative justice is not something that people necessarily need to have degrees to do. I am a case in point. In fact, I think it would limit who would step up from the community if we started requiring that people had degrees. Because there is a place for the grandmother. There is a place for the mother. There is a place for my neighbor. And that's what restorative justice really is, because it is not just about restoring things back into balance for that one person or for those two people who have some kind of interaction. It's about restoring things back into balance for the larger community and that nothing that we do is just about us. Everything that we do affects other people. So I would love to see cadres of people in neighborhoods trained to be circle keepers, so when something goes down in the neighborhood the neighborhood takes care of it. My justice is very much tied to my community and to justice for my community.

Sunny: I wonder if some of the work we are doing around circles is not effective because a basic foundational level of respect and community is not in place. Some students ultimately feel they can do what they want to do. And it's such a conflict because that's a good thing—you do want students to feel like they are in control of their lives. But at the same time you've also got eighteen-year-olds who have got zero high school credits and you're trying to help them graduate.

I think some teachers are frustrated because they can taste, like, the next level of growth but feel that what's holding them back is not going to be dealt with in circles. They are saying that sometimes teenagers need to be kicked into line. And then those circles will work even better because there's been this foundation and this sort of shared sort of agreement.

Anita: It seems that there's a wide spectrum of restorative justice. There are people who feel that we should never have a student kicked out of the community and "we don't do detention." Whereas there are others who say, "When you really harm the community, you could be put out of the circle for a while to figure out what to do, but you are always welcomed back."

If someone asked, "Why should we use restorative justice in our school to address our disciplinary issues?" What would you say?

Curtis: I would start by saying that this would actually help get students more involved with each other. When we started doing restorative justice in our school and we started getting comfortable with it, at first we were doing just the community circles and that alone was getting us involved with each other in our social lives, allowing the little posses to become a whole community. You create a relationship between students and teachers that evolves with the community circles as well. You get kind of a bond between students and teachers, and that bond helps you understand where other people come from.

Janet: Curtis spoke to empathy, the understanding of one another's feelings and where somebody comes from and how that can shift the way you look at them. When we start off in the Justice League by reading off the person's strengths, it shifts the whole lens of how people then look at this young person and shifts your mind in terms of what solutions you might come up with. It is not to discount the infraction but to know that the person is more than that infraction and that they have these strengths and that those strengths are going to be what can help them make this thing right.

It really is a return to the teachings. If you were visiting your grandmother and you broke her neighbor's window, what would happen?

Curtis: Oh man!

Janet: You would go over with your grandmother and you would apologize to those people. You would have to help them put that window in. If you were too young to have a job and pay for it yourself, then your grandmother would pay for it but you would have to find a way to work that off. So it's really kind of old school.

Laurent: Restorative justice came into my life during a really bad period. I was at the point in my life where I didn't care. I'd given up. Then when I got arrested; it was the worst thing that could have ever happened to me. It was horrible. And I needed an outlet just to talk about my feelings. Restorative justice was just that outlet for me. If Janet hadn't come back into my life, with the whole restorative justice thing, I wouldn't have turned things around like I have. It was a huge opportunity for me, and I feel like I took advantage of it. I was into restorative justice before, but it wasn't until I got in trouble that I noticed what kind of opportunity I had with restorative justice.

Anita: Why was it that by getting in trouble you could better understand or appreciate restorative justice?

Laurent: I was constantly getting in trouble, and everything was building up—a bunch of animosity was building up, and it was building up and building up. It was just like my cup was overflowing and I didn't know like where to pour it out at. And I was just like looking for a real outlet. Getting arrested was the last straw. I thought, "What the hell am I doing? I have this restorative justice where people will listen to me, but why wasn't I getting it?" I guess it's not until you really understand how serious things are that you can use restorative justice.

   I felt like I was trailing off and you all supported me in your own ways. You guys held on long enough until I was ready to really stride on my own. I feel like restorative justice means you don't give up on me.

Janet: You don't give up. That's exactly true. You don't give up and you keep going back. And that's sometimes what makes it hard in school. But we can't throw people away. And that's what we're doing. When we suspend a kid, we're throwing them away. We are throwing people away when we lock them up in DYS [Department of Youth Services], instead of saying, "What do you need to belong? What do you need? We support you."

Laurent: "How can we hold you?"

Janet: Right. "How can we hold you?"

NOTES

1. This participant's name has been changed to protect his identity.
2. Diploma Plus is a national organization that "seeks to develop, implement, and sustain, in partnership with school districts and communities, innovative educational

approaches and small schools that provide rigorous and student-centered alternatives for youth who have been failed by the traditional system in order to nurture their power as learners and enable them to complete high school college- and career-ready." See http://www.diplomaplus.net

3. Social Justice Academy was a Boston public school located in Hyde Park. It closed its doors in 2011.

4. Victim Offender Dialogue, or Victim Offender Mediation, is a restorative justice practice in which conversations are facilitated between victims of a crime and their offenders. These dialogues provide a safe space in which victims can share their stories and receive answers to questions and in which both victims and offenders can work together to develop plans for restitution and accountability (Shenk, 2004; Umbreit & Greenwood, 2000).

5. The Diploma Plus learning community.

REFERENCES

Center for Restorative Justice at Suffolk University. (n.d.). What is restorative justice? Retrieved from http://www.suffolk.edu/research/6953.html

Dignity in Schools. (2009). Fact sheet: School discipline and the push out problem. Retrieved from *www.dignityinschools.org/files/DSC_Pushout_Fact_Sheet.pdf*

Gregory, A., & Cornell, D. (2009). "Tolerating" adolescent needs: Moving beyond zero tolerance policies in high school. *Theory into Practice, 48*(2), 106–113.

Jordan, J., & Bulent, A. (2009). Race, gender, school discipline, and human capital effects. *Journal of Agricultural and Applied Economics, 41*(2), 419–429.

Martinez, S. (2009). A system gone berserk: How are zero tolerance policies really affecting schools? *Preventing School Failure, 53*(3), 153–156.

McCold, P. (2005). The recent history of restorative justice: Mediation, circles, and conferencing. In D. Sullivan & L. Tifft (Eds.), *Handbook of restorative justice: A global perspective* (pp. 23–51). Hoboken, NJ: Taylor & Francis.

Shenk, A. H. (2004). Victim-offender mediation: The road to repairing hate crime injustice. In P. B. Gerstenfeld & D. R. Grant (Eds.), *Crimes of hate: Selected readings* (pp. 299–311). Thousand Oaks, CA: Sage.

Umbreit, M. S., & Greenwood, J. (2000). *Guidelines for victim-sensitive victim-offender mediation: Restorative justice through dialogue.* Washington, DC: U.S. Department of Justice, Office for Victims of Crime.

Wald, J., & Losen, D. (2003, May). *Defining and redirecting a school-to-prison pipeline.* Paper presented at the School-to-Prison Pipeline Research Conference, Institute on Race and Justice, Northeastern University, Boston.

Zehr, H. (2002). The little book of restorative justice. Intercourse, PA: Good Books.

EDUCATION

■

ELIZABETH A. REID

What did education mean to me as a child? Well, education meant effort. Being in school required too much effort. Effort to wake myself up. Effort to wake my sisters and brothers up. Effort to look for the cleanest dirty clothes for all of us to wear. Effort to find anything at all to eat. Effort to get to school on time without a ride. Effort to explain why I had no homework to turn in and no school supplies to use. Effort to stay out of the free lunch line with its scornful looks. Effort to assure, with a smile (*Oh, that smile!*), that I didn't bring a lunch because I just wasn't hungry. Effort to get excused from PE on a regular basis so the bruises and marks wouldn't show. Effort to pretend that I was happy and carefree, the way all kids should be. Effort to lie about my life, with a smile (*Yes, that smile!*). Effort to keep the secrets. Effort not to wonder why I was all alone in the world. Effort not to cry.

All of this effort turned into fear. School was the place where I would be revealed. If I slipped up, they would split our family up. My brothers and sister had no one else but me to take care of them. If they saw my black eye, I would go to jail with the policeman. An eight-year-old standing in front of the mirror, putting on cover-up to hide a black eye. That was me. That was my life. The constant state of fear I lived in at home traveled with me to school. It was just fear of another kind. My fear of school led to a lifelong fear of education. And this fear of education followed me all through the years. But that smile (*Yes, that smile!*)? I lost that somewhere along the way.

The years went by. I grew up and became what I was expected to become. When you grow up surrounded by a world of drugs, dealers, violence, and poverty, it becomes hard to believe that there is anything better for you. I accepted my role in that world and did whatever I had to for survival. I managed to make it to prison three times as an adult. But I found that the life I had made for myself also required too much effort. After becoming a drug dealer, I had to worry constantly about the police, about the drug users, about getting robbed, about re-upping, about getting taken advantage of because I was a girl, about hiding what I was doing, and about getting killed. Education became the only option left. It was the only thing I hadn't tried in order to make my life better. If anything was going to save me from returning to prison, it was going to have to be education.

After all the years, though, I was still afraid of it. I was doing my best to deny that fear, but it was there. You see, I was still carrying around all of those feelings about school I'd had as a child. There are scars that never fade. There are unfulfilled needs that linger inside of us. That childlike need for acceptance (*somewhere!*) remained. I wished for a place to belong. I couldn't go back to prison again. I didn't have it in me anymore. This was it—*my last chance.* I felt that sick fear in my stomach. *You are not gonna measure up!* That old voice, my constant crippling companion, whispered incessantly to me that I couldn't do it. I would fail. Again.

But this time I did not listen. I had too much to lose. This time my life was on the line.

I began attending Green River Community College in Auburn, Washington. A friend told me that there were excellent professors there and that they would help me. Things began to change right away for me. I would write papers and receive A's on them. The responses to my efforts surprised me. I began to feel like a different person. I was surprised at how easily learning came to me when I wasn't forced to worry all the time. Slowly but surely my confidence grew. During the first quarter I earned straight A's. Then I earned a perfect 4.0 during the next quarter. Hope took root. Awareness of previously unknown worlds entered my mind. The dark world I had known all my life started to recede. There were people and places I wanted to know. There were words I wanted to read and write. I finally felt I had something worth saying. Life began to take shape.

That fear? It is gone for the first time in my life. Education has changed my life—it has changed *me.* This campus is where I feel safe. I don't have to hide anything here. There is acceptance. There is friendship just for the sake of being friends. It is where I know I belong. It opened up its doors and gave me a place where I was welcome. My future awaits me and I am *running* towards it. And, finally, the fear I've been dragging along my entire life has been left behind. And my true smile (*No, not that OLD smile*)? I finally found it, for the first time, right here on my face.

PART II

■

EDUCATION IN DETENTION

TIPPING THE BALANCE

■

JOSEPH CAMBONE

"Anne" is a teacher at a residential and day school for boys with severe emotional and behavioral challenges, an extremely complex learning environment that remains little known to the rest of society and the educational community at large. In this chapter, Joseph Cambone presents a portrait of Anne and her struggles to succeed and help her students learn. Anne works hard, thinks critically about her teaching, attempts to meet her students where they are, and holds a love for her students and her work that helps her maintain her focus on "strength and health, not pathology" in the teaching and learning process. Through Cambone's portrait, we bear witness to Anne's personal growth and professional development, her students' development as learners and members of a community, and the ways in which teaching and learning happens in this complex educational community.

> Especially in times of darkness,
> that is the time to love, that an act of love might
> tip the balance.
> — *Aeschylus*

CHAOS

"I was some of the problem. My expectations were wrong." It is early October, a week after the lesson took place, and we are getting ready to watch it together on the videotape I have made. Anne sits with her Diet Coke, I with my pad and video paraphernalia. It is our first meeting, and I am struck (as I will be throughout our months of videotaping lessons and talking about them afterwards) by how honestly self-critical she is. "I remember thinking that I was glad we would see this on videotape," she says with a little laugh. She seems nervous, perhaps even embarrassed, about watching together what was clearly a difficult lesson. I had anticipated that. What I had not anticipated was her curiosity. More than anything, she is curious. She wants to see for herself where she made her errors, how she was part of the problem. For that opportunity, she is glad.

But I am puzzled: how could she have been the problem? I had obviously seen the lesson differently through the lens of the camera. These children

Harvard Educational Review   Vol. 60   No. 2   Summer 1990

are so difficult to manage, and the lesson seemed such a reasonable one to attempt! This group of five boys is the youngest in the long history of this residential treatment center. By all accounts, they are the most violent and disturbed for their age.[1]

Six-year-old Jeremy was born in a state institution and already has been in nearly ten foster homes. Small and thin, his dark hair is cut in a spiky brush-cut top that sets off his pale olive skin; he is cute, spunky, and talkative. Adults and children alike are drawn to him. But he is frequently confused and frustrated by almost all social situations and often becomes physically assaultive or sexually provocative.

Paul is seven. He and his family have been homeless until just recently, and there is evidence that he has been sexually abused in one of many shelters. The school is the first place that he has lived for any extended period of time. His round, deep-brown face is full of expression; his large almond-shaped eyes are always wide with what seems to be confusion and panic—and sometimes, thankfully, the glee of a little boy. He is known by almost all of the adults in the school by now, because his tantrums have been so exceedingly violent, frequent, and prolonged.

Six-year-old Steve had also been sexually abused before his adoption. Unlike the other boys, he is not a child who has tantrums often. Instead, he becomes oppositional, automatically shouting "NO!" at small requests or even when offered opportunities for fun. Often he sits, jaw set in his long, delicate face, brows furrowed, eyes squinting, whispering obscenities and taunts at the other boys. He is the only boy at grade level in his school work.

Samuel, eight years old, is a unique child, with average intelligence but pervasive neurological difficulties. In one-to-one situations, he is sweet and affectionate, never hesitating to hug adults or tell them how much he loves them. But he has spent very little time in classrooms or with groups of any kind. He is given to screaming episodes at the slightest provocation, leaving adults and students alike wondering at the cause.

Blond, blue-eyed, freckled Jamie is five years old, full of energy and continually on the move. He is unable to sit still for more than a few seconds at a time, always bumping into others, teasing and taunting them, poking his fingers at their sides. His activity level can escalate rapidly, easily disrupting the whole class; he is placed in "time-out" frequently. He is bright and verbal and quite engaging.

None of the boys has spent substantial time in school. Taken on their own, they are difficult to manage, demanding, and impulsive; put together, they interact explosively, provoking each other in a variety of ways—fighting, striking out at adults, throwing furniture and objects, and running away. Whenever I have seen the five together, chaos has not been far away. I thought the lesson went pretty well, considering the boys' behavior.

"Was this a bad lesson?" I betray my incredulity through my tone of voice. She laughs her laugh, intelligent and perceptive, always with the slight touch of apology, and answers, "Well, this was not as good a lesson as it could have been!" She explains:

> In terms of the process of a teacher . . . this has been a really hard group for me 'cause I've needed to change a lot of the things I'm doing. I'm constantly critiquing what I'm doing. And the group has been so out of control most of the time! On one level, I know that a lot of other people who have been here at the school even longer than I have said, "Oh my God! I can't believe that group!" And "I don't know how you deal with them every day." And "This is the most difficult group I've ever had in the art room!" And blah blah blah! So I know it's not me. But at the same time, I'm constantly knowing that I do need to change what I'm doing and that there are things that I can change to make it better. So I'm sort of constantly replaying that in my head.

Her eagerness to be self-critical seems layered, like so much of what she does; perhaps being self-critical helps fend off the impulse to blame the boys for their difficulties, as others sometimes do. Given their extremely troublesome behavior, it is easy to blame them. Perhaps, too, she is self-critical because she knows that, in a way, she is in the spotlight; people are watching closely and with a certain amazement at how she'll handle the most difficult group they've seen in years.

Yet, the self-analysis goes much deeper, to what being a teacher means to her. Anne believes that being self-analytical is part of the "process of being a teacher." This process involves constantly re-evaluating assumptions about what works and what does not work in the classroom, not settling on one method; rather, developing a curriculum *in response to* the children. Anne believes that this year's plans cannot be based on last year's students.

So she is "glad" as we watch the tape of the lesson—glad for the opportunity to think over her assumptions, glad to think over her methods. And I am glad for the opportunity to watch her think as we begin to watch the videotape together.

Cathy's voice is getting tighter. It's the third week of school and already Anne has given this new teaching intern plenty of responsibility. The boys are getting restless, whispering, fidgeting on the L-shaped bench that wraps around the far left corner under the windows. There are usually five boys in the group, but Jeremy has already been removed from the room for trouble. Anne is setting up a new lesson and has not given them her full attention for just over a minute. The boys' energy is palpable, unfocused. She pulls the table out and puts the apples on it before them.

The PAUSE button gets pushed. "I wasn't well organized enough. I mean that is an immediate hindsight reaction . . . ." At first, I think she is referring to having the apples ready and the table in place. But she is referring to her disorganized mind-set: she wasn't planning for the right children. "I've done this lesson at least twice before with other groups, and kids loved it. They were totally motivated to eat the apples . . . it was fun, a great lesson! . . . I sort of was stupid in saying ' . . . I can just do it off the top of my head!'" She watches the frozen action on the screen. ". . . I didn't really think enough about how different this group is from last year's—just how because it was successful last year . . . !"

She has focused on her interior organization for the lesson, while I have focused on how not being ready with materials causes tension to mount in the room. Ordinarily, a teacher can take at least sixty seconds or so of class time to arrange supplies for an activity, but not in this class—trouble begins brewing in those sixty seconds. Any time spent talking instead of doing something tempts fate; transitions between activities can be tortuous. I begin to understand her comments about organization. If she can move the boys smoothly from activity to activity, keeping them focused on objects by using their hands and eyes, she can divert their attention away from their own thoughts or each other. Nevertheless, it has to be the right activity. I push PLAY.

Samuel, strange and distant, starts making gulping noises, moving his head forward and back like a chicken when it walks. "Samuel, I can't put in a good sticker for you until you're not making noises. Samuel, look at me." Cathy is trying to regain his attention. He doesn't hear, lost in his own rhythm. Anne is moving quicker now but says nothing. Paul and Jamie are laughing together on the bench, mostly ignoring Cathy. Jamie makes small kung-fu gestures. Paul laughs at the gestures Jamie uses and makes a few of his own. Jamie laughs and ups the ante; leaning back in his chair, he spreads his legs and pretends to play with his penis.

Over the voices on the tape, Anne comments on Samuel. "It's very frustrating to figure out what to do with him! His biggest problem is being overstimulated, and he's in a group of extremely acting-out kids. The other kids are probably scary. . . ." She isn't sure he should remain in the class—maybe this school is the wrong place for him, maybe he needs something even more specialized. And Jamie is such a baby, not even six years old. He is so bright and eager, but overrun with impulses. She sees him play with his penis and wishes she could just let it pass by without comment. "It's something that [seems unimportant]. He plays with his penis on top of his pants . . . in some ways it is not atypical for a five-year-old. But with this group and knowing him. . . ." Cathy, who is less experienced, and less philosophical, seems frantic.

"Jamie, it looks to me that you need to go to time out." He leans toward her, purses his lips, sticks his tongue out a little, and makes a growling noise. Samuel mimics him, although he makes no sound. The defiance is contagious and Paul starts fidgeting wildly. Karen, the milieu therapist who is the third member of this team, takes Jamie by the hand and leads him out. Jamie hesitates and looks at Anne and says, "Ohhhh! What am I gonna do?" He seems befuddled. Was I doing something wrong, he seems to say; what did I do? "But when can I get my 'good' sticker?" he whines as he is withdrawn from the room. Anne turns to the remaining boys, face set in a serious look.

When a child does something like what Jamie did, something that she thinks in itself is minor or manageable but could upset the others, she is distressed. "How much do you send one kid away from the group for something you think might upset the others in the group?" She returns to this question again and again, unable to answer it. The tension of this uncertainty about what approach to take marks the first weeks of school.

> By now, Paul is in motion again, kneeling on his bench on all fours, swaying his buttocks back and forth. He is a ball of energy, but when he sees the adults' attention shift from Jamie back to him he jumps into a perfect sitting position.
>
> "Today we're going to talk about apples," she begins. She stands behind the table and puts out four different types of apples. The three boys give her rapt attention, as if they'd never seen an apple before. "Who can tell me something about these apples?" Hands shoot up in a great start to the lesson. Samuel says, "There's a red one, a green one, and [pointing to a golden delicious apple] a white one." "So they have different what . . .?" Samuel: "Colors." Anne: "Paul, what can you tell me about these apples?" He leaps off his bench and lurches toward the apples, leaning in as he goes. "No, stay in your seat, you'll get to touch them later." "But I have to show you!" He is pleading, he can't say it without touching. But she just continues speaking to the boys about the lesson. He inches backwards and sits down.
>
> Fully animated, he points at one, learning forward, twisting in his seat, trying to find something important to say about the apple. His hand is outstretched, feeling the apple in the air as she calls on him again. "What can you tell me about these apples?" "They got skin on 'em? And stems?" Am I on the right track? He seems to ask as he works himself up to standing on one leg, knee still on the bench. His movement is getting larger; he can't sit still. "Good job, Paul." Now standing, he starts to sway, swinging his arms and hands up and down in the front of his body, then around to his back, then in front again. A little louder. "They have skin all around them." Anne acknowledges quickly, "Yes, they have skin all around them." Paul, voice filled with drama, "To make them warm!"

"What are you thinking?" I ask, hitting PAUSE. "Just how constantly in motion he is, that he has not been still once! . . . He's doing okay . . . although he is moving so fast . . . would it help him, would it be better or worse to make him stop and sit still?" She has him involved. His energy is ample but she is keeping it within boundaries. She makes a decision: "Right now, Paul moving his body around a lot is a minor problem compared to Paul being typically aggressive. It's sort of like saving my battles." She is constantly vigilant, watching them closely, collecting information, and sorting it on the fly.

> She simply gestures to him to sit. Paul climbs back on the bench and kneels on it, facing away from the group, his head as a third point touching the bench. Samuel starts moving in his chicken motion, stops, starts again. Is he paying attention? "I like the red one and the dotted one," Steve says. Paul, up and moving again toward the apples asks, "You mean this one?" Anne loses none of her own momentum as she points and says, "Back on your seat, Paul." Once again he returns and lies across the bench.
>
> The idea for the lesson is to use the senses to experience what is different and what is the same about apples. "We're going to see how they look, how the apples smell, how the apples feel, how the apples taste . . . ," she says. Paul is on the move again. "Sit down," she says calmly and firmly without missing a beat. "This is a Macintosh. We're going to pass the

apple around, and we're going to look with our eyes and say some words that tell what a Macintosh apple looks like."

Steve holds the apple and smiles. "It's cold!" he says. "There's a word for what it feels like. Remember that. But right now let's look at how it looks." She has a chart ready to write down words that tell how it looks, then feels, smells, and tastes. But it is too late, she has given them the apple to hold and the wheel's in motion. Paul takes the apple, gazing dreamily out the window as he rubs it between his hands, then smooths it against his face. "Now you guys are looking and feeling," Anne says aloud to herself. It's a statement of fact—things are already happening differently from what she planned. In truth, they are not "looking" at all, they are feeling. She planned a structured, sequential lesson on the five senses; they're interested only feeling.

She tries again to focus them, to redirect the lesson, to organize their learning. "I want boys to remember to look with their eyes. Now who can tell me a word about how this apple looks." Steve has caught on. He says, "It's red." Samuel says, "It's juicy." But Anne is concentrating again on getting the squirming Paul back on track, "Paul, what's a word about how the apple looks?" "It looks funny!" He is on his knees in front of her in a flash. "This could be a mouth and this could be a head." This time she lets him stay. After all, he has told her what it looks like. "Yes, but what color is it?" she asks. "It's red." Steve complains that he had already said that. No one hears him over Paul so he says, barely audible, his eyes slitted and angry, "It looks like a bum!" Paul has moved back to the bench and is walking on it like a crab with excitement. The tone in the room has changed but she isn't yet sure why. "I need everybody sitting quietly on the bench and eyes on me." There is a brief moment of stillness.

When her simple request to sit quietly works, Anne decides not to make a big deal about everyone talking at once. She just stops and regroups. She wants to get on with the lesson and give each boy a chance to participate, but she needs a moment to get a handle on the tone of the room. She did not hear Steve's comment, and Samuel's was overshadowed by Paul's voice as well, but she picked up the change in tone, a shift away from exuberance and toward agitation. "Tone" is important to many of her decisions. It is an indication of the group's mood and level of tolerance. When she is made confident by the group's tone that they are doing well, she knows she can give an individual boy a little more latitude in his behavior, as she has with Paul. She draws on "knowledge of the individual kids and knowledge of the group dynamics. . . . If I feel like [a boy is] doing something that is going to set off the rest of the group, it's gotta stop right away. And if it looks like it's something that nobody else is paying attention to and the kid is still with what is going on, and it's going to cause a bigger problem to stop it than it is to let it keep going, then I might let it go." But in this case she misreads the tone, misunderstands why it has shifted, misses that the constant motion and commotion seem to be masking the boys' underlying confusion about what she wants. The tension is mounting among the children. They are offering ideas, talking about the apples. What does she want? They are mumbling what is important to them— "it's cold," "it's juicy"—but she is trying to focus them on seeing. Samuel is squirming and Steve has turned around in his seat, yawning, inattentive. She has lost them somehow.

After the lesson she realizes her error—the lesson was not suited for them. "We needed to cut out like twenty-five steps . . . . I've always taught the youngest kids who were emotionally disturbed and learning disabled and I felt like I had already pared everything down to the barest minimum. With this group, I need to go twenty steps below that." But in the moment, she wants to push them, "I'm used to pushing kids to that next level of thinking. . . . But the task I was asking them to do didn't make sense. I mean forget the difference between the eyes and the hands! Save the five senses for another lesson! That's a prerequisite skill they don't have yet." In this case, she has misjudged; has pushed too hard too soon, and the delicate balance of control was quickly lost.

"Paul, can you say what the apple looks like?" He jumps up and comes to her. She lets it go. He kneels. "There are little green spots and flat on the bottom. Flat here, flat here, and here it's busted." "Good job, Paul, now sit down." Paul, the showman, takes a bow before the group. Steve has been trying to speak again and gets pre-empted by Paul. Samuel giggles. Steve has been continually thwarted by Paul's misbehavior and when Paul, perpetual motion on the bench, bounces around the bench toward Steve, Steve punches him in the side. Not hard, just enough. Paul hits him back. Anne is firm, calm, "Now Steve and Paul, each of you have three minutes to sit quietly and we're not going to go on until you're finished." The room bursts into pandemonium.

Anne's mind races to meet the crisis.

"It's moving so quickly and I don't feel I have time to think about what I'm saying. . . . "

Paul leaps up to run from the room but Cathy grabs him. Samuel starts rocking back and forth, head like a rag doll. Paul is yelling, "Fuck you, leave me alone, fuck you." "Paul, you have to the count of three to be back on your bench or you will leave the classroom. One, two . . ." Paul stops screaming and cursing, smiles at his classmates, cocky. Samuel gets quiet but then laughs and seems like a willing participant in the misbehavior. "Now the whole group is going to sit." When they hear this, the room bursts into chaos again. Paul grabs his crotch wildly and starts shouting suggestive words. Samuel laughs hysterically. Paul lifts his shirt and displays his stomach provocatively to Samuel, sing-songing, "BELLYBUTTON!!" Anne takes his arm and begins to remove him.

"He's going to do something either dangerous or so outrageous that it is going to cause more of a problem."

Samuel starts to make noises. As Paul moves past the table with the apples on it, he picks one up and, still shouting sexual epithets for the boys, throws it at the wall. Anne takes both arms and walks him to time-out. Steve jumps from his chair and runs for the apple.

"This shouldn't be happening. I'm a bad teacher! If this is happening in my classroom, I should be able to have better control than this!!"

Samuel starts shrieking "FUCKER" over and over while he starts rocking. Finally, he jumps up and tries to run away.

"Can't we do anything to shut him up! He has good reason to be anxious . . . but we can't even be supportive!"

Cathy catches his arm, tries to hold Samuel and to get Steve back in his chair at the same time. Anne, at the other side of the room, has Paul pinned in a chair.

"An adult needs to put hands on him and physically stop him because otherwise he's going to run out of the classroom, knock something over, or do something potentially dangerous!"

He is kicking her and attempting to head-butt her, screaming.

"There's a part of me that is dealing with the physical reality—of not being able to physically put Paul down."

Karen returns Jamie to the room at just this moment.

" . . . this is a stupid time to bring Jamie into the room!"

Apparently, he has calmed down. Karen leaves Jamie in a chair on the far side of the room, takes Samuel from Cathy, and leaves the room with the shrieking Samuel. At the same time, Anne sees that Paul cannot remain and removes him from the room to the Crisis Center. Steve remains, looking innocent, on the bench.

"I can't remember whether Steve had been part of the initial problem or not. It all happened so quickly."

The class is over in ten minutes. It takes another thirty minutes to calm the children down and get on with the day. As we finish the tape, Anne is visibly frustrated, struggling to find what is going wrong, why she can't teach in the way she knows best and interact therapeutically with the boys as she has done in the past. "So much is happening at once . . . I need to be juggling so many things at once!" In the end, she circles back to where she began: "I was some of the problem. My expectations were wrong."

INSIGHT

The huge old oak stands majestic in the center of the sprawling lawn, its last leaves driven away by the first rainy day of November. The manicured lawn, stretching gradually up the hill from the tree to the large, beige Victorian mansion, is dying green and sepia, and the last struggling marigolds are beginning to fade in the big barrel planters along the walks. Even in the rain, the campus is pretty. Sitting on a bluff over the river, the property was once a wealthy dairy farm. Now it is a school for emotionally disturbed boys, and the barn, with a copper weathervane atop its cupola, has been tastefully refitted for offices. The old carriage house matches the main house in style and

color and is used as a crisis center. The very modern school building sits far-
ther back on the prooperty, near the pasture that stretches up and out, rolling
away toward the river; it is conservation land filled with birds. The mansion
itself, called The House, is a residence for the boys, and although the inside
is revamped for that purpose, the exterior retains its original grace. Canada
geese fly overhead, leaving the river behind for the winter, and I breathe it all
in as I amble up the walk, past Anne's classroom window, to my appointment
with the principal to speak about Anne's work.

"FUCK YOU!"

Paul's voice pushes through the wall and crashes into the landscape. Samuel's piercing wail follows. Furniture is pushed over, and Paul's obscenities fuse
with Samuel's sustained cries. I think about the video session Anne and I have
planned for the afternoon, the conversation we will have, and the struggle she
is involved in. I look one more time at the lovely campus and take another,
deeper breath.

In the staff room at lunchtime, Anne is propped on the end of her seat,
leaning toward her colleagues, talking rapidly, loudly, her food half eaten.
Her usually pale face is drained further of color, tears fill her eyes. She is
furious. Whatever I overheard an hour before led to something even more
serious. I've never seen her angry—even when the children are outrageously
provocative, she remains calm, her voice measured. I hesitate to ask what has
happened and instead watch her two teacher colleagues listen carefully, offer
words of encouragement, and validate her feelings of frustration and anger.
They are good listeners, long practiced at "giving space," letting anger wind
down before trespassing with their own thoughts and opinions. Yet it is clear
that they are not listening out of obligation. They are sincere, they share her
worry about the children, and they share many of her beliefs about teaching
practice.

Almost in unison, all three look up at the clock. It is 11:55. By 11:56 they are
gone. As always, they must be ready when the boys return from lunch, ready
to maneuver them smoothly into the afternoon activity. Predictability, consistency, and challenge are words they use to explain their work, conditions they
believe are requirements for these children. But making those beliefs manifest
puts tremendous pressure on them; it requires them to wolf down meals, communicate economically, and quickly move on—even though they are person-
ally upset. The heart of this school beats fast, pushes hard; it is difficult not
to get caught up in the rapid-fire thinking, talk, and movement. Invariably,
within twenty minutes of arriving, my pulse is racing, too.

At 3:00 that afternoon, Anne is still upset as she tells me the story. It began
at "wake-up." The boys were resistant to getting out of bed and doing their
morning routines. Breakfast was disagreeable, and by the time they reached
the classroom, Anne, Cathy, and Karen had a difficult time settling the boys
in. They had a full day ahead: reading, math, and writing, as usual. But a special event was planned for the morning. The "Animals as Intermediaries" folks

were coming. These people are a group of naturists who come to the school with live, usually wild, but injured animals as part of a school-wide science program. Today they brought a field mouse and a dog. Anne had high hopes for this period. When they had come the week before, the activity was a great success. But today, Jeremy, in a rage because Steve got to hold the dog's leash and he did not, picked up a stapler and threw it at the dog, beginning a chain of problems that reverberated throughout the morning. Karen took Jeremy to the crisis center, where this behavior escalated, and before long Jamie was removed by Cathy for misbehavior as well.

Left alone with the three remaining boys, Anne continued with the planned curriculum and moved on into Big Books period. Big Books are just that: three feet tall, colorful, with large type. They are the basis for multiple language and reading activities. This is usually a successful time for all, but today the negative momentum of the morning pushed hard against the fun of Big Books. Steve ended up in time-out, Paul began running around the room, climbing on the window sill, and Samuel began to shriek, "because that's what he does whenever someone else is having trouble." Refusing to sit down when he was told to, Paul became physically abusive toward Anne, requiring her to hold him in a chair. When his behavior became even more assaultive, kicking and head-butting her, she attempted to put him in a full restraint, in which the child is maneuvered into a position where he cannot move his body, thus preventing harm to himself and others. He proved too wild and strong for her, and she was unable to control him. In the back of her mind, she knew the other two boys were watching closely to see if she could safely restrain Paul, and she knew she could not. She pulled back and let him run out of the room. The situation had shaken her and the other boys badly. "That was an upsetting scene because the other kids were watching me not be in control, physically in control of this situation. And then he [Paul] was running around campus being out of control."

To make matters worse, about five minutes after Paul was finally calmed down, his therapist insisted on having her regularly scheduled meeting with him, even though he had just assaulted a teacher and run around campus. Against Anne's strong objection, the therapist relieved Paul from his consequences and took him to get his lunch—in front of the boys who have just seen him assault their teacher. Anne was outraged. She tells me:

> . . . [he] sort of pranced into the lunchroom and got his lunch and all the other boys sort of looked at him and said "he just hit a teacher and ran around campus, what is he doing here?" And it was really very confusing. I was very angry because I didn't agree with that happening. So that was sort of the straw that broke the camel's back . . . here was this child who had just done, in my mind, the two worst things he could have done! And there he was. And so I told his therapist to take him out of the lunchroom, that he couldn't be there, that he couldn't be near other boys and that I didn't want boys in my class to see him at all right now. And it was a little bit tense. . . .

She laughs a laugh that almost apologizes for her passion. But she is extremely serious: how can she be expected to make her classroom a safe place to learn if everyone doesn't give the children the same message about their behavior? These children can't differentiate the therapy session from the classroom; all adults are the same to them, and what the therapist sees as unconditional positive regard for Paul seems to seven-year-old Paul like getting off the hook. Anne's argument is quite persuasive; it has the force of belief, and her frustration is real.

Anne's frustrations are mounting. She is frustrated because it is already November and the chaos is continuing, frustrated that she can't deal with the children individually and therapeutically because so many things happen at once, frustrated that she cannot keep everyone safe, and particularly frustrated when she sees adults not working as a team. That, in fact, is the "straw that broke the camel's back."

Even though the feeling of chaos claims the balance of the day, there is a difference in the class. I had felt the difference earlier as I taped her lesson, felt that she might be making inroads into the chaos. Yet, it is evident as we begin to watch the tape together that she is not yet feeling any positive difference. The class still feels like bedlam to her. But it is clear to me that she is more confident about how to proceed. Closely watching her work with the children as she responds to whatever surprises they toss at her, I realize how intellectually agile she is. She enters a given period with a plan and a terminal goal, but her intellectual and emotional stance is open and ready: What will they do? What will they say? How will I respond so that I can keep them moving toward the goal and not lose them to answer or frustration? Each situation the boys present is a fresh problem to be solved in a series of steps toward a final goal. She draws on her earlier repertoire of activities, but she applies them in new ways, for different purposes.

Her work is not just responsive in the moment, though. Threaded through her talk about the class and evident in her actions with the boys are three principles that she has extracted from the chaos: these boys, individually, are clearly capable of higher intellectual and behavioral functioning; the problems they are presenting are group-management problems; the schedule of the day must be altered accordingly. By keeping these three ideas in mind, she limits the field of possible approaches: focus on their individual strengths, work to improve their interaction skills, and modify their environment to enhance their strengths and promote healthier interaction.

Three children and three adults sit huddled on the bench together, first an adult, then a child, then an adult, child, adult, child. Jeremy and Paul, she explains to Cathy and Karen, and for the ears of the three remaining boys, have been separated for the remainder of the day for their violent behavior.

I'm surprised. The remainder of the day? "[I am] trying to preserve the classroom space as a safe, calm space. Even if that means that four out of five need to leave it and then gradually come back one at a time. . . . But this . . . space needs to be preserved as a place where learning happens and where crazy behavior can't happen. . . ." I think back to her recurring dilemma: "How much do you send one kid away from the group for something you think might upset the others in the group?" She seems to have made a decision about how to proceed—make the classroom a place of learning and pull them back one at a time. This is a methodological decision that reflects Anne's adjustment to who these children are and the ways they think—they are young, inexperienced in school, and still unsure of what is required of them, and they are easily confused by what others say and do. She has decided to structure the environment in unambiguous, stark terms. The group-management problems can be resolved only if the children understand the environmental requirements: in this class, we learn; in this class, we do not act crazy. It is simply stated, over and over, in word and deed. It is for this reason that she is angry with Paul's therapist. By giving the message that consequences for violence could and will be suspended by one adult, but not another, the therapist undermines Anne's efforts.

> *Anne is finishing a read-aloud book. All five children seem mellow and affectionate. Jamie sees me and my video camera and comes up to look. Anne suggests that if the boys are interested and do a good job cleaning up and getting ready for the next period, I will demonstrate the camera. They hop to it, the transition goes smoothly, and one by one they sit on my lap and film their teachers and classmates. Then, just as easily, they hop back to their benches and begin writing class.*

Anne shows them a large manila envelope, addressed and ready to go. It is a thank you letter to a museum they had toured the week before. "Remember yesterday we wrote a thank you letter to the Children's Discovery Museum. I got a big envelope. . . ." In it she put the oversized card that they had written as a group the day before. She tells them how she addressed the envelope and will send it. It is a brief lesson in letter writing. Quickly, she moves on and shows them the book they had made yesterday filled with the photos taken at the museum. On every page, a boy had pasted a photo of himself doing some fun thing at the museum. Under each photo he dictated a short sentence about what he did. "Here's Steve's picture. It says 'Steve liked the chain-reaction room!' and there's Samuel's picture, and it says, 'Samuel is jumping on the giant water bed!'" As she reads the captions under each picture, they give her all their attention, giggling with glee when their picture comes up.

"They said what to write and I *wrote* it, and they could *read* it," she says with excitement. "It was a record of their experiences: Jamie liked this, Paul liked this, Jeremy liked this. . . ." There is a remarkable difference in the presentation of this book from the presentation of lessons earlier in the year— the apples, for instance. Here, the short lesson is focused directly on the boys, what they thought, felt, saw, and did. The children laugh, ask questions, make comments. This way of doing things makes sense to them. They are in positive frames of mind. Characteristically, Anne decides to push them a little, to try something they don't like as much, and she pulls out the easel to begin a group lesson. She is always looking for an opportunity to push them harder, to acclimate them to school-like activities, to shift the balance in favor of academics.

"We'll keep this on the shelf in our room so that if you want to show anyone about our trip, you can." Anne sets up the easel as she speaks, "I thought that it is nice to have things to show about special things you've done. And this morning we did something special. Who can remember some of the things that we did this morning when the animals came to the class. . ." At the slightest hint of a structured lesson, where questions will be asked and answers required, the boys' anxiety level goes up. Samuel starts rocking and making low noises; Jamie whines and sprawls on the bench. Cathy goes to Jamie, Anne to Samuel. Each talks quietly to the boys and they sit up. But Jamie is still fidgety. "I don't want to do this," he complains. Anne pushes ahead and asks Samuel what he liked about this morning. "I liked patting the dog." Anne writes the sentence on the easel. Not to be outdone, Jamie's hand shoots up. "I'm glad you've thought of something you liked, Jamie. What did you like?" His words spill from his mouth, he has so much he liked. "Wait, wait," says Anne with a smile, "let me get this all down!"

They finish recording all the fun things they did. The lesson lasts less than three minutes. Anne gives them paper and markers and they draw pictures of what they remember, dictate sentences about the pictures to Anne, then copy what she has written under the pictures themselves.

I run down with Anne what I've learned in the first moments of taping: the boys were able to look through my camera without incident, they have gone to a museum in another town on a field trip, and have engaged in a short lesson that, a month ago, would have led to a disruption. "How is it you were able to accomplish these things two days in a row?" First, she reminds me the period would never have been successful if all five children had been present. She would have had to do everything differently in that case. Then, as she speaks, she seems to be putting a name on what she has been doing, has been knowing, but did not yet put into words. "[I could do it] because there were these really salient things. We had gone on this trip and had this experience with the animals. They had been powerful or exciting or different experiences. It seemed like too good an opportunity to pass up! . . . I wanted to capitalize on these things and get them to do this . . . If they're gonna be able to do it [writing] at all, they'll be able to do it best when there's something they're really excited about." She has decided that, in part, managing the behavior of the group means getting them interested in what they are doing in class. The more they are interested, the more leverage she has to keep them out of trouble and in the group.

Using "salient" things make the difference. She has searched for and located what excites the boys in school, and has put more of the same in their way. Yet "salience" does not translate to doing whatever they want—an activity may be fun, but not salient. For Anne, salient activities are interesting to the boys *and* fulfill her academic or social goals for them as well. Her goals are clear. In the case of language arts, the older three boys (whom she considers first graders) will be writing stories on their own by June. The younger, kindergarten-aged boys will be dictating stories. From the beginning of September, "that's been the same goal. My feelings about how realistic it is go up and down a little bit." She laughs. Sometimes, it seems she laughs because her words sound absurd to her own ears, her beliefs and hopes incongruous in the current situation. Perhaps she should be happy with the small accomplishments and forget the terminal goals. "I'm too product-oriented!" she says, and laughs again.

Finding the salient content for her classes is important, but the day's organization is equally important to managing the group's behavior. Keeping them interested alone will not solve her problem of group management; when and how they do activities is just as important. Very early in the year, she decided that the afternoon schedule was too intense for these young children. With the slightly older children she had taught in the past, a half-hour each of language arts, science, and social studies activities made sense. For this year's youngsters, these artificial differentiations by content area didn't make sense. She believed the more important skills were learning to use language, to listen, to function as a group, and do group lessons, at least for now. Science, social studies, and writing became the materials she used, but what really mattered to Anne was ". . . balancing out each individual kid's academic, cognitive potential versus their behavioral, social needs . . . figuring out how to get them to do what they are capable of doing, [and] at the same time, keeping them in a group and having reasonable behavioral expectations for the group. . . ." She still had their academic goals in mind, but, "I needed to find a way to get all those experiences and all those goals done differently." And so she abandoned her formal writing period, as well as formal science and social studies, replacing them with a series of structured experiences in which the emphasis was less on content and more on group process. The activities she chose were still academic, but more spontaneous, more dependent on the prevailing moods of the class. The afternoon began to look more like pre-school or kindergarten and less like first or second grade.

The five boys loved being read to and would remain calm and attentive all through a picture book. So she read books about Pilgrims and Fizzwiggle the Cat. They enjoyed filmstrips, too, especially about insects or dinosaurs. They loved to draw. After each activity, the boys drew pictures and made things with their hands. All around the room hung drawings of Pilgrims and dinosaurs, insects and cats. Yet underneath each drawing or on a label beneath a string of clay beads were always words—a sentence about the art work. The early creations were labeled in an adult's neat hand; the later ones gradually gave way to the prehensile scrawl of kindergartners, silent testimony to the slow progression of the year, to "taking turns a little bit, not trying to accomplish all as quickly as I might have last year, by doing sometimes language art things, sometimes science things, sometimes social studies things. But the goals are still there. . . ."

Anne had set her goals for them long ago; it just has been unclear how to get to those goals. She is used to older children, and to setting goals for first and second graders. These children are kindergartners; the types of things she can teach, the ways she prefers to teach don't seem to work. Yet, she is making slow progress. She can keep three in the room at one time, sometimes without fights. Slowly, one by one, she will bring them back into the classroom. She can regroup them after a terrible morning and lead a productive afternoon. But the activity must be salient. She can cover some content with them. She just has to be flexible about when and how. She has to have the freedom to maneuver the schedule to match the mood.

REGRESSION

"Yak! Yak! He's a Lego maniac!!
Yak! Yak! He's a Lego maniac!!
Yak! Yak! He's a Lego maniac!!"

Over and over, for nearly ten minutes, Jamie chants the phrase. He is flung across Anne's lap and she holds him tightly, a rag doll spent from anxiety, awaiting his state social worker's visit. The worker does not visit unless there is news, usually bad news: "We can't find your mommy." "We can't find your daddy." "We have a new foster home." "You'll be moving to a residential school." He doesn't know what Anne knows, that they have found his mommy and she has sent him some presents. She wants him back, is going to fight the state, which wants to put him up for adoption. This news will only overwhelm him more.

Anne is overwhelmed, too. As the weeks of struggle have turned into months, it is harder to hold on to the belief that she can make a difference, harder to resist being tipped into despair. And so she labors to balance herself between despair and belief. Now, she sits silently and Jamie chants his mantra in his futile battle to focus on one thing instead of the million thoughts and worries that are rushing at his mind. She is not unlike him. The desperate events of the past months rush at her and she does battle with them, she forces them into perspective by reminding herself why she does what she does. She is thinking, she tells me later, about nothing in particular and everything that has happened, numb and anguished at the same time.

> The past two weeks have been a complete regression back to less than zero. And until two days ago, pretty literally no teaching academics happened at all in the classroom. Two of the boys, Jeremy and Steve, we found out, have been involved in fairly extensive sexual activity on the weekends with one another. Both of them were pretty much basket cases for about two weeks and practically unable to be in class at all. [When they are in class] . . . the severity of [their] sexual and aggressive acting out [is so disruptive to others, that] Jamie has also, pretty much [been] unable to be in school. And with that much going on, Samuel, of course, spends a lot of time shrieking and has a lot of difficulty because things

were pretty chaotic. So for almost two weeks, I did little else than restrain kids all day. And it was really miserable, and really awful.

I finally felt that we were *getting* somewhere, like we were progressing toward some of the goals, that we were doing better as a group, and then everything fell apart, and it didn't make any sense, and I couldn't understand why. And then finding out why, having one of the boys disclose some of these things that were going on, on the one hand made it feel better because at least there was a reason for it! You know, it wasn't me, it wasn't the classroom, it wasn't just out of the blue!! But it also felt really bad. It was like we couldn't even keep these kids safe! That things were happening that are making their lives worse while they're in residential care! And that felt yukky—even though it wasn't my personal thing. It left me feeling very unhopeful about Jeremy's prognosis, very disheartened.

In choosing to work with these kinds of kids, clearly I'm not just interested in academic teaching. I'm interested in social/emotional growth of kids. So I expect that some proportion of my time is gonna be spent dealing with social/emotional/behavioral issues with kids and not just with teaching. But there is that part of it that feels like, "Well, for two weeks, all I did was restrain kids. I didn't have a classroom, I wasn't a teacher!" You know, I planned all this great curriculum that I didn't get a chance to do. . . . The neat curriculum isn't as important to me as how the kids are doing altogether. It's frustrating to feel like you're working so hard to plan . . . here I am, I revamped all these things. I have all these new ideas and we're not even getting to try them because everyone is out of control all the time. And that feeling of, like I said in the beginning of the year, I said to my team who were new [this year], at Thanksgiving we're really going to see improvement. We didn't. That was wrong.

For pretty much two weeks, I've thought about the kids twenty-four hours a day. I've gone home and had dreams about them and felt very hopeless. It was a little bit better at the end of this week, 'cause better things started happening the past couple of days. At the same time that this is happening, I found out about a kid who graduated from here last year whose parents are about to terminate his adoption. And this was like a kid who wow! Here was one of our success stories! I had just told one of the parents of one of the kids in my class about this wonderful [story]: This boy came when he was seven-and-a-half, graduated when he was ten and went to public school, and he was doing so much better. Look how there is hope and success! And here his life is falling apart! And Jeremy is back to sucking the dicks of his friends when he is out of eyesight for ten seconds! And he is being really violent and really aggressive. And on one level, it made me feel really hopeless, and it's really shitty to feel hopeless about six-year-olds! And it's really hard to maintain the kind of energy that it takes to do this work when you're not feeling hopeful about it.

I guess I remind myself of the times when I feel hopeful, of the good things that can happen, and of my real belief that things will get better. I don't think I can fix them. I think I can help be part of making them healthier people. And if I didn't think that, I don't think I would do this kind of work. I think it's one of the reasons I like working with younger kids. . . . I wonder sometimes, especially with some of the more damaged kids, how much of that damage can be undone. The damage is there and it's always going to be there. But he's *six years old*! I'd like to think that all the time and effort and energy that's going into everything that I'm doing and that others are doing with him is going to mean that ten years from now he can lead some sort of productive, more normal life where he is not completely overrun by sexual and aggressive impulses 80 percent of the time! So I think . . . that [the] definition of success is different. . . . I've felt differently about it at different points in my professional growth. I feel differently about it for different kids. And it's really hard with such young kids to project what the ultimate hope might be for what they might be like.

I think [I have] high standards and push the kids and maybe cause more behavioral problems 'cause I'm pushing them to do things. It wouldn't be worth doing that if they were always going to be at a place like this for their whole lives. Like *who cares*, you know, how much socially appropriate behavior they learn, and if they learn how to read and do math and those kind of things! I think that there is always in the back of my head the thought and the hope that at some point down the road they're gonna go to some more normal setting. Whether they're gonna be adopted and stop living here or they go back to a public school at some point. Or that they stay at a place like this and are more successful there. You know or whatever. That there is a goal, that each one of these kids is capable of more higher functioning."

"Yak! Yak! He's a Lego maniac!!
Yak! Yak! He's a Lego maniac. . . ."

PROGRESS

"Guess what? Our first book is about to be published!" She sits before the group, her voice full of excitement. Just one minute before, she had begun the transition from read-aloud time to writing. Everyone had enjoyed the book, had been huddled together on the bench, like puppies warming themselves against each other. Yet when Anne announced the transition, Paul threw himself back on the bench, spread his legs and started gesturing to his anus. Jeremy started yelling at him to stop. Jamie began yelling his request to get a book. Samuel started screaming. In a flash, without speaking, the three adults moved into action. Paul was removed to a chair on the other side of the room; Jeremy, refusing to move to time-out, needed to be quickly lifted off the bench and carried out. An adult sat next to Samuel and touched his arm and he quieted. As quickly as the disruption began, it was over. Paul was brought back to his seat—he had regained control quickly. Jeremy remained in the time-out chair but listened to what was going on. As if nothing has happened, Anne begins what will be a positive lesson.

> "Guess what? Our first book is about to be published! Samuel decided that he was going to write about his dog and he wrote "Samuel and His Dog." Then he thought of a lot of different things all about his dog and he wrote them in his book. Samuel, can you come here and sit next to me while I show them your book? "My dog lived in the forest. My dog likes bones. . . . My dog's name is Sunshine!"

111

By early January, Anne had reinstituted a formal writing time at the boys' request. The first time one of the boys asked to write a book was during a free-choice period back in November (free choice comes at the end of every day; if they have done all their schoolwork, they can choose an activity of their own to do). Given their great love for read-aloud, it did not come as too big a surprise. Anne did not leap on the opportunity then; instead she "let this excitement keep on building on its own. A couple of months from now I will introduce it as a formal activity because they will be excited." She also waited because they still could not sit at a table together in November. They could listen to books, loved listening, in fact, but if they moved to work at tables, everything fell apart. She still needed to work on their ability to spend time together as a group.

The tone of the class seems very different. She finishes reading Samuel's book and begins to explain how boys can publish books they've written. She demonstrates how the books are constructed, with contact-paper-covered cardboard serving as a book jacket, shows how to glue the pages. She shows them the press-on letters they can use on the front for a title. Each page, she reminds them, must be illustrated as well. The explanation takes time and they sit paying attention. Occasionally, Paul bounces on his seat and Anne stops for a moment. "I'm going to wait until everyone pays attention." Paul immediately quiets down and gives his attention to the activity. "When each boy finishes his story, he can do this to his story to publish it." They like that idea a lot!!

Anne divides the group in two; Jamie and Jeremy go with Cathy, the others remain with her. This is a chronological division, the younger children will not be required to write. If they want to write, they can. What is important is for them to tell stories and have Cathy write them down. However, Anne believes that the other three boys need to begin to do their own writing and not just tell stories. She feels a pressure to get them to do first-grade work, but not at the expense of their learning to dislike writing. She worries about this being their first writing experience. She wants to guarantee that it is positive. Hence, they can write about whatever they choose and illustrate with the pictures they love to draw. Anne will then type their stories and ready them for "publication." Each finished story means the class has an "Author of the Day" who sits with the teacher in front of the group and has his story read. Only positive comments are allowed from the audience. Within a few weeks, fifteen or so books have been "published" and sit on the class bookshelf, to be taken out and read aloud, over and over again.

Paul dances to his chair at the table, swaying his buttocks back and forth. "Paul, go back to your bench. And when I see you sitting the right way, you can come up to the table." He sits for a brief moment while she settles Steve in. "OK, Paul, you can come over." He runs across the room and leaps on his chair. One leg goes up on the tabletop and he starts to climb. Anne calmly tells him to sit correctly and keeps reading from Steve's story of yesterday. "'Steve and Karen have a snowball fight.' That's good. Think about what you want to write today." Steve is not in a very good mood, it seems. When Anne turns to help Paul,

Steve mumbles an obscenity toward Paul under his breath. Anne tells him to go back to his bench and to sit for a minute for speaking that way. As he leaves the table, he pretends to spit on Paul's work. Paul retaliates and pretends to spit on Steve's work. "Now, you have one minute on your bench as well." Paul erupts verbally, "He fuckin' spit on my fuckin' paper!" "Well," says Anne calmly, almost nonchalantly, "that doesn't mean you should do the same thing." "Loudmouth," says Steve toward Paul. I tense up and focus the camera closely on what will be a violent episode . . . nothing. They both sit back and wait quietly while Anne turns her attention to Samuel, who has ignored this whole altercation, busily readying the pieces of his publishable book.

No screaming, no desks pushed over, no fists flying. Has she "fixed" them, I ask myself.

Steve moves his legs up underneath himself cross-legged. Paul does the same. Steve folds his hands, Paul does the same. One sticks out his tongue, the other sticks out his tongue. Anne and Samuel continue to talk about his story; they are laughing together and having fun, talking about the illustration that he needs to do. Miraculously, both Steve and Paul abandon their taunting and watch Anne. She finally brings Paul back to the table, opens his book with him and begins to read it. "What does this say?" she asks. He reads a page to her. "What will come next?" she asks. He falls to the work and starts writing his sentence. She has two of them working now. "Okay, Steve, now you can come to the table. What do you want to write about you and Karen today?"

Earlier in the year, she had to send them out of the room for difficult behavior, get fun things happening in the room, then bring them back one at a time. Now, she can accomplish this same thing with them remaining in the room. " . . . It just took longer than I expected to get them acclimated into being in a classroom. I think in some ways, when I do look back on the year as a whole, I will say the first three months were spent getting the kids comfortable with the concept of being civilized in a classroom setting. It took that long to have them feel safe in a class and be able to contain themselves well enough to start doing anything else."

They do seem to feel safer, seem more confident in Anne, calmer in the environment. They seem to know what they are doing, the activities make sense. And it is clear that Anne feels good about them. Her frustration is not apparent, her body seems more relaxed, her voice almost gentle. Since safety and control no longer dominate the period, she can begin to push a little harder to get the boys to produce. For each boy, the issue to push on is different.

"Steve, what do you want to write?" "Me and Karen . . . uh . . ." He hands her a paper and demands she write down what he is saying. "You know what Steve, I don't have to write the word 'Karen,' you can copy it from right here." He flares up, "NO, you write Karen!!!" She ignores him, he is being obstinate, and she refuses to help. He takes it out on Paul. "Pussy!" he says at Paul, who just keeps working. Anne points to Steve's bench, and he goes there quietly. Samuel, in the meantime, is calling for her attention. He wants to show his drawing of his dog. It is just a bunch of legs in space. "Where is his body?" she asks. "I don't want to draw a body," Samuel replies. "Well, it's gonna be awfully hard for

people to understand your picture, then." He draws another picture, but now only a body and no legs! "Now where are the legs?"

When she brings Steve back to the table, she still quietly insists that he copy words that he already knows or are written for him somewhere else in his story. As soon as he has trouble with a word that he doesn't yet know or hasn't written before, she is there to write it down. With Samuel, she continues to insist that he make a dog with legs, and the correct number of legs as well. The conversations overlap, the boys interrupt her, she deals with three questions at once. Instead of safety and control problems, these are new and welcome troubles, problems she is more accustomed to dealing with. Now that they are engaged in their work, they all want her attention simultaneously, they want their questions answered first, they cannot wait. This is, to her, "the classic writing time. Writing time in all of my classes felt that way, even with kids who can write and were further along. I know they are all working on their own thing and they all need my help all the time. They have no ability to understand you need to be helping other people as well. I pretend to be listening to all three of them constantly all of the time." She thinks about the problem that Steve is having today, his easy frustration and impatience with the task and with her. She wonders if it is because she is doing something wrong.

She lets Steve dictate a difficult sentence. "Anne . . . Anne . . . Anne," Samuel calls in his drooping whine. She responds, finally, when she has finished with Steve. But no sooner has she turned to Samuel than Steve is demanding from her that she spell the word 'to.' She moves back immediately and spells it. But he makes an error writing it, tries to erase, tears his page. "See! This fuckin' paper. . . ." She tries to help, suggests he tape the tear. "I hate you. . . . I'm going to stab you . . . no tape. . . . I want you to erase that damn letter!!!" Behind him, Samuel is droning over and over, "I'm on my last page, Anne . . . I'm on my last page, Anne . . . I'm on my last page, Anne." Paul asks for help. She speaks with Samuel, she answers Paul's question, she tapes Steve's page. . . .

The PAUSE button gets pushed on the video machine. "At this point, I was upset that Steve was getting as frustrated as he did, partly, I feel, with the way the writing program is set up, nobody should be getting frustrated. Partly, I was feeling that I was moving too fast with Steve in terms of what he was doing. But then I wasn't sure if his frustration was because I was moving too fast or if it was because he was having a cranky, needy day and even if it was not too hard for him, he would be feeling that way."

I smile to myself, and think back to September: "I was some of the problem. My expectations were wrong." I am amazed that she is being self-critical, now. Steve is being nasty even though she is being as helpful as seems possible. But it is a part of her personality, a drive within her, part of her "process of being a teacher." She believes these boys are capable, that learning for them should be fun, creative, exciting; it should focus on strength and health, not pathology. Teaching skills and competencies, she says, can be the most therapeutic thing of all. Yes, I think, for the teacher and the taught.

BELIEF

When I get out of my car on this April morning, about twenty boys are running up to class to begin their school day. Jostling, teasing, and generally doing what young boys do; they all race ahead of Samuel, who is struggling hard, and failing miserably, at doing what young boys generally do. His parents have tried to dress him "*a la mode.*" He has new sneakers, a good windbreaker; he is holding a backpack along with the books that didn't fit in it, and straining to get his Walkman over his ears. All the while, he is trying to run and keep up with the others. But the Walkman slips off his head and falls to the ground. When he bends to reach for it, his books fall from his hand and the backpack follows. He flops on the sidewalk, not yet warmed after winter, and tries to reassemble his "look." His lack of coordination would be farcical if it were not so real.

In the front office, I pass young Jamie. He is angry as he walks with his therapist. "Where can I buy a gun?" he asks her. "I really need a gun!" His words smash against my ears like cymbals. My eyes meet his therapist's and she smiles wanly, takes him by the hand, and walks on.

I look at the children and I think about Anne and the work she does. How sustaining the power of belief must be for her! Although her resolve wavers, she believes in the children, in their ability to heal. She is convinced, truly, that she *must* make a difference. "I wonder sometimes, especially with some of the more damaged kids, how much of that damage can be undone. The damage is there and it's always going to be there. But he's *six years old*!" She possesses a kind of love for the children, some might say a foolish love, that keeps her pushing against the weight of their troubles, always trying to tip the balance in their favor.

NOTE

1. I have changed the names of all adults and children to protect their confidentiality,
   However, to faithfully depict their experience, I have purposely retained their language.

I would like to acknowledge Dr. Sara Lawrence-Lightfoot, Donald Freeman, and Dr. Richard Small for their insightful critiques of earlier drafts of this portrait. Especially, I would like to thank "Anne" for generously fitting me into her already busy schedule, and for engaging in the reflective process with such vigor.

TEACHING
"ON THE INSIDE"

LESSONS FOR DISRUPTING THE SCHOOL-TO-PRISON PIPELINE

■

DOUGLAS W. PRICE

Every single day I'm amazed by my students' self-reflection, intelligence, and ability. These talents are evident in their personal narratives, short stories, poems, and persuasive and expository essays. My students are male felons awaiting disposition of their cases in Albuquerque's Metropolitan Detention Center. I teach English for the Gordon Bernell Charter School, the second charter school in the nation to be founded in a jail. We help inmates complete the credits they need for high school graduation, an important goal for them that we celebrate in December and June of each year. We also prepare and support them in the specific steps for successful transitions to postsecondary training and education.

When new students enter my room, they are greeted with their names learned and matched to their faces. Often I explain to students the three aspects of my job: to help them complete the English credits they need for their diploma; to further develop their language skills for clear thinking and self-expression; and to teach them to use writing skills to help them develop and reach goals. They also receive a folder with three questions to help me get to know them. What do you want me to know about you? What is most important to you? What do you want to be or do or accomplish and what is your plan? A student once asked, "Suppose I don't want to write anything?" I told him, "Write nothing if you want. It's up to you." Like everyone, he wrote in a truthful and straightforward way. I save every piece of their first writing. Sometimes my students leave jail but return again, despite their best intentions and our best efforts. Recently a student who returned came in with less than an ideal attitude. I met with him to discuss his answers to those questions I had given him months earlier, addressed one of his main issues about gang involvement, and connected him to a student who had written a contest-winning essay on that issue. He became observably more settled and more mature. With connection comes focus.

116

I tell these inmates, ages nineteen to sixty-two, almost all of whom struggle with drug or alcohol addiction and the criminal behavior that those generate, that I always get good writing from my students. Every time. Even from those who didn't receive more than a fourth-grade formal education. The reason, I explain to them, is because everyone writes from his experience, from what he knows and feels, and from what he believes and hopes.

When each student completes a piece of writing, I insist on listening to him read it to me before I look at it. Often men are unsure of themselves or nervous at this first reading. Some refuse. I explain that when I hear what they have to say, I hear the heart. If I look at it, I see through the eyes of an English teacher and notice grammar, punctuation, and spelling, which aren't the most important things. I assure them that I will compliment them after I hear their writing, and I always do because their strong effort deserves that. If they're still unwilling to read their writing to me, I take as long as necessary to build their trust and point out that my job is to help them polish their writing so they can be even more proud of it. "This is the first time I've ever done anything like this," I often hear with nervousness evident in the unsure glance, the bouncing knee, the vulnerable shyness. This process works, and emerging confidence is visible in their smile and receptive eyes. Reading their writing becomes normal. Our school recently self-published *Writing from Within*, a collection of student work. It's a strong formal recognition of their abilities, creates well-deserved pride and self-respect, and is definitely within reach of anyone who wants to work through the writing process.

One of my students recently wrote in his personal narrative that he needs structure, a schedule, or a rhythm. They all do. We all do. School "on the inside" provides these things and is supported by daily life in honor residence "pods," which offer strong, clear, consistent incentives for adhering to a code of conduct. "Am I late?" I'm asked. Avoidance of a demerit is important. A glance at the smallest disruption quickly brings "Sorry" and back-on-target behavior. In the pod, "a busy inmate is a good inmate," says our security officer. The men not only work independently on packets of curriculum, they help one another, too. Best of all, they share their writing with each other. They behave in the pod (for the most part) because being in the honor pod is so much more worthwhile than being in the general jail population. This makes school discipline simple, direct, and effective, especially when combined with quietly handled infractions. Private, personalized discipline signifies and generates considerable respect.

Our school has boarding students in orange uniforms. Most have hard-earned wisdom and sincerely want to focus on what our motto calls "Changing Lives from the Inside Out." Hopefully, students' previous experience "on the outside" can be developed through our self-paced curriculum, individualized instruction, and constantly motivational practices to bring out focus and commitment for individual reform. Hopefully, the work of our teachers and students will contribute to the insight and planning needed to disrupt the school-to-prison pipeline into which young people, families, and even small communities can fall too easily. Hopefully, these men, our students, can be examples of genuine and effective change heading toward a clearer path to freedom and self-respect, not slipping into a free-fall toward incarceration. Together we work on developing pro-social, productive goals and the attitudes, behaviors, and skills needed to attain them.

I share with my students essays read by the writers on ThisIBelieve.org for motivation and for learning skills of organization, grammar, and the clarity that correct punctuation brings. Inspiration is as critical as good instruction. Yesterday I showed *Admittance to a Better Life,* in which a self-described "semi-thug," who hung out on street corners with drug dealers and who's become a college professor, used this as his lead sentence: "I believe that education has the power to transform a person's life." There was spontaneous applause at the end. A few days ago my students provided punctuation in this passage, which I had given unpunctuated after they had seen and heard the essay "Bessie Mae: Nobody Famous": "The day I left for basic training my mother told me, a skinny, nervous black kid, four simple words, 'Just do your best.' That expression may be a cliché, but coming from her, it has given me a lifetime of powerful inspiration." Just now I am reading lines from the recently deceased Chuck Colson: "I shudder to think of what I'd been if I had not gone to prison. Lying on the rotten floor of a cell, you know it's not prosperity or pleasure that's important, but the maturing of the soul." I tell them, as I often do, that jail is a training camp for the next part of their lives, so they can get ready to be what they most want for themselves and their families. I tell them that I'm their offensive and defensive coach. One man said, "Let me see the electrolytes." "Let me see the sweat," I replied. The root meaning of *to educate* has two meanings, both of which must always be honored: to instill and to draw out.

Our mobility rate is high, and we have relatively few graduates, but among them the recidivism rate is far less than a tenth of the national average. This is one measure of success. The willingness our students bring to class every day is an indicator that our students believe we will help them toward achieving worthwhile goals. Individualized instruction and advancement just as quickly as they can earn it, sustained challenge and support—this type of education is a better way out by developing the better person within.

APPLYING UNIVERSAL DESIGN FOR LEARNING

TO THE EDUCATION OF YOUTH IN DETENTION AND JUVENILE CORRECTIONS FACILITIES

■

JOANNE KARGER, DAVID H. ROSE, AND KATHLEEN B. BOUNDY

In this essay, Joanne Karger, David H. Rose, and Kathleen B. Boundy examine the poor quality of education inside detention and juvenile corrections facilities. They detail the legal right to a high-quality education for incarcerated youth and propose the framework of Universal Design for Learning (UDL) to help actualize this right and improve the learning environment for students. In outlining the main principles of UDL, the authors show how the framework can ensure that youth are taught to high standards and can fundamentally transform education in detention and juvenile corrections facilities.

The school-to-prison pipeline is a phenomenon that channels youth who are disproportionately students of color and from low-income backgrounds out of their regular school environments into the juvenile justice system (Advancement Project, 2005; NAACP Legal Defense and Educational Fund, 2005). Many of these youth become trapped in an ongoing cycle in which they move in and out of detention or juvenile corrections facilities,[1] ultimately becoming incarcerated in the adult prison system.

The early stages of the school-to-prison pipeline are characterized by various school-based push-out policies and practices, including the constructive exclusion of low-income students of color from high-quality learning opportunities through the overidentification of these students for special education (NAACP Legal Defense and Educational Fund, 2005) and the assignment of these students to low-level classes by means of tracking (McCord, Widom, & Crowell, 2001; Oakes, 1987). Schools further push out youth by implementing zero tolerance disciplinary suspensions and expulsions (ABA, 2009; APA Zero Tolerance Task Force, 2008; Skiba, 2000) and the criminalization of minor, school-based behavior through inappropriate referrals to law enforcement or juvenile court (Advancement Project, 2005; New York Civil Liberties Union, 2007; Ordover, 2001).

119

In this essay we discuss a later stage of the school-to-prison pipeline—namely, the education provided to youth *inside* detention and juvenile corrections facilities that is so critical to the successful reintegration of youth into school. We first describe the legal basis for the right to a high-quality education for all school-aged youth who are incarcerated. We then argue that Universal Design for Learning (UDL), an innovative educational framework that combines advances in technology with research from the learning sciences, can serve as a powerful mechanism to actualize this right. The UDL framework promotes the design of flexible learning environments that plan, from the beginning, for anticipated learner variability in order to reduce barriers in the curriculum that impede the active participation of students in the learning process. This framework can transform the education provided to youth in detention and juvenile corrections facilities by ensuring that they are taught to high standards and are supported in becoming independent and successful learners.

The right to a high-quality education for all school-age youth is grounded in Title I of the Elementary and Secondary Education Act (ESEA, 2011) and the Individuals with Disabilities Education Act (IDEA, 2011). The legal mandates of these two statutes that give meaning to a high-quality education can be implemented and enforced when read in conjunction with the federal civil rights statutes (Boundy & Karger, 2011). The latter call for examining an institutional policy or practice that has a disparate effect based on race, national origin, gender, or disability and then shifting the burden to the institution either to justify the educational necessity of the policy or practice or to eliminate it. Moreover, some states recognize education as a fundamental right under their constitutions, a recognition that, in the absence of a compelling state interest, guarantees all eligible school-age youth a public education (Blumenson & Nilsen, 2003).

Although incarcerated youth have the right to a high-quality education, in reality the education provided to youth in detention and juvenile corrections facilities is characterized by significant shortcomings that further contribute to the school-to-prison pipeline (Boundy & Karger, 2011). For example, the curriculum is often not aligned with grade-level standards and assessments (Gagnon, Barber, Van Loan, & Leone, 2009); instruction typically focuses on low-level skills rather than higher-order thinking and comprehension skills (Howell & Wolford, 2002; Leone & Cutting, 2004); students with disabilities often do not receive appropriate special education and related services (Burrell & Warboys, 2000; Leone, 1994; Leone, Meisel, & Drakeford, 2002); and transition planning is inadequate to enable youth to reenter school and the community successfully (Baltodano, Mathur, & Rutherford, 2005; Brock & Keegan, 2007; Mears & Travis, 2004; Stephens & Arnette, 2000). These failings have ramifications for the large numbers of youth incarcerated each year. During the 2009–2010 school year, there were approximately 226,921 youth in detention facilities and approximately 117,876 in juvenile corrections facilities (Seiter, Seidel, & Lampron, 2012).

In this essay we present the UDL framework as a promising new approach to address many of the challenges that may be impeding the actualization of the right to a high-quality education for youth held in detention and juvenile correctional facilities. The first section presents a brief overview of the legal requirements comprising the right to a high-quality education for youth confined in detention and juvenile corrections facilities. The second section examines serious shortcomings in the educational programming provided to incarcerated youth that have been identified in the literature and explores ways in which UDL can address these challenges. The third section discusses the implications of incorporating the UDL framework into the education systems of detention and juvenile corrections facilities—namely, that UDL has the potential to promote enhanced levels of student engagement, to raise the expectations that teachers and administrators have of incarcerated youth, and to change the image and expectations about learning that incarcerated youth have for themselves.

THE RIGHT TO A HIGH-QUALITY EDUCATION FOR INCARCERATED YOUTH

There is a strong legal basis for requiring the provision of a high-quality education for school-age youth confined in detention or juvenile corrections facilities. In addition to rights stemming from the education clause of the constitutions in some states (Twomey, 2008), Title I of the ESEA establishes the right to a high-quality education for all school-aged youth, with a particular emphasis on improving educational outcomes for disadvantaged youth, while IDEA affords specific protections to students with disabilities. The mandates of these two statutes—when interpreted together with the disparate impact provisions of the federal civil rights laws and regulations focused on race (Title VI of the Civil Rights Act of 1964), national origin/language (Equal Educational Opportunities Act of 1974), gender (Title IX of the Education Amendments of 1972), and disability (Section 504 of the Rehabilitation Act of 1973 and the Americans with Disabilities Act of 1990)—create strong legal handles to implement and enforce the right of incarcerated youth to a high-quality education (Boundy & Karger, 2011).

Title I of the Elementary and Secondary Education Act

Title I of the ESEA (2011), most recently reauthorized as the No Child Left Behind Act of 2001, provides substantial financial assistance to states and local educational agencies (LEAs) to improve the academic achievement of disadvantaged students. The purpose of Title I is "to ensure that all children have a fair, equal and significant opportunity to obtain a high-quality education and to reach, at a minimum, proficiency on challenging state academic achievement standards and state academic assessments" (20 U.S.C. § 6301). The express reference to "all children" includes those confined in detention and juvenile corrections facilities. There are several sections of Title I that have particular implications for this population of students.

Under Title I, Part A, each state educational agency (SEA) must establish a single statewide system of accountability[2] with the goal of reducing the achievement gap between higher and lower performing children. As part of this accountability system, states must adopt challenging academic content and achievement standards that will be the same for all children in the state. States must also implement "a set of high-quality, yearly student academic assessments" aligned with the academic standards established for all children (20 U.S.C. §§ 6311(b)(1)-(3)). Moreover, Title I, Part A delineates the parameters of a high-quality education for schoolwide programs and targeted assistance school programs that receive these funds to provide an enriched, accelerated curriculum, highly qualified teachers, and effective interventions for struggling learners (20 U.S.C. §§ 6314(b), 6315(c)).

Title I, Part D provides additional financial assistance for prevention and intervention programs for children and youth who are neglected, delinquent, or at risk. Underscoring the need to provide delinquent youth with a high-quality education, the purpose of Part D includes: (1) improving educational services and opportunities for such youth to meet the same challenging state academic content and achievement standards that all children are expected to meet; (2) providing these youth with services to transition successfully from institutionalization to further schooling or employment; and (3) providing youth returning from corrections facilities with a support system to help ensure their continued education (20 U.S.C. § 6421).

For SEAs to receive and allocate Title I, Part D funds to other state agencies that operate free education programs for youth in detention or committed to juvenile and adult correctional facilities, the SEA must ensure that youth in these institutions or facilities "have the same opportunities to achieve as such children would have if such children were in the schools of local educational agencies in the State" (20 U.S.C. § 6434(a)(2)(B)). These federal funds can also be used for programs and projects that provide detained and delinquent youth with the knowledge and skills they need to make a successful transition to secondary school completion, vocational or technical training, further education, or employment (20 U.S.C. §6435(a)(1)(B)).

Eligible SEAs may award subgrants to LEAs with high numbers or percentages of children and youth in locally operated corrections facilities for youth, including facilities involved in community day programs for delinquent youth (20 U.S.C. § 6452(a)). An LEA seeking these funds must describe how its participating schools will coordinate with locally operated corrections facilities to ensure that delinquent children are participating in an educational program comparable to the one operating in the local school such child would otherwise attend (20 U.S.C. § 6453(3)). LEAs must also describe how the program will involve parents in efforts to improve the educational achievement of their children and how participating schools will inform corrections facilities of a youth's existing Individualized Education Program (IEP) for delivering special education and related services to help enable youth with disabilities to learn to the standards set for all students (20 U.S.C. §§ 6453(8), (12)). Moreover, key to using civil rights protections to eliminate barriers to learning for the disproportionate number of males, youth of color, and youth with disabilities being educated in state and locally operated institutions and facilities, each state agency and LEA conducting a program with Part D funds must evaluate the educational program; disaggregate data by race, ethnicity, gender, and disability; and report the results to the SEA with overriding responsibility and to the U.S. Department of Education (ED) (20 U.S.C. § 6471(a), (d)).

Thus, the collective provisions of Title I, Parts A and D establish the legal foundation from which states and local educational agencies must provide a high-quality education consistent with state standards to youth confined in detention and juvenile corrections facilities. The second and third sections of this essay will discuss how the UDL framework can help operationalize these legal requirements.

Individuals with Disabilities Education Act

Students with disabilities who are confined in detention and juvenile corrections facilities are afforded specific rights pertaining to the provision of a high-quality education under IDEA. These rights are significant in light of the overrepresentation of students with disabilities in the population of incarcerated youth. A large, national study conducted in 2005 found that approximately 33 percent of youth in juvenile corrections facilities received special education services under IDEA (Quinn, Rutherford, Leone, Osher, & Poirier, 2005). Among the disability categories represented in juvenile corrections facilities, emotional disturbance (48%) and specific learning disabilities (39%) accounted for the highest percentages (Quinn et al., 2005). In 2011 the ED reported that approximately 13 percent of students in the overall population received special education and related services under IDEA (ED, 2011c). Mental health challenges have also been found to be prevalent among incarcerated youth (Cocozza & Skowyra, 2000; Teplin, Abram, McClelland, Dulcan, & Mericle, 2002), including post–traumatic stress disorder (Wood, Foy, Layne, Pynoos, & James, 2002).

SEAs receiving federal funding under IDEA must ensure that a free appropriate public education shall be provided to all eligible students with disabilities, even if these students have been suspended or expelled from school (20 U.S.C. § 1412(a)(1)(A)). The requirements of IDEA apply to all political subdivisions of the state that are involved in the education of students with disabilities, including "State and local juvenile . . . corrections agencies" (34 C.F.R. § 300.2(b)(1)(iv)).[3]

Under IDEA, SEAs must also identify, locate, and evaluate all students with disabilities residing in the state who are in need of special education and related services, known as "child find" (20 U.S.C. § 1412(a)(3)). The Office of

Special Education Programs has specifically stated that child find systems must include incarcerated youth who would be eligible to receive a free appropriate public education (OSEP, 2003). Moreover, IDEA requires that students be evaluated in all areas of suspected disability with valid and reliable assessments (20 U.S.C. § 1414(b)(3)(A), (B)).

Once it is determined that a child has a disability and is in need of special education and related services, an IEP must be developed, containing a written statement of all the services and supports that are necessary to meet the unique needs of the child (20 U.S.C. § 1414(d)(1), (3)). IDEA requires the new public agency to take reasonable steps to obtain the child's educational records from his or her previous placement in a prompt manner (34 C.F.R. § 300.323(g)). Schools must release school records to juvenile detention facilities educating youth (*Alexander S. v. Boyd*, 1995; *Smith v. Wheaton*, 1998). IDEA contains different timelines for the development of IEPs depending on whether the IEP represents an initial determination of disability at a given facility, the transfer of a student from one program or facility to another within the state, or the transfer of a student to a facility in a new state (DOJ, 2010).

Eligible students with disabilities, including those being educated in detention or juvenile corrections facilities, also have the right to be provided a curriculum aligned with the same state standards established for all students under Title I and applicable state law (20 U.S.C. § 1401(3)(A)) and to have the opportunity to be involved and progress in the general education curriculum (34 C.F.R. § 300.320(a)(2)(i)(A)). Reflecting the fact that these requirements are not always satisfied in juvenile corrections facilities, an investigation of the Indianapolis Juvenile Corrections Facility (IJCF) by the Department of Justice's Civil Rights Division (2010) found that the IJCF had violated IDEA by denying students with disabilities access to the general education curriculum through: (1) failure to enroll students in classes for fourteen days after intake; (2) failure to provide students with certain courses that are required in Indiana; (3) denial of appropriate instruction as a result of inadequate teacher planning, lack of instructional adaptations, and inadequate recordkeeping; (4) failure to afford students the same amount of instructional time provided to other students in Indiana; and (5) failure to provide students with access to academic work during periods of removal from learning, such as administrative or disciplinary segregation.

To address the social and emotional needs of students with disabilities whose behavior has resulted in their exclusion from public school and placement in a delinquent facility, the public agency must provide a range of targeted, individualized services. IEP teams must consider special factors in developing the IEP, including whether the child's behavior impedes his or her learning or that of others; and if it does, the team must consider "the use of positive behavioral interventions and supports [PBIS], and other strategies, to address that behavior" (20 U.S.C. § 1414(d)(3)(B)(i)). Students with disabilities may also require the provision of "related services" in order to benefit from special education, including, for example, psychological services, physical and occupational therapy, and speech-language services (20 U.S.C.§ 1401(26)).

IDEA further mandates the provision of "transition services," defined as a coordinated set of activities to be implemented through a results-oriented process (20 U.S.C. § 1401(34)). The court in *Smith v. Wheaton* (1998) stated that "equipping disabled children with the skills and ability to function *outside of an institution* and, if possible, within the mainstream of society, is a goal of the IDEA" and noted that "an 'appropriate' education for a child . . . is one that gives him a reasonable chance to acquire the skills that he needs to function outside of an institution" (citing *Rettig v. Kent*, 1981, p. 777; emphasis added).

Thus, IDEA includes additional requirements specific to the provision of a high-quality education that apply to incarcerated youth with disabilities. Although students with disabilities educated in detention and juvenile corrections facilities have specific rights under IDEA, these rights are not fully realized.

AN OVERVIEW AND APPLICATION OF UDL FRAMEWORK IN DETENTION AND JUVENILE CORRECTIONS FACILITIES

While incarcerated youth have the right to a high-quality education, the educational programming provided in detention and juvenile corrections facilities is largely substandard (Boundy & Karger, 2011). In the following sections, we discuss how the UDL framework has the potential to bring about a sweeping transformation in the education of youth confined in detention and juvenile corrections facilities. We first introduce UDL and then explain how serious shortcomings in the education provided to youth in detention and juvenile corrections facilities can be addressed with this framework.

UDL Background

UDL grew out of the universal design movement in the field of architecture that began in the 1970s. At the time, public buildings were frequently constructed without any consideration of the needs of individuals with disabilities. To obviate the necessity of retrofitting expensive and unattractive adaptations after the fact, universal design advocated for the creation of structures that were accessible to the widest possible range of users from the outset (Story, Mueller, & Mace, 1998).[4]

Improvements stemming from the universal design movement in architecture ultimately resulted in advantages for individuals with disabilities, the creation of more attractive buildings, and the extension of benefits to additional groups of individuals beyond those with disabilities. For example, ramps originally designed for persons in wheelchairs were also found to be helpful for persons with baby strollers, travelers with luggage, individuals with delivery carts, and older individuals struggling with mobility issues.

125

Universal Design for Learning extends the concept of universal design to the field of education by applying information about the brain and the science of learning to the design of educational curricula and instructional strategies. Although the term UDL does not currently appear in IDEA, this term has been defined under federal law in the Higher Education Opportunity Act of 2008 (HEOA) as a scientifically valid framework for guiding educational practice that:

1. provides flexibility in the ways information is presented, in the ways students respond or demonstrate knowledge and skills, and in the ways students are engaged; and
2. reduces barriers in instruction, provides appropriate accommodations, supports, and challenges, and maintains high achievement expectations for all students, including students with disabilities and students who are limited English proficient. (20 U.S.C. § 1003(24))

The HEOA also refers to UDL in the context of teacher preparation programs—for example, by requiring states to describe how these programs prepare future teachers to integrate technology effectively into curricula and instruction, including the use of activities that are consistent with the principles of UDL (20 U.S.C. § 1022d(b)(1)(K)).

Following the passage of the HEOA in 2008, UDL has begun to appear more prominently in federal education policy. In 2010 the appendix to the Common Core State Standards (CCSS) stated that UDL could be used as a way to implement the CCSS with respect to students with disabilities (NGA Center for Best Practices, 2010). In addition, the U.S. Department of Education's (2010b) "National Education Technology Plan 2010" highlighted UDL as a framework that can benefit all learners, in particular those that have been underserved. UDL was also identified as a promising practice in the Obama administration's "Blueprint for Reform of the ESEA" (ED, 2010a) and, most recently, in guidance on the ESEA waivers (ED, 2012a).

As a framework, UDL can transform the way that educators view and interact with students and that students, in turn, experience education. Although UDL had its origins in special education, it has the potential to benefit students without disabilities as well. Rather than explaining deficits as intrinsic to the individual student, UDL considers traditional, inflexible learning environments as the source of barriers that impede successful learning. In this manner, UDL moves away from the medical model of disability, a paradigm that pathologizes the individual by viewing disability as a condition within the individual that needs to be "treated" or "cured" (McDonnell, McLaughlin, & Morison, 1997). In contrast, UDL conceptualizes learning differences as following a predictable pattern of systematic variability, with variability being the norm rather than the exception. Accordingly, flexible learning environments are planned and designed from the beginning to anticipate learner variability by providing alternative routes or paths to success.

FIGURE 1   UDL principles and guidelines

I. Provide Multiple Means of Representation	II. Provide Multiple Means of Action and Expression	III. Provide Multiple Means of Engagement
Perception	Physical action	Recruiting interest
Language, expressions, and symbols	Expression and communication	Sustaining effort and persistence
Comprehension	Executive function	Self-regulation

Source: National Center on Universal Design for Learning, http://www.udlcenter.org/aboutudl/udlguidelines

The UDL framework combines the latest advances in technology with research from the learning sciences—education, developmental psychology, cognitive science, and cognitive neuroscience (Rose & Meyer, 2002). While technology is not required for the implementation of UDL, technology can significantly facilitate the development of flexible curricula and instructional strategies. Moreover, new digital media offer the promise of creating dynamic learning opportunities for students and teachers (Meyer & Rose, 2005). The ultimate goal is to raise expectations for the academic performance of all students in order to enable them to grow into independent and successful learners.

UDL is based on three broad principles that are aligned with three networks identified in the brain as involved in learning (see figure 1):

- Provide multiple means of representation (corresponding to recognition network, or the "what" of learning)
- Provide multiple means of student action and expression (corresponding to the strategic network, or the "how" of learning)
- Provide multiple means of student engagement (corresponding to the affective network, or the "why" of learning) (Rose & Meyer, 2002)

Within these three principles, the UDL framework encompasses a set of guidelines to help educators create flexible learning experiences that address learner variability.

In the following sections we will explain how these three principles and guidelines can be used to bring about educational change in detention and juvenile corrections facilities.

UDL Can Address the Variability in Learning of Incarcerated Students and Ensure High Standards

One of the challenges identified in the literature with respect to the provision of high-quality learning experiences for youth in detention and juvenile corrections facilities is the wide variability in age and academic level exhibited by these youth (Houchins, Puckett-Patterson, Crosby, Shippen, & Jolivette, 2009; Leone & Cutting, 2004). Incarcerated youth can range in age from younger than twelve (middle school age) to older than eighteen (high school graduation age) (OJJDP, 2011a). The difference in age level in one classroom can be as large as four to five years (MA EOHHS, 2002). Youth in detention and juvenile corrections facilities also function at different academic levels, with many experiencing large deficits in reading and mathematics (Foley, 2001; Krezmien, Mulcahy, & Leone, 2008). Contributing to the heterogeneity of classrooms in juvenile delinquent facilities is the fact that in some facilities, youth are assigned to classes according to gang affiliation for perceived safety concerns, regardless of age or academic level (Vaught, 2011). In short, "the typical juvenile justice classroom resembles a one-room schoolhouse. Students ranging in age, grade, and ability are placed in the same class taught by a single teacher. Under these conditions teachers must have access to a variety of multi-level curriculum materials" (Florida Legislature, 1998).

Rather than addressing the wide variability among the population of incarcerated youth, the education provided in these facilities typically consists of curricular and instructional strategies that are based on low expectations and not aligned with state standards. In a national survey of principals of juvenile corrections facilities, almost one-third reported that the instructional materials used by teachers in their facilities were only "somewhat, very little, or not at all aligned with state assessments" (Gagnon et al., 2009, p. 688), and more than half stated that they believed that "grade level expectations *should not* apply to all students with LD [learning disabilities] and EBD [emotional behavioral disabilities] in their schools" (p. 685). In a related study of state directors of special education, Gagnon (2008) reported that "a discouragingly high percentage of . . . JC [juvenile corrections] schools appear to be developing or individualizing curricula rather than providing students with access to more standard . . . curricula" (p. 213).

Moreover, although youth in juvenile delinquent facilities tend to have large deficits in reading and mathematics (Foley, 2001; Krezmien et al., 2008), instruction in these subjects fails to focus on the cultivation of higher-level critical thinking skills essential for students to be able to graduate from high school and obtain successful employment (Maccini, Gagnon, Mulcahy, & Leone, 2006). Rather, instruction in reading and mathematics usually consists of low-level busywork, with unmotivated students working mechanically on unengaging worksheets based on drill and practice (Coffey & Gemignani, 1994; Leone & Cutting, 2004; Leone, Krezmien, Mason, & Meisel, 2005; Maccini et al., 2006). This kind of instruction has been described as leading to "inactivity, boredom (for students and teachers), limited emphasis on learning, and little true individualization" (Howell & Wolford, 2002, p. 14). The provision of quality instruction taught to high standards is critical for incarcerated youth given the strong relationship between academic achievement and a reduction in recidivism (Katsiyannis & Archwamety, 1997; Katsiyannis, Ryan, Zhang, & Spann, 2008).

UDL will enable educators in detention and juvenile corrections facilities to implement curricular and instructional practices that are aligned with high-level state standards while concomitantly being responsive to the wide variability characteristic of incarcerated youth. Consistent with the right of incarcerated youth to receive a high-quality education, UDL begins with the expectation that all students will be taught to high standards. Expectations are not lowered; rather, students are afforded the opportunity to attain high standards with the help of enhanced levels of support and multiple paths toward success.

Digitized curricular materials with built-in supports based on the three UDL principles can assist with targeted literacy and mathematics instruction as well as instruction in the content areas by presenting information in multiple ways (first UDL principle). For example, embedded supports can help with difficulties in the areas of decoding and vocabulary through features such as text-to-speech and built-in glossaries. Additional scaffolding can assist with challenges in the area of comprehension through features such as clear headings and advance organizers, models that supply background knowledge, and reading prompts that guide students by highlighting key concepts and ideas. Moreover, digitized curricular materials can be designed to allow for multiple options for students to demonstrate what they have learned (second UDL principle)—for example, using different methods of response, such as writing, drawing, audio, or video. Finally, such digitized materials have the potential to be highly engaging for incarcerated youth (third UDL principle).

Research has shown that there are benefits associated with the use of technology in juvenile delinquent facilities. Bewley (1999) found a positive association between the use of multimedia and attitudes, motivation, and participation on the part of incarcerated youth. In addition, technology has been shown to support the teaching of higher-level mathematical concepts among youth in juvenile corrections facilities, in particular when there is a connection to real-world problem solving (Coffey & Gemignani, 1994; Maccini et al., 2006). Moreover, the use of video conferencing has been used in corrections facilities to promote communication between youth and their communities (Gilham & Moody, 2001).

Notwithstanding the documented benefits associated with the use of technology in juvenile delinquent facilities, these facilities do not always provide for the use of computers and other technology because of perceived safety concerns (namely, that confined youth could use the Internet to contact gang members or engage in illegal activities) (McIntyre, Tong, & Perez, 2001). UDL, however, provides a way to deal with concerns regarding potential misuse of technology by incarcerated youth. Rather than infantilizing these youth and expecting that they will automatically misuse technology, the use of technology can be transformed, in accordance with the UDL principles, into learn-ing opportunities that build self-control and self-regulation (such as through a system of earned privilege, recognition, and respect). Ultimately, any concerns that may be raised regarding inappropriate uses of technology by incarcerated youth are greatly outweighed by the potential benefits that digitized curricula with embedded supports can have on the education of this population.

The application of UDL to the education of youth in detention and juvenile corrections facilities in fact capitalizes on the main asset of these educational programs—namely, time. In contrast to traditional public schools, which have begun to focus on the need for extended learning time (Khankeo van der Graaf, 2008), the education provided in detention and juvenile corrections facilities does not suffer from a lack of time for education because the youth are unable to leave. The introduction of flexible learning environments will enable youth to make better use of the time during which they are incarcer-ated by engaging in high-level and meaningful learning experiences.

UDL Can Improve Services for Underserved Populations, Including Students with Disabilities, Students from Diverse Cultures, and English Language Learners

Failure to provide appropriate special education and related services to incar-cerated students with disabilities has been identified as a particular shortcom-ing (e.g., Leone, Meisel, & Drakeford, 2002). As noted earlier, students with disabilities comprise a large percentage of the youth in detention and juvenile corrections facilities. Although the large numbers of students with disabili-ties who are confined in delinquent facilities have procedural and substantive rights under IDEA, they often do not receive appropriate special education and related services (Burrell & Warboys, 2000: Leone, 1994; Leone, Meisel, & Drakeford, 2002). Students with disabilities may experience challenges with respect to issues such as the timely transfer of student records, administra-tion of special education evaluations, and development and implementation of appropriate IEPs. These problems may be due in part to the division of responsibility in some states, where oversight of the education of incarcer-ated youth with disabilities is divided between the state corrections and the state educational agency (Blomberg & Pesta, 2008), resulting in unclear lines of accountability, lack of collaboration, and administrative delays (Farrell & Meyers, 2011).

UDL has the potential to improve instruction for students with disabilities in detention and juvenile corrections facilities by removing the focus from the individual student and providing appropriate scaffolding in areas in which stu-dents with disabilities typically struggle. While the UDL guidelines in figure 1 can be read vertically according to the three UDL principles, the guidelines can also be read horizontally according to increasing levels of independence on the part of the student. With a horizontal perspective, the first level, pertain-ing to increased accessibility for the student, has particular relevance for students with disabilities. The three guidelines that relate to accessibility include instructional strategies that take into account considerations such as providing options with respect to the presentation of auditory and visual information (representation), optimizing access to tools and assistive technology (action/ expression), and minimizing threats and distractions (engagement). These strategies can make a difference in the extent to which students with disabilities are able to participate in the curriculum. At the same time, the second horizontal level of guidelines, focused on providing increased opportunities for students to practice new skills, is also important for students with disabilities. This level includes options such as supporting decoding and mathematical expressions (representation), allowing students to have multiple opportunities to build fluencies with graduated levels of support (action/expression), and varying demands and resources to optimize challenge (engagement). Finally, the third horizontal level of the guidelines, focusing on the development of higher-level skills, provides support for students with disabilities in areas in which they may be struggling and for which independence in learning is critical—namely, comprehension (representation), executive functioning (action/expression), and self-regulation (engagement).

A particular challenge affecting incarcerated youth with disabilities is the fact that detention and juvenile corrections facilities often fail to address the behavioral challenges of students with disabilities as an *education* issue. Delinquent facilities tend to use a behavioral point system and/or psychopharmacologic treatment rather than strategies that have been shown to be effective in helping to improve problematic behavior among incarcerated youth. The inappropriate treatment of behavior in these facilities is due in part to the disconnect between security and teaching personnel (Houchins et al., 2009; Leone et al., 2005). There may be tension between the competing philosophies of these two departments: "corrections and education personnel working within the same juvenile facility may have conflicting perspectives about whether punishment and control or rehabilitation and treatment should be the governing principles for youth incarceration" (Leone et al., 2005, p. 93). Moreover, despite the high percentages of youth with emotional disturbance and mental health needs, there is also a lack of collaboration between teaching and clinical personnel, with frequent removals of youth from class for counseling or other clinical support services (Houchins et al., 2009).

UDL has the potential to improve behavioral challenges among incarcerated youth with disabilities by promoting increased engagement through attention to students' underlying learning challenges, which may have been largely ignored for years. When students become more engaged in learning, they may be less likely to act out in frustration. Moreover, behavioral challenges of students can themselves be addressed through a UDL lens, in particular in conjunction with other approaches to behavior that have proven to be effective. The latter include: positive behavior supports, which take a pro-

131

active and preventive approach to address behavior (Houchins, Jolivette, Wessendorf, McGlynn, & Nelson, 2005; Scott et al., 2002); "wraparound" services, including mental health and counseling, which provide various community-based supports and services to address the individualized needs of the student and family (Leone, Quinn, & Osher, 2002); and restorative justice, which focuses on community building in an attempt to repair the harm that has resulted from an alleged incident by engaging all those involved in the incident in the formulation of an appropriate resolution (Bradshaw & Roseborough, 2005; Ryals, 2004). In a manner similar to these other approaches, UDL views learning from the perspective of the student and takes into account considerations such as environmental factors and antecedent behaviors.

Furthermore, UDL can help teachers provide appropriate support for students from diverse cultures. Students of color and students from culturally and linguistically diverse backgrounds are disproportionately represented among the population of incarcerated youth (Bilchik, 2008; Gavazzi, Russell, & Khurana, 2009; Piquero, 2008). In 2010 the custody rate for Latino youth in juvenile corrections facilities was almost two times that for White youth, while the rate for African American youth was almost five times that of White youth (OJJDP, 2011b). Although there is an overrepresentation of students of color in juvenile delinquent facilities, the teachers in these facilities do not always reflect the racial and ethnic diversity of their students (Spry, 2003) and often do not use culturally competent instructional and disciplinary strategies that value students' experiences and cultures (Harris, Baltodano, Artiles, & Rutherford, 2006).

In contrast, the UDL framework acknowledges cultural differences by recognizing that affect may come into play when students feel that their culture is not being respected. The UDL principle of engagement calls for the promotion of relevance, value, and authenticity in learning by providing options that are culturally relevant and responsive. UDL also has the potential to address the diverse needs of English language learners (ELLs) by offering appropriate language support. For example, digital tools that are infused with UDL-based scaffolding can promote understanding across languages and provide clarification of vocabulary as well as syntax and sentence structure. Support in language and literacy for ELLs is particularly important for students who have come to this country as teenagers and who therefore have only recently begun to acquire basic language and reading skills while at the same time trying to comprehend complex content (Collier & Thomas, 2001; Ruiz-de-Velasco, Fix, & Clewell, 2000).

UDL Can Help with the Successful Transition and Reintegration of Youth into School and the Community

Although IDEA and Title I, Part D contain important requirements concerning transition planning, detention and juvenile corrections facilities often do not have effective policies in place to support the reintegration of youth into school and the community. As a result, there can be a lack of coordination between the facility and the student's community school, delays in the transfer of the student's records from the facility to the community school, or instances in which the community school refuses to accept academic credit for classes taken during incarceration (Baltodano et al., 2005; Brock & Keegan, 2007; Mears & Travis, 2004; Stephens & Arnette, 2000). These factors can contribute to students feeling "unwanted and unsupported" on reentering their schools (Baltodano et al., 2005, p. 119). Moreover, in order for youth to reintegrate successfully into the community, there need to be clear lines of communication among the various community agencies (Stephens & Arnette, 2000).

UDL's emphasis on promoting independence in learners can help facilitate improved transition planning for youth about to exit delinquent facilities and return to the community. The goal of effective transition services should be to create a coordinated and seamless system of support that enables youth to resume their education in their local schools, where they can continue to learn and attain college- and career-ready standards expected for all other students. Preplanning has been found to be a critical factor for successful reintegration (Baltodano et al., 2005). The process should therefore begin long before youth exit the facility and continue for a period of time after the departure, all the while allowing the youth to play an active role in the process. By supporting incarcerated youth to become motivated, resourceful, and strategic learners as they transition back into the community and by focusing on the future of these youth, rather than on their pasts, UDL can help reduce recidivism rates.

The UDL framework further supports the transition of incarcerated youth back into the community by promoting the use of relevant and authentic learning opportunities that enable students to make real-world connections to their own lives (Newmann & Wehlage, 1995) as an important aspect of the principle of engagement. The implementation of enhanced vocational training can be used to help incarcerated youth contextualize and personalize their learning experiences as part of the transition process. Although research has shown a relationship between vocational training and reduced recidivism rates among delinquent youth (Wilson, 1994), juvenile delinquent facilities typically provide few vocational opportunities (Moody, Kruse, Nagel, & Conlon, 2008; Platt, Casey, & Faessel, 2006). While some community-based job vocational training programs exist, a comprehensive, systematic approach to vocational training is not always taken (MA EOHHS, 2002). Vocational opportunities for incarcerated youth that are implemented through a UDL lens would be used as a means to recruit interest in future learning as well as in the development of improved self-regulation skills such as personal goal setting to support motivation. Similarly, while less than 25 percent of juvenile corrections facilities offer some form of arts programming (Williams, 2008), in accordance with the UDL framework, art classes can be used as a way to recruit interest, including through the use of technology (e.g., introduction of graphic design elements).

In summary, in spite of the strong legal requirements concerning the provision of high-quality learning opportunities for youth confined in detention and juvenile corrections facilities, the literature has reported significant shortcomings in the education being provided in these facilities. These shortcomings contribute to the perpetuation of the school-to-prison pipeline. This section has demonstrated how implementation of the UDL framework can play a major role in breaking this pipeline.

THE IMPLICATIONS OF APPLYING UDL TO THE EDUCATION OF YOUTH IN DETENTION AND JUVENILE CORRECTIONS FACILITIES

As we have shown, UDL can effect radical changes in the education provided to youth confined in detention and juvenile corrections facilities. Through the application of UDL in the manner described above, the following transformations can occur: (1) incarcerated youth who have experienced many years of academic failure can become engaged in their education; (2) educators in detention and juvenile corrections facilities can embrace a reconceptualized view of incarcerated youth and promote high expectations for the educational achievement of these youth; and (3) incarcerated youth can change the views they have of themselves by becoming independent learners rather than victims of learned helplessness.

Incarcerated Youth Who Have Experienced Many Years of Academic Failure Have the Potential to Become Engaged in Their Education

UDL holds the promise of addressing a significant barrier to learning that is pervasive among the population of delinquent youth—namely, widespread disengagement and lack of motivation to learn. By the time youth enter the juvenile justice system, many have had numerous years of negative school experiences. These youth are more likely to have experienced poor school attendance, received low or failing grades, and been retained in a grade (Foley, 2001; Wang, Blomberg, & Li, 2005). Approximately 21 percent of youth who enter juvenile corrections facilities are not enrolled in public school at the time, and 61 percent have been suspended or expelled during the year prior to their incarceration (Sedlak & McPherson, 2010). Many of these youth have been educated in substantially separate classrooms or alternative schools designated specifically for students with behavioral challenges. These programs and schools tend to provide instruction that is focused primarily on low-level skills, emphasizing the provision of behavioral modifications at the expense of learning (ACLU & ACLU of Mississippi, 2009) and providing virtually no opportunity for student engagement. What has evolved is a separate system of education that is segregated and stigmatizing for students with behavioral challenges, who are disproportionately from low-income and racially and ethnically diverse backgrounds.

As a result of their long history of negative experiences with school, many youth confined in detention and juvenile corrections facilities are likely to have adverse emotional associations with learning. The education provided in detention and juvenile corrections facilities may be the last opportunity for delinquent youth to reconnect with learning in light of the fact that large percentages of incarcerated youth do not return to school when they exit these facilities (Brock & Keegan, 2007; Cusick, George, & Bell, 2008). Yet, as described in the second section, the learning environments in detention and juvenile corrections facilities are not engaging or appropriately challenging. Without a focus on engagement, it is likely that many of these youth will continue to feel disconnected from learning and be more likely to recidivate and ultimately drop out of school. Dropping out has been described not as a discrete event but as a long-term process that unfolds over time and is the result of a combination of factors that contribute to students' feeling disconnected from their education (Rumberger, 2004).

UDL provides a potent mechanism by which the learning experiences in detention and juvenile corrections facilities can be shaped to be more engaging for youth and, at the same time, consistent with state standards. The use of digital technology with embedded UDL supports can counteract the toxicity that delinquent youth often associate with traditional learning that takes place in static classrooms heavily reliant on printed material. When curricula and instructional strategies provide students the affordances to balance the demands of the environment with their personal strengths, they feel appropriately challenged and are able to become engaged in optimal learning. UDL creates a responsive educational system in which students' strengths, rather than their weaknesses, are recognized.

A Reconceptualized View of Incarcerated Youth That Promotes High Expectations

By changing the focus from stereotypical deficits perceived to be intrinsic to the individual student to contextual barriers inherent in the learning environment, UDL can raise the expectations of teachers and administrators for the educational achievement of their students. UDL advances the belief that incarcerated youth are able to achieve at high levels and that they have the right to do so. When learning is viewed through a UDL lens, past failed learning experiences are considered irrelevant to the broader goal of helping *all* students, regardless of their situation in life, to become successful, independent learners. In this way, UDL is similar to what Minow (1990) has referred to as the social-relations approach to the treatment of difference. According to Minow, perceptions of difference are a function of the relationships between individuals wearing the label "different" and those in positions of power who do the labeling. Similar to UDL, the social-relations approach rejects the view that the stigma of difference is located in the person labeled "different." Rather, Minow's approach locates the burden of difference in the relationships of power that have given meaning to this difference. As a result, individuals who were previously excluded from the norm are able to become full participants in the broader community.

UDL has the power to change how teachers and administrators interact with students in detention and juvenile corrections facilities. In order to facilitate the promotion of high expectations on the part of teachers and administrators for the academic performance of incarcerated youth, detention and juvenile corrections facilities need to implement high-quality professional development opportunities to build the capacity of educational and corrections staff to understand UDL and how to teach the wide variety of learners in their classrooms. In addition, in light of the high percentages of racially and ethnically diverse students among the population of youth confined in detention and juvenile corrections facilities, attention should be given to the inclusion of UDL-related professional development that focuses on culturally responsive teaching and discipline strategies.

Incarcerated Youth Have the Potential to Change the Views They Have of Themselves

It is significant that UDL has the potential to change not only the views that teachers and administrators have of incarcerated youth but also the views that these youth have of themselves. Because incarcerated youth have experienced many years of being labeled negatively, there is the strong possibility that they may have internalized these labels (Bernburg, Krohn, & Rivera, 2006). With respect to education, these youth may have developed learned helplessness, characterized by lack of motivation and lowered cognition as a result of having experienced numerous years of academic failure (Abramson, Seligman, & Teasdale, 1978; Sideridis, 2003). Students who have repeatedly failed academically begin to believe that it is inevitable that they will continue to fail.

UDL can help change the negative views that incarcerated youth have of themselves by fostering independence and self-sufficiency in learning, in contrast to learned helplessness. UDL promotes the development of executive functioning skills, which can help students reduce impulsive behavior and learn to plan, strategize, organize, and manage their time more effectively. UDL addresses the improvement of executive functioning by scaffolding lower-level skills so that these require less executive processing while simultaneously supporting the development of improved higher-level executive functioning skills. Specific supports to help with executive functioning can be built into digitized curricular materials—for example, prompts to assist with appropriate goal-setting, coaches that model think-aloud strategies, prompts to help with categorizing information, and rubrics and authentic self-assessment guides. Moreover, data collected from digitized materials can be used to inform students about how their performance has improved over time (CAST, 2011).

On a final note, UDL prepares incarcerated youth to use contemporary technologies and twenty-first-century skills that hold great power and currency in today's labor market. Virtually any job interview in which delinquent youth will participate will ask about their computer literacy skills. By valuing technology as a means of learning, UDL helps to position these youth to become more marketable when seeking employment in the future. Ultimately, youth who are able to change the views they have of themselves, to take ownership of their own learning, and to develop enhanced computer skills will be better equipped to break out of the school-to-prison pipeline and embark on a path toward successful adulthood.

CONCLUSION

Once youth become caught in the school-to-prison pipeline, including as a result of school push-out policies and practices, it is difficult for these youth to extricate themselves. All youth, including those confined in detention and juvenile justice facilities, have the right to a high-quality education, as mandated by Title I of the ESEA and IDEA. Federal civil rights statutes based on race, national origin/language, gender, and disability provide support for enforcement of these legal mandates. Notwithstanding the right of incarcerated youth to a high-quality education, the education provided inside detention and juvenile corrections facilities is substandard. Serious shortcomings include, among others, low-level curricula and instruction that are not aligned with state standards, failure to provide appropriate educational services to students with disabilities and other diverse learners, and inadequate transition planning that can result in recidivism rather than successful reintegration into the community.

UDL views static learning environments—such as the environments these youth encounter in detention and correctional facilities—as the source of barriers to learning. Incorporation of the UDL framework into the education of youth in detention and juvenile corrections facilities is especially appropriate because it can reengage incarcerated youth in the learning process, promote a reconceptualized view of incarcerated youth based on high expectations by teachers and administrators, and help incarcerated youth change their negative views of themselves.

Given the widespread nature of the failings characterizing the education provided in detention and juvenile corrections facilities, minor adjustments will not be sufficient to eliminate the school-to-prison pipeline. What is needed is radical change to the juvenile justice education system. The UDL framework has the potential to bring about a dramatic transformation in order to actualize the right to a high-quality education for youth confined in detention and juvenile corrections facilities.

NOTES

1. Detention facilities are shorter-term institutions providing care to youth "who require secure custody pending court adjudication, court disposition, or execution of a court order, or care . . . after commitment," while juvenile corrections facilities are generally longer-term placements for youth who have already been adjudicated delinquent or in need of supervision (NDTAC, 2011).
2. On September 23, 2011, the U.S. Department of Education offered SEAs the opportunity to request flexibility with respect to specific requirements of the ESEA, with the goal of focusing greater attention on improving student learning and increasing the quality of instruction (ED, 2011b). Among the requirements that have been waived are the annual measurable objectives for determining adequate yearly progress (AYP) by 2013–2014 and the accompanying sanctions imposed for schools and LEAs that are recipients of Title I funds who fail to make AYP (ED, 2011a). By February 15, 2012, eleven states that had previously submitted requests for ESEA flexibility had been granted approval. On February 28, 2012, twenty-six additional states plus the District of Columbia submitted requests for ESEA flexibility. These requests are currently being assessed by a group of peer reviewers (ED, 2012b). While the ESEA waivers extend flexibility to states with respect to specific requirements, the long reach of Title I has been preserved, and the underlying right of all youth, including those confined in detention and juvenile corrections facilities, to receive a high-quality education has remained intact.
3. See also *Alexander S. v. Boyd* (1995); *Donnell C. v. Illinois State Board of Education* (1993); *Handberry v. Thompson* (2000); *Nashua School District v. State of New Hampshire* (1995); *Smith v. Wheaton* (1998); *Unified School District No. 1 v. Connecticut Department of Education* (2001).
4. Under IDEA (2011), the term *universal design* has the same definition as under the Assistive Technology Act: "a concept or philosophy for designing and delivering products and services that are usable by people with the widest possible range of functional capabilities, which include products and services that are directly accessible (without requiring assistive technologies) and products and services that are made usable with assistive technologies" (20 U.S.C. § 1401(35) (incorporating by reference 29 U.S.C. § 3002(3)).

REFERENCES

Abramson, L. Y., Seligman, M. E. P., & Teasdale, J. D. (1978). Learned helplessness in humans: Critique and reformulation. *Journal of Abnormal Psychology, 87*(1), 49–74.

Advancement Project. (2005). *Education on lockdown: The schoolhouse to jailhouse track*. Washington, DC: Author.

Alexander S. v. Boyd, 876 F. Supp. 773 (D. S.C. 1995), *aff'd in part, rev'd in part on other grounds*, 113 F.3d 1373 (4th Cir. 1997).

American Bar Association [ABA], Commission on Youth at Risk. (2009). *Report on resolution 118b: Right to remain in school*. Retrieved from https://docs.google.com/viewer?url=http://www.cleweb.org/sites/default/files/ABA.118B.RighttoRemaininSchool.pdf&pli=1

American Civil Liberties Union [ACLU] & ACLU of Mississippi. (2009). *Missing the mark: Alternative schools in the state of Mississippi*. Jackson, MS: Author. Retrieved from http://www.aclu.org/pdfs/racialjustice/missingthemark_report.pdf

Americans with Disabilities Act, as amended by the ADA Amendments Act of 2008, 42 U.S.C. § 12101, *et seq.* (2011).

American Psychological Association [APA] Zero Tolerance Task Force. (2008). Are zero tolerance policies effective in the schools? An evidentiary review and recommendations. *American Psychologist, 63*(9), 852–862.

Baltodano, H. M., Mathur, S. R., & Rutherford, R. B. (2005). Transition of incarcerated youth with disabilities across systems and into adulthood. *Exceptionality, 13*(2), 103–124.

Bernburg, J. G., Krohn, M. D., & Rivera, C. J. (2006). Official labeling, criminal embeddedness, and subsequent delinquency: A longitudinal test of labeling theory. *Journal of Research in Crime and Delinquency, 43*, 67–88.

Bewley, R. (1999). The use of multimedia and hypermedia presentation for instruction of juvenile offenders. *Journal of Correctional Education, 50*(4), 130–139.

Bilchik, S. (2008). Is racial and ethnic equity possible in juvenile justice? *Reclaiming Children and Youth, 17*(2), 19–23.

Blomberg, T. G., & Pesta, G. (2008). *Massachusetts juvenile justice education: Case study results.* Tallahassee: Center for Criminology and Public Policy Research, Florida State University.

Blumenson, E., & Nilsen, E. S. (2003). One strike and you're out? Constitutional constraints on zero tolerance in public education. *Washington University Law Quarterly, 81*, 65–118.

Boundy, K. B., & Karger, J. (2011). The right to a quality education for children and youth in the juvenile justice system. In F. Sherman & F. Jacobs (Eds.), *Juvenile justice: Advancing research, policy, and practice* (pp. 286–309). Hoboken, NJ: Wiley & Sons.

Bradshaw, W., & Roseborough, D. (2005). Restorative justice dialogue: The impact of mediation and conferencing on juvenile recidivism. *Federal Probation, 69*(2), 15–21.

Brock, L., & Keegan, N. (2007). *Students highly at risk of dropping out: Returning to school after incarceration.* National Evaluation and Technical Assistance Center for the Education of Children and Youth Who Are Neglected, Delinquent, or At-Risk. Retrieved from www.neglected-delinquent.org/nd/resources/spotlight/spotlight200701b.asp

Burrell, S., & Warboys, L. (2000). *Special education and the juvenile justice system* (Juvenile Justice Bulletin NCJ 179359). Washington, DC: Office of Juvenile Justice and Delinquency Prevention, U.S. Department of Justice.

CAST. (2011). *Universal Design for Learning guidelines version 2.0.* Wakefield, MA: Author. Retrieved from http://www.udlcenter.org/aboutudl/udlguidelines

Civil Rights Act of 1964, Title VI, 42 U.S.C. § 2000d.

Cocozza, J. J., & Skowyra, K. R. (2000). Youth with mental health disorders: Issues and emerging responses. *Juvenile Justice, 7*(1), 3–13.

Coffey, O. D., & Gemignani, M. G. (1994). *Effective practices in juvenile correctional education: A study of the literature and research, 1980–1992.* Washington, DC: U.S. Department of Justice, National Office for Social Responsibility.

Collier, V. P., & Thomas, W. P. (2001). Educating linguistically and culturally diverse students in correctional settings. *Journal of Correctional Education, 52*(2), 68–73.

Cusick, G. R., George, R. M., & Bell, K. C. (2009). *From corrections to community: The juvenile reentry experience as characterized by multiple systems involvement* [Final report to the Illinois Criminal Justice Information Authority]. Chicago: Chapin Hall Center for Children, University of Chicago.

Donnell C. v. Illinois State Board of Education, 829 F. Supp. 1016 (N.D. Ill. 1993).

Education Amendments of 1972, 20 U.S.C. § 1681 *et seq.* (2011).

Elementary and Secondary Education Act, No Child Left Behind Act, Title I, 20 U.S.C. § 6301 *et seq.*; 34 C.F.R. § 200.1 *et seq.* (2011).

Equal Educational Opportunities Act, 20 U.S.C. § 1703(f) (2011).

Farrell, A. F., & Myers, D. M. (2011). Collaboration in the service of better systems for youth. In F. Sherman & F. Jacobs (Eds.), *Juvenile justice: Advancing research, policy, and practice* (pp. 433–455). Hoboken, NJ: Wiley & Sons.

Florida Legislature. (1998). *Review of education services in juvenile residential facilities* (Report No. 98-28). Tallahasee, FL: Office of Program Policy Analysis and Government Accountability. (ERIC Document Reproduction Service No. ED 426 335)

139

Foley, R. M. (2001). Academic characteristics of incarcerated youth and correctional educational programs: A literature review. *Journal of Emotional and Behavioral Disorders, 9*(4), 248–259.

Gagnon, J. C. (2008). State-level curricular, assessment, and accountability policies, practices, and philosophies for exclusionary school settings. *Journal of Special Education, 43*(4), 206–219.

Gagnon, J. C., Barber, B. R., Van Loan, C., & Leone, P. E. (2009). Juvenile correctional schools: Characteristics and approaches to curriculum. *Education and Treatment of Children, 32*(4), 673–696.

Gavazzi, S. M., Russell, C. M., & Khurana, A. (2009). Predicting educational risks among court-involved black males: Family, peers, and mental health issues. *Negro Educational Review, 60*(1–4), 99–114.

Gilham, C., & Moody, B. (2001). Face to face: Videoconferencing creates opportunities for incarcerated youth. *Journal of Correctional Education, 52*(1), 29–31.

Handberry v. Thompson, 92 F. Supp. 2d 244, 248 (S.D.N.Y. 2000).

Harris, P. J., Baltodano, H. M., Artiles, A. J., & Rutherford, R. B. (2006). Integration of culture in reading studies for youth in corrections: A literature review. *Education and Treatment of Children, 29*(4), 749–778.

Higher Education Opportunity Act of 2008, 20 U.S.C. § 1001 *et seq.* (2011).

Houchins, D. E., Jolivette, K., Wessendorf, S., McGlynn, M., & Nelson, C. M. (2005). Stakeholders' view of implementing positive behavioral support in a juvenile justice setting. *Education and Treatment of Children, 28*(4), 380–399.

Houchins , D. E., Puckett-Patterson, D., Crosby, S., Shippen, M. E., & Jolivette, K. (2009). Barriers and facilitators to providing incarcerated youth with a quality education. *Preventing School Failure, 53*(3), 159–166.

Howell, K. W., & Wolford, B. I. (2002). *Corrections and juvenile justice: Current education practice for youth with learning and other disabilities.* Monograph Series on Education, Disability and Juvenile Justice. Washington, DC: Center for Effective Collaboration and Practice, American Institutes for Research. (ERIC Document Reproduction Service No. ED471211)

Individuals with Disabilities Education Act [IDEA], 20 U.S.C. § 1401 *et seq.*; 34 C.F.R. § 300.1 *et seq.* (2011).

Katsiyannis, A., & Archwamety, T. (1997). Factors related to recidivism among delinquent youths in a state correctional facility. *Journal of Child and Family Studies, 6*(1), 43–55.

Katsiyannis, A., Ryan, J. B., Zhang, D., & Spann, A. (2008). Juvenile delinquency and recidivism: The impact of academic achievement. *Reading and Writing Quarterly, 24*(2), 177–196.

Khankeo van der Graaf, V. (2008). *A five year comparison between an extended year school and a conventional year school: Effects on academic achievement.* (ERIC Document Reproduction Service No. ED505912)

Krezmien, M. P., Mulcahy, C. A., & Leone, P. E. (2008). Detained and committed youth: Examining differences in achievement, mental health needs, and special education status. *Education and Treatment of Children, 31*(4), 445–464.

Leone, P. E. (1994). Education services for youth with disabilities in a state-operated juvenile correctional system: Case study and analysis. *Journal of Special Education, 28*(1), 43–58.

Leone, P. E., & Cutting, C. A. (2004). Appropriate education, juvenile corrections, and No Child Left Behind. *Behavioral Disorders, 29*(3), 260–265.

Leone, P. E., Krezmien, M., Mason L., & Meisel, S. M. (2005). Organizing and delivering empirically based literacy instruction to incarcerated youth. *Exceptionality, 13*(2), 89–102.

Leone, P. E., Meisel, S. M., & Drakeford, W. (2002). Special education programs for youth with disabilities in juvenile corrections. *Journal of Correctional Education, 53*(2), 46–50.

Leone, P. E., Quinn, M. M., & Osher, D. M. (2002). *Collaboration in the juvenile justice system and youth serving agencies: Improving prevention, providing more efficient services, and reducing recidivism for youth with disabilities.* Monograph Series on Education, Disability and Juvenile Justice. Washington, DC: Center for Effective Collaboration and Practice, American Institutes for Research. (ERIC Document Reproduction Service No. ED471210)

Maccini, P., Gagnon, J. C., Mulcahy, C. A., & Leone, P. E. (2006). Math instruction for committed youth within juvenile correctional schools. *Journal of Correctional Education, 57*(3), 210–229.

Massachusetts Executive Office of Health and Human Services [MA EOHHS], Department of Youth Services. (2002). *Delivering effective education to youth: A report on education services in the Massachusetts Department of Youth (A Report to the Massachusetts House and Senate Committees on Ways and Means).* Boston: Author.

McCord, J., Widom, C. S., & Crowell, N. A. (Eds.). (2001). *Juvenile crime, juvenile justice.* Washington, DC: National Academies Press.

McDonnell, L. M., McLaughlin, M. J., & Morison, P. (Eds.). (1997). *Educating one and all: Students with disabilities and standards-based reform.* Committee on Goals 2000 and the Inclusion of Students with Disabilities, National Research Council. Washington, DC: National Academies Press.

McIntyre, T., Tong, V. M., & Perez, J. F. (2001). Cyber-lock down: Problems inherent with the use of internet technology in correctional education settings. *Journal of Correctional Education, 52*(4), 163–165.

Mears, D. P., & Travis, J. (2004). *The dimensions, pathways, and consequences of youth reentry* [Research report]. Youth Reentry Roundtable Series. Washington, DC: Urban Institute.

Meyer, A., & Rose, D. H. (2005). The future is in the margins: The role of technology and disability in educational reform. In D. H. Rose, A. Meyer, & C. Hitchcock (Eds.), *The universally designed classroom: Accessible curriculum and digital technologies* (pp. 13–35). Cambridge, MA: Harvard Education Press.

Minow, M. (1990). *Making all the difference: Inclusion, exclusion, and American law.* Ithaca, NY: Cornell University Press.

Moody, B., Kruse, G., Nagel, J., & Conlon, B. (2008). Career development project for incarcerated youth: Preparing for the future. *Journal of Correctional Education, 59(3),* 231–243.

Nashua School District v. State of New Hampshire, 23 IDELR 427 (N.H. 1995).

National Association for the Advancement of Colored People [NAACP] Legal Defense and Educational Fund. (2005). *Dismantling the school-to-prison pipeline.* New York: Author.

National Evaluation and Technical Assistance Center for the Education of Children and Youth Who Are Neglected, Delinquent, or At-Risk [NDTAC]. (2011). *State and national fast facts.* Retrieved from http://data.neglected-delinquent.org/index.php?id=01

National Governors Association [NGA] Center for Best Practices, Council of Chief State School Officers. (2010). *Common Core State Standards: Application to students with disabilities.* Washington, DC: Author. Retrieved from http://www.corestandards.org/assets/application-to-students-with-disabilities.pdf

New York Civil Liberties Union. (2007). *Criminalizing the classroom: The over-policing of New York City schools.* Retrieved from http://www.aclu.org/pdfs/racialjustice/overpolicingschools_20070318.pdf

Newmann, F., & Wehlage, G. (1995). *Successful school restructuring.* Alexandria, VA: Association for Supervision and Curriculum Development.

Oakes, J. (1987). *Tracking in secondary schools: A contextual perspective.* Santa Monica, CA: RAND. (ERIC Document Reproduction Service No. ED298643)

141

Office of Juvenile Justice and Delinquency Prevention [OJJDP]. (2011a). *OJJDP statistical briefing book: Online* (Custody Data: 1997–Present: Age Profiles). Retrieved from http://www.ojjdp.gov/ojstatbb/corrections/qa08204.asp?qaDate=2010

Office of Juvenile Justice and Delinquency Prevention [OJJDP]. (2011b). *OJJDP statistical briefing book: Online* (Custody Data: 1997–Present: State custody rates by race/ethnicity). Retrieved from http://www.ojjdp.gov/ojstatbb/corrections/qa08203.asp?qaDate=2010

Office of Special Education Programs [OSEP], U.S. Department of Education. (2003). Letter to Mr. Geoffrey A. Yudien from Stephanie S. Lee, Director, Office of Special Education Programs. Washington, DC: Author.

Ordover, E. (2001). *When schools criminalize disability: Education law strategies for legal advocates.* Boston: Center for Law and Education.

Piquero, A. R. (2008). Disproportionate minority contact. *Future of Children, 18*(2), 59–79.

Platt, J. S., Casey, R. E., & Faessel, R. T. (2006). The need for a paradigmatic change in juvenile correctional education. *Preventing School Failure, 51*(1), 31–38.

Quinn, M. M., Rutherford, R. B., Leone, P. E., Osher, D. M., & Poirier, J. M. (2005). Youth with disabilities in juvenile corrections: A national survey. *Exceptional Children, 71*(3), 339–345.

Rettig v. Kent, 539 F. Supp. 768 (N.D. Ohio 1981), *aff'd in part, vacated in part,* 720 F.2d 463 (6th Cir. 1983), *cert. denied* 467 U.S. 1201 (1984).

Rose, D. H., & Meyer, A. (2002). *Teaching every student in the digital age: Universal Design for Learning.* Alexandria, VA: ASCD.

Ruiz-de-Velasco, J., Fix, M. E., & Clewell, B. C. (2000). *Overlooked and underserved: Immigrant students in U.S. secondary schools* [Research report]. Washington, DC: Urban Institute.

Rumberger, R. W. (2004). Why students drop out of school. In G. Orfield (Ed.), *Dropouts in America: Confronting the graduation rate crisis* (pp. 131–155). Cambridge, MA: Harvard Education Press.

Ryals, J. S. (2004). Restorative justice: New horizons in juvenile offender counseling. *Journal of Addictions and Offender Counseling, 25,* 18–25.

Scott, T. M., Nelson, C. M., Liaupsin, C. J., Jolivette, K., Christle, C. A., & Riney, M. (2002). Addressing the needs of at-risk and adjudicated youth through positive behavior support: Effective prevention practices. *Education and Treatment of Children, 25*(4), 532–551.

Section 504 of the Rehabilitation Act of 1973, 29 U.S.C. § 794 (2011).

Sedlak, A. J., & McPherson, K. S. (2010). *Youth's needs and services: Findings from the survey of youth in residential placement* (Juvenile Justice Bulletin NCJ 227728). Washington, DC: Office of Juvenile Justice and Delinquency Prevention, U.S. Department of Justice.

Seiter, L., Seidel, D., & Lampron, S. (2012). *Annual performance report for school year 2009–10: Program for the education of children and youth who are neglected, delinquent, or at risk of educational failure.* Washington, DC: National Evaluation and Technical Assistance Center for the Education of Children and Youth Who Are Neglected, Delinquent, or At-Risk.

Skiba, R. J. (2000). *Zero tolerance, zero evidence: An analysis of school disciplinary practice* (Policy Research Report No. SRS2). Bloomington: Indiana Education Policy Center. Retrieved from www.indiana.edu/~safeschl/ztze.pdf

Smith v. Wheaton, 29 IDELR 200 (D. Conn. 1998).

Sideridis, D. (2003). On the origins of helpless behavior of students with learning disabilities: Avoidance motivation. *International Journal of Educational Research, 39*(4–5), 497–517. (ERIC document Reproduction Service No. ED313854).

Spry, S. A. (2003). Making diversity in correctional education classrooms work for correctional educators and incarcerated students and workers. *Journal of Correctional Education, 54*(2), 75–78.

Stephens, R. D., & Arnette, J. L. (2000). *From the courthouse to the schoolhouse: Making successful transitions* (Juvenile Justice Bulletin NCJ 178900). Washington, DC: Office of Juvenile Justice and Delinquency Prevention, U.S. Department of Justice.

Story, M. F., Mueller, J. L., & Mace, R. L. (1998). *The universal design file: Designing for people of all ages and abilities.* Raleigh, NC: Center for Universal Design. Retrieved from http://design-dev.ncsu.edu/openjournal/index.php/redlab/article/view/102

Teplin, L. A., Abram, K. M., McClelland, G. M., Dulcan, M. K., & Mericle, A. A. (2002). Psychiatric disorders in youth in juvenile detention. *Archives of General Psychiatry, 59*(12), 1133–1143.

Twomey, K. (2008). The right to education in juvenile detention under state constitutions. *Virginia Law Review, 94,* 765–811.

Unified School District No. 1 v. Connecticut Department of Education, 780 A.2d 154 (Conn. App. 2001).

U.S. Department of Education [ED]. (2010a). *A blueprint for reform: The reauthorization of the Elementary and Secondary Education Act.* Washington, DC: Author. Retrieved from http://www2.ed.gov/policy/elsec/leg/blueprint/blueprint.pdf

U.S. Department of Education [ED], Office of Educational Technology. (2010b). *Transforming American education: Learning powered by technology.* National Education Technology Plan 2010. Washington, DC: Author. Retrieved from http://www.ed.gov/sites/default/files/netp2010.pdf

U.S. Department of Education [ED]. (2011a). *ESEA flexibility.* Washington, DC: Author.

U.S. Department of Education [ED]. (2011b). *ESEA flexibility: Frequently asked questions.* Washington, DC: Author.

U.S. Department of Education [ED], National Center for Education Statistics. (2011c). *Digest of education statistics, 2010* (NCES 2011-015). Washington, DC: Author.

U.S. Department of Education [ED]. (2012a). *Summary of considerations to strengthen state requests for ESEA flexibility.* Washington, DC: Author. Retrieved from http://www.ed.gov/sites/default/files/considerations-strengthen.pdf

U.S. Department of Education [ED]. (2012b). Status of state requests. Washington, DC: Author. Retrieved from http://www2.ed.gov/policy/eseaflex/status-state-requests.pdf

U.S. Department of Justice [DOJ], Civil Rights Division, Special Litigation Section. (2010). Letter of investigative findings: Indianapolis Juvenile Correctional Facility. Washington, DC: Author.

Vaught, S. E. (2011). Juvenile prison schooling and reentry: Disciplining young men of color. In F. Sherman & F. Jacobs (Eds.), *Juvenile justice: Advancing research, policy, and practice* (pp. 310–330). Hoboken, NJ: Wiley & Sons.

Wang, X., Blomberg, T. G., & Li, S. D. (2005). Comparison of the educational deficiencies of delinquent and nondelinquent students. *Evaluation Review, 29*(4), 291–312.

Williams, R. M. C. (2008). The status and praxis of arts education and juvenile offenders in correctional facilities in the United States. *Journal of Correctional Education, 59*(2), 107–126.

Wilson, P. R. (1994). Recidivism and vocational education. *Journal of Correctional Education, 45*(4), 158–163.

Wood, J., Foy, D. W., Layne, C., Pynoos, R., & James, C. B. (2002). An examination of the relationships between violence exposure, posttraumatic stress symptomatology, and delinquent activity: An "ecopathological" model of delinquent behavior among incarcerated adolescents. *Journal of Aggression, Maltreatment and Trauma, 6*(1), 127–147.

MYSTORY

A PUBLIC EDUCATIONAL EXPERIENCE

■

BOBBY DEAN EVANS, JR.

In 1954, the Supreme Court case *Brown v. the Board of Education* ruled against arbitrary discrimination in education, stating, "Separate is not equal education." Within integrated schools, segregation continued to operate in the form of special education classes. The *mystory* is that even though there were two landmark cases decided against segregation in public schools, for over fifty years African Americans have found themselves in school environments similar to the legal segregation scheme outlined in *Plessey v. Ferguson.*

In 1975, Congress acknowledged the damaging effects of segregation on students who were educated in separate environments. Legislation was put into place to protect the rights of children with disabilities. The Individuals with Disabilities Education Act (IDEA) was designed to enhance education, not as a form of punishment. Students with disabilities are to be placed in normal classroom settings with relevant language and cultural literacies. According to the IDEA, if an education program in a segregated setting can be applied in an integrated setting, it is inappropriate *not* do so. Without an appropriate education, special education students are catapulted into a life that "promises a form of punishment that is often more difficult to bear than prison time: a lifetime of shame, contempt, scorn, and exclusion" (Weatherspoon, 1991, p. 139). An inappropriate education for me resulted in "civic death"—the curse of living as an illiterate felon at the time.

In the 1970s, I was placed in special education classes at Crockham Elementary School in Winton, California. Being labeled and being excluded from regular classes and students had a crippling effect on my educational development. The stigma of being placed in special education has left a scar deep in the gray matter of my heart. Not only did this misdiagnosis impact me and my family, it also warped society's thinking and interactions toward me. My placement in special education kept me from learning social behaviors by excluding me from interacting with my peers and from participating in advanced educational courses. This also impacted my high school experience: my tests scores decreased, and, ultimately, my chances of graduating also decreased. I believe my exclusion from an appropriate public education contributed to, and influenced, the criminal activity in my life that eventually carried me away from the American Dream and onto a path of incarceration.

I was labeled as dysfunctional and stereotyped as deviant, hostile, and oppositional. My lack of enthusiasm for education, and no doubt my skin color, along with the simple childish trouble I would get into, seemed like the only logical justifications for my placement in a segregated special education class. As a child, I knew something was different about me, and this became evident in how I was treated in school. Trying to find myself, I rebelled in the only ways I knew how, such as being disruptive and picking on other children to get attention. In retrospect, I was not less smart than the other kids, nor did I have a learning disability. In my mind, as one of a few Black children in my school, I did not feel encouraged, and school seemed irrelevant. I did not see a reason to apply myself. I felt different than—less than—others. I fell into a trap and reinforced the negative labels that were put on me. I rebelled and acted in ways that exemplified a dysfunctional, stereotypically deviant, hostile child.

Public education failed to ensure me an appropriate education. My placement in a segregated class designed for low academic achievers contributed to my low self-esteem and did not prepare me with the skills necessary to continue and to value my education. I was insufficient as a student, and my academic accomplishments lagged substantially behind the educational accomplishments of non–special education students. Without an appropriate education, special education students are relegated to second-class citizen status (Weatherspoon, 1991). This underclass status increased my chances of getting suspended or expelled or of dropping out of school entirely (Weatherspoon, 1991). These factors no doubt had a negative impact on my desire to remain in school and graduate.

Without education, my liberty was in jeopardy. Without education, my mind was enslaved. Without education, my destination was incarceration.

In high school I was assigned to a "sports curriculum" because of my above-average athletic skills. I was nourished and developed to play sports at the expense of my education (Weatherspoon, 1991). As a sophomore, I had a hernia and had to quit sports. My failure to succeed in sports, my poor attendance, and my failing grades resulted in my expulsion from high school.

Because of my expulsion, I was bused to Merced to a continuation school designed for low-achieving students. There I was among the most negative students in the district. The rates of expulsion and dropouts were phenomenal. My special education and continuation placement had become a crucible for the development of a criminal mind-set. The continuation school offered no challenge to getting marijuana, speed, or powdered cocaine. I also drank beer regularly and stole to support my alcohol and drug abuse. My placement in a continuation school was no doubt a motivating factor for my dropping out of school.

Among the reasons why I dropped out of school was a curriculum that failed to motivate and stimulate me so I could appreciate the immediate and

145

long-lasting rewards of education. As a dropout, I gravitated toward other dropouts. Without a structured educational environment, the long-term effects of being an uneducated dropout were underemployment, drug use, criminal behavior, and increased chances of incarceration. Like many special education students, I did not graduate. And we hardly ever graduate as *valedictorians* of our class.

The terrible truth is that the public school system would have allowed me to graduate with failing grades and ill prepared for life had I not dropped out of school voluntarily. My younger uncle, John, graduated from high school, but he had difficulty reading. One day Grandma asked me if I would help John get his driver's license. I did not see it as a problem. John and I hung out a lot. He knew how to drive and had a job. I never knew him to have a problem with reading or writing. I figured Grandma wanted me to take him to the DMV, let him use my car for the driving test, or perhaps even help him study for the written portion of the test. Whatever it was, I was willing to help my uncle. It was then that I understood that Grandma wanted me to take the written exam for John because he had trouble reading.

As Alexander has described, my experience as a young Black man meant that "police supervision, monitoring, and harassment were a fact of life for me; and not only for all those labeled criminals, but for all those who 'look like' criminals" (Eberhardt, Goff, Purdie, & Davies, 2004, p. 132). My label as a dysfunctional student rolled into being labeled as a criminal. I was about fourteen years old when I had my first run-in with the police. One evening, returning from watching the Friday-night varsity football game, I was about a block away from my house when a Merced County sheriff stopped me. I was asked what I was doing out after curfew. Fearfully, I explained where I was coming from and where I was going. Subsequently, I was taken in to the sheriff's department and my mother was called to come and pick me up. It was suggested to her that she should contact the Probations Office and make an appointment. They had impressed on her that I needed supervision—implying that I was deviant, hostile, and oppositional. As a single mother, she expected to find help with her only son. What she found was that that would not be the last time her son would be placed in the back of a police car.

Life in the streets had become normal for me. For years I refused to involve myself with life beyond the walls of prison and knew nothing of the "invisible cage" that had become my life. I saw myself as a "worthless human being not expected to aspire to excellence; expected to make peace with mediocrity" (Alexander, 2010, p. 247). Without an education, I was on track to fail and found it difficult to "succeed in life" (Weatherspoon, 1991, p. 4). Incarcerated for many years of my life, I had the fortitude to pick up some good behaviors from the programs offered in prison. I enrolled in GED classes while in prison and retained vital academic information. When I paroled in 1993, I was motivated by my mother to take a GED test at Merced School District, and, *to my surprise*, I passed.

In 1990, before paroling on a seven-year prison term, I enrolled in a prerelease class and was instructed on life skills, setting goals, and achieving success. As a result, I had a short period of success. I bought a car before I paroled, collected resources to obtain a job, a place to live, and a bank account. Within six months after I paroled, I successfully achieved all of my goals. Yet, without insight into my behaviors and reasons for criminal activity, I relapsed and found myself back in prison on a parole violation.

Research by Weatherspoon (1991) and Alexander (2010) has assisted me in understanding my plight as it pertains to recidivism rates. This information has also revealed to me that just as I had been tracked into special education classes, I was targeted for incarceration. I am at a disadvantage because of the color of my skin—no different than "the stigma of race, condemnation, scorn heaped upon [my forefathers] for no reason other than the color of their skin" (Alexander, 2010, p. 137). Alexander (2010) explains how the proverbial hand of an inappropriate education was laid on me and, consequently, how no education equals no basic human rights. Today, education is inextricably woven into the fabric of every developed country. Yet, in the light of schools closing in places that desperately need them, it appears that education is not of value in the United States.

Having changed my mind-set and had a revelation about my criminal behavior, I now fully understand the need to assist incarcerated people for successful community reentry. Today I am a granddaddy. In addition, I care very much for my Mama, my sisters, my children, and everyone in my family. The person I was before redemption from a criminal mind-set—I would not want that man living next to my loved ones. But as a redeemed prisoner, I know the value of life and have learned to appreciate, love, care, and give of myself.

My son Daylon is sixteen years of age. He has been put out of school for reasons I do not quite understand. He has been placed on independent studies and says he has to make up some credits. My question is, How is he to educate himself without a teacher? By excluding him from school, he is pushed further away from the importance of an education and further into the streets. I see myself in him.

As a child, I could never keep my hands off other people's stuff. I took from my mother's purse and would borrow money from my sisters, hoping they would never know. In high school I would take things from the 7-Eleven, like two-liter sodas and Doritos, to impress my football buddies. For years I was locked into a criminal mind-set and a street mentality. My MO was one of a thief, robber, jacker, burglar—what I took you owed me, and I felt nothing of the impact my crime and violence had on you. Eventually I graduated to burglary, taking money that some class at the local grade school raised selling cookies or something. From there I burglarized houses and moved on to strong-arm robbery and kicking in doors of drug dealers. The home invasion on the drug house (two counts of robbery and a burglary) was used to strike me out. In 1995 I was sentenced to twenty-five to life for three strikes.

In many ways, I am thankful for this prison experience. It allowed me a place and space to change and develop my mind-set and has assisted me in valuing myself as well as others. I have gained insight into my criminal behavior and have made positive corrections in my thinking and life's purpose. I no longer minimize my criminal behavior. What I called "taking" or "borrowing" is theft! I stole from my family, and I cared for no one's personal space or possessions. I stole from myself. When I think about it, I am a big hypocrite. I abhorred and wanted to hurt the person who stole the bicycles that I bought for my two sons. Today, I have that same bitterness in my soul when I think of the economic pain and personal suffering I caused the multitude of people I robbed and stole from.

I have gained a firm understanding of myself through the many self-help programs I have participated in during my ten-year prison experience here at San Quentin State Prison. My reward will be seeing people like my Uncle John, my son Daylon, and myself become successful and productive members of our society.

Being under the structured academic tutelage of the Prison University Project and self-help programs at San Quentin, I have attained a solid educational foundation with resources and support. I have earned an associate of arts degree from Patten University (Oakland, California). I continue to take classes toward a bachelor's and want to attain a master's in social work to eventually work in reentry programs assisting those in my situation transform their lives for positive change.

These programs have provided teachers and professionals who inspire, motivate, and encourage me to be involved in my personal transformation. I completed programs for the first time in my life and graduated *valedictorian* of my class. This has positively impacted my desire for making positive changes. Having a keen understanding of myself and my triggers, as well as a relapse prevention plan, is essential in assisting me to stem the long-term negative impact of being mainstreamed into lower-level classes that were designed for my demise. The appropriate programs in San Quentin stimulated me and involved me in cultural norms and positive connections between myself, my family, and my community. The effect will undoubtedly be no more in and out of prison. I will continue to stay involved in education and self-help programs when I am physically freed from this concrete and steel world that has become my institution of higher learning.

Education has changed my life. Graduating as class valedictorian from Patten University has raised my level of consciousness, increased my sense of self-worth, and given me a clear path for my future. With the insight I have gained into the causes of the destructive lifestyle of my past and into the importance of educating incarcerated persons, I am now painfully aware of the need to serve others. Accordingly, I am involved in the organization and administration of several GED programs for our incarcerated community here at San Quentin. In addition, I was instrumental in building and organizing a nonviolent self-help group called No More Tears. This group gives former per-petrators of crime the tools and opportunities to transform their lives by becoming nonviolent facilitators within these prison walls, better preparing them to return to their communities. My present work involves helping incar-cerated persons reenter society as productive citizens. I aspire to create pro-grams for at-risk youth, troubled persons, and the elderly in order that they may be successful and viable members of society. Upon parole, I will continue to work in crime prevention. I will work to keep our communities safe, to unify people with common interests, and to organize them to assist in the growth and improvement in our communities. I will establish forums that give people opportunities to educate themselves and will develop programs to help them find alternative, nonviolent ways to deal with conflict in their lives.

REFERENCES

Alexander, M. (2010). *The New Jim Crow.* New York: New Press.
Eberhardt, J. L., Goff, P. A., Purdie, V. J., & Davies, P. G. (2004). Seeing black: Race, crime, and visual processing. *Journal of Personality and Social Psychology 87*(6), 876–893.
Weatherspoon, F. D. (1991). *Principle-centered leadership.* New York: Summit Books.

INSTITUTIONAL RACIST MELANCHOLIA

A STRUCTURAL UNDERSTANDING OF GRIEF AND POWER IN SCHOOLING

■

SABINA E. VAUGHT

In this article, Sabina E. Vaught undertakes the theoretical and analytical project of conceptually integrating Whiteness as property, *a key structural framework of Critical Race Theory (CRT), and* melancholia, *a framework originally emerging from psychoanalysis. Specifically, Vaught engages* Whiteness as property *as an analytic tool to examine data from a larger ethnographic study of juvenile prison and schooling. She suggests that the psychoanalytic framework of* melancholia *enriches and complicates this analysis and proposes a theoretical move toward understanding structural affective processes in the scholarly effort to map schooling, race, and power. Throughout, Vaught illustrates the significance and utility of such an approach through multifaceted data-driven analyses.*

> We might then say that melancholia does not simply denote a *condition* of grief but is, rather, a *legislation* of grief.
> — Anne Anlin Cheng

In the formation of the early United States, Whiteness was attached to property through multiple mechanisms. This process, Critical Race scholar Harris (1993) argues, produced the organizing racial category of "Whiteness as property"—the cornerstone of White supremacy. This specific construction of race was exercised legally, ideologically, and socially. Of all people in the republic, only certain White males could own legally recognized and protected property, including tracts and buildings. "Courts established whiteness as a prerequisite to the exercise of enforceable property rights" (Harris, 1993, p. 1724). Notably, this legal maneuver helped establish Whiteness as definitively and singularly racially capable and deserving of property ownership and therefore established it as superordinate to Indigenous "race"—constructed by Whites as fundamentally antithetical to ownership. That ownership, or possession, of race and property—and the attendant rights to dispossess Others—produced another possession: citizen status and rights. Such White men were given exclusive civic rights and recognition, such as voting and representation. The right to vote made one a citizen and therefore a full human in the initial fictional construct of representational democracy (Guinier, 1994).

However, it was through the violent institutionalization of chattel slavery that Whites consolidated race, rights, and material possession into the single property of exclusive humanity. Specifically, through the White commodification of Black peoples through slavery, a distinction of race came to indicate who could be made the property of another and who could own another. The White creation, organization, and practice of American slavery produced and protected the White right to own Black bodies and provided a guarantee against ever being owned. Whiteness became the right to own property *and* to never be owned. Blackness became the property that legally defined Whiteness as exclusively human—that is, property-owning, free citizens protected from commodification. In other words, Whites owned the right to humanity. The right to determine meaning—to decide who was human and what was truth— was prized, exclusive, and guarded property. As Harris (1993) explains, the legal formalization of racialized slavery rested on affording "whiteness actual legal status"; this legal action worked to transform race as identity into race as property, "moving whiteness from privileged identity to a vested interest" (p. 1725). The rights to craft and instantiate meaning, to accrue benefit, and to expect exclusivity and legal protection continue to be cornerstones of the contemporary exercise of Whiteness as property.

Indeed, Whiteness as property theoretically (and highly complexly) explains many of the structures and mechanisms that characterize White institutions, including schools and prisons. However, in the context of ethnographic research I conducted at a school housed inside a prison for juvenile males, I began to understand the need to expand on this theory—to create an explanatory conceptual dialogue between Whiteness as property and a framework that accounts for the affective features of institutions. Specifically, while doing this ethnographic work, I was struck by the need to produce analytic tools that situate systemic, institutional analyses as not abstracted from the emotive characteristics of violent oppression. This became quite evident as I encountered my own analytic limitations in this regard. For example, I found myself, on the one hand, able to detail the power dynamics functioning within the prison school policy as grounded in propertied White supremacist structures and, on the other hand, able to draw out the affective actions of individual teachers and inmates/students as institutional members and representatives, but I was utterly unable to make the two analyses meet. This inability left me with a stark view of the theoretical chasm between institutional analysis and macro affective meaning. I wondered, How did the institutionalization of the extraordinarily brutally racist incarceration of children and youth of Color not only corrosively form the individual psychic and ideological condition of supremacist participants (Morrison, 1992) but in fact shape the institutions themselves?

In searching for an answer to this, I landed, with no small amount of resistance and trepidation, on psychoanalytic theories of grief. In part, this came from a persistent rendering of grief within the White power structures. This grief—this iteration of the unreconciled, contradictory loss that marks grief—reverberated through the policy and practice of juvenile incarceration. This was not the grief of personal sadness or vulnerability. Rather, in this case, it was the loss produced when the defining, self-requisite features of Whiteness—liberty and equality—exist (as they always do) in unmitigated opposition to the functional, essential features of Whiteness: domination and oppression. So, the questions that began to emerge from my work included: How might we recognize and account for the affective features of institutions? How might the structure and practice of Whiteness as property contain mechanisms and trajectories of grief? How might we understand the ways in which those mechanisms and trajectories are expressed through organization, policy, and practice? How might we begin to map the White supremacist institutional shape of loss and unresolved grief so as to better understand and disrupt it?

In this article, I engage these questions and describe the ways in which *melancholia* (Cheng, 2001; Rickman, 1957)—a psychoanalytic conceptualization of unresolved grief—can be understood at the institutional level, rather than individual or even cultural level, as an integral part of Whiteness as property. I engage in a dialectical explication of Whiteness as property and melancholia, identifying how melancholia refines and extends structural and legal understandings of Whiteness. Also, I consider why this engagement is important. Next, I explore the application of this integrated conceptual frame to data from the prison school, with an analytic eye to White narratives and White institutions' organizational practices. Finally, I consider the implications and further questions suggested by the process of integrating psychoanalytic and structural/material conceptual frames and bodies of theory.

WHITENESS AS PROPERTY: RIGHTS OF FIRST POSSESSION

Whiteness as property is a conceptual frame that emerged from a scholarly movement known as Critical Race Theory (CRT; Crenshaw, Gotanda, Peller, & Thomas, 1995; Matsuda, Lawrence, Delgado, & Crenshaw, 1993; Valdes, Culpe, & Harris, 2002). CRT was originally the project of a group comprised largely of legal scholars of Color who responded to the absence of critical analyses or even recognition of race and racism in both the law and legal studies. They produced a rigorous scholarly conversation around race. Through their scholarship, early Critical Race scholars established working tenets of the movement that have informed ensuing scholarship. Among these tenets are: racism is permanent and is endemic to U.S. ideological, legal, cultural, and institutional structure; scholarship must act to disrupt reigning notions of objectivity and neutrality, in part by privileging the epistemologies of people of Color through narrative and other methods; and productive societal transformation must take place through radical, rather than incremental, change (Bell, 1992; Crenshaw et al., 1995; Delgado & Stefancic, 2001; Matsuda et al., 1993; Valdes et al., 2002). CRT became an interdisciplinary scholarly movement and was introduced by Ladson-Billings and Tate (1995) to the field of education, where it gained traction (Dixson & Rousseau, 2006; Lynn & Parker, 2006; Parker, Deyhle, & Villenas, 1999).

Harris (1993), whose conceptualization of Whiteness as property was foundational to the movement, argues that in the early republic, U.S. racialized societal power arrangements were codified into law, and humanity was collapsed with rights. Property thus became a condition of humanity, not an object of marketplace exchange, not fungible. This collapse occurred through the reification of race as a signifier of humanity. In fact, Harris points out that in the law and in dominant philosophy, property is anything to which value is attached. Whiteness acquired a quality of property, exclusivity: what one owns, one can enjoy and does not have to share. Today, one of the most highly prized values of Whiteness and White institutions is the exclusive right to make meaning, to define truth and the social order. Like intellectual property, meaning-making property is not necessarily directly attached to material items but to the regimes of truth that determine and organize the material world. Meaning is produced through all dominant societal mechanisms. Chief among those in schooling, and acting most often in concert, are curricula, pedagogy, law, discipline, organization, and policy. For White institutions, this highly guarded, exclusive property is, in part, the right to construct Blackness as the subhuman, criminal, noncitizen antithetical to Whiteness. Exceptions to the rule only serve to prove the rule.

EMERGENCE OF A CONCEPTUAL FRAMEWORK FOR UNDERSTANDING INSTITUTIONAL GRIEF

Context, Data, and Methodology

Over the course of a year and a half that spanned 2008–2009, I conducted an ethnographic study at a school housed inside Lincoln Treatment Center, a prison for juvenile males located in the northeastern United States, and was part of a compulsory "treatment" program for the young men incarcerated there. Lincoln prison[1] was a high-security facility run by the state Division of Juvenile Affairs (DJA) and was designated to hold young men ages thirteen to twenty-one who carried sentences of six months or more and who were described as the state's "worst offenders." When I arrived, eighty young men were incarcerated at Lincoln; seventy-eight of them were African American or Black Latino/Afro-Caribbean and two were White. Most had sentences that well exceeded six months, had had their sentences extended while incarcerated, or were on their third or fourth stint in lockup. Significantly, these young men were from a larger metropolitan area whose population was over 50 percent White and in a state in which all youth of Color made up only approximately 20 percent of the juvenile population but over 60 percent of all incarcerated youth.

Teachers at Lincoln were White, young, and often not credentialed in their area of instruction. Moreover, the rate of teacher turnover was astronomical, such that when I arrived, the most senior-ranking teacher—a White man in his mid-twenties—had been at Lincoln for just two and a half years. The school's curricula were drawn loosely from local and state ninth-grade guidelines and were repeated so that young men incarcerated for six months or more or detained at multiple facilities consecutively encountered a recurring curriculum. For example, during the first several months I was at Lincoln, I noted that a number of the young men had previously been assigned and read materials for the language arts class—several of them multiple times.

The school was located on the first floor of the three-story prison building and was organized as a series of about ten small classrooms lining one side of a very long hallway. This layout allowed for surveillance camera and security staff viewing of the entire hallway at all times. Classroom doors remained closed, and inmates transitioned between classes through a complex security protocol. Security staff monitored all areas of the facility, including classrooms. Notably, while the teaching staff was White, security was staffed entirely by people of Color.

I negotiated entry into the DJA through a ten-month review process. Although I was initially interested in working primarily at a female juvenile facility, DJA senior personnel—all of whom were White—directed me to Lincoln. The full range of reasons for this decision was unavailable to me. My race, gender, and class location informed these negotiations and my role at Lincoln. Though I am mixed, or multiracial, my appearance is ambiguous. My institutional race in the northeastern United States in particular is unquestionably White. Moreover, my professional status as both a professor of education and a former high school English teacher, in conjunction with my gender-conforming female appearance, served to solidify that institutional race, as those are professions associated with White womanhood. So, in spite of DJA administrative concern about providing a long-term researcher access to the system, I received consistent cues that my race, gender, and profession made me admissible, even though not an insider.

Because my scholarly aims included understanding race institutionally (rather than as individual identity), in this context I allowed myself to be raced just as I raced others—in other words, I chose not to disrupt or complicate the process of racialization in any direction. In research contexts where inmates or security staff eventually inquired into my race (White participants never inquired), I answered transparently. However, while their understanding of me as mixed affected our individual relationships, such understandings had no impact on how race—mine or theirs—functioned institutionally.

My central aim was to undertake a critical race ethnography (Duncan, 2005; Vaught, 2011) to begin to map the institutional arrangements (Guinier & Torres, 2002; Smith, Miller-Kahn, Heinecke, & Jarvis, 2004; Stein, 2004) that produce both juvenile prison and prison schooling and the larger system of criminalization and racism in U.S. public schooling (Ferguson, 2000; Kim, Losen, & Hewitt, 2010; Lyons & Drew, 2006; Noguera, 2008). I did this through observations at Lincoln prison school, the DJA juvenile detention center, and other sites, and through interviews with inmates, security staff, teachers, principals, DJA administrators, police officers, family members, advocates, and community leaders. Additionally, I examined curricula, assisted young men with schoolwork, assisted in classes, and reviewed reports both inside Lincoln and at DJA.

I began my analyses of the data through the Whiteness as property framework (Harris, 1993). The various ways in which the young men incarcerated at Lincoln were both the property of the state DJA and White society, and tools in the construction and protection of Whiteness as property, were complicated but clear. For example, although according to DJA officials the most common charge carried by the young men was assault and battery *without* a weapon (a typical school or street fight),[2] I was told repeatedly that the young men were "dangerous," "predators," and "a threat." I was warned severely about my personal safety, and the overarching narrative around schooling within DJA was one of "safety." Capturing this elaborate contradiction, teachers in Lincoln school often made comments to me containing sentiments such as the following from my field notes:

> I asked if [the teacher] enjoyed his work, and he said, "Depends on the kids. I like my job more often than not. Every once in a while these kids make me enjoy the death penalty . . . 'cause every once in a while these kids will do something so fuckin' bad it warrants that."

This teacher defined the young men's behavior—which he left unnamed and undescribed—through a description of a punishment. In this way, he, like many of his colleagues, cast the young men at Lincoln as extraordinary criminals by conjuring punishments that assume a deserving offense. In other words, he drew on the state's most extreme punishment—execution—to depict the young men at Lincoln as the most extreme of predators and in so doing managed to avoid real discussion of the young men and the system that removed them from society. Additionally, this depiction of punishment cemented the boundary between Whiteness and civil society and Blackness and criminality.

Similarly, after I asked another teacher to explain to me why he thought almost all the young men incarcerated were youth of Color, he referred to "attitudes" and "drugs" and then explained by saying, "When I look at my students, I see kids who need to be locked up . . . They're just not ready to be in society." This and many similar comments were seemingly absurd, but were received convention within Lincoln. They were expressions of larger systems of belief that not only criminalized young Black and Brown men (Ferguson, 2000; Williams, 1987, 1995) but also mobilized that criminalization to deny the oppressive and often genocidal White structures that push young men of Color into prison (Casella, 2003; Meiners, 2007; Skiba & Knesting, 2001; Skiba, Michael, Nardo, & Peterson, 2002; Vaught, 2011; Wald & Losen, 2003). Those larger systems of belief were foundational to Whiteness as property. The young men were objectified and controlled through, in part, the labels of *crime* and *criminal* to produce the meaning-making boundaries against which civil, human Whiteness established its exclusive humanity and ostensible benevolence. This exercise in meaning making is central to the contemporary function of Whiteness as property. Therefore, as these examples illustrate, the young men's collective racial criminalization was a mechanism by which White society protected the propertied right to make meaning and, in so doing, protected the inheritance of the property of civic and civil humanity exclusively for its White children. Juvenile incarceration had to be understood by institutional members as obvious and necessary in spite and because of its primary function—to guard the racialized property of White children, whose very absence from the prison marked them as not criminal.

However, in analyzing these narratives and related policies and practices at Lincoln and across DJA, it became clear to me that the dynamics of racialized property alone did not explain the institutional practices that characterized property relations in the juvenile prison system and in the prison school. The use of the young men in the construction of race as property could be expected to result in extreme disengagement on the part of the White institution and its members. There is no obvious compelling interest for an oppressing group to act otherwise. Indeed, one might understand the work of domination, oppression, and/or genocide to be driven by a calculated, even if highly contradictory, disregard for the objects of its oppression. In fact, we witness this the world over. Concern—even though feigned—has not been central to many oppressive projects from slavery in the West Indies to the Holocaust. Furthermore, oppressing groups always maintain a justification for their violence, but not always a justification that hinges on benevolence toward the oppressed group(s). Yet, what I observed throughout DJA and within Lincoln was that the institution was seemingly *overly* involved and engaged in the destructive meaning making and practices illustrated above. Moreover, this overinvolvement was accompanied by a blanket discourse of White benevolence and support for criminalized youth.

I conceived of this pronounced institutional attachment to the objects of oppression as an ongoing unresolved grief around locking up children as a mechanism of Whiteness as property—a grief that was connected to institutional and structural Whiteness, not individual experience. This idea that what I was observing could be interpreted as institutional grief was further illuminated on a day that I spoke with a DJA education administrator. A White woman in her forties, she spoke to me ardently about a recent city police presentation to DJA administrators in which they used geographic information system maps to identify, by last name, the families from which they suggested the majority of juvenile crime emerged. It was known by some as the "criminal surname map," and, according to this administrator, the map enabled police to "trace all the juvenile crime, or you know, 85% of it really, to just a few—really just a small number—of families." It was a DNA mapping of the city that singled out specific "Black" and "Dominican" families as inherently criminal. "And with this map," explained the administrator, "we can—the police, and us—we can intervene, you know take the kids out of those family environments or at least be watching . . . Really powerful. That map was really powerful."

As she spoke, I noticed on her desk two framed photographs of her with White children. I did not ask if the children pictured were hers, but I did note the violent juxtaposition of her warm, smiling hug of White youth and her unrestrained excitement at removing youth of Color from their homes. I wrote in my field notes, "I cannot describe her reaction and the institutional practice of mapping crime onto racialized people as anything but grief." Here I did not and do not mean grief as used in common parlance when we individually describe the untenable sadness we experience when a loved one dies or a friend betrays us. And I did not mean *her* grief. Rather, I meant that the representation of middle-class White family life, institutionally protected and valorized, in concert with the narrative and mapping of institutionally targeted and criminal Black and Brown family life highlighted the larger institutional contradiction of valuing children.

She spoke of "treating" and "saving" the mapped youth and imprisoning children—an act of ideological, material, and physical violence on families and communities of Color. This contradiction was rife with grief, as it eviscerated any semblance of "juvenile justice." The creation of the map reproduced the contradiction, and the animation of the map as a meaning-making tool revealed it. The map and the institutional reaction to it captured the fundamental, unresolvable contradiction at the heart of Whiteness. I recognized this as grief. The collective or institution experiencing or characterized by grief is not necessarily a victim suffering the loss of power. By grief, I mean loss unattached to obvious sadness or vulnerability. This grief is attached to the inability to reconcile ideals, practices, and structures. While psychoanalytic theory would use this conceptualization of loss to explain the experience of an individual, I suggest here that this loss is an organizing mechanism of institutions that exist in the service of fundamental White societal principles. Juvenile prison systems are massive White institutional conglomerates that serve White propertied principles of exclusivity. Yet their mere existence concurrently signals the loss of the White principle of equality. Whiteness is consti-

157

tuted by contradictions, and those active contradictions mean that Whiteness is defined by permanent, irreconcilable loss and is therefore organized by the grief such loss produces. So, as an analytic tool, loss, or grief, can be mobilized to make sense of the affective ways in which White institutions organize themselves and function vis-à-vis dominated peoples and their own survival. The White DJA administrator above was not experiencing individual grief but was in fact describing how grief shaped the practices of DJA.

Melancholia and Grief: An Emerging Institutional Framework

As a result of these reflections, I began to explore what had been previously written about this idea of grief. In 1917, Freud published an essay on mourning and melancholia (Rickman, 1957). In it, he conceptualized mourning as a psychological process produced by loss, characterized by its finite trajectory and the individual's ability to ultimately release the object of loss and substitute it with another object and so culminating in the resolution of grief. Melancholia, he suggested, is the state of unresolved grief. He conceived of melancholia as a response to loss characterized by the inability or unwillingness to surrender the object of loss. In this state of psychic stasis, the individual—unable to let go—must find means to incorporate the lost object into her or himself. The melancholic individual psychologically consumes or devours the lost object—often a person to whom emotion was attached. In this way, the melancholic subject maintains the object as part of herself or himself—though as a ghostlike object that is utterly denied any subjectivity. Freud posited that this produces a split in the ego and that the internalized object or objects become the foundation of the superego, or conscience. Later, Freud considered how this might function on a collective, or cultural, level.

My cursory description of melancholia is just that. In quite complex and nuanced ways, scholars of culture have grappled with the psychoanalytic frame of melancholia. At the turn of the twenty-first century, scholars—particularly those in cultural and literary studies—took up this psychoanalytic frame of melancholia to help explain dynamics of race and sexuality (Bhabha, 1992; Cheng, 2001; Crimp, 2002; Eng, 2001; Eng & Han, 2000; Eng & Kazanjian, 2003; Mercer, 1991; Muñoz, 1997, 1999; Parikh, 2002). This analytical move produced scholarship around what Butler (in Bell, 1999) calls "culturally instituted forms of melancholia" (p. 170). In considering melancholic understandings of race via the racialized subject, Butler argues that a constitutive component of melancholia occurs when what the subject is "confronting is the loss of the loss . . . So it becomes an impossible referent, it becomes an impossible object of grief" (p. 171)—that is, *racial melancholia*.

Other scholars expand this notion of racial melancholia to characterize the melancholic relationship between and among the racialized subject/object and Whiteness (Cheng, 2001). Authors have fully or partially deployed a melancholic frame to consider complex postcolonial racial power dynamics, often

through the cultural or artistic representations by which Blackness is reproduced as an object of White male cultural power, fear, and desire, and as a
consumed and constitutive signifier of loss for postcolonial subjects (Bhabha,
1992; Mercer, 1991; Muñoz, 1997). Considering scholarship on melancholia
and immigration and assimilation (Eng & Han, 2000), Cheng (2001) explored
and expanded on the melancholic function of assimilation in Asian American
cultural and literary tropes. According to Cheng (2001), "melancholia alludes
not to loss per se but to the entangled relationship with loss" (p. 8). Cheng was
concerned primarily with the experience of racial melancholia by people of
Color, and more specifically with Asian American struggles with racial power
dynamics. As such, she was interested in the melancholic loss produced by
one's inevitable engagement with Whiteness and Whites.

These illustrations represent just a fraction of the rich body of scholarship
exploring the psychic dynamics of cultural interaction through the framework
of melancholia. Cultural and literary studies have long-standing theoretical
psychoanalytic traditions out of which these complex analyses emerge. My
aim here is not to capture or contribute to that conversation but, instead, to
borrow the scaffold of melancholia to begin to analyze dominant *institutional*
structures within the field of education. I am cognizant that psychoanalysis and
psychoanalytic frameworks are widely contested and thoughtfully disputed. My
coordination here is not with the practice of psychoanalysis but, rather, with
the explanatory framework that might inform affective institutional analyses.
In particular, I am bringing to bear a framework that maps collective, systemic
psychic mechanisms onto institutional organizations and systems of power.
I am interested here in mapping the superego of the society's structure—in
particular, a kind of systemic melancholia that works to shape dominant institutions. Specifically, I am interested in how the foundational contradictions
inherent in White racist loss and grief affectively shape institutions. So in this
initial foray, I construct an institutional conceptualization of melancholia that
is grounded in Whiteness as property (Harris, 1993).

Envisioning an Institutional Form of White Racist Melancholia

Institutions, including prisons and schools, have created and maintained
Whiteness as property in part through an incessant process of discursively creating sense out of nonsense, reconciling the irreconcilable: only some humans
are human; people are inherently free and people can be owned; freedom *and*
slavery are fundamental to the nation; and so on. The right to make meaning
is a cornerstone of the way Whiteness exists within these institutions and but-
tresses its ongoing legally and culturally protected status as an exclusive form
of property. But what shapes the process of propertied meaning making? The
institutional form of White racial melancholia, or what I call *institutional racist melancholia*, describes the structural psychic, or affective, underpinnings of
Whiteness as property within institutions. As a partial description of White-

ness, institutional racist melancholia conceptually suggests that the irreconcilability of dominant meaning making creates an unresolvable institutional grief.

INSTITUTIONAL RACIST MELANCHOLIA: NARRATIVE FUNCTIONS

School (In)Equality

In the construction of the White nation, the declaration of freedom *from* subjugation to England was *for* freedom to subjugate: to create a slave state (Cheng, 2001). This declaration of independence contained an unresolvable contradiction: the ideals of freedom were predicated on the denial of freedom and as such could never be reconciled. In their construction of independence, Whites lost the truth of independence. Such loss is absolute and becomes the basis of all national narratives. It becomes unresolved discursive grief—a form of institutional racist melancholia.

In the realm of education, this melancholia is reflected in the dominant narrative that characterized pre–*Brown v. Board* Black society as "separate but equal," rather than *subordinate and disenfranchised,* vis-à-vis White society, schools, and other institutions. The White legal and systemic correction of this melancholic narrative was equally melancholic, as it borrowed from other ideologies situated in grievous irreconcilability: meritocracy and the American Dream, among others. Ostensibly integrated schools measured equality through narratives, policy, and organization of access rather than outcomes. As a result, dismantling the melancholic structures and narratives of "separate but equal" did nothing to dismantle inequity in schooling and society. Nor did it challenge dominant narratives around Blackness.

This specious narrative of equal access is codified into law in many ways. For example, Crenshaw (1988) writes that antidiscrimination law is characterized by two viewpoints: "The expansive view stresses equality as a result and looks to real consequences for African-Americans . . . The restrictive vision, which exists side by side with this expansive view, treats equality as a process, downplaying the significance of actual outcomes" (pp. 1341–1342). The restrictive view of law and society protects Whiteness as property by discursively and organizationally protecting White institutions, and elides the possibility for structural equity. Applying this to the educational context, school itself goes unchallenged, as long as the front door of the school building is ostensibly open to all. Once inside that front door, children of Color are meritocratically made responsible for their success or failure. Yet, restrictive equality not only describes the structuring of Whiteness as property into our institutions but also signals an irreconcilability that is not fully explained by the dominant failure to comprehend expansive equality. In fact, restrictive equality is explicitly shaped by institutional racist melancholia. The racist melancholic institutional narrative of school equality relies on the precarious balancing of freedom and oppression. The concept of Whiteness cannot reconcile the fantasy of freedom with the lifeblood of oppression. There is no Whiteness without the story of liberty and justice. There is no Whiteness without supremacy over Blackness (Bell, 1987; Bonilla-Silva, 2005; Gotanda, 1991; Harris, 1993; Leonardo, 2004). As such, restrictive equality in schooling allows for the narrative stability of justice, democracy, and freedom (Vaught, 2011). Moreover, it supports the defining feature of Whiteness: supremacy. Whiteness maintains its superiority as citizen (read: human) as constructed singularly against the concocted failure of Blackness to attain citizenship (and so humanity) (Williams, 1991). Narratives of the racialized culture of poverty, such as the Moynihan Report and No Child Left Behind, flourish.

This institutional narrative reflects the racist melancholic mechanisms by which the subjects—White society and its constructed institutions—cannot release their object of grief. Black Americans become the embodiment—in flesh, as a political organ, as imagined and real culture, and so on—of irretrievably lost freedom, justice, and truth. White narratives must consume the Black Other to construct narratives that somehow maintain both Blackness and freedom in order to maintain the White national superego. Explicitly, the superego—the conscience, the moral faculty meant to restrict or repress immoral predilections and desires—telescoped to a societal context reflects the formal and informal White policing institutions (law, law enforcement, schooling, and prison, among others) that both mediate and create racist melancholic narratives. The way in which these narratives are embedded in Whiteness as property allows the naturalization of oppression through the purchasing power vested in exclusive humanity. Because melancholia, unlike mourning, is infinite, the object of loss must be both incorporated and denied. Specifically, Winant (2001) writes, the "world racial system will therefore simultaneously incorporate and deny the rights, and in some cases the very existence, of the 'others' whose recognition was only so recently and incompletely conceded" (p. 35). In melancholia then, there is, as Cheng (2001) writes, a "slip from *recognizing* to *naturalizing* injury" (p. 5). Recognition would necessitate other recognitions—of racial subjectivity, for example—that in turn necessitate the recognition of irreconcilable ideals and practices. This naturalization of racial injury is both produced and confirmed through multiple institutional structures and is revealed in the melancholic narrative production and representation of those structures.

State as Parent

In a society organized by property, children have no independent rights (Williams, 1991). They cannot purchase or protect their propertied rights. In fact, these rights are always activated and navigated by proxy—by the propertied "parent." The parent, writ large, is not an isolated agent but a representative of a propertied collective. In some cases, this might be the individual White parent of the individual White child who can generally mobilize her exclusive property to promote her vested interest in her child's property value. Take, for instance, the case of *Parents Involved in Community Schools v. Seattle School District No. 1* (2007; Vaught, 2011; Dumas, 2011). The propertied White Seattle parent of a White child felt that she and her White child (and by extension other White children) should not have to lose their exclusive right to access to and control over the public education system as they wished—to go to the school of her "choice." Indeed, she interpreted the infringement of her rights—the trespassing on her property—as originating in the district's consideration of student race as a tie-breaking factor in assigning students to "oversubscribed" schools. In the case of oversubscription (too many students ranking a certain school as their school of choice), the race of the students was considered in an effort to make the district's schools racially "balanced"—that is, reflecting the racial percentages of the district at large and broken down only by "White" and "non-White." Such consideration of race, the argument of the White plaintiff went, gave unfair preference to children of Color and resulted in the denial of her son's White property rights. The Supreme Court's definitive determinations against the consideration of student race (i.e., against the most minimal recognition of students of Color and against recognition of any structural racism) safeguarded the property rights of White parents via their children, and vice versa, in a seemingly impenetrable vault. Clarence Thomas buried the key to that vault when he crafted his argument in large part around the claim that the dissent in *Parents Involved* was using the same strategies and discourse of the "segregationists" in the *Brown* case (*Parents Involved*, 2007).

While this convoluted White narrative and resulting White policies and legal precedent were many things—false, anti-affirmative action (Lawrence & Matsuda, 1997; Yosso, Parker, Solórzano, & Lynn, 2004), and color-blind (Gotanda, 1991; Haney López, 2007)—they also took on the shape of melancholic fantasy. Children of Color, Black children in particular, were invisible objects narratively and truly consumed by the school, the courts, and White parents and then resurrected as objects of threat in the White debate around schooling and equity. White society—the White mother protecting her child's property, the White court valorizing her righteousness and admonishing the district, and the White district determining its own policies in relation to students of Color who were being failed miserably in its schools—raised the specter of the Black child and bandied it about alternately as the specter of threat and the specter of need. The ghost of the Black child was violently used as bait to chum the swampy waters of propertied racial conflict among Whites. This conflict is foundational to the existence of Whiteness. Without the consumed, object Black child, the White child, and his guarantee to exclusive educational rights, does not exist. A thing is not exclusively owned unless there is some Other that does not or cannot own it. The generational racial wealth of Whiteness relies on the very endangerment and degradation but maintenance of Blackness that shapes the indicators of propertied White schooling—the achievement gap (Berlak, 2001), disproportionate discipline (Casella, 2003; Fenning & Rose, 2007; Skiba & Knesting, 2001), and so on. This racist melancholic condition of dependence on and oppression of Blackness is manifest in the desperate White institutional narratives that mechanize keeping Black youth alive and extrasocietal. The narrative function contributes to the two primary functions of institutional racist melancholia: elaborate explanations or justifications for oppression and assertions of benevolence in oppressive acts.

Where were the actual Black children in Seattle? Where were the actual Black families? First, as Bell (2004) points out, Black families and communities are not party to the construction of education policy, so any policy benefit is fortuitous and any lack of benefit is held to no account. But also, there is the shape of that mechanism of Whiteness as property. Structurally, the White state is and always has been the usurping "parent" of Black children. This was codified into law early in the nation, when the condition of the Black child was linked to her or his mother while the condition of the White child was linked to her or his father. The Black child was linked to her or his mother to guarantee not only the continuation of slavery through the reproductive and other control of Black women, but also the perpetuation of Whiteness as property through the Black woman's body. Black slave women's children were the literal property of White men and therefore of the White state that legally organized and supported slavery. And, they were melancholic ghosts of the White state's construction.

Black children today continue to have their "condition" linked to the White legal, institutional, and narrative status of their mothers. This is evidenced in various welfare policies (Augustin, 1997), health-care policy and practice, school organization (Blanchett, 2006; Vaught, 2009), and juvenile prison (Ayers, 1997). In a racist patriarchy, this ensures their subhumanity, their three-fifths condition, their absolute melancholic structural liminality. Children of Color are simultaneously never propertied and always the object cornerstone of Whiteness as property through various institutional paternal proxies. The White state as parent to the child of Color is profoundly melancholic, practicing a widespread structural infanticide while claiming such practice is in the best interest of its child. Child prison is the ultimate institutional expression of White state parenting of Black children. In true institutional racist melancholic form, the White state parent constructs a narrative of paternal benevolence that seeks to positively and morally explain the oppression of child incarceration.

"Treatment" of Prisoners: White Benevolence Narratives

The racist melancholic narrative construction of juvenile prison in many U.S. states is that of "treatment." The appropriate punishment of the criminal in Euro-White societies has long been a question of moral and political debate (Loury, 2008). In describing the history of this controversial issue, Foucault (1995) writes, "The day was to come, in the nineteenth century, when this 'man,' discovered in the criminal, would become the target of penal intervention, the object that it claimed to correct and transform" (p. 74). Echoing that moral position, many proponents of juvenile incarceration during portions of the twentieth century conceived of such imprisonment variously as correction, treatment, and rehabilitation (Ayers, 1997; Loury, 2008). In the United States, such conceptualizations of juvenile prison are always linked to racial meaning making. Young men of Color are narratively cast and legally codified as criminals (Ferguson, 2000; Noguera, 2008; Williams, 1995) resulting in and melancholically explaining away wildly disproportionate rates of arrest and incarceration (Alexander, 2010). Therefore, the criminal to be treated or rehabilitated is a young man of Color, and he is most often conceived of in the dominant narrative as Black.

Yet, juvenile prisons are state-run facilities in which young criminalized men are locked in against their will, without property defense against the state, without reprieve, where they are monitored and controlled incessantly and are punished with "civil death" (Meiners, 2007). Civil death is achieved through the denial of formal civil rights and informal markers of civil life: employment, housing, social status, etc. Thus, civil death transforms young men of Color into extra-societal ghosts who must exist for the binary-dependent existence of young White citizens. Their incarceration is a process of White institutional consumption by which the White superego of freedom and civilization flourishes. The maintenance of young men of Color as living ghosts—zombies of the White world—underwrites the ongoing narrative of liberty, justice, and White supremacy. In this way, the incarceration of young men of Color upholds the meaning-making authority of Whiteness, an exclusive and potent property. *It does so by structuring melancholy into the dominant societal narratives and the institutions those narratives describe.* As Cheng (2001) mentions, such injury is normalized. Here I suggest it is normalized through the frenetic stasis of institutional racist melancholia.

Treatment is contingent on the freedom, agency, and humanity of the treated subject. But Black and Brown children cannot be subjects of White institutions. They are, by definition, objects (Bell, 2004). This objectification is fundamental to the survival of Whiteness. In detailing the historical evolution of Whiteness as property, Harris (1993) writes that slavery

> produced a peculiar, mixed category of property and humanity—a hybrid possessing inherent instabilities that were reflected in its treatment and ratification by the law. The dual and contradictory character of slaves as property and persons was exemplified in the Representation Clause of the Constitution. Representation in the House of Representatives was apportioned on the basis of population computed by counting all persons and "three-fifths of all other persons"—slaves. (pp. 1718–1719)

To create so-called democratic processes founded on liberty and equality, White power brokers had to devise narratives that would make sense of other nonsensical narratives and the institutional practices they described. If freedom and representation describe the citizens of the United States, thereby designating them human, and if all men are created equal, how can men be slaves and be the property of other men? As Whiteness as property worked out its exclusive particularities, it did so in the shape of institutional racist melancholia. Rather than designate Black people who were enslaved as *non*human, Whites chose to designate them as *sub*human. This effort to reconcile slavery and humanity produced the absolute legal and institutional structure within which Black people were consumed objects. They were liminally suspended through the White construction of humanity because they were consumed into the institutional corporeal body of White society, signifying untenable boundaries of humanity, freedom, and equality. If Black people could neither be constitutionally nor institutionally alive or dead, human or nonhuman, then their structural position was organized by ghostlike stasis, moved at the melancholic whim of the oppressive White structure as it variously interpreted and interprets the object of its consumption. Like a ghost, their object status is neither dead nor inanimate. The melancholic process of consumption produces subhuman liminality. The construction of Black subhumanity is essentially irreconcilable but is fundamental to the existence of White society.

INSTITUTIONAL RACIST MELANCHOLIA: RACIST MELANCHOLIC NARRATIVES AT LINCOLN TREATMENT CENTER SCHOOL

In order to ground this institutional racist melancholia in tangible illustrations, I return to my discussion of the Lincoln prison school. This discussion of institutional racist melancholia and Whiteness as property is meant to connect the abstract theorizations above to more concrete explications. In particular, the explorations here generate an initial conversation out of which a more detailed understanding of the frame might occur.

The Narrative of "Treatment"

The narrative subhumanization of the young men incarcerated at Lincoln was frequent and consistent. I was told succinctly by Lincoln prison administrators that "these are not kids. These are predators." This subhumanization took on many forms, from animalization to criminalization. For example, when I was first escorted into the prison by the interim principal, as one heavy metal door shut behind us and we stood in the liminal space between doors, between the unlocked world and the prison, the interim principal jingled his large key ring and said, "Welcome to the jungle." Such practices consistently positioned the young men as extra-civil beings, meant to give ethereal shape to the space beyond the rigid boundaries of racialized humanity.

Within this context, prisoners were "treated." This racist melancholia was intrinsic to the institutional narratives around youth incarceration in the state. Juvenile prisons were called "treatment" centers or facilities; and when I referred to them as "prisons," I was met with rebuff by state authorities and correction from youth legal advocates and scholars with whom I interacted at external sites, such as advocacy group meetings and universities. In one interview, the DJA director described the state's practices solely as a form of treatment and recognized any issues or concerns only within this framework. So, the circumscribed salient question for the director was, "How can we better serve the populations committed or remanded to our custody?" The melancholic elision of state-produced structural oppression was absolute—again, the White institution leveraged its propertied right to own meaning, to enjoy its permutations, and to exclude others from its production and use.

The young men at Lincoln Treatment Center became commodities of melancholic exchange on the marketplace of White meaning. This commodification was complex. It did not appear simply in the external abject objectification that might be conjured by concepts such as property. However, property here has been collapsed with humanity, and the purchase of meaning does not occur in an abstract marketplace but within the emotive faculties of society—institutions. And, because, as I am suggesting, affective features are integral to Whiteness as property, and because those features are melancholic, the commodification of persons in the process of buttressing racialized property rights is deeply objectifying in an entangled way. The tension between subhuman and nonhuman, rather than their stark categorization, is the site at which racist melancholia sits. This is a site of oppressive irreconcilability. Subhumanity calls for partial recognition, but that recognition is granted by the subject force, which means the grantee is already an object in the construction of the subject—a lifeblood referent. The grantee is consumed in the desperate effort toward resolution, but melancholia is defined by the impossibility of resolution. Therefore, White law, ideology, and institutional practice make Black Americans simultaneously subhuman and a commodity. The paradox that arises is the paradox that preceded the practice: White racism is a contradiction for and constitutive fact of Whiteness.

One young man I worked with, Anthony, explained that he was locked up for beating up his mother's boyfriend. He arrived home to his mother's Section 8 apartment one night to find that she was being severely beaten by her boyfriend. He defended her and beat down the man. Consequently, he was incarcerated for almost two years. On release, he was forced to plea as a "menace to society" and was denied even a visit to his mother's apartment, lest she lose her lease. Criminals cannot return to Section 8 housing. The boyfriend did, however. Anthony was released from prison at eighteen years old a civil ghost: jobless, homeless, and without a high school diploma (as the prison refused to administer a GED program). He was a commodity for building the White architecture of who is a menace and who is a member, who is an object (consumed and denied) and who is human.

Rather than simply designate Anthony a menace, the White institutions undertook "treatment" of Anthony to engage in seeming benevolence because their mechanisms of property are driven by racist melancholia. Echoing other young men, Anthony said to me, "All this 'workin' on your treatment,' it's all fake. This ain't no treatment." Yet in an act of institutional racist melancholia, the state engaged in both denying and devouring Anthony within its system of supposed treatment. Anthony became both the spectral object of purchase of fictive White benevolence and the boundary-making object of denial in the melancholic dynamic of unresolved grief around impossible contradictions. In support of the reigning narrative, Anthony was both treated and made a menace to society, an extrasocietal ghost simultaneously absorbed and denied by the practice of institutional racist melancholia.

Treatment was compulsory and administered by young, White, female clinicians. According to the young men and teachers at Lincoln, treatment stridently and exclusively emphasized inmate "anger." One young man said of the clinicians what many other young men echoed:

> They look for certain things and don't look at the whole picture. They think everything's an anger problem . . . A lot of them, they try to figure out what's wrong with you. They sum it up to, "Oh, so you caught this charge. Reason you caught this charge is 'cause you was angry."

Importantly, the treatment constructed and drew on a myopic melancholic narrative of Black pathology. By pretending to treat anger (thereby assuming anger is both a pathology and a source of pathologic behavior), clinicians contributed to narratives of rage that completely eclipsed structural oppression—a real source of undeniable and important rage.

Treatment normalizes pathology and so normalizes the injuries inflicted by White supremacy. It assumes that there is an illness in need of treatment. When young men of Color agree to their pathology—"I am a menace to society"—they are released. They must accept the narrative categorization that permanently affixes to them their subhuman status. Narratives of pathology alleviate White institutions (e.g., racialized poverty, racist schooling) not only of critique but, more importantly, of existence. Structural inequality and racial oppression disappear under the narrative force of *treatment*. What emerges instead is the illusion of White state benevolence. Institutional racist melancholia functions through the grief-driven control and consumption of the racial Other, and the object invention of that Other as part of the foundation of the structural superego of White America. Here, young men of Color are constructed as criminals, as antithetical to what is White, civilized, and good. Therefore, their incarceration for *fighting* becomes a pathologically logical expression of institutional grief.

As we discussed treatment, a Lincoln inmate said to me, "It don't never help, if you lock somebody up. Letting me out would help. Jobs would help." Said another inmate, "Take away somebody's freedom, not going to change them." But taking away illusive and elusive freedom is precisely the end goal of racist melancholic institutional narratives, because by denying Black and Brown freedom, they affirm Whiteness as property. Moreover, they affirm this property while maintaining the façade of benevolence. Treatment is the melancholic entanglement with the unfree, consumed Other. It is the exercise of nonsense that makes sense inside the closed loop of institutional racist melancholia.

Williams (1987) alludes to the practiced violent amnesia and dishonesty of this institutional racist melancholic injury. She details the dynamics following the incident in which White Bernard Goetz shot (with an unregistered firearm) and injured four young Black teenagers on a New York City subway because one of the young men approached Goetz to ask him for five dollars. At trial, Goetz was found guilty only of firearms possession violations. Williams (1987) writes:

> In the process of devaluing its image of black people, the general white population seems to have been socialized to blind itself to the horrors inflicted by white people. One of the clearest examples of the mechanics of this socialized blindness is the degree to which the public and the media in New York repeatedly and relentlessly bestialized Goetz' victims. Images of the urban jungle, of young black men filling the role of "wild animals," were favorite journalistic constructions. Young white urban professionals were mythologized, usually wrapped in the rhetorical apparel of lambs or sheep, as the tender, toothsome prey. The corollary to such imagery is that the fate of those domesticated white innocents is to be slaughtered in confrontation, the dimensions of which thus become meaninglessly and tragically sacrificial. Locked into such a reification, no act of the sheep against the wolves can ever be seen as violent in its own right, because active sheep are so *inherently* uncharacteristic, so brave, so irresistibly and triumphantly parabolic. (p. 152)

The young White women who "treated" the prisoners at Lincoln and the young White men and women who "taught" them were cast not only as innocents (sheep) but also as altruistic ambassadors of White society. Their imagined selflessness in the face of incessantly constructed criminality worked in lockstep to secure the logic of that one master narrative. The real-world implications for the young men incarcerated at Lincoln (wolves) were many and far reaching. One of those was that "anger" was used by the clinicians as a rationale to extend inmate sentences, and the clinicians were able to act individually, without judicial process or review, to extend sentences. This occurred in spite of the fact that the young men had a right to legal representation and review. However, not one of the young men I encountered understood that this right existed, let alone knew how to go about accessing it. So those in charge of delivering treatment in fact capriciously and extrajudiciously extended incarceration of youth. The White melancholically produced narrative of anger resulted in the frequent extension of inmate sentences, and most of the young men with whom I spoke were serving prison terms far longer than their original sentences. This process could have been seen as rampant institutionalized violence, as indeed it was. Instead, the paternalistic White melancholic context legitimized extended incarceration as necessary for "treatment."

Racist Melancholic Structures at Lincoln: Extracivil Ghosts and Paternalism

Institutional racist melancholic paternalism was practiced with precision through the "no touch" and "security" policies of the Lincoln prison. The following counternarrative (Ladson-Billings, 2000; Solórzano & Yosso, 2002) is composed of sections drawn directly from my field notes. It highlights some of the racist melancholic functions inherent in the practice of Whiteness as property at Lincoln and in relation to young Black men in society. This narrative is offered as an illustration of how scholars might consider data in relation to the emerging frame of institutional racist melancholia.

One winter morning, before making the trip to Lincoln prison, I sat to read the news online and came across a headline indicating that the killers of a young, middle school student had been apprehended. As I read, I understood that the arrests of the three indicated were based on what the police euphemistically called "community tips." And, as I read further, I saw the name of a young man incarcerated at Lincoln: Desmond.[3] Though he was a teenager and had not faced any judicial process in the case, he was being charged as an adult and his name was printed in the paper. I was certain that, with an adult charge, Desmond would be immediately transferred out of Lincoln, a juvenile facility.

Later, when I arrived at Lincoln, the principal told me that the police had arrived early during the first period of classes and had handcuffed Desmond and walked him out of the building, without any of his belongings and with no goodbyes. I asked how Desmond's best friend, Ricky, was holding up, and the principal sort of shrugged, because he and I both knew the answer to my question. From the principal's office, I walked into the long school hallway. I saw Ricky sitting in a chair, his head in his hands and his knees against the wall.

Lincoln was governed by a DJA, statewide no-touch policy. In other words, no adult was to touch an inmate, and no inmate could touch another inmate. No handshakes, no high-fives, no pats on the back, no hugs. No touch. This policy was accompanied by a more complicated policy that forbade all adults from discussing with the inmates any topic that might cause them upset.

Ricky had just lost his best friend. Being marched out in handcuffs by the police is a death. For fifteen-year-old Ricky, Desmond was gone forever. Desmond and Ricky had helped one another in the longest of minutes and hours and days and in the absence of mothers they missed, younger siblings they yearned to care for and play with, and freedom. Ricky was in grief and alone. There was no security guard in the part of the hall where Ricky sat, no clinician, no teacher. So I walked up to Ricky, my back to the security camera, and asked quietly if he was okay. He didn't speak and barely moved. Then I said, "I'm really sorry." Ricky sniffled. My words were meaningless in the face of his grief. So I carefully touched his back. And, then, he looked up. The injury in his expression was complete. He said, "I'm so sad."

The state, Ricky's racially propertied parent, was working to continuously crush Ricky's spirit by removing or destroying, one by one, each person and experience

169

that gives a child life and hope. My fleeting and meager efforts to support Ricky were a violation of state policy. And when I entered the classroom outside of which Ricky sat and the young men whose table I joined quietly and with concern asked me if I knew what happened and if Ricky was okay in the hallway, I was reported to the warden by the teacher for talking with the inmates about possibly upsetting subjects. My access to the prison was reviewed, and I was given a first and only warning. Ricky was left alone.

This counternarrative to juvenile "justice" and "treatment" certainly reflects only a fraction of the brutal psychological and social conditions faced by incarcerated youth. The force of isolation at Lincoln was unquestionably extreme. This story of the no-touch policy also captures the ways in which institutional racist melancholia functioned in the larger system of Whiteness as property. The young, Black middle school student who was a victim of a murder over one year earlier was valorized in the press as an honors student, a respectful and wonderful son at home, and a great friend to all he encountered. As a middle school student, he was also characterized as young—a quality suggestive of innocence and one never afforded the inmates (regardless of their age) or *living* Black middle school boys. There are no young Black men; there are no innocent prisoners; there are no young prisoners. Only dead is the Black child afforded the possibility of the innocence and value that inhere nearly uniformly in living White children. Only dead is the young Black man touchable—deserving of empathy, concern, and support. This is particularly true when he is the supposed victim of another Black male child. The living Black male child is the melancholically consumed ghost of White ownership of what is civil and civic. The living Black male child is the object spectacle to distract from the culturally genocidal White institutions of schooling, labor, health, law, and so on that collude to result in the conditions that make the shooting death of a Black middle school child so possible in the United States (Williams, 1987). The living Black child is an untouchable. The no-touch policy reveals the architecture of institutional racist melancholia. Specifically, it illustrates the blueprint by which denial and consumption function in White institutional contexts.

For a "free" and "democratic" society to so endanger its children, it must enact the irreconcilable. It must paternalistically degrade the racial Other and offer its criminal youth "treatment" through the absolute denial of freedom. There must be young Black killers, and there must be young Black killed. The constructed dynamic of such crime protects the democratic infrastructure of Whiteness as property that is in fact a house of cards. "Indeed," writes Cheng (2001), "melancholia offers a powerful critical tool precisely because it theoretically *accounts* for the guilt and the denial of guilt, the blending of shame and omnipotence in the racist imaginary" (p. 12). Institutional racist melancholia must normalize the injury of street violence and state violence to allow Whiteness to survive.

Institutional racist melancholia forms the affective map of Whiteness as property. Lincoln Treatment Center itself could not be located on any map, print, or satellite. It was a ghost edifice in the heart of the highly mapped White world. The young men in it were corporeally consumed into the belly of Whiteness and projected out as objects of newspaper articles, state reports, policy meetings, and even activist organization work. As such objects, they were mobilized to maintain the superego of White society. They were both buried subjects and hypervisible objects consumed to continuously form and reform the antithetical barriers to the highly exclusive property that is White humanity. This objectification and object-consumption/production institutionally patterned the racist melancholia shaped by the White *loss* of humanity as it attempted to define rights by denying them in others, valorize freedom by refusing it to others, and make exclusive what fundamentally cannot be: humanity.

CONCLUSION

Institutional racist melancholia cements the relationship between loss and the ongoing creation of loss. Unresolved grief is created and recreated in order to evade the irreconcilable foundational grief of Whiteness. Whiteness as property—its exclusive grip on humanity—requires the presence of the subhuman, objectified, consumed Black Other. In addition, it requires faith in its own myths—justice and freedom for all, among others. Prison schooling is not an isolated location of institutional racist melancholia. Institutional racist melancholia is foundational to White institutions and can be conceptually mobilized to analyze the narratives, policies, and practices of schooling and related institutions.

In this article I have used the psychoanalytic frame of melancholia to help map the institutional topography of grief onto the structural frame of Whiteness as property, to understand how institutional narratives and practices are infused with and informed by collective affective forces. This application of a psychoanalytic concept to a structural analysis has rich implications for education research. By engaging psychoanalytic frames in structural analyses, scholars may begin to better understand the shape of the particular mechanisms of social and cultural reproduction of race, class, gender, and other categories of analysis. While structural frames are powerful tools for explicating with detail the mechanisms of power in schooling, they have the potential to become even more illuminating when functioning in concert with affective frames. The resulting richness and complexity of such a theoretical dialogue could better help us understand, describe, challenge, and transform inequitable structures. For example, here I examined the policy and practice of prison treatment through the combined analytic lens of property and melancholia. One resulting implication is that challenges to such policies and practices must strategize identifications and disruptions of the vulnerable mechanisms of DJA. These disruptions cannot simply refer to law or justice or equality but must also target melancholic productions and exercises.

NOTES

1. It is important to note that the state did not refer to any of its locked facilities as "prisons" and that I have chosen this term. My choice to refer to Lincoln as a prison and the young men as prisoners, not "residents," is meant to reflect the real material, ideological, and political conditions of incarceration that were as present at Lincoln as they are at any prison in the United States, and that are in fact defining features of prison and imprisonment.

2. I want to note that my discussion of charges is itself problematic, because the statement of an offense both reifies the truth of that offense and, in the Foucauldian sense, creates the reality of the offender. While it is not within the purview of this article to elaborate both the speciousness of specific charges and fallaciousness of the mechanisms by which these charges are produced and attached to discipline, I do wish to make note of this problem. Furthermore, I contend that even the more obvious "crimes"—murder, manslaughter, robbery—were narratively and ideologically decoupled from the social, material conditions of systemic racism and poverty that contextualized the lives of *all* young men incarcerated at Lincoln, thereby rendering them meaningful only in their utility in forming racialized and gendered categories of criminal and not in understanding individual decision making or circumstances.

3. I later noted that while Desmond's name and the unverified accusations against him were printed without his consent in the paper, another family could not afford the cost of an obituary in that same paper for a young Lincoln inmate who was murdered shortly after his release.

REFERENCES

Alexander, M. (2010). *The new Jim Crow: Mass incarceration in the age of colorblindness.* New York: New Press.

Augustin, N. A. (1997). Learnfare and Black motherhood: The social construction of deviance. In A. K. Wing (Ed.), *Critical race feminism: A reader* (pp. 144–150). New York: New York University Press.

Ayers, W. (1997). *A kind and just parent.* Boston: Beacon Press.

Bell, D. (1987). *And we are not saved: The elusive quest for racial justice.* New York: Basic Books.

Bell, D. (1992). *Faces at the bottom of the well: The permanence of racism.* New York: Basic Books.

Bell, D. (2004). *Silent covenants:* Brown v. Board of Education *and the unfulfilled hopes for racial reform.* Oxford: Oxford University Press.

Bell, V. (1999). On speech, race and melancholia: An interview with Judith Butler. *Theory, Culture and Society, 16*(2), 163–174.

Berlak, H. (2001). Race and the achievement gap. *Rethinking Schools Online, 15,* 10–11. Retrieved from http://www.rethinkingschools.org

Bhabha, H. K. (1992). Postcolonial authority and postmodern guilt. In L. Grossberg, C. Nelson, and P. Treichler (Eds.), *Cultural Studies* (pp. 56–66). New York: Routledge.

Blanchett, W. (2006). Disproportionate representation of African American students in special education: Acknowledging the role of White privilege and racism. *Educational Researcher, 35*(6), 24–28.

Bonilla-Silva, E. (2005). "Racism" and "new racism": The contours of racial dynamics in contemporary America. In Z. Leonardo (Ed.), *Critical pedagogy and race* (pp. 1–36). Malden, MA: Blackwell.

Casella, R. (2003, Fall). Punishing dangerousness through preventive detention: Illustrating the institutional link between school and prison. *New Directions for Youth Development, 99,* 55–70.

Cheng, A. A. (2001). *The melancholy of race: Psychoanalysis, assimilation, and hidden grief.* New York: Oxford University Press.

Crenshaw, K. (1988). Race, reform, and retrenchment: Transformation and legitimation in antidiscrimination law. *Harvard Law Review, 101*(7), 1331–1387.

Crenshaw, K., Gotanda, N., Peller, G., & Thomas, K. (Eds.). (1995). *Critical race theory: The key writings that formed the movement.* New York: New Press.

Crimp, D. (2002). *Melancholia and moralism: Essays on AIDS and queer politics.* Cambridge, MA: MIT Press.

Delgado, R., & Stefancic, J. (2001). *Critical race theory: An introduction.* New York: New York University Press.

Dixson, A., & Rousseau, C. (2006). *Critical race theory in education: All God's children got a song.* New York: Routledge.

Dumas, M. J. (2011). A cultural political economy of school desegregation in Seattle. *Teachers College Record, 113*(4), 703–744.

Duncan, G. (2005). Critical race ethnography in education: Narrative, inequality and the problem of epistemology. *Race Ethnicity and Education, 8*(1), 93–114.

Eng, D. (2001). *Racial castration: Managing masculinity in Asian America.* Durham, NC: Duke University Press.

Eng, D. & Han, S. (2000). A dialogue on racial melancholia. *Psychoanalytic Dialogues, 10*(4), 667–700.

Eng, D. & Kazanjian, D. (Eds.) (2003). *Loss: The politics of mourning.* Berkeley: University of California Press.

Fenning, P., & Rose, J. (2007). Overrepresentation of African American students in exclusionary discipline: The role of school policy. *Urban Education, 42*(6), 536–559.

Ferguson, A. A. (2000). *Bad boys: Public schools in the making of black masculinity.* Ann Arbor: University of Michigan Press.

Foucault, M. (1995). *Discipline and punish: The birth of the prison* (2nd ed.). New York: Vintage Books.

Gotanda, N. (1991). A critique of "our constitution is color-blind." *Stanford Law Review, 44*(1), 1–68.

Guinier, L. (1994). *The tyranny of the majority: Fundamental fairness in representative democracy.* New York: Free Press.

Guinier, L., & Torres, G. (2002). *The miner's canary: Enlisting race, resisting power, transforming democracy.* Cambridge, MA: Harvard University Press.

Haney López, I. F. (2007). "A nation of minorities": Race, ethnicity, and reactionary colorblindness. *Stanford Law Review 59*, 985–1063.

Harris, C. (1993). Whiteness as property. *Harvard Law Review, 106*(8), 1709–1791.

Kim, C., Losen, D., & Hewitt, D. (2010). *The school-to-prison pipeline: Structuring legal reform.* New York: New York University Press.

Ladson-Billings, G. (2000). Racialized discourses and ethnic epistemologies. In N. Denzin & Y. Lincoln (Eds.), *Handbook of qualitative research* (2nd ed., pp. 257–277). Thousand Oaks, CA: Sage.

Ladson-Billings, G., & Tate, W. (1995). Toward a critical race theory of education. *Teachers College Record, 97*(1), 47–68.

Lawrence, C., & Matsuda, M. (1997). *We won't go back: Making the case for affirmative action.* Boston: Houghton Mifflin.

Leonardo, Z. (2004). The color of supremacy: Beyond the discourse of "white privilege." *Educational Philosophy and Theory, 36*(2), 137–152.

Loury, G. C. (2008). *Race, incarceration, and American values.* Cambridge, MA: MIT Press.

Lynn, M., & Parker, L. (2006). Critical race studies in education: Examining a decade of research on U.S. schools. *Urban Review, 38*(4), 257–290.

Lyons, W., & Drew, J. (2006). *Punishing schools: Fear and citizenship in American public education.* Ann Arbor: University of Michigan Press.

Matsuda, M., Lawrence, C., Delgado, R., & Crenshaw, K. (Eds.). (1993). *Words that wound: Critical race theory, assaultive speech, and the first amendment.* San Francisco: Westview Press.

Meiners, E. R. (2007). *Right to be hostile.* New York: Routledge.

Mercer, K. (1991). Review: Looking for trouble. *Transition, 15,* 184–197.

Morrison, T. (1992). *Playing in the dark: Whiteness and the literary imagination.* New York: Vintage.

Muñoz, J. (1997). Photographies of mourning: Ambivalence and melancholia in Mapplethorpe, Van der Zee and looking for Langston. In H. Stecopoulos & M. Uebel (Eds.), *Race and the Subject of Masculinity* (pp. 337–358). Durham: Duke University Press.

Muñoz, J. (1999). *Disidentifications: Queers of color and the performance of politics.* Minneapolis: University of Minnesota Press.

Noguera, P. (2008). *The trouble with black boys . . . And other reflections on race, equity, and the future of public education.* San Francisco: Jossey-Bass.

Parents Involved in Community Schools v. Seattle School District No. 1 et al., 551 US 701 (2007).

Parker, L., Deyhle, D., & Villenas, S. (1999). *Race is . . . race isn't: Critical race theory and qualitative studies in education.* Boulder, CO: Westview Press.

Parikh, C. (2002). Blue Hawaii: Asian Hawaiian cultural production and racial melancholia. *Journal of Asian American Studies, 5*(3), 199–216.

Rickman, J. (Ed.). (1957). *A general selection from the works of Sigmund Freud.* Garden City, NY: Doubleday Anchor Books.

Skiba, R. J., & Knesting, K. (2001). Zero tolerance, zero evidence: An analysis of school disciplinary practice. *New Directions for Youth Development, 92,* 17–43.

Skiba, R. J., Michael, R. S., Nardo, A. C., & Peterson, R. L. (2002). The color of discipline: Sources of racial and gender disproportionality in school punishment. *Urban Review, 34*(2), 317–342.

Smith, M. L., Miller-Kahn, L., Heinecke, W., & Jarvis, P. F. (2004). *Political spectacle and the fate of American schools.* New York: RoutledgeFalmer.

Solórzano, D., & Yosso, T. (2002). Critical race methodology: Counter-storytelling as an analytical framework for education research. *Qualitative Inquiry, 8*(1), 23–44.

Stein, S. J. (2004). *The culture of education policy.* New York: Teachers College Press.

Valdes, F., Culpe, J. C., & Harris, A., (Eds.). (2002). *Crossroads, directions, and a new Critical Race Theory.* Philadelphia: Temple University Press.

Vaught, S. E. (2009). The color of money: School funding and the commodification of black children. *Urban Education, 44*(5), 545–570.

Vaught, S. E. (2011). *Racism, public schooling, and the entrenchment of White Supremacy: A critical race ethnography.* Albany, NY: SUNY Press.

Wald, J., & Losen, D. (2003 Fall). Defining and redirecting a school-to-prison pipeline. *New Directions for Youth Development, 99,* 9–15.

Williams, P. (1987). Spirit-murdering the messenger: The discourse of fingerpointing as the law's response to racism. *University of Miami Law Review 42,* 127–157.

Williams, P. (1991). *The alchemy of race and rights: Diary of a law professor.* Cambridge, MA: Harvard University Press.

Williams, P. (1995). Meditations on masculinity. In M. Berger, B. Wallis, & S. Watson (Eds.), *Constructing masculinity* (pp. 238–249). New York: Routledge.

Winant, H. (2001). *The world is a ghetto: Race and democracy since World War II.* New York: Basic Books.

Yosso, T. J., Parker, L., Solórzano, D., & Lynn, M. (2004). From Jim Crow to affirmative action and back again: A critical race discussion of racialized rationales and access to higher education. *Review of Research in Education, 28*(2004), 1–25.

I thank my university and department for both the grant and sabbatical leave that facilitated my travel to and time spent at research sites.

THE BIRTH OF HOPE

EDUCATION INSIDE AND OUTSIDE A NEW JERSEY PRISON

■

MICHAEL SATTERFIELD

I did not have hope for the future until I came to prison. There are numerous reasons for this. However, I feel that the education I am receiving here is a key reason why I began to consider working toward a better life than the one I had before. The availability of a formal education began to redefine the perception I had of the world around me. One could easily believe that in a prison environment, such as the one I am in, a person's options for future successes are limited. Yet, I believe this is far from the truth. Outside of here, while there might be the appearance of having endless opportunities, this wasn't the case for me and, I am sure, a great many people. I'll not attempt to explain why so many people come to prison, or grow up without hope for the future; instead, I'd like to simply focus on education. Education, while not the sole factor that determines the course of a person's life, is certainly helpful in ensuring that a person will move toward some form of financial stability. So I wish to relate some of my own educational experiences and give my opinion of the difference between education on the outside and education behind prison walls.

Our society largely attempts to instill the belief that so long as a person works hard at something, success is inevitable. However, from what I've witnessed and have seen throughout my life, I believe this is a falsehood. If a person is poor, grows up in a neighborhood rich in crime, or is merely raised in a bad home, their options are limited. For such people, including me, the only impressions of a different sort of life than their parents' and those around them come from two main sources: the media and school. The media, of course, offers an unreal version of the world that one either can't believe in or leads to disillusionment. School, while offering knowledge of alternate routes one might take in life, also sets limits on a person's aspirations and dreams. I believe that there are very few teachers who actually encourage students to wish to have different lives than those of their parents or the other people they are surrounded by. Instead of trying to instill hope in students' hearts, they try to simply treat them as the class they are born into. Poor students are expected to be disruptive and automatically fail. Now, I do not know if this is the same everywhere, but I do know that it seemed to be the norm in the schools I attended in both Georgia and New Jersey.

I once had a teacher make a snide comment about the fact that the clothes I wore had once belonged to my brother. She told me I dressed like him; I dressed in his clothes and acted just like him. She believed that he was a loser and that I probably was one too. She said this to me only a few weeks after school had begun. This was not a random occurrence. Most of my teachers, like my clothes, were similarly passed down to me by my brother. However, most of the teachers I had expected me to fail in some fashion. My teachers expected me to be a disruption, to get poor grades, and perhaps to eventually drop out. The teachers I had seemed to believe my parents had failed in some way and that I would as well. It was easy to not care about my education when no one seemed to care about it either. It was easy to be a disruptive student when I was already expected to be a problem child.

I felt school was useless, as I am certain did many of the people in the town where I lived. I could not see the point in trying to achieve academic success when I couldn't believe I would benefit from it. I lived down to the expectations of those around me, as many people do, I'm sure, because while it is unpleasant to fail in life, it is far less enjoyable to strive toward a goal you can't even begin to hope to achieve. As I saw it, and many people in this facility saw it, the only way to gain any form of financial security was through criminal activities. After I dropped out of high school, as it seemed everyone expected me to, I could only find work doing menial jobs with little possibility of advancement. Despair was quite easily instilled within me, as life seemed fairly pointless.

I am unsure exactly when I began to possess hope, at what exact point I came to truly believe that I might be able to do something that mattered with my life. It was certainly not the first night I spent in a jail cell, or even a few months after I was arrested, that I began to have hope for the future. I do know that when I received my scores for the GED test, I felt hope clearly then. It was only a small accomplishment, but it was more inspiring than anything I'd done up to that point. The notion that I might be able to do more with my life was firmly planted then. Even if I still had seven years left to spend here, I knew that I would not, and could not, waste them.

I started working as a teacher's aide almost immediately after receiving my GED. It seemed like a method to help others feel what I felt, and feel, now: hope for something better. It isn't always the easiest job, and too few are able to break free from the belief that there is anything they can be other than criminals. Not every teacher who works in this facility is devoted to helping students desire to achieve more. That is understandable. It is not an easy thing to lift people up and make another person want something. All anyone can do is try to ignite a spark within another, which may blossom into a voracious appetite for knowledge and something better than being in prison. Admittedly, I've come to a point where I assess each student and decide whether

176

or not I can truly help them. It is something that most teachers here do. The teachers here do not merely ignore students they feel aren't ready to try and break away from self-destructive beliefs about what they are capable of. They instead wait and hope, as I do, that such students will at least begin to consider bettering themselves.

In here the teachers largely act as war doctors, saving as many as they can. They might at times overlook the worst or unready cases, but they do work hard to help those they believe they can help. I believe that is in large part the difference between the teachers who work in the public education system outside of here and those who work in here. Teachers on the outside look on the majority of their students as hopeless cases. Those that work here at least try to find a way to keep their students from coming back to prison. This is a generalization, and I am certain that there are good teachers who work in public education. I just haven't met any of them. Good teachers are a rarity in public schools, but it is bad teachers who are difficult to find here.

Also, in here, once one actually does have some hope and a GED (or high school diploma), prison offers something else many inmates previously were terrified to even dream of: a college education. Where the GED and high school teachers plant those precious seeds of hope, the college instructors here offer the water and the light that allows hope to truly flourish in prisoners' souls. It is not only hope but also a path toward redemption that is born here. Isn't that what education is supposed to do? Move society forward toward a better future?

I didn't have hope for the future until I came to prison. I'm sure many other inmates here, whether they admit it or not, know or have known despair intimately. Despair is not bred in public schools but elsewhere in this world. It is only that schools, which are meant to act as beacons of light that guide people, such as myself, out of the darkness are failing to do so. Education may not be the only thing that helps ensure that people succeed in this world, but it is almost certainly the start to becoming something better than we are. It is a strange thing that the path to hope is often found in a prison, but it is.

PARTICIPATORY LITERACY
EDUCATION BEHIND BARS

AIDS OPENS THE DOOR

■

KATHY BOUDIN

In this article, Kathy Boudin recounts her story as an inmate and literacy educator at Bedford Hills Correctional Facility for women. While the standard literacy education curriculum for the facility emphasized instrumental, workbook-based reading skills, Boudin sought to make the literacy program more relevant to the women's lives and experiences. By working with the women in the literacy program, Boudin incorporated critical literacy teaching practices into the skills-based curriculum, using the subject of AIDS in prison as a means of linking the women's experiences with their acquisition of literacy skills. Although the article focuses on prison education, the women in Bedford Hills are like other women in urban communities for whom literacy is only one of many problems. Thus, the pedagogical and social issues raised here have many implications that extend beyond the prison bars.

> I started hanging out and not taking school seriously when I was a teenager. At seventeen I met my first baby's father, and he had a lot of control over me. After he went to jail, I started using drugs. I had a job for one or two years on and off in a grocery store, running a cash register. But I left that job to sell drugs, because I could earn more money that way. I always wanted to be a bookkeeper, but you have to know how to read, filing, math. Now I think about a porter job in a hospital. Nothing I have to use reading for. I would like to think of nice things: nice clothes, an investigator, a secretary, nice jobs. I see ladies all dressed up, legs crossed. I like things like that, bubble baths, but I can't be thinking too many dreams cause I got five kids. I hope I can make it when I go home
>
> — *Anna, Adult Basic Education student, Bedford Hills Correctional Facility*[1]

Prison lies at the end of a road taken. Although women arrive for many reasons, we have one thing in common: we share a deep desire to leave prison and not return. Many of us are looking for alternatives to the actions that brought us here. We are working to imagine new choices, to widen options, and to figure out how to make these real.

When Anna spoke, she was in an Adult Basic Education (ABE) literacy class, hoping it would open doors for her. She was not alone with her literacy problem. In Bedford Hills Correctional Facility, New York State's maximum security prison for 750 women, 63 percent of the incoming women do not have a high school diploma and almost 20 percent do not read at a fifth-grade level (Nuttall, 1988).

Although having limited literacy proficiency is a serious problem, it is only one of many that women in Bedford Hills face.[2] Prior to their imprisonment, most were confronting more pressing problems: poverty, drugs, domestic abuse, neighborhood violence, single-mother parenting, and immigration issues. Many, feeling permanently locked out of the economic mainstream, were trying to make fast money illegally, usually through involvement with drugs. Basic literacy education meant a time commitment, a slow, long-term investment in a life moving fast, so fast that it got out of control, and ended up with imprisonment. In prison, life slows down enough for these women to take time for such things as a literacy class, yet the women know that when they leave here, most will return to the same broad problems, problems that loom as permanent and intractable. Improved literacy will not be the miracle that will change their lives, especially since the average stay in prison is less than three years (Division of Program Services, 1992) and literacy growth is a slow process. It is rare for a woman to leave Bedford with a goal of changing social conditions, even if she believes those very conditions contributed to her ending up in prison. "You can't change the world" is a commonly held attitude. Trying to deal with immediate issues such as housing, jobs, and child raising are foremost in most women's minds when they leave. The urgent need many of us from a diversity of backgrounds feel is to change the things inside ourselves that landed us here, to be more able to negotiate the system and to cope with the problems we will face when we leave. Improved literacy is part of something bigger, part of their whole struggle to grow. As one woman said, "The only way out . . . is in."

What kind of literacy education would best meet the needs of the women in prison who face these issues? This is the question I grappled with some years ago, when I came to prison, as I became involved in studying and teaching adult literacy. I am an insider, a prisoner myself, a woman and a mother, serving a twenty-to-life sentence. I am also something of an outsider—White, from a middle-class background, college educated, and a participant in the social movements of the 1960s. I had not shared some of the most common realities of the women in the ABE class, realities including racism, drugs, family violence, immigration, or poverty. Nevertheless, twelve years of prison life has broken down barriers: living through the daily experiences such as lock-ins or cell searches, cooking or gossiping; deep friendships; working on AIDS, foster care, and literacy; and sharing the life events such as mothering, deaths, and graduations. All of this has created for me windows into the lives, past and present, of women from different backgrounds and has also led to a new commonality among us.

Early in my master's degree work in adult education (which I undertook when I first entered prison), I learned about Paulo Freire's problem-solving approach to literacy education, an approach that places literacy acquisition in the context of learners' daily concerns and social reality (Freire, 1970, 1974). I hypothesized that it would be effective at Bedford because it could offer an education in which women could think and act around urgently felt needs while developing their literacy ability.

I, like many other prisoners, wanted to be productive and to do something meaningful with my time in prison, and I looked to teaching literacy as one way to do this. Yet prison administrators usually limit the amount of responsibility and independence a prisoner can have, and teachers who have inmate teacher aides usually use them only in very limited roles. Would I, a prisoner, as a teacher's aide to a civilian teacher, be able to create the space to do meaningful work?

Would it be possible in a prison classroom to create conditions for self-awareness, a space where people felt safe to identify and address their own problems and then struggle toward solutions, to imagine the world as it could be otherwise? Prisons are founded on assumptions of control, obedience, and security. Thus, independent thinking and individual and collective initiative create sharp tensions around these assumptions.

Prison is a metaphor for failure, the failure of those who end up there, while a sense of self-worth is a foundation for active learning, for being willing to take risks. Would it be possible, in the prison atmosphere, to break through the prevailing ideology about prisoners as failures, an ideology that had been internalized to varying degrees by the women themselves, and to release their psychological energy for creative learning? These were among the questions I faced as I began to think about becoming a literacy educator in prison.

In this article, I tell the story of what happened between 1986 and 1990 at Bedford Hills Correctional Facility as I struggled to develop a literacy program that was meaning-based, problem-posing, and relevant to learners' lives. Written from my perspective and observations as both a teacher and a prisoner, with quotes drawn from my detailed journal entries over a five-year period, I start by examining the prison environment, and then relate my experience of teaching while evaluating which educational approach best met the needs of incarcerated women at Bedford. Finally, I discuss the possibilities and constraints that the prison context creates for establishing participatory education.

THE PRISON CONTEXT

The primary missions of prison—control, punishment, and deterrence through social isolation (Sullivan, 1990)—serve to intensify the powerlessness and dependency that many women prisoners have already experienced out-side of prison. The loss of the ability to make decisions permeates every aspect of prison life cumulatively in the way it increases powerlessness. The authori-ties move women freely among the nine female prisons in New York State; thus, within a moment, a woman's entire world may shift. Lack of control over where one lives means lack of control over all the pieces of a life—friends, work, education, routine, possessions, environment, and, of central impor-tance to women, contact with children and family. If a woman is in prison near her children, she can maintain an active relationship with them; when she is moved, the ties are ruptured.

Prison policies dictate what clothing to wear and what colors are permit-ted. When the telephone rings, a prisoner cannot pick it up. Only guards can open doors. Intimate relationships are illegal and must be hidden. This lack of control extends to life outside prison as well. For example, a woman may learn that her child is in the hospital, but cannot be present to comfort her or him. When a child runs away from home, the mother is helpless to work on the problem. We as prisoners must rely on people outside to help with the details of daily living—from buying clothes, food, and presents for children, to phoning lawyers who don't accept collect calls.

While women's prisons can be brutalizing, they are often infantilizing.[3] The social conditioning in a women's prison encourages a childlike dependency (Burkhart, 1976). For example, at Bedford Hills we constantly have to ask permission to do some of the most basic things: when at work or at school we must ask an officer for toilet paper, and she or he will then tear off a few pieces and hand them to us; we must wait for an officer to turn the lights off or on in our cells, since cell lights are controlled by a key that the officer has; we may stand by a gate or a door for five minutes or more until an officer feels we are quiet enough, and only then will she or he open it. Women operate within the confines of power and control, reward and punishment; women typically express their overall sense of having no control when they refer to authorities and say, "This is *Their* jail."

Although prison intensifies powerlessness, for many women it paradoxically also offers a space for growth. There is a release from the pressures of every-day survival, abusive relationships, family responsibilities, and drug addiction; some women have their first drug-free pregnancy while in prison. Incarcera-tion can be a time for women to reevaluate and reflect on their lives, to get an education and acquire skills they never had a chance or didn't want to get, and to think about issues they may never have thought about.

There are numerous educational and social programs that women can make use of in prison.[4] These programs are shaped by the conflicting goals of security, control, and punishment on the one hand, and rehabilitation or self-development on the other (Bellorado, 1986; Sullivan, 1990). The various basic education programs at Bedford Hills—ABE, pre-GED, GED, ESL, Bilin-gual Literacy—can serve either as a means of control (primarily used to keep prisoners occupied and having limited educational goals) or as a fruitful context for deep growth. It was in this environment of constraints and possibilities that I set out to teach.

ENTERING THE CLASSROOM: EDUCATION FOR CONTROL

I started to work as a teacher's aide in the ABE class in February 1986. I requested to work in this class because the teacher had expressed support for my teaching ideas and, from my observation, seemed to have a strong rapport with the students. By this time, I had spent a year-and-a-half in both graduate study and individual tutoring of ABE, GED, ESL, and college students. This range of experience led me to define three goals for my work in the ABE classroom: first, to teach reading and writing; second, to foster participants' intellectual and emotional strengths (e.g., analytical ability, imagination, and self-esteem); and third, to create a context for exploring and possibly acting on personal and social issues faced by women in the prison. When I entered the classroom, I was in for a rude awakening.

On an average day, the women in the ABE class ranged in age from seventeen to seventy, with the vast majority in their mid-twenties. They were primarily African-American or Hispanic, coming from a variety of cultures and places: New York City, the South, Puerto Rico, Jamaica, Colombia, and the Dominican Republic. A few were working-class White women from upstate New York, and some came from other countries (Hong Kong, Yugoslavia, and Israel).

Typically, women arrived in class and took their individual folders and workbooks from a shelf. Their work consisted of reading paragraphs or short passages on various unrelated themes (e.g., popcorn, insects, and newspapers), and then answering multiple-choice questions that focused on skills (e.g., finding the main idea, understanding a particular word, or locating a detail). When a student finished a designated amount of work, the teacher or aide checked the answers against the answer key. The student then tried to correct her wrong responses.

The class was silent, except when the teacher spoke to individual students or when friends exchanged a few words. There was no instruction to the whole class by the teacher. What mattered most was whether the students answered workbook questions correctly. The answer key and the teacher were the only sources of knowledge. The learning process was entirely defined by the teacher, and it was narrowly confined to a limited body of information.

Occasionally, group discussion followed a movie; the teacher might encourage writing a few times a year, for example, during Black History month. Once in a while there was a lesson on a life skill relating to the state-mandated functional competency program or computer work, but these activities were not the norm. Day after day, year after year, women came to class and silently read workbooks in which they repeated discrete skills in preparation for periodic tests.

My first reaction to the classroom was physical. My eyes strained from try-ing to match up answer sheets with hundreds of tiny boxes, and my mind went dull. I found myself de-skilled and transformed into a clerk. I was nei-ther expected nor able to use any intellectual or emotional aspects of myself. I found no room for choice, judgment, or authentic interaction. The experi-ence of almost two years in this role contributed to passivity, conformity, and a feeling of uselessness, which, as a prisoner, I was constantly struggling against anyway.

For the women in the literacy class, reading paragraphs day after day and taking tests with similar paragraphs resulted in incremental improvement on test scores over time, and, therefore, in some sense of progress and satisfac-tion. Yet communication and meaning, the essential core of reading, were not the point of the classroom experience. There was no writing, no explicit development of strategies to enhance construction of meaning from texts, no exposure to various literary genres such as poetry, stories, or drama, and no building on interaction between the different language processes of reading, writing, listening, and speaking.

I asked myself what we were telling women about the importance of literacy, when there was no link between literacy and self, no development of literacy as a powerful means to construct a world. What message were we giving the women about themselves and their lives in this classroom, where their think-ing and all their experience were irrelevant? The women I taught brought into the classroom a rich tapestry of knowledge, experience, and cultures. They knew first-hand about the social problems of crack, homelessness, the crisis of being mothers behind bars, the immigrant experience; they shared basic human conditions of love and friendship, betrayal, death, community, work. If learning materials did not portray a life that was familiar, did not reflect their reality, did not contain their voices or their languages, what did that tell them about their cultures? If the teacher and the workbooks were the only sources of knowledge and authority, what did that say about their capacity to know and to create?

I believe that this approach, with its excessive emphasis on obedience and limited possibility for initiative or constructive learning, with its lack of atten-tion to self and its undervaluing of affect in learning, was detrimental to basic mental health. This kind of instruction could not foster self-esteem or self-con-fidence. And, in denying the possibility of making choices, solving problems, looking at different options, or figuring out one's own opinion, it thwarted the possibility of helping women to change their lives.

Educational policy and curriculum for all New York State prisons is set by the Department of Education of the New York State Department of Correctional Services (Nuttall, 1988). The approach used in the prison literacy classes, like that used in many adult literacy programs throughout the country (Fingeret, 1984; Hunter & Harman, 1979), is a decontextualized, subskill model of read-ing in which content, real life issues, creativity, and imagination are all irrelevant. It is individualized and programmed, precluding interaction or social action (Nuttall, 1983). The reading process is conceptualized as a bottom-up process in which comprehension of the message of the text is slowly built up by accumulating small pieces, sound by sound, word by word, moving from lower to higher levels of complexity (LaBerge & Samuels, 1985). An adult who has failed to learn to read adequately is presumed to be lacking in particular subskills. Initial testing identifies those particular weaknesses, remediates for them and then retests in this diagnostic prescriptive model (Nuttall, 1983). The concept of literacy that guides the curriculum in the ABE class is based on grade level: a literate inmate is defined as one who scores at or above the 5.0 reading level on the standardized achievement tests used throughout the system (Nuttall, 1983).[5]

As in any other teaching context, the rationale for the choice of approach to prison literacy education is informed, in part, by assumptions about learners. A report from the Education Department of the New York State Department of Correctional Services states:

> The most serious obstacle to a successful program and "habilitation" or "rehabilitation" is the make-up of the population itself. For the most part, commitments to the Department represent individuals who have little education, who have no viable occupational skill, who have a history of substance abuse, and who often have a long history of criminal activity. (Nuttall, 1988, p. 2)

This policy statement characterizes prisoners themselves as the main obstacle to their own rehabilitation. Although it identifies objective problems, it fails to recognize strengths that prisoners bring to the learning process. From my observation, viewing prisoners primarily as a problem meant that correctional services' education personnel were unlikely to involve prisoners in their own education, let alone to think they might make a contribution to society. I knew from my years in prison that this perception of women exclusively as "problems" was inaccurate, and that this prevailing view would never lead to a process of meaningful educational growth.

Women who have committed serious crimes may well have survived serious pressures. Many women have not just survived, but have actively refused to accept a passive or victimized role. While women may have acted in a destructive and/or self-destructive way, assertiveness can be a lever that opens options for new action. The ability to survive and fight back may be a strength on which to build. It is crucial to discover and work with this and other strengths because, however deeply hidden, they are, in the end, women's greatest allies. And so a question began to form and to follow me: Could I create a process whereby the potential and strengths of the women could be expressed and developed, becoming part of the literacy process and fueling it with energy?

AN ALTERNATIVE VISION

I developed an alternative vision through a combination of my past history as a community organizer, my experience in the individual tutoring and ABE class, and the theory and methods that I learned through my graduate studies. In the 1960s, I had been involved in teaching about welfare rights, housing, and health issues. I had worked with women who had little formal education and who were regarded by society as inadequate, or as "victims" to be helped by those who were more educated by formal academic standards. Yet these women and people like them throughout the United States were learning together, acting on their own problems, and, at the same time, providing social insights that affected the entire society. I brought to my classes a certain optimism from my experience as an educator outside the classroom. I believed that, even in the controlled prison environment and in a different historical period, it might be possible to create a participatory learning process in which people felt a relative sense of empowerment.

My studies confirmed that, when literacy was taught as a collection of skills outside of any meaningful context and divorced from any importance in the learners' lives, the work would not fully tap their intellectual capacity. Neither would it draw on their prior knowledge, which, as schema theory had taught me, is so critical in the development of reading proficiency (Anderson, 1985; Bransford, 1985). Taken together, my community organizing experiences, my graduate studies, and my observations of prison classrooms led me to hypothesize that a meaning-driven, whole-language orientation might be more effective in the prison context (Altwerger, Edelsky, & Flores, 1987; Goodman, 1973, 1985; Smith, 1973).

I believed that such an approach would be stronger not only cognitively, but affectively as well. The women whom I taught were once the children who had failed in school or, more accurately for many of them, whose schools had failed them. From my interaction with the women in and out of class, I learned that they brought with them negative feelings about education and about themselves as learners. Attitudes about race, class, and gender undermined their confidence to learn academically, compounding the insecurities about school. I knew from conversations that many were only in the ABE class because it would look good for the parole board or because they had been assigned to be there. It was critical to use an approach that built on the women's intelligence, experience, and culture in order to counter these forces.

The existing classroom process, depending as it did on passivity and the rote learning of isolated skills, did not link literacy learning with the daily needs of the women, nor did it equip them to take an active role in their own education. As such, it ran counter to what we know about adult learning in general: (a) the complexity of adult social roles and related responsibilities (spouse, worker, parent, community member) means that adults want learning to be applicable to their needs; (b) the broad knowledge and life experience that adults have acquired mean that they have a great deal of prior knowledge that can be used as a strength in developing literacy ability; and (c) the independence and self- direction that characterize adults mean that learning—both in content and in process—should be participatory (Ellowitch, 1983; Knowles, 1984).

For the women with whom I worked, the general needs of all adult learners were magnified by the multitude of urgent issues they faced; thus, the need to overcome powerlessness and to create new choices was essential. Freire's approach to literacy education was particularly relevant, as it is rooted in work with marginalized and oppressed groups. His ideas influenced my work in several ways. First, his approach begins with students developing the ability to analyze their experiences and their social reality, as they explore the meanings of this reality in the words and the sentences they are learning to read and write. The literacy class can, at times, become a place where students may even act on issues, using and further developing their literacy ability. Second, his work raises issues about teachers, their methods, and their relationships with their students. I had been frustrated with the one-way street of teaching that left the ABE students in a passive situation. Freire argues that this passivity comes, in part, from the tendency of many middle-class teachers to feel superior to their students from poorer backgrounds. He proposes a "dialogic" method, in which students and teachers together explore a shared set of issues. This dialogue, while not removing the teacher's responsibility to teach a body of knowledge, can unleash an active role for the learners, enhancing not only their present learning, but also their lives beyond the classroom (Freire, 1970, 1974).

These views resonated with my community work with African-American and poor White women, largely from Appalachia, prior to my incarceration. As I had come to know these women and their life stories, I became acutely aware that my formal education represented only one kind of knowledge; in fact, my own background, while having given me certain advantages, also had left me with certain blinders. My work with these women had been a two-way street— we learned from and taught one another. I wanted now to build on both the reality we shared as women prisoners and the differences in our backgrounds and experiences.

THE STRUGGLE FOR CHANGE

For almost two years as a teacher's aide, I struggled to implement this alternative vision. Sometimes I worked with small groups of women, reading a particular text of interest, striving always to keep meaning in front of us. We read plays, did interviews, and read stories. Although each project engaged women and taught them a wider range of literacy skills, nothing altered the overall routine. The women frequently did not want to work with other women, feeling either embarrassed and ashamed of themselves or contemptuous of the others.

In many cases, they did not want to attempt any writing, which was rarely required by the teacher. The classroom context was still set by the teacher and the sub-skill approach; the approach I was using was simply not considered "real work." Moreover, I found myself experiencing the same frustration as other teachers with the "call-out" system (in which students could be pulled from class at any time for appointments). This system, along with transfers to other prisons, pushed the curriculum toward individualized work and away from a content focus, since it was difficult to develop a cohesive unit of study with a constantly changing group of people.

Slowly, the sub-skill model began to seduce me. Although I never lost my aversion to this limited sense of education, I began to become preoccupied with how women were doing in their workbooks and on the tests, measuring my worth as a teacher in these terms. I lost a strong sense of initiative. The structure and machinery of school were undermining my vision of education. I was turning into the teacher I did not want to be. I understood what had happened to other teachers, many of whom encouraged me and seemed to identify with my vision, but didn't have the energy to implement it.

The existing curriculum materials, testing apparatus, and overall conception of literacy set terms for success and failure that brought all of us—teachers and students alike—into its orbit. From my observations in class, and from conversations with the students, it appeared that the students had internalized years of failure in school, and without the confidence in themselves as thinkers they were very open to the safe routine of workbooks. In addition, prison, with its system of rewards and punishments (the ultimate of which was meted out by the parole board), contributed to students' willingness to accept a rote method of learning. By the fall of 1987, after almost two years of trying, I wanted to quit.

While I was wrestling with whether or not to leave teaching, the ABE teacher resigned; the Educational Supervisor then asked me to teach the class for four months until a new teacher could be hired. This offer was unexpected and unprecedented, since prisoners are permitted only to be aides to civilian teachers. I saw the opportunity to try to implement my vision of education, and I took it, as I felt it would allow me to define the approach to literacy education for the class as a whole, rather than as a side project.

The Education Supervisor, as an educator, was supportive of a problem-posing approach. He knew of my graduate work and was willing to take a risk with me. In allowing me to teach the class, the prison authorities had to balance their personal interest in my ideas about education with the system's policy of limiting an inmate's level of responsibility and influence over other inmates, along with concern not to threaten the civilian teachers' job security and sta-

187

tus.[6] According to prison authorities, the decision was possible because it was limited in time, and I would officially remain in the position of teacher's aide to the other ABE teacher who worked with students at a tested reading level of K–3.[7]

THE ISSUE OF AIDS ENTERS THE CLASSROOM

The most important challenge facing me was to create a reading class in which concerns that had meaning to the women would "drive" the learning process. The issue of AIDS opened this possibility. In September 1987, the ABE reading class watched a television show on the National AIDS Awareness Test. At that time, AIDS was still largely an issue prisoners did not discuss, although it was deeply affecting their lives. Close to 20 percent of incoming women inmates tested positive for the HIV virus (New York State Commission on Correction, 1988). Women lived in a state of anxiety over whether they might be HIV positive and whether to take the test. Many women had used intravenous (IV) drugs, and many had lovers or spouses who still did. Women were sisters, mothers, daughters, and homemakers for people with AIDS. Here, women shared cooking areas, showers and toilets, and a life together. People were scared—scared of each other, scared for their lives. The stigma that AIDS carried reenforced a sense of guilt and shame that the women already felt as prisoners pronounced "guilty" by the courts and society. There was a fear of just being associated with AIDS. This fear created both a collective silence and a desperate need to talk.

During the television show, I noticed that the women were riveted to the screen, trying to write down information, their voices sounding out rapidly staccato, one after another: "How do you spell 'pneumonia'?" "How about 'disease'?" "And 'infection'?" "What's an antibody?" "What do they mean, 'immune system'?" "Spell 'protection,' 'hemophiliac'." While they tried to hold on to the meaning of new terms, I went to the blackboard to write down all the words they were calling out. AIDS was a powerfully emotional issue; a new sense of urgency entered the classroom.

That night I focused on everything I had learned but, until then, been unable to implement. I prepared a vocabulary worksheet, an activity that was familiar to the women. While the words were typically drawn from a textbook list for children at different grade levels, the words on this list came from the AIDS show. The women studied avidly, learning words far above their difficulty level in their workbook lists. Some words were conceptually familiar but difficult to spell, such as *transmit, doctor, disease, patient,* and *pneumonia;* some led to learning new concepts, such as *immune system, antibody,* and *hemophiliac.*

In addition to the vocabulary, I asked three questions that were on all of our minds: *What are the pros and cons of taking the AIDS test and how do you feel about it? If you tested positive would/should you tell somebody and who would you tell? What*

do you think would be a good program for AIDS here at Bedford Hills? These questions created an environment in which the students related to real life emotional and social issues; they began addressing problems that they faced both
individually and communally. I asked the women what they thought.

"I don't want to take the test. I'm scared to find out. I used needles."

"You have to tell your lover, otherwise you might hurt her."

"I don't even know what the test tells you, do you?"

"I'm not worried now, but what about when I go home? My man, he's been
with women while I'm here. Even though he says he hasn't, he's like any other
man. I know the real deal."

"I shot up with some people and now they're dead. I don't want to know
and then again I do."

Everyone participated. The women speaking to one another turned their
orderly rows into an informal circle. I also talked, feeling my commonality
with the women because I too had feelings about testing, safe sex, and fears of
rejection. I also felt our differences as women spoke about IV drugs in their
lives and decided to speak to these differences, making explicit the fact that
I didn't know about IV drugs and wanted to know more. This was the first
of many times that I would try to make the differences in our backgrounds
a point for exchange. In that first discussion, I began to change my role as
teacher: I was a prisoner, exploring shared problems; a facilitator, guiding
learning and discussion; and a person with specific information I wanted to
learn and impart.

Soon, women began to write about personal experiences with AIDS, and
even brought unsolicited writings to class. For example, Lucia wrote:

> My friend died from AIDS last year. . . . Since then I've been scared. This is a
> disease that they haven't found the medicine for. I would like to be one of those
> persons from the big laboratory to help find the medicine for those people who
> have AIDS. I'm trying not to think about the disease, but I have a brother and
> a sister and they are into drugs. They say they don't use anybody's syringe, but
> still I'm afraid.

Lucia had never written anything in class and had difficulty writing in her
native Spanish, as well as in English. When she presented her piece, she was
sharing a hidden secret about her family, her fears and her dreams, as well as
asking for help in English and writing. The drive to express her intense feelings had led her to take real risks in her writing and use of English.

With reading centered on AIDS-related materials, the women contributed
to the curriculum, something that had not happened previously. They brought
in newspaper articles and pamphlets to share with the class, which I developed
into reading lessons. One day Juana, who was about to transfer to the GED
class, came to me holding pages of paper tightly in her hand. She said, "I've
written something; it's a story, maybe the class would like it." She had a look

of triumph on her face, and a triumph it was! Juana's story, called "Chocolate and Me," was about a relationship between two women in jail, one of whom had AIDS.[8] When she read it, the women listened intently as they felt their own lives being described by one of their class members, and clapped enthusiastically when it was over. Juana worked on it, learning the concept of paragraphs, struggling with sentence structure and spelling. Then I typed it, made copies, and developed a reading lesson from it. The class felt proud that one of their members had written something that they were studying. This was the first of many times that the women's own writings became the reading materials for our class.

WRITING A PLAY: BUILDING ON THE STRENGTHS OF AN ORAL TRADITION

During this time, I proposed to the class that we write our own play.[9] I had several goals: to develop literacy through the process of creating a play in which women would be communicating important thoughts and feelings; to broaden literacy ability through studying the genre of a play and integrating the language forms of reading, writing, talking, and listening; and to develop the strengths of working in cooperation with others.

We began by talking about what a play is, learning about the elements of plot, character, conflict, dialogue, and setting. I gave out vocabulary worksheets with words related to theater. We read plays from a literacy program facing issues similar to those in our own community.[10] This encouraged us: if another basic literacy class could write a play about issues of housing, health, and drugs, then we, too, could write such a play. When one woman asked, "What should the play be about?", another responded, "It should be something about us, our lives." This was one more step by participants in gaining confidence that their own life experiences were significant. When it came time to decide on a focus, the women chose AIDS, because we were increasingly involved with it in class.

During the next weeks, the conflicts around which to base the plot emerged from our real questions and anxieties about AIDS: Should a person take the HIV test or not? If she tests positive, should she tell her parents? Her lover? The work on the play allowed women to reflect on their day-to-day experiences, and the play changed along with their reflections. One day Elena said, "A friend of mine told me last night that she just tested positive. She's supposed to go home in four months. She had so many dreams—traveling, having kids—now those dreams have all gone down the drain. Maybe I shouldn't push so hard for testing."

Jackie added, "Yeah, I agree, here I am in the play, pushing Anna to take the test, but I'm scared. I'm not ready to deal with it; I know I'm not, and I bet I'm not the only one." From this discussion, the group decided to make the dialogue in the play less pressured toward taking the test.

As we improvised dialogue around each conflict, plot and characters slowly developed. When it was time to create a script, two or three people followed each person's spoken words and wrote down whatever they could. We then pieced the entire dialogue into a whole. Finally we put all the scenarios on the blackboard and made choices as to the sequence of action.

The theater framework allowed participants to try out different resolutions to conflict, to experience the emotions they most feared, and to learn from the process. During one rehearsal, we focused on the woman who was the counselor in the play. "Try to get into it more, try to really put yourself into it," the women coached and pushed. Suddenly Teresa burst into tears. "I think I'm afraid," she said, "afraid to put myself in it completely because then it makes it real, and I guess no matter how calm I seem to all of you, really I'm afraid to think about AIDS." Women went to her and hugged her. After that moment, she did put herself more into the acting and was more open about her experiences and fears.

Work on the play further molded my changing role as teacher. The women urged me to take a part in the play. For a moment I hesitated, wondering if it was appropriate for a teacher to do that. Then I laughed at myself, realizing I was feeling afraid I might lose my authority. Taking the part strengthened my teaching, as I identified with the women in working on a shared problem.

Theater gave the Hispanic and African-American women an opportunity to build on a strong oral tradition. They were able to use their own language, dialects, informal speech, and body language. Some of the women who had the greatest problems developing their reading and writing were outstanding in the development of dialogues and acting. The theater process accentuated the strengths of some women, while valuing the strengths of each as language, communication, reading, and writing all developed.

A COMMUNITY DEVELOPS IN THE CLASSROOM

The students' growing consciousness of themselves as part of a community, first in the classroom and then in the prison, became a positive factor in literacy development. The classroom had been a place in which each person individually felt locked into her own sense of failure. "I hate being in this class, people think it's for dummies. Maybe it is," Anna had said. No one wanted to be identified with being in the ABE class, "the lowest spot on the totem pole," just as no one wanted to feel like they were part of the prison.

But as people began to talk about their fears and questions concerning AIDS, something changed in the classroom. A sense of community, an awareness of common experiences, and a feeling of support began to grow. The most emotional moment reflecting this came when Lucia shared with the class that she had just found out that her brother was hospitalized with AIDS. I wrote in my journal:

When Lucia came back into the classroom, people said they were sorry and wanted to be there for her. Elena suggested that Lucia write about her feelings. So Lucia spent the rest of the class writing about what is happening with her brother.

When people arrived at class in the morning, they now spoke with each other differently, with an openness, a sense of identification, and growing trust. As one woman wrote, "In our class we talk about a lot of things and learn a lot of reading. Sometimes we talk about real things that make our tears come out. . . ."

The support for one another expressed itself in the classroom in many ways. For example, when a woman got sick, everyone made a card for her; when a woman made parole, people had a celebration for her. The class organized a Christmas party, something that had never before happened in an ABE class. The most significant articulation of community occurred when we were picking a title for the play. When someone said, "Let's call it *Our Play* because it is about us," there was enthusiastic agreement. That sense of there being an "us" had never existed before, and the title expressed a pride in the "us" that had emerged.

ABE class members carried this ethos of support beyond the class and into the prison population. Word began to get out that the ABE class was talking about AIDS in a supportive way; other prisoners now sought out women in the ABE class as confidantes on their living units. One day Ching came to class and said to me, "A woman on my floor found out she has AIDS and tried to kill herself. I'm the one person she told. I know why she tried. She came to me, I'm the person she talks to." Ching's eyes filled with tears. I saw then that the knowledge that the ABE class was accumulating was also bringing with it awesome responsibilities.

The feeling of community influenced literacy ability, as well as intellectual and emotional growth. People took risks in reading and writing because they were no longer afraid. They felt less ashamed of themselves and were willing to express their thoughts more freely. As they brought increasingly complex reading materials to class and began to teach one another, recognizing that each one could teach as well as learn, a tentative grouping of learners and teachers emerged. One of many examples of this occurred when the women were preparing for a spelling test. "I'll help Jamie," said Ms. Edna, who was seventy years old. They worked for a while, and then Ms. Edna brought the test over to me. They had gotten 100 percent on it. They were beaming at their mutual success.

A growing social awareness laid the basis for the next critical leap: the desire to change the conditions that were causing problems. "What can we do with everything we're learning?" Jackie asked. "People are coming to me, asking me things," Alicia added. Instead of seeing AIDS as an individual problem, people began to see it as a common one, and one they could work on together. First the women worked on an article for the school journal, hoping to share what they had learned. I took the class through the process of writing a composition, focusing on what they wanted to say about AIDS. After five hard-working sessions, the article, *Alert to Aids*, was done, and was published not long after with all the class members' names on it. Although the feeling of community had first grown inside the class, it now extended beyond the class into the prison as a whole. The women continued to use their developing literacy skills to make a difference. *Our Play* became the means of accomplishing this.

ARE WE REALLY LEARNING TO READ AND WRITE?

The transformation that was taking place in the classroom challenged participants' notions about what counts as education. In place of filling out multiple choice questions from workbooks, the women were learning from their own experiences and reading materials that did not have "yes" or "no" answers. The range of literacy activities was far beyond those normally carried out in the ABE class. Yet, it was not an easy transformation, and not everyone was comfortable with the process. The students had questions, and so did I. Randy said, "I feel I've learned a lot about AIDS, I'm learning to write a composition, I'm reading lots of articles, and I'm actually writing a play, but I'm just not sure I'm really learning." Many women wanted a clear sense of right and wrong answers. The workbooks had provided this, as well as a sense of progress because of the movement through the book and from one level to the next. Some women did not like working in groups. Others wanted to know whether their progress would show up on the test scores.

During the work on the play, one woman playing a major role did not do as well on the quarterly TABE test as she had hoped. She announced that she was quitting the play to go back to the workbooks. Everyone wanted her to come back to the play and eventually she did, with renewed commitment. However, I knew that I had to take her concerns seriously, and that they were shared by others. I, too, was worried about whether this work would give them the needed test preparation.

During this period, when I encountered both a variety of student resistance and my own insecurities as a relatively new teacher of literacy, I asked myself whether I was imposing on the women an educational approach that I thought was best for them, but that they didn't want. Perhaps my views were linked to the differences in my background. Would it give them adequate test preparation? With time, the range of reading materials, the explosion of writing, and the students' engagement and personal growth all made me more confident about my approach. And now, having established a meaning-driven context within the classroom, I was able to begin focusing on problem areas. I took readings and developed lessons similar to those in the workbooks. This, I felt, would allow the women to feel a relationship between the past and the new learning experiences. I tried to develop a better balance between group and individual work, spending time with each person on specific areas of need.

Many of the women needed work on both the sound symbol relations and the basic structure of English language. Finally, I developed lessons on test-taking skills.

PERFORMING THE PLAY: EMPOWERMENT WITHIN A PRISON

By mid-December of 1987, we were ready to put on the play. We were all nervous. AIDS was still a subject associated with fear and stigma. Those who were taking the risk to open up a hidden subject were not seen by either themselves or other inmates as potential educators, because they were in the lowest level academic class.

The play was performed six times, and each time the audience reacted beyond all dreams. It brought into the open fears, questions, and issues in a safe social setting, breaking the silence so that people could together begin to deal with the epidemic. Women cried as a father rejected his daughter, moving his chair away from her after she told him she had tested positive. Yet the tears were mixed with embarrassed laughter, because they knew that they, too, might move away from someone whom they thought to have AIDS. When a woman told her lover she had tested positive, there was a dead silence as people waited for the lover's reaction. Everyone was able to identify with one of the women or the other; they were living through what they themselves might face. When the support group in the play came together for the last scene and told each other of the good and of the difficult reactions they had gotten from family and friends, the audience stood up and cheered, feeling the strength that came from people supporting each other.

After several performances, we held discussions with the audiences about what could be done to deal with the crisis of AIDS here at Bedford Hills. The audience asked for support groups and a program to be built like the one depicted in the play. Members of the prison administration came to watch one of the performances. The superintendent requested that the class put on the play for the civilian counselors in the prison, and the class made a video of it.

Several months later, a group of women separate from the ABE class, including myself, formed an organization for peer education and counseling called AIDS Counseling and Education (ACE). The ACE Program has created a major difference in attitudes, medical care, mental health, knowledge, and support in the prison around AIDS-related issues.[11] It uses the video of *Our Play* to help women deal with the emotional issues that AIDS raises.

After the play, the ABE class did its first evaluation of their learning experience, another step in the women's self-consciously helping to mold their own education. The Education Supervisor, who facilitated the evaluation, asked, "What did the work in the AIDS unit accomplish for you?" The answers included, "Writing skills, vocabulary, recognizing words, spelling, how to write a play, learning about conflicts and resolutions."

"Learning about AIDS."

"How to put on a play and how to act."

"How to respect people's feelings, how to speak louder, and how to express our feelings."

"I liked the counseling group because it involved counseling each other."

"We gave people a message, we helped people."

"The play brought a level of emotions, awareness to help learn."

"I feel wise, learning how other people feel."

"The play gave me a mirror to look at my own life."

I believe that these quotes reflect how the women in the ABE class felt empowered in different ways, both as individuals and as a group. The classroom experience allowed individuals to understand their own lives more clearly. Their self-concept changed from being poor learners to people who could teach others. Although the process had begun with one peer educator, myself, the participatory problem-posing approach generated many others, as women taught one another in the classroom, and as the ABE class educated the population through informal discussions and writing the play. A sense of efficacy and agency developed for all of us—myself as teacher, the women in the class as students, and all of us as prisoners. As a group, the class knew that they had made a major contribution to the entire prison population by breaking the silence about AIDS, using their growing literacy ability to do so. The play had helped to create conditions whereby an ongoing program developed. Three years later, I asked one of the ABE class participants in *Our Play*, who is presently a member of ACE teaching others about AIDS, how she felt about her experience in the ABE class and the play. She said to me:

> The play made people more aware. Some people didn't want to face it, some people went around judging people that have AIDS. The play helped change that. I felt good about myself. I didn't know what AIDS was before I came to Bedford. It made me feel good that I'm educated and how I can help educate others. I grew in the process, that was a step, and a step makes for progress.

THE MODEL REPEATS: A MULTICULTURAL COMMUNITY EXPRESSES ITSELF

Was the intense student involvement during the unit on AIDS tied only to the issue of AIDS, or was it linked to the new way of teaching? Clearly AIDS was an issue of great emotional urgency, and it did provide the initial energy to transform the educational approach. Once the ABE class openly embraced the issue of AIDS and owned it as a shared human problem instead of as a badge of guilt, then, paradoxically, the very issue that led to oppressing and denying people their humanity became a vehicle of transformation and hope. As women freed themselves from the dehumanization of stigma and prejudice, proclaiming their own self-worth and humanity, an energy was created that drove the learning process, the desire for knowledge, the confidence to create.

Once the women had experienced a literacy education that focused on issues of importance, they wanted it to continue. Fundamentally, it was the educational approach that had provided the glue to overcome the fragmented reality that is debilitating to prisoners and teachers alike. Fragmentation was overcome when the learning process tapped into the whole person, and when a sense of community was created so that people felt committed to each other, as well as to broader goals.

An indication of the power of such an educational approach occurred when the new teacher was hired and reestablished the individualized, basic skills model, sending all of us—students and myself—back to the workbooks and multiple-choice questions. I felt a sadness, almost as if there had been a death of a fragile new life. The students evidently felt the same way and, as the weeks went by, many of them complained to the teacher and to administrators, asking for a return to teaching in which their ideas and issues mattered. This active role of ABE students requesting a certain type of education was unprecedented at Bedford Hills.

The AIDS unit had generated enough support for a participatory approach that not only the education supervisor, but also higher prison authorities were interested in seeing it continue in some form. The new teacher, who was troubled by declining attendance, and was also open to the problem-posing approach, agreed to let me teach the class two out of five days, during which time he would be present in the classroom. This arrangement left him in authority, yet gave credence to my work.

The model repeated itself as the ABE class explored other thematic units over the next year. In one called "Mothers and Daughters," we explored our mothers' lives, our relationship to them as daughters, and our own role as mothers. In another, we explored issues of personal experiences and values with money. Finally, for a six-month period, we took on a major project—writing a handbook for incoming inmates, entitled *Experiences of Life: Surviving at Bedford Hills*.

For two days a week, the class became a writers' workshop. It began with the women, myself included, sharing what was on our minds the first night we arrived in prison. Then we brainstormed about what we had known, feared, and wondered about prison life in Bedford Hills before arriving here. I found writings by other prisoners about these concerns and used them as the basis for structured reading lessons. They triggered intense writing, from several sentences to several pages, until enough material was created for the book. The chapters included, "Advice for How to Survive in Prison," "Coming from Another Country," "Being Pregnant in Bedford Hills," and "Mothers and Children."

The exploration of each new issue deepened participants' sense of themselves and of shared realities. Out of the cumulative experience of feeling our commonality as prisoners and women, a trust developed that made it possible for us to explore our cultural, racial, ethnic, and linguistic differences.

Literacy acquisition interacted with the exploration of cultural identity. One among many examples of this occurred when it came time to edit the handbook. We looked at the different forms of language that were found in the writings of the women in the handbook: Standard American English, informal speech, Black English, and slang. For the first time, many women heard that the Black English, which always had been corrected as "wrong," was a dialect reflecting a culture.

The class had a long discussion about what style of language to use for the handbook. Some wanted it to be in Standard American English because they felt that new women coming in should see that the ABE students knew the standards of accepted grammar. Other women wanted to leave some of the informal language or slang and Black English dialect in order to facilitate communication with the new women. A Chinese woman proposed a solution: to leave it in the style that the particular woman had written if she wanted, but to explain in the beginning of the book that the decisions about language had been a conscious, educated choice. Thus, the readers would know that the ABE students knew enough to distinguish between and to choose different types of language. This was how it was done.

PRISONERS AS EDUCATORS

As a prisoner teaching, I experienced a shifting of roles and identities. I was an inmate, reminded of that reality by a twenty-to-life sentence and the day-to-day experiences of being strip-searched after a visit, separated from my son, and locked down; yet, at times I felt myself to be a teacher in training, headed for an identity as an educator, occasionally asked by another inmate, "Are you a teacher or a prisoner?", until they noticed my green pants and gave me a knowing nod. In my role as educator, teachers would sometimes speak to me with respect, almost as a peer; some were genuinely excited about the work and supported my educational growth. Yet there was an ambivalence about me as an educator. One example can be seen in the words of a teacher who was familiar with the quality of the AIDS work, yet who introduced me as her "inmate clerk." At times I would be a translator, negotiating between two worlds. Then the reality of control and limits would bring everything back into focus. Although there was a shifting of roles, I found that the primary tendency of the system was to define me as prisoner. It was always a struggle to transcend the limitations of that role.

To what extent was the participatory approach tied to a prisoner being the one teaching? In the class evaluation, the women addressed this issue, responding to the Education Supervisor's question, "How was Kathy's teaching like past teachers or different from them?" The women responded, "In the past a teacher was always just a teacher, but she (Kathy) was both part of it and also a teacher."

"She was learning also. She was also like a counselor."

"Teachers never participated in learning, past teachers taught 'what to do,' not 'how to'." The Education Supervisor asked, "Could a civilian do it, not just a prisoner?" One woman said, "Yes, but they would have to be sympathetic to the group and have to pick up on the vibes. It wouldn't happen as fast, have to build rapport, that takes time." To the question, "How do you build rapport?", someone responded, "Show care, speak what you're about, you open up to us, we'll open up to you, forget that you're a civilian."

There was a strength in the peer education process, of a prisoner teaching prisoners. It allowed for a shared exploration of issues that became the basis of literacy curriculum development. Additionally, as a prisoner I shared the powerlessness felt by the students and had a deep stake in creating a participatory learning process, in which we as prisoners were ourselves making decisions, taking on problem-posing and problem-solving.

Yet the very strength of the peer education process was also its weakness in the prison context. Although most of the prison administrators with whom I dealt expressed personal enthusiasm toward the educational approach I was using, they also expressed a dilemma when the question of whether I could actually teach arose: how could they permit me real responsibility as an educator without giving me too much responsibility as a prisoner? How could such an empowering group process be initiated by prisoners without it becoming a threat to security?

FUTURE PROSPECTS

The paradox of education is precisely this—that as one begins to become conscious, one begins to examine the society in which one is being educated. The purpose of education, finally, is to create in a person the ability to look at the world for oneself, to make one's own decisions, to say to oneself this is black or is white, to decide for oneself whether there is a God in heaven, or not. To ask questions of the universe, and then to learn to live with those questions, is the way one achieves one's own identity. But no society is really anxious to have that kind of person around. What societies really ideally want is a citizenry which will simply obey the rules of society. (Baldwin, 1988, p. 4)

If creating a liberating education is difficult and paradoxical within the society at large, as James Baldwin writes, then it is all the more so within a prison, an institution of authoritarian control. Yet, after a year-and-a-half of utilizing a problem-posing approach in the classroom, there was change. The experience was so positive that it moved not just inmates, but also some teachers, educational administrators, and some prison officials towards supporting more of this kind of teaching.[12] This support led me to ask: could a problem-posing approach to literacy become an ongoing part of the educational programs in the prison? Was the experience simply a chance occurrence, or was it consonant enough with the prison goal of rehabilitation to imagine extending it to involve more classes and more inmates as peer educators?

Three education supervisors agreed to work with me on a proposal to implement a problem-posing curriculum more widely. We addressed the question: Who were the most appropriate people to do the teaching? We agreed that inmates would bring particular strengths to the process, namely that of identification with the learners. Moreover, a program using peer educators meant extending the rehabilitative process beyond the students in the literacy classes to those women with higher educational backgrounds. In this prison alone, more than one hundred women are either in college or have bachelor degrees; therefore the potential number of literacy peer educators was large, and developing teaching skills, carrying out work that required self-reliance, and contributing to the broader community was clearly within the concept of penal rehabilitation.

The final proposal involved training peer educators from among prisoners to work four hours per week in every basic education class, using a problem-posing curriculum developed in cooperation with the students. The Superintendent approved the program and productive meetings began with education administrators, teachers, and interested peer educators. Then, midway through the planning period, the prison Administration disapproved it.

Both the support and the withdrawal of support for the peer education program can only be understood as aspects of the broad contradictions among the primary prison goals of control, punishment, and deterrence, and that of rehabilitation. These conflicting goals manifest themselves in many ways, including what type of behaviors are rewarded or sanctioned, the perspective towards inmates, and different education models. How this contradiction is resolved at any moment in time depends on specific conditions. In this case, a number of conditions as diverse as personnel and social climate changed between the time of approval and disapproval: (1) The key education supervisor, who was the critical link between the teachers and our group of inmate peer educators and who supported the program, left the prison for another job; (2) The New York State financial crisis led to education cutbacks, and teachers were laid off. I knew from conversations with teachers and administrators that this increased anxiety among remaining teachers about their jobs made them more resistant to, and threatened by, inmates teaching or even inmates playing an active role in their own learning; (3) There was an increasing tendency towards law and order policies and attitudes within the society with concomitant social-service cutbacks. The general political climate was more antagonistic towards prisoners, inmate initiative, and program innovation. The prison administration reacted to all these factors by canceling a program involving inmates' critical thinking and initiative.

The current education crisis facing most prisons illustrates the impact of these conflicting goals. Prison populations are swelling due to drug-related crimes—in New York State, they have grown from 35,000 to 55,000 since 1985, when crack became a driving force in crime, and prison officials estimate that 75 percent of the inmates are incarcerated for drug-related offenses (Browne,

1991). The need for basic education programs has grown with the population increase.

Conversely, the budget cutbacks in education mean elimination of classes taught by civilian teachers. The first layoffs at Bedford Hills, in January 1991, led to the elimination of the ABE class for those inmates reading at the K–3 level and also of the ESL class; the GED class has also suffered significant cutbacks. Between 1989 and 1993 the number of academic and vocational teachers was cut from 25 to 9. The crying need for educational services could be alleviated by allowing inmates to be peer educators and by using participatory methods in which learners actively work on problems they face. Yet prison authorities are reluctant to allow such a problem-posing curriculum to develop or to allow inmates to teach classes. In short, while prison administrators may talk about providing an education for rehabilitation, they rarely do what is necessary to make it happen.

These contradictory needs and goals are integral to the structure of the prison system and, as such, cannot be transcended. At the same time, however, they frame the conditions under which struggle can occur; the very existence of these contradictions offers possibilities for change.[13]

Prisons, like other societal institutions, contain cracks and openings for change—conflicting goals and policies, a diversity of people, changing historical directions. At Bedford Hills, due to a particular combination of these variables, it became possible to create a liberating form of education that lasted for several years. This experience is now an immutable part of the educational history at Bedford Hills, a basis upon which to build.

The enormous expansion of prison populations suggests that prisons mirror and are part of a larger social crisis. This connection is reflected in the words of one New York State Department of Corrections spokesperson who said that prisons "probably give out more high school equivalency diplomas than ninety percent of the high schools in the state. Why do people have to come to prison to learn to read and write and get drug treatment?" (Browne, 1991). Human potential, which will be wasted or encouraged, is crowding into prisons. The challenge that problem-posing education raises in prison is part of a larger challenge facing the entire society: will social problems be dealt with by measures of control from above or through mobilization and education from below?

CONCLUSION

One never knows what improved literacy ability in itself will do for women in prison. One person may gain in self-esteem, while another will make practical improvements in letter writing, filling out forms, or reading to her child. For some, the ability to compete in the job market may increase, but indications are that for most it will not. For the adults with whom I work, the kinds of improvements necessary to increase job opportunities involve great effort over an extended period of time.

What if one embeds literacy acquisition in a broader education that has at its heart problem-posing, critical thinking and acting on shared problems? How might that affect people's personal growth, family relationships, jobs, and their ability to create the lives they want? Although the answer to this clearly depends on many unknowns, these are questions I have asked myself as I have thought about the struggle to build a problem-posing approach and about the women with whom I work and live.

One story in particular illustrates the complexity of this issue. When Anna was here, she participated fully in the AIDS unit, in the play, and in every successive unit during the year-and-a-half that the educational program existed. She, as much as anyone, felt empowered by the entire experience. When Anna went home, she started by getting a job in a flower shop. When the father of her children came out of prison, she made a decision to go back to him in spite of their problems with drugs, because he offered economic and emotional security. Soon afterward she became pregnant and, during her pregnancy, her husband began seeing another woman. Anna went back to drugs. She was rearrested on a parole violation and came back to Bedford Hills for eight months before going home again.

When Anna was in the play and learning to read and write, while also learning about AIDS, this approach to education seemed like the answer. There were moments when I felt that the human potential and creativity that were emerging in the classroom would allow the women to take on the world, or at least in their own lives, and remake them to fit their dreams. Then, when Anna came back and told me her story, I felt the crushing limitations of even the most positive educational experience in light of what Anna and other women face, including personal scars and the need for social and economic changes.

As educators, we are often forced to accept more limited results than we envision in our hopes and dreams. The success of a short-term literacy program, one that meets our best vision, cannot be measured by one set of tangible standards; the social forces are too complex. Thus, despite Anna's return to prison, I believe that her learning experience and that of the others in the ABE class affirms an approach to teaching literacy based on the lives and experiences of the women themselves. Anna and the others so often have spoken with great pride of what they read and wrote, of the things they learned and taught to others. The participatory approach encouraged a feeling of their own worth and capacity. Although it contains no guarantees, it does offer a powerful hope, because it involves the full potential of participants. Lucia, who is among the many who have not returned to prison, said before she left, "I never thought I would be doing this. I never even did it on the street. I never thought I would act in a play and here I am reading everything. I can go home to my kids and say, 'I've done something!'"

NOTES

1. This quote is a verbatim statement taken from an interview with an ABE student with whom I worked. Some of the quotes in the article come from similar interviews, while others come from my own journal entries. Although this article was written when almost all of the women quoted had already left prison on parole, or had transferred to a different prison, I was able to get in touch with the majority of them to tell them that I was doing public writing and to get their permission to use material about or by them. Because some of the women consented to have their real names used and others preferred to remain anonymous, I used fictitious names throughout. The one exception is Juana Lopez, who previously had material written for the ABE class that was published using her real name.

2. The prisoners in Bedford Hills Correctional Facility are overwhelmingly Black and Hispanic women, mothers, undereducated in a formal sense, frequently poor, and usually single heads of households. The ethnicity of the general prison population in New York State prisons is 50 percent Black, 31 percent Hispanic, and 19 percent White. (The United States population as a whole is 12 percent Black and 7 percent Hispanic.)

   The ethnicity of those prisoners with serious reading problems, that is, those under the 5.0 reading level, is 54 percent Black, 37 percent Hispanic, 9 percent White, and 5 percent other. In terms of the education levels of the women who enter the New York State prison system, 18 percent read below a fifth-grade level; 16 percent have math skills below a fifth-grade level; 77 percent dropped out while in high school; and 63 percent do not possess a high school diploma (Nuttall, 1988).

   Seventy-three percent of the women in Bedford Hills are mothers (Division of Program Services, 1992), and the majority were single heads of households (Humphrey, 1988). One study showed that over half the women in prisons have received welfare payments during their adult lives (Craig, 1981); in a National Institute of Corrections study of men and women, 80 percent of those who were employed before arrest made less than a poverty-level salary (Bellorado, 1986).

   Forty-four percent of the women in Bedford Hills Correctional Facility were convicted of a drug offense; however, the warden at Riker's Island, which is the largest feeder jail to Bedford Hills, estimates that drugs underlie the incarceration of 95 percent of the female inmates there (Church, 1990). Lastly, in a study done at Bedford Hills in 1985, 60 percent of respondents said they had been victims of abuse (sexual, physical, or emotional) (Grossman, 1985).

3. Recent examples of women's prisons in which repressive measures such as extreme isolation or sexual abuse have been documented include the underground prison in Lexington, Kentucky, and the Shawnee Unit in Maryanna, Florida.

4. In addition to the basic education programs, some of these programs include: The Parenting and Foster Care Programs of the Children's Center, where women learn about issues related to being mothers; the Family Violence program, where women examine violence in their personal lives and some of the social values and roles that permit or even encourage such violence; the AIDS Counseling and Education (ACE) program, where women have struggled to build a community of support around AIDS-related issues and have trained themselves to become peer educators and counselors; and the four-year college program run by Mercy College, where women can earn bachelor degrees.

5. The Department of Education of the New York State Department of Correctional Services defines literacy by using a combination of grade level and functional competency definitions. The functional competency definition was crystallized into a Life Skills curriculum (Nuttall, 1983). However, in the three-and-a-half years during which I was involved in the ABE class, the Life Skills curriculum was not put into practice except in an occasional lesson.

6. A recent policy statement of the New York State Department of Correctional Services states, "Although the Department has been reluctant to place inmates in positions where they might possibly acquire influence or authority over other inmates, we have used inmates as teacher's aides and vocational aides and in recent years have begun to employ them as pre-release peer counselors and ASAT aides (Division of Program Services, 1991, p. 3). This statement is comparable with the long-standing practice of not permitting inmates to teach academic classes, but of encouraging them to do one-on-one tutoring, either as a teacher's aide or volunteer tutor.

7. In the summer of 1987, the ABE class was divided into two classes defined by level K–3 and level 3–6. I was working with the 3–6 level, and it was this class that I was offered to teach. Beginning with the winter of 1991–1992, the K–3 teacher was laid off, and once again there is one ABE class, level K–6.

8. Juana's story, "Chocolate and Me," was published by the PWA Coalition in *Surviving and Thriving with AIDS: Collective Wisdom*, vol. I (1988).

9. The sources of the suggestion and the guidance in using theater with literacy instruction were Dr. Ruth Meyers, my graduate study mentor, who worked with the Creative Arts Team (CAT), a professional educational theater company in residence at New York University, and Klaudia Rivera, who at the time was Director of the Community Language Services Project of the Adult Learning Center at LaGuardia Community College, where literacy and theater work was developed.

10. The plays were written by different classes of the Community Language Services project (CLS) of the Adult Learning Center at LaGuardia Community College in 1986, under the coordination of Klaudia Rivera, coordinator of the program.

11. For more information about the ACE Program see J. Clark and K. Boudin (1990), "A Community of Women Organize Themselves to Cope With the AIDS Crisis: A Case Study From Bedford Hills Correctional Facility," and K. Boudin and J. Clark (1991), "A Community of Women Organize Themselves to Cope with the AIDS Crisis: A Case Study from Bedford Hills Correctional Facility."

12. In December 1987, Educational Supervisor Rob Hinz wrote about my teaching after the completion of the AIDS unit: "Her use of Dr. Freire's theoretical work on praxis combining thought and action in a dialectical approach to the teaching of reading to adults has had remarkable results. The women with whom she was working are technically classified as technically illiterate, yet she was able in three months' time to provide classroom instruction on AIDS . . . and to, using the vehicle of a play, have these women writing and reading while at the same time boosting their self-image and confidence."

   In the spring of 1988, the prison authorities gave permission for the ABE class video to be shown at an ABE conference of educators in New York City, with a presentation of the teaching methods done by Klaudia Rivera.

   In the winter of 1988–1989, the Bedford Hills Correctional Facility Education Department sent a copy of the ABE class handbook to Albany as an example of an education product.

13. An example of how the contradictory needs and goals present opportunities for change is reflected in a recent development in the New York State Department of Correctional Services. The enormous increase in the prison population has created the need for a greatly increased work force inside the prison. Looking toward inmates to partially meet this need has led to a reformulation of a philosophy about inmates: "In keeping with our new emphasis on training inmates to meet the needs of the Department and encouraging and recognizing individual inmate responsibility, it is now our intention to make even greater use of properly trained and qualified inmates. We plan to establish new job titles of 'Inmate Program Associates.' The Program Associates will work in such areas as classrooms, orientation, pre-release, libraries, and counseling" (Division of Program Services, 1991, p. 3). It is too soon to know how this new philosophy will actually manifest itself.

REFERENCES

Altwerger, B., Edelsky, C., & Flores, B. M. (1987). Whole language: What's new? *The Reading Teacher, 41,* 144–145.

Anderson, R. C. (1985). Role of the readers' schema in comprehension, learning and memory. In H. Singer & R. B. Ruddell (Eds.), *Theoretical models and processes of reading* (3rd. ed., pp. 372–384). Newark, DE: I.R.A.

Baldwin, J. (1988). A talk to teachers. In R. Simonson & S. Walker (Eds.), *The Graywolf Annual Five: Multi-cultural literacy.* St. Paul, MN: Graywolf Press.

Bellorado, D. (1986). *Making literacy programs work: Vol. I. A practical guide for correctional educators* (Grant No. FZ-7). Washington, DC: U.S. Government Printing Office (Stock No. 027-000-1293-1).

Boudin, K., & Clark, J. (1991). A community of women organize themselves to cope with the AIDS crisis: A case study from Bedford Hills Correctional Facility. *Columbia Journal of Gender and Law, 1,* 47–56.

Bransford, J. D. (1985). Schema activation and schema acquisition: Comments on Richard Anderson's remarks. In H. Singer & R. B. Ruddell (Eds.), *Theoretical models and processes of reading* (3rd. ed., pp. 385–397). Newark, DE: I.R.A.

Browne, A. (1991, February 10). Cuomo: Release nonviolent cons. *The Daily News,* pp. 3, 24.

Burkhart, K. W. (1976). *Women in prison.* New York: Popular Library.

Church, G. J. (1990). The view from behind bars [Special Issue: Women: The road ahead]. *Time,* pp. 20–22.

Clark, J., & Boudin, K. (1990). A community of women organize themselves to cope with the AIDS crisis: A case study from Bedford Hills Correctional Facility. *Social Justice, 17* (2).

Craig, G. M. (1981, July). The development of literacy/conscientization program for low-literate women in prison. *Dissertation Abstracts International, 42,* p. 68. *(University Microfilms No. 81-12, 793)*

Division of Program Services. (1991). *Division of Program Services action plan.* New York: New York State Department of Correctional Services.

Division of Program Services. (1992). *Female cluster program services action plan.* New York: New York State Department of Correctional Services.

Ellowitch, A. (1983). *Women and the world of work.* Philadelphia: Lutheran Settlement House Women's Program.

Fingeret, A. (1984). *Adult literacy education: Current and future directions.* Columbus: Ohio State University, National Center for Research in Vocational Education.

Freire, P. (1970). *Pedagogy of the oppressed.* New York: Seabury Press.

Freire, P. (1974). *Cultural action for freedom.* Cambridge, MA: Harvard Educational Review (Monograph Series No. 1).

Goodman, K. (1973). Psycholinguistic universals in the reading process. In F. Smith (Ed.), *Psycholinguistics and reading.* New York: Holt, Rinehart & Winston.

Goodman, K. (1985). Unity in reading. In H. Singer & R. B. Ruddell (Eds.), *Theoretical models and processes of reading* (3rd. ed, pp. 813–840). Newark, DE: I.R.A.

Grossman, J. (1985). *Domestic violence and incarcerated women: Survey results* (Prepared by New York State Department of Correctional Services; administered in July 1985 to female inmate population at Bedford Hills Correctional Facility). New York: Department of Correctional Services.

Humphrey, C. (1988). *Female, new court commitments (1976–1987).* New York: Department of Correctional Services.

Hunter, C., & Harman, D. (1979). *Adult illiteracy in the United States: A report to the Ford Foundation.* New York: McGraw Hill.

Juana. (1988). Chocolate and me. In *Surviving and thriving with AIDS: Collective wisdom* (vol. 1). New York: PWA Coalition.

Knowles, M. (1984). *Androgeny in action.* San Francisco: Jossey-Bass.

LaBerge, D., & Samuels, S. J. (1985). Towards a theory of automatic information processing in reading. In H. Singer & R. B. Ruddell (Eds.), *Theoretical models and processing of reading* (3rd ed., pp. 689–718). Newark, DE: I.R.A.

New York State Commission on Correction. (1988). *Acquired immune deficiency syndrome: A demographic profile of New York State inmate mortalities 1981–1987.* New York: Author.

Nuttall, J. H. (1983). *Reducing inmate illiteracy in New York State.* New York: Department of Correctional Services.

Nuttall, J. H. (1988). *An update of illiteracy in New York's correctional system.* New York: Department of Correctional Services.

Smith, F. (1973). *Psycholinguistics and reading.* New York: Holt, Rinehart & Winston.

Sullivan, L. E. (1990). *The prison reform movement: Forlorn hope.* Boston: Twayne.

I would like to acknowledge the invaluable role of Ruth Meyers who, as my mentor during my graduate program, helped shape the thinking, practice, and interpretation of experience described in this article. I am grateful to Klaudia Rivera, who shared with me her own experience in adult literacy education and also played an important role in the use of theater in literacy work. I owe a special debt to Elsa Auerbach and Bill Ayers, who took considerable time and effort editing the many drafts of this article and who helped inform its content and style. I wish to acknowledge the contributions of Susan Kessler, Paul Mattick, Rose Paladino, Margaret Randall, Ruth Rodriguez, Ann Seidman, and Ruth Wald, each of whom raised critical questions of content and organization. I want to thank the numerous women from Bedford Hills Correctional Facility, both prisoners and civilian employees, who took the time to read the article and who brought the particular perspective of people who were living and/or working inside a prison. Finally, I owe a special debt to the women in the ABE class and to the group of twelve prospective peer educators, without whom the educational process would not have been possible.

PROGRESS

EDUCATION IN PRISON

∎

CHRISTOPHER DANKOVICH

I have been incarcerated since I was fifteen years old. Before that I had completed three-quarters of my freshman year of high school. Prior schooling taught me grammar, the laws of thermodynamics, how to play "Happy Birthday" on a recorder, and basic algebra. However, I never had the opportunity to learn these subjects in-depth at school. I had a desire to learn, though, and during my initial incarceration I bridged the long, lonely canyons of time by reading everything I could, from religious and pop philosophy to an entire set of encyclopedias and discarded high school and college textbooks. After turning sixteen I took my GED tests at the first opportunity and passed them all with perfect or near-perfect scores.

Fortune alone allowed me to take college courses by correspondence, which were paid for by my father, while fate led me to the first job of my life as a tutor in the prison school. I regularly tutored five students per class, or around twenty students per day. The majority of the students were from the "youthful side" of the prison, Michigan's only prison units set aside for adult prisoners ages thirteen to twenty-one, which is where I was held. The students that I tutored were prisoners who I socialized with outside of school. Most of the GED students were young black men from the cities of Detroit, Flint, and Pontiac.

The classroom that I worked in was a "special education" classroom, which meant that some, though not all, of our students were assigned to us because they had diagnosed emotional or developmental problems. From my experience, the hardest aspect of working with any student was in getting them focused at the beginning of class and then keeping their attention on the work for the entire period. Instead of running our groups as a cohesive whole, my fellow tutors and I would instead give each individual direct, one-on-one attention and instruction, divided up by short assignments which allowed us to give that same attention to the others.

The general euphemism among the students was that the GED was the "Good Enuff Degree." Both the prisoners and staff shared this mentality. Most of the students, even after sometimes years of tutoring and teaching, would just barely pass the tests. Coming in, most did not know the basics of grammar or spelling, arithmetic, science, or history. They rarely went to school while growing up, and the ones that did went to some of the worst schools in the country. The young men from the suburbs could usually pass the GED within a few months, while those from the cities were pressed to pass at all. At our most optimistic, we felt no hope for those who couldn't earn their GED, and little hope for those who could.

I had one very special student, though. He came to our class because he was diagnosed with attention deficit disorder. I didn't have much hope for him. When Blake[1] initially came to class, I gave him a math "locator" test, which has problems of increasing difficulty and which is used to help determine which class a student belongs in. He could only consistently perform addition. Blake had some basic multiplication facts memorized, but he could not divide or complete any subtraction problem involving borrowing. Deciding that I did not yet want to embark on a possible year-long (or longer) teaching endeavor with him, I chose to first work with him on social studies and science. I remember asking him what war Abraham Lincoln was president during. Looking me directly in the eyes, he confidently said, "World War II."

Since my other students were doing well on their own, I spent the rest of the time going over all of the American wars and their major details with Blake. He seemed interested but didn't take notes. Though I felt like I might have been wasting my energy on him, I continued.

The next day I started him on a U.S. history textbook. He focused quietly on it throughout the hour-and-a-half class before shocking me by asking to check it out for the weekend. I agreed. I also told him that he would be charged for ripping pictures out of the book, which I assumed was his intention.

The next time that we had class, I quizzed Blake. I asked him about the Civil War, and he repeated nearly word-for-word what I had taught him the previous week, along with direct quotes from Lincoln given in the book. In turn he explained the Revolutionary War and World War II with similar enthusiasm and detail.

I had Blake return to math, beginning with subtraction. After he learned how to borrow, he did about twenty long problems before I moved him to multiplication and division. I demonstrated the procedures for both once, after which he completed numerous problems of increasing difficulty without help. And he retained it. Fractions, decimals, and percents—he learned them all over the next couple days. He completed algebra after that. Finishing geometry qualified him for the GED math test.

We reviewed social studies again, the subjects of which Blake recited details perfectly from the book that he had not seen in weeks. I had never witnessed progress like his from a student before. I had never witnessed such retention like his before in a human being. Before I had him move on to science, the last subject that he needed to learn, I asked Blake how, with the abilities that he had, did he not know all of these things already at age seventeen.

"Nobody ever took the time to teach me anything before."

NOTE

1. A pseudonym.

PART III

■

TRANSFORMING THE PIPELINE

GRASSROOTS ORGANIZING AND THE SCHOOL-TO-PRISON PIPELINE

THE EMERGING NATIONAL MOVEMENT TO ROLL BACK
ZERO TOLERANCE DISCIPLINE POLICIES IN U.S. PUBLIC SCHOOLS

■

KAVITHA MEDIRATTA

In this essay Kavitha Mediratta examines the emerging growth and success of grassroots organizing to roll back zero tolerance school discipline policies in U.S. public schools. Over the past two decades, zero tolerance policies have pushed increasing numbers of children out of school and into the juvenile and criminal justice system, with a disproportionate impact on children of color. Mediratta documents how students, parents, and their legal, research, and philanthropic partners influenced the creation of a federal joint agency initiative to improve disciplinary practices in schools. She argues that grassroots organizations were central to the Obama administration's decision to acknowledge and address the role of zero tolerance school discipline in accelerating school push-out and juvenile justice involvement. They framed zero tolerance as a problem, highlighted examples of reform, and helped to create a political context that made it possible for federal leaders to act. The essay concludes with a discussion of three main challenges for the field: (1) improving policy alignment between the administration's school discipline reform plan and its major education reform strategies; (2) articulating the need for zero tolerance reform in ways that build alliances with teachers and school administrators; and (3) addressing racial disparities in school discipline and student achievement.[1]

In May 2011, in the third-floor conference room of the U.S. Department of Justice in Washington, DC, Attorney General Eric H. Holder Jr. met with members of his Coordinating Council for Juvenile Justice and Delinquency Prevention. Representatives of twelve federal agencies, along with nine field practitioners, were assembled to discuss ways of coordinating efforts to improve policy and services for at-risk youth and their families (U.S. Department of Education, 2011). That day, the agenda included an advance briefing on a statewide study of school discipline in Texas from Michael Thompson, director of the Council of State Governments Justice Center (CSG).

Thompson's presentation on CSG's report *Breaking Schools' Rules* (Fabelo et al., 2011) was short and to the point: 59.6 percent of all Texas public school students and 75 percent of all African American students had been suspended or expelled between the seventh and twelfth grades. Only 3 percent of these disciplinary actions were serious enough to require removal from the classroom under federal law; the vast majority, instead, were cases in which local administrators and teachers had discretion over whether or not to suspend or expel. Schools in the same district, serving similar populations of students, were making markedly different choices about school disciplinary strategies, suggesting that high suspension rates were more a reflection of administrative approach than the actual rates of student misbehavior. Most troubling, however, the use of out-of-school suspensions to punish student misbehavior was associated with dramatically higher risk of course failure, dropping out of school, and future involvement in the juvenile justice system.

Although CSG's findings mirrored those from previous research, the magnitude of school suspensions they revealed was stunning (Losen & Skiba, 2010). Texas educates one in ten U.S. public school students, and so the high number of suspensions from that state alone warranted federal officials' attention. But data on school discipline suggested that the Texas findings were not unique and, in fact, their suspension rates were likely lower than other states' (Fabelo et al., 2011). The explosive number of suspensions and expulsions found in Texas thus signaled a growing national threat to the educational attainment and future success of U.S. public school children.

The discussion following Thompson's briefing was sober. As one news organization later reported, the attorney general was "visibly shaken" by the study's findings (Kelly, 2011, para. 6). Holder and the Council weighed possible responses for more than an hour, discussing the need for policy guidance to jurisdictions cautioning them against excessive use of suspensions and the importance of educating "teachers of the country about the negative impact of their discretionary disciplinary actions on students" (U.S. Department of Justice, 2011a, p. 8).

At the attorney general's urging, two months later, the Departments of Justice and Education jointly announced a new federal Supportive School Discipline Initiative (SSDI). The announcement came at the July 21 meeting of the Coordinating Council in a public session attended by national media, civil rights advocates, and agency staff. In his opening remarks, Holder observed a troubling "relationship between school discipline and later involvement in the juvenile justice system." Excessive and inappropriate school disciplinary practices too often contribute to a "school-to-prison pipeline," he said (U.S. Department of Justice, 2011b). Secretary Duncan expressed similar concerns, recalling his own surprise when, as CEO of the Chicago Public Schools, he learned about the high rate of school-based arrests for minor misbehaviors in his district (field observation, July 21, 2011). "People wanted to do the right thing. They just didn't know better," he said. "When our young people start getting locked up early . . . they start to move out of schools, out of the pipeline to success . . . So many of these children need assistance. What they don't need is to be pushed out the door" (Shah, 2011).

In response, Holder and Duncan outlined four key action steps to help schools craft better disciplinary strategies to "engage students in learning and keep them safe."

- Building bipartisan consensus for action among federal, state, and local education and justice stakeholders
- Collaborating on research and data collection necessary to shape new policy, such as evaluations of alternative disciplinary policies and interventions
- Issuing policy guidance to ensure that school discipline policies and practices comply with federal civil rights laws and to promote positive disciplinary options to improve the climate for learning and keep students in school
- Promoting awareness and knowledge about evidence-based and promising policies and practices among state judicial and education leaders. (U.S. Department of Justice, 2011b)

Judith Browne-Dianis was sitting in the third row of the conference room, barely ten feet away from Attorney General Holder and Secretary Duncan when they announced the new federal school discipline initiative. A civil rights lawyer, she founded the Washington-based Advancement Project in 1999 and led its work to end the "schoolhouse-to-jailhouse track." She was part of the effort to bring Chicago school arrest data to Duncan's attention in 2005, in collaboration with a local youth organizing group, the Southwest Youth Collaborative, and lawyers at Northwestern University. Nationally, Advancement Project, along with the Alliance for Educational Justice (AEJ), Dignity in Schools Campaign (DSC), and the NAACP Legal Defense and Educational Fund (LDF) issued reports, circulated petitions, staged press events, organized mass marches, and held closed-door meetings with public officials to call attention to the role of school suspensions in fueling a pipeline of young people from schools to prison. Listening to Secretary Duncan acknowledge the reality of that pipeline and his intention to confront it felt like a watershed moment to her, Browne-Davis said.

> I had been working on this issue for more than ten years, from before it had a name and when few people cared about it. After all these years, I was so moved to see the federal government—and Arne Duncan—taking on school discipline and the school-to-prison pipeline. I could hardly believe it. It put my work in perspective—that all of the organizing, research, reports, and advocacy we'd done had not been in vain. Change really could happen. (personal communication, March 16, 2012)

213

The new federal school discipline initiative indeed marks a major step forward in recognizing and addressing the school-to-prison pipeline as a national problem. While this story might be read as an example of research-driven policy making at its best, the underlying impetus for the Supportive School Discipline Initiative was in fact a growing grassroots movement for change, led by students, parents, and dedicated legal advocates like Browne-Dianis. A close look at the events leading up to the initiative's announcement reveals how grassroots organizing, and social science research can work in concert to influence policy at the local, state, and federal levels. This central role of grassroots organizing in efforts to end the school-to-prison pipeline underscores the necessity of foundations and other allies to increase support for the organizations that make up this burgeoning movement.

This essay begins with a brief review of exclusionary discipline policies and their role in the school-to-prison pipeline. Next, it describes the emergence of grassroots activism around this issue, cataloging the number and types of organizations involved and the factors that supported their expansion from state and local to national campaigns. It then probes the ways that organized youth, parents, advocates, and researchers created a "policy window" (Kingdon, 1995) for national reforms by naming and framing the problem of the school-to-prison pipeline, uncovering viable alternatives, and demanding action. The essay concludes with a discussion of challenges facing this emerging national movement and identifies immediate and longer-term questions that grassroots organizations, advocates, and their reform allies must address.

I write from the perspective of a long-time researcher of youth and community-led organizing for public education reform and also as a grant maker involved in supporting current reform efforts. The essay draws on my personal involvement in events, field observations of the Justice Department's Coordinating Council meetings, and interviews with key officials who developed the SSDI. It also draws on personal communication with leading grassroots organizations and national advocates in the course of developing and implementing a grant making strategy at The Atlantic Philanthropies (Atlantic). Since early 2010, Atlantic has supported efforts to reform school discipline policies in U.S. public schools as a means of improving educational opportunities for the nation's most vulnerable children and avoiding their unnecessary placement in the juvenile and criminal justice systems. The foundation has provided resources for grassroots and legal advocacy for local, state, and federal school discipline policy change. It also has initiated projects to increase knowledge about effective alternatives, build exemplars of better policy and practice, and engage educators and justice leaders as allies in reform. This experience offers a unique vantage point from which to assess the breadth of reform efforts under way around the country as well as how the groundswell of activity is influencing policy makers' understanding of the school-to-prison pipeline as an urgent national issue.

PUBLIC EDUCATION AND THE PIPELINE TO PRISON

At the center of the school-to-prison pipeline is a troubling increase in exclusionary discipline strategies (i.e., disciplinary actions that remove a child from the classroom for an extended period of time) as a reflexive response to adolescent misbehavior in schools. Data from the National Center for Education Statistics (NCES, 2009) show that more than 3.3 million students were suspended in 2006—nearly one in fourteen and double the rate of school suspensions in the 1970s. While high suspension rates are a concern for all students, they are particularly concerning for students of color. Analyses of school discipline indicate that African American students are suspended at very high rates—in Milwaukee, for example, 50 percent of the school district's black middle school students were suspended in 2007 (Losen & Skiba, 2010). They also are disproportionately more likely than their white peers to receive a suspension for a first-time violation of their school's code of conduct; to be punished more severely for nonthreatening categories of offense; to be overrepresented in school-based arrests, referrals to the courts, juvenile detention centers and "disciplinary schools"; and to drop out of school (Skiba, Michael, Nardo, & Peterson, 2002; Rafaele Mendez & Knoff, 2003; Wallace, Goodkind, Wallace, & Bachman, 2008; Fabelo et al., 2011; NCES, 2011).

Educational attainment is the single-most-important predictor of an American child's prospects in life. More than any other factor, success in high school determines one's life earnings and reduces the chances that a young person will be incarcerated in the future. High school dropouts are at greater risk of incarceration (at an annual cost of roughly $23,000 per inmate per year) and earn 96 percent less over their lifetimes than those with a bachelor's degree (Schmitt, Warner, & Gupta, 2010; NCES, 2011). Keeping children in school is therefore a paramount concern, not only for their individual success but also for the economic and civic health of society as a whole.

Few believe that schools should put up with dangerous or abusive behavior from students. Yet, while serious misbehavior warrants a serious response, young people who commit minor mistakes also are being swept up in the push to "get tough on crime." Using profanity in the classroom or violating the dress code—actions that typify the modus operandi of adolescent life—are increasingly triggering out-of-school suspensions under zero tolerance school discipline policies that emphasize a swift and severe response when students break school rules.[1] In Colorado, for example, legislators observed cases where "students have been referred to police for bringing a wooden replica of a rifle to school or unintentionally hitting a teacher with a bean bag chair" and called for a return to a culture of "reasonableness" (Moreno, 2011, para. 4–6). Similarly extreme cases have been documented in other parts of the country (Miller et al., 2011; VOYCE, 2011; Youth United for Change & Advancement Project, 2011; Sullivan & Morgan, 2010; Padres y Jovenes Unidos & Advancement Project, 2005).

215

Consider the following examples from students in Philadelphia:

> Robert was an eleven-year-old in fifth grade who, in his rush to get to school on time, put on a dirty pair of pants from the laundry basket. He did not notice that his Boy Scout pocket knife was in one of the pockets until he got to school. He also did not notice that it fell out when he was running in gym class. When the teacher found it and asked whom it belonged to, Robert volunteered that it was his, only to find himself in police custody minutes later. He was arrested, suspended, and transferred to a disciplinary school.

> Kevin was a tenth-grader who was "caught" with a small pair of scissors in his backpack while going through the school's metal detector. He had forgotten to remove it after wrapping Christmas presents at his girlfriend's house the night before. Kevin was arrested, suspended, and transferred to a disciplinary school.

> Gerald, fifteen, was a ninth-grader who was arrested, suspended, and sent to an alternative education program for having a butter knife in his backpack. He only learned it was there when he was entering school and placed his bag on the scanner as he walked through the metal detector. When the scanner went off, his bag was searched, the utensil was found, and he was handcuffed to a chair until the Philadelphia police came and arrested him. (Youth United for Change & Advancement Project, 2011, p. 14)

A growing body of research suggests that the strict imposition of penalties regardless of individual circumstances does little to improve student behavior (APA Zero Tolerance Task Force, 2008; Osher, Bear, Sprague, & Doyle, 2010; Rausch & Skiba, 2006). Young people in the Philadelphia-based student organizing group Youth United for Change (YUC), which conducted research on disciplinary policies in partnership with Advancement Project (2011), observe that rigidly punitive disciplinary approaches can actually produce the opposite effect. The accusatory and capricious nature of the punishments makes students feel uncared for at school and angry at the adults involved, especially the police, leading them to slowly disinvest from school and making their behavior worse. YUC youth leaders explain:

> When I got suspended for four days, I lost focus on work and I lost out on a lot of credit. But when I went to my teachers for extra credit or work that I missed, they acted like it was not their problem.

> [On entering Daniel Boone for the first time,] I had to take off my shoes and they searched me like I was a real criminal . . . [After that] I was making up every excuse not to go to school. (Youth United for Change & Advancement Project, 2011, p. 17)

How and why did schools get here? The literatures on school safety and discipline generally trace the rise of exclusionary discipline in schools to two federal laws: the Drug-Free Schools and Communities Act in 1986 and the Safe and Gun Free Schools Act in 1994. These laws provided the legal framework for a swift and severe ("zero tolerance") response to student behavior by establishing possession of firearms, explosives, and certain drugs on campus as mandatory expulsion offenses. Although focused principally on the school context, these federal mandates paralleled shifts in the treatment of criminal offenders in the justice community. The Sentencing Reform Act of 1984, followed by the 1986 Anti-Drug Abuse Bill and the 1991 Crime Bill, reframed justice from a focus on rehabilitating offenders to a focus on retribution and deterrence through mandatory minimum sentences and stiffer penalties for nonviolent offenses (Sterling, 2009; Kalstein, McCornock, & Rosenthal, 1992). These policies also limited judicial discretion in determining the severity of punishment in favor of a uniform and more punitive response to infractions. This national swing toward harsher criminal sentencing, combined with a spate of highly publicized and tragic school shootings (including an incident at Colorado's Columbine High School in 1999), influenced the public's and policy makers' perceptions of how best to respond to adolescent behavior. The result was to accelerate the spread of zero tolerance policies and to broaden the application of these policies in schools (Blumenson & Nilsen, 2002; Thurau & Wald, 2010).

Consequently, school districts across the nation embraced get-tough discipline policies intended to deter misbehavior and hired security officers ("school resource officers") in order to prevent "another Columbine from happening here" (Fowler, Lightsey, Monger, & Aseltine, 2010, p. 3). By the early 2000s, local zero tolerance disciplinary policies were going beyond federal law, permitting suspensions for all manner of less threatening offenses, such as wearing hats or bringing plastic weapons, aspirin, paper clips, or nail files to school (Advancement Project & Harvard University Civil Rights Project, 2000; Blumenson & Nilsen, 2002; Thurau & Wald, 2010).

Although the larger atmosphere of hypercriminalization is one reason for the growing application of zero tolerance strategies on adolescent behavior, there are multiple forces behind the rise in suspensions, expulsions, and arrests in U.S. public schools. A second reason relates to the growing presence of law enforcement on school campuses.[2] In New York City, for example, there are now more than five thousand school safety officers in the city's public schools (Mukherjee, 2007). Law enforcement–based security measures, such as metal detector machines and wand scanning, are regular features in students' lives, with an estimated 99,000 New York City students passing through permanent metal detectors to enter their school buildings each day (New York Civil Liberties Union, n.d.). Although the literature on school resource officers emphasizes multiple roles for police in schools, including mentoring students, advocates report that police officers receive little training on youth development, conflict resolution, positive school climate, or the needs of students with disabilities (ACLU & ACLU of Connecticut, 2008; Fowler et. al., 2010; Wald & Thurau, 2010). Thus, their presence in schools can create flashpoints for conflict with students and encourage police involvement in minor school-related issues. Routine student misbehaviors that might once have been resolved by a teacher or school principal are instead viewed as criminal offenses, with terminology like "disorderly conduct," "theft and robbery," and "assault and battery" creeping into the vocabulary of schools (Freeman, Neill, & Guisbond, 2010).

A third reason for the expansion of exclusionary discipline relates to the growing pressure on schools to raise student standardized test scores. Beginning in the mid-1990s, the federal government began to assert stronger accountability mandates for schools receiving federal Title I funds to demonstrate gains in student achievement. This pressure intensified with the passage of the No Child Left Behind Act (NCLB) in 2001, which required annual testing in grades 3 through 8 and set performance targets that schools were required to meet or lose funding. The heightened pressure on schools to improve test scores, coupled with budget cuts, led to a scaling back of nontested academic subjects, such as science and social studies, along with arts and gym programs, in order to devote more time to test-prep activities (McMurrer, 2007). The result, students say, are academic programs that are less interesting and that reward those students who are more willing (or developmentally ready) to sit quietly in the classroom (AEJ, 2011). Significantly, the pressure on schools to produce higher achievement scores—initially to meet Adequate Yearly Progress standards under NCLB and, increasingly, as a measure of teaching effectiveness—creates an incentive to remove low-performing children from the classroom who require extra time or effort. Indeed, a study of school discipline data in Florida found that suspensions and expulsions increased in the months preceding the state's assessment test, with lower-performing students consistently more likely to receive harsher punishments than their higher-achieving peers (Figlio, 2006).

A fourth reason for the growing numbers of disciplinary actions relates to the long history of racial inequity in U.S. public schooling. Numerous studies have documented the disproportionate use of punitive school discipline on children of color, despite statistical evidence that these children are not misbehaving at higher rates than their white peers (Advancement Project, 2010; Advancement Project & Harvard Civil Rights Project, 2000; Children's Defense Fund, 1975; Losen & Skiba, 2010; Monroe, 2005; Skiba et al., 2002; Skiba, Peterson, & Williams, 1997; Wald & Losen, 2003). In 2000, Advancement Project drew parallels between the use of corporal punishment in Mississippi schools and the state's history of slavery and disenfranchisement of its black populations (Padres y Jovenes Unidos & Advancement Project, 2010). Others have noted racial undertones behind the myth of the black and brown "super predator," which fed national fears of youth violence in the early 1990s and justified the criminalization of adolescent behavior (Ginwright, 2001; HoSang, 2003). If students of color are willfully disobedient thugs, went the thinking, a get-tough approach is not only appropriate but necessary (Males,

1996). Indeed, young people and advocates observe the widespread use of stop-and-frisk policies in their communities as evidence of a persistent pattern of viewing youth of color with suspicion and as less deserving of the supports and second chances afforded to their white peers (Stoudt, Fine, & Fox, 2012). Such suspicion, they argue, contributes to the rising use of suspensions for vaguely defined behaviors, like "defiance," that are subject to wide-ranging interpretation by teachers and administrators. In such a context of pervasive racial discrimination, it is hardly surprising that suspensions, expulsions, and arrests in schools are on the rise, and racial disproportionality within them increasing, at a time when the numbers of students of color in U.S. public schools are growing (U.S. Department of Education, 2012).

In sum, substantial evidence suggests that, regardless of intent, zero tolerance disciplinary policies do more harm than good. Out-of-school suspensions, arrests, court referrals, and expulsions decrease in-class learning time, compound academic failure and drop-out, and increase children's chances of involvement in the juvenile and criminal justice systems (APA Zero Tolerance Task Force, 2008). Zero tolerance discipline policies harm all students, not only the growing numbers of students who have been suspended, by undermining children's sense of connection to and safety in school (McNeely, Nonemaker, & Blum, 2002). These policies are especially harmful to students of color, who are more likely to attend schools that use punitive discipline policies and more likely to receive tougher sanctions than their white counterparts, even for the same offenses (Skiba et al., 1997; Welch & Payne, 2010). LGBT students, too, are at increased risk of punishment by school authorities, police, and the courts, particularly when they challenge mainstream norms of gender expression (Himmelstein & Bruckner, 2010).

GRASSROOTS ORGANIZING FOR FEDERAL POLICY CHANGE

John Kingdon's (1995) theory of public policy agenda setting asserts that policy windows open at moments of alignment among the problem stream (issues recognized as significant problems that need to be addressed), the policy stream (what is regarded as a good and actionable idea), and the political stream (dynamics in the larger political environment that facilitate action). Alignment across these streams creates the opportunity for new ideas to enter into the policy-making discourse. The emerging trend to rethink zero tolerance policies attests to advocates' success in framing zero tolerance as a problem, providing concrete examples of a "better way," and creating the necessary political context of pressure and support to move their agenda forward. In this section I outline the ways in which local and state-level organizing by grassroots organizations, together with their legal, research, and foundation partners, fostered the national movement that captured the Obama administration's attention.

Young People Push Back: State and Local Efforts Build the National Movement

Among the earliest advocates to record racial disproportionality in disciplinary practices was the Children's Defense Fund (1975), which published a report observing the prevalence of suspensions that were "unnecessary, made no educational sense and disserved the interests of the children involved" (p. v). However, the current movement of grassroots organizing on pipeline issues did not begin until the late 1990s when young people—and later parents and civil rights advocates—began to fight back against what youth organizer Jasmin de la Rosa described as the "growing feeling across the country that young people are out of control" (Chow, Lizardo, Olsen, & Dowell, 2001, p. 65).

In California, grassroots youth organizations formed a statewide Schools Not Jails campaign in 1999 to call public attention to a pattern of youth criminalization that, through the confluence of increased police presence on school campuses, stiffer penalties for first-time youth offenders, and decreased educational resources, created a direct path for children of color from schools into the state's penitentiary system (Chow et al., 2001; Ginwright, 2004). Writing of the student mobilizations, researcher Mamie Chow and her colleagues (2001) observed that "the question put on the table during [the Schools Not Jails] campaign was: 'What is our society doing to the future of youth of color by choosing to incarcerate rather than educate them?'" (p. 65).

In Chicago, high school student members of Generation Y produced a report, *Suspended Education: A Preliminary Report on the Impact of Zero Tolerance on Chicago Public School Students* (Lahoud, 2000), examining how school suspensions were counterproductive and undermined their education. As a high school student observed in the report, "Teachers are getting strict, but are suspending kids for stupid reasons. During suspension or expulsion, students never do anything, so how could that punish them? It's just taking away time from their education" (Davenport, 2001, p. 38). Generation Y's advocacy with Chicago's board of education persuaded the school district to implement conflict resolution programs, including peer courts, to reduce disciplinary actions in schools (HoSang, 2006).

Three years later, in 2003, the intergenerational organizing group Padres y Jovenes Unidos began documenting how disciplinary practices in the Denver Public Schools threatened the academic success of the district's black and Latino students (Padres y Jovenes Unidos & Advancement Project, 2005). Working with Advancement Project, youth publicized the problems with the district's discipline policies and held events to pressure school district leaders, the teachers union, and the Denver City Council to enact a reform agenda. Their successful advocacy led to a new disciplinary policy in 2008 limiting the offenses for which students could be suspended or arrested in schools and implementing an alternative disciplinary program, called restorative practices, in district schools.[3] The district also pledged to work to eliminate racial disparities in discipline and began providing suspended students the opportunity to complete classwork missed due to suspension without penalty. These reforms reduced out-of-school suspensions in the district by 40 percent and police ticketing for discipline code violations in schools by 68 percent.

In New York City, Youth Force and the Prison Moratorium Project collected data linking disciplinary actions and state-level investments in juvenile incarceration to show how rising suspension and expulsion rates were feeding the prison-industrial complex, a term used to describe, "a set of bureaucratic, political, and economic interests that encourage increased spending on imprisonment, regardless of the actual need" (Schlosser, 1998, para. 7; Landsman, 2011). These groups were joined later by the Urban Youth Collaborative, a citywide coalition of youth-led organizations that formed in 2005 to challenge the growing intrusion of police in New York City schools and to propose alternatives—such as the hiring of additional guidance counselors and the creation of student-run academic support centers—to keep students in school (Mediratta, Cohen, & Shah, 2007).

And in south Los Angeles a four-year campaign by the grassroots parent organizing group Community Asset Development Re-Defining Education (CADRE) led the school district in 2007 to mandate schoolwide Positive Behavior Support programs in Los Angeles public schools to reduce suspensions and improve the climate for learning.[4] Leading up to the disciplinary policy change, CADRE (n.d.) organizers collected stories from students and parents about the impact of suspensions on students' trajectories in school, coproduced a report on school push-out in Los Angeles with a national human rights organization, staged a "people's hearing" on school discipline, and met repeatedly with school district officials to press the case for reforming the district's discipline policy.[5] Following the adoption of the new policy, suspensions dropped by 13 percent and expulsions by 56 percent (CADRE, 2010).

Today, more than one hundred organizations are working on school-to-prison pipeline issues across the country. Roughly half these groups were not doing this work two years ago, and more than three-quarters were not doing this work five years ago (Advancement Project, 2011). The majority of them are grassroots organizations led by high school students and public school parents (DSC, 2012).

From Local to National: The Role of Research and Policy Organizations

What fueled the development of school-to-prison pipeline organizing from its initial phase of youth-led state and local activism into a burgeoning national movement? A crucial element in the expansion was the growing number of legal, research, and policy organizations taking on pipeline-related issues and lending their particular forms of expertise to explicate the factors at play. In 1999, following an incident in Decatur, Illinois, where seven black students were expelled for a scuffle at a football game, civil rights advocates, including the Reverend Jesse Jackson and lawyers at the Advancement Project and Harvard Civil Rights Project, convened a national summit that explored the racially disparate impact of zero tolerance suspensions in schools (Advancement Project, 2010). These organizations, along with others—including the American Civil Liberties Union (ACLU), Education and Juvenile Law Centers of Pennsylvania, NAACP LDF, and Southern Poverty Law Center—explicitly linked zero tolerance school disciplinary policies to longer-term struggles for equity and educational opportunity for children of color and worked in partnership with grassroots groups to produce reports and develop litigation to challenge school district practices.[6]

In addition, prominent scholars such as Pedro Noguera began linking school disciplinary practices to poor educational outcomes, particularly for black boys. Russell Skiba at Indiana University (IU), Anne Gregory at Rutgers University, and other researchers produced statistical and qualitative studies disentangling race and poverty in order to show the pernicious effects of racial bias in producing disparities in disciplinary sanctions. The Civil Rights Remedies Initiative at the Civil Rights Project (CRP), under the direction of Daniel Losen, began releasing regular analyses of public data sets demonstrating trends in school discipline disparities. IU and CRP launched, with Atlantic support, a Research-to-Practice Collaborative of scholars and advocates in 2011 to build knowledge about causes of and remedies for discipline disproportionality and to provide timely research and data analysis for the field. At least three books have been published in recent years by university presses related to the school-to-prison pipeline, along with a steady stream of reports and articles by advocates and scholars.[7]

Two major national advocacy coalitions also have emerged to provide a coordinated and nationwide response to end the pipeline. The Dignity in Schools Campaign formed in 2007 to unite the emerging network of youth, parents, educators, civil rights organizations, lawyers, and social justice advocates under an umbrella vision of challenging school push-out and promoting alternatives to a culture of zero tolerance, punishment, and student removal in schools (DSC, 2012). The Alliance for Educational Justice (AEJ) launched in 2009 to provide a national platform for young people to express their views on educational policy. Comprised of twenty youth-led, multigenerational, and multiracial organizations from across the country, AEJ's member organizations include some of the first to organize nationally against zero tolerance discipline policies, such as Padres y Jovenes Unidos, as well as organizations newer to the issue, like Voices of Youth in Chicago Education (VOYCE).

The DSC and AEJ provide on a national level what social movement scholars McAdam, McCarthy, and Zald (1996) call "mobilizing structures"—a key factor in the emergence and development of social movements. These coalitions serve as formal structures for collective action, enabling local community organizations to insert their views into federal policy discussions on a consistent and ongoing basis. The DSC, for example, convenes annual Days in the Capitol for members to meet with federal officials and has developed a structure of cross-site working groups and issue-specific webinars to ensure that participating local organizations contribute to its work. Similarly, AEJ brings youth together in national summits, regional retreats, and monthly membership calls to plan campaign strategy and share their views with policy makers.

The commitment of financial resources from foundation supporters also helped to coalesce a national movement. The Surdna Foundation and Edward W. Hazen Foundation invested deeply in youth-led education organizing across the country and, together with the Funders Collaborative on Youth Organizing, convened youth organizations in national gatherings to share analyses and campaign strategies.[8] Other foundations, including the Charles Stewart Mott Foundation, Schott Foundation for Public Education, and Open Society Foundations (OSF) provided support to parent organizing while also making grants to legal advocates. In 2003, Mott, OSF, the Levi Strauss Foundation, and, later, the Jeht Foundation and Surdna joined in an effort to provide targeted funding on zero tolerance (Surdna Foundation, personal communication, May 29, 2012). In 2007, Mott, together with Hazen and the Ford Foundation and Schott Foundation, among others, launched a national funding collaborative, Communities for Public Education Reform (CPER), at Public Interest Projects to assist grassroots groups in scaling-up their work, first to reach state-level influence and later to engage in federal policy advocacy.

The ecosystem of school-to-prison pipeline organizing currently draws its resources through the combined efforts of multiple foundations, all of which are vital to the continued growth and success of this burgeoning movement. CPER and its sister fund, the Just and Fair Schools Fund (JFSF), which began in 2010 with Atlantic support, now support a total of one hundred grassroots groups, forty of which are working on school discipline and climate reform (JFSF Donor Materials, personal communication, March 5, 2012). In addition, several foundations are supporting programmatic interventions to complement the advocacy by their grassroots organizing grantees. The California Endowment, for example, has provided extensive resources to implement restorative justice in California high schools, in addition to supporting policy research and communications across the state. Similarly, Open Society Institute–Baltimore has invested deeply in promoting disciplinary alternatives in the Baltimore public schools.

From "Violence" to "Push-Out": Framing Zero Tolerance School Discipline as a Problem

Collective action in any movement depends on an interpretive process of framing, or "sense-making," among movement participants about problems and viable responses (McAdam et al., 1996). Framing theory suggests that it is not just the presence of an injustice that motivates people to act but how that grievance is interpreted. Frames are a crucial part of movement building; they are crafted and embedded in organizational materials and activities to "activate adherents, transform bystanders into supporters, exact concessions from targets, and demobilize antagonists" (Snow, 2004, p. 385). In this section, I examine advocates' efforts to frame zero tolerance as a problem and how that frame has begun to influence the media and policy makers.

The push to adopt a zero tolerance approach to school discipline in the 1990s was driven by a framing of the policy as necessary to protect children from youth perpetrators. For groups that opposed this policy, the initial challenge was to articulate a counternarrative that communicated the injustices of zero tolerance school disciplinary strategies—that they were racially biased and counterproductive to educative ends and produced enormous social costs by pushing children unnecessarily into the juvenile and criminal justice systems. The school-to-prison imagery resonated with young people in part because it described a tangible reality in their lives. As organizer Jasmin de la Rosa observed in 2000:

> You're starting to see a direct link between schools and prison. Youth get in trouble for smoking a cigarette, and then get taken to the Youth Detention Center and get in that cycle. In Oakland, the school district even rented cells out of the Juvenile Detention Center especially for high school students. (Chow et al., 2001, p. 66)

The "school-to-prison pipeline" language also appealed to young people's desire for fairness and to fight injustice. The term was agitational, provoking youth to consider the structural forces at play behind individual students' experiences of punishment in schools. It encouraged them to repudiate the national rhetoric of dangerous youth, and to join in collective protests in California and elsewhere for an equitable distribution of funding for their schools at a time when government investment in the criminal justice system had begun to outstrip allocations for public education (HoSang, 2006).

Importantly, the school-to-prison frame also linked the experiences of young people of color to a history of racial disenfranchisement and helped them to forge alliances with other influential organizations. Civil rights groups like Southern Echo in Mississippi had begun working on a Schoolhouse to Jailhouse project to confront corporal punishment, de facto segregation in schools, and a rise in juvenile incarceration (Lambright, 2001). Through the Oakland, California–based Applied Research Center's Racial Justice Initiative and Advancement Project, youth organizations networked with organizations in Mississippi and others around the country (Mediratta & Fruchter, 2001).

Against the backdrop of public safety concerns, however, the pipeline imagery was insufficient to shift policy makers' perceptions of zero tolerance as a necessary tactic in schools. Indeed, anti-school-to-prison organizing continued under the radar for much of the 2000s. With the formation of national coalitions in 2007 and 2009, the framing of the issue began to widen, and so too did its visibility in the media. First, the Dignity in Schools Campaign's (2012) problem framing linked school discipline to push-out and explicitly demanded students' right to be treated with dignity "as human beings . . . to participate in decisions affecting them and their education, and to attend school free from discrimination of any kind." The Alliance for Educational Justice pushed this framing further, linking school discipline and push-out to inequitable funding of public education, an overreliance on high-stakes testing, and low levels of academic rigor and expectations in schools. The expanded framing of school discipline—not just as a path to prison for undeserving children but as a case of schools deliberately pushing the most vulnerable children out of school, struck a dissonant chord with the Obama administration's goal of the United States producing the highest proportion of college graduates in the world by 2020 (White House, 2009). A review by Advancement Project in 2011 found a noticeable shift in the attention of news organizations to zero tolerance school discipline. News media stories on the topic increased by 70 percent between 2010 and 2011 from 549 to 935. Many of these stories reported on advocacy and data analyses by youth and parent-led grassroots organizing groups and legal advocates, in addition to publicizing instances of overzealous punishment.[9]

Most significantly, media articles from 2011-2012 reflect a perceptible shift in coverage of zero tolerance, from being a necessary strategy to keep children safe from youth perpetrators to a policy that has gone too far. An in-depth analysis of coverage by twelve major newspapers nationally conducted by Advancement Project (2011) found that of the 77 stories on zero tolerance, only 11 favored the use of such policies in schools in 2011, compared with 13 out of 38 stories in 2010. From the federal government on down, observed Advancement Project researchers, "law enforcement officials, education officials, and state legislators, both Republican and Democrat, have written opinion pieces or been quoted in articles using very strong language condemning the school-to-prison pipeline" (slide 17).

Offering Viable Alternatives

Grassroots groups and their allies not only framed and publicized the problem of the school-to-prison pipeline. They also catalyzed and built legitimacy for exemplars showing how zero tolerance could be rolled back in schools without unleashing chaos in schools. The implementation of the schoolwide Positive Behavior and Intervention Supports (PBIS) and Restorative Practices called for by CADRE in Los Angeles and Padres y Jovenes Unidos in Denver offered concrete and nonpunitive alternatives to zero tolerance policies and practices as well as a new stream of data demonstrating their effectiveness.

What gives a given policy solution traction in a larger landscape of competing ideas? The partnership among parents, students, lawyers, and researchers certainly added legitimacy to grassroots efforts. Research studies showing PBIS's success in improving school climate and student behavior played a role in persuading Los Angeles school district leaders to adopt the program, as did the implementation studies from leading scholars that echoed CADRE's monitoring reports (CADRE et al., 2010; Sprague & Vincent, 2011). Importantly, the growing number of advocates engaged on this issue helped to keep school discipline in the news and to convey not only growing public concern about the excesses of zero tolerance but also the existence of credible and more effective alternatives. A succession of effective advocacy efforts in different states created a sense of urgency and momentum for reform in the months leading up to the SSDI announcement by the U.S. attorney general and secretary of education.

For example, in April 2011, one month prior to Thompson's presentation to the Justice Department's Coordinating Council, the Los Angeles Police Department announced an agreement to end its practice of issuing summons ("tickets") and fines to students for missing school or coming late. This work was spearheaded by CADRE's longtime ally, the Labor Community Strategy Center, and involved multiple youth organizations and a legal partner, Public Counsel. Police ticketing had emerged as a critical impediment to student success because of the sheer expense of resolving them (costing students up to $1,000 with penalties and court fees). The problem, as a *Los Angeles Times* editorial observed,

> is that students, especially poor ones, often can't afford to pay the fines. Indeed, some choose to avoid school altogether rather than risk being cited for showing up late. So rather than deterring truancy, such fines may be fueling absenteeism. Statistics are hard to come by, but what's known is that between 2005 and 2009, the police issued more than 47,000 tickets; the truancy rate during the same period increased from 5 percent to more than 28 percent, according to the California Department of Education. ("L.A.'s Truancy Trouble," 2012, para. 4)

The ticketing campaign and subsequent agreement with the Los Angeles Police Department received extensive media coverage, including in-depth stories on National Public Radio and in the *Los Angeles Times* and *Huffington Post*.

In Colorado, Padres y Jovenes Unidos used the school discipline reforms in Denver as a springboard to revise the state's school discipline statutes. In September 2010, the organization launched a statewide coalition to advocate for reform and built alliances with a wide variety of organizations across the state. Following a vigorous campaign, on May 23, 2011 (the same day as Thompson's presentation to the Coordinating Council), Colorado governor John Hickenlooper signed a bill authorizing the creation of a bipartisan legislative task force to review the state's school discipline trends and policies and make recommendations to "reduce the student dropout rate, make schools safer and more effective, and reduce the number of youth entering the juvenile and criminal justice systems" (Colorado Senate, 2011).

These community-driven reforms were aided by a high profile, although unconnected, effort by Baltimore Public Schools superintendent Andres Alonso to reduce school suspensions through programs to build a positive school climate and address individual student needs. Steep gains in African American male attendance and achievement resulting from Alonso's reforms brought national attention, including lengthy stories in *Education Week* and the *New York Times* (Sparks, 2010; Tavernise, 2010). Baltimore's success underscored what advocates had earlier observed, that higher suspension rates tended to reflect a school's approach to discipline rather than the extent of student misbehavior. Shifting the focus to keeping students in schools could drive gains in attendance and achievement without compromising school safety. Media coverage of Superintendent Alonso's work, in concert with the problem frames advanced by advocates, helped to position the Los Angeles and Denver reforms as mounting evidence that school district and state leaders were themselves recognizing the need for action.

Creating Political Pressure at the Federal Level

With the problem framed and valid alternatives in the policy stream, grassroots organizations and their partners also created a context of political pressure and support to move key policy makers. The convergence of problem, policy, and politics opened a "policy window" (Kingdon, 1995) for the federal initiative announced on July 21, 2011.

Key staff members involved in the federal SSDI assert that while the Texas study provided the impetus for federal action, the ground was prepared by the growing chorus of demands for action on school push-out from students, parents, legal advocates, and researchers around the country. Beginning in 2010, Dignity in Schools and Alliance for Educational Justice staged coordinated actions around the country and met repeatedly with federal officials to share their experiences in schools and to offer recommendations for what education policy makers could do to move schools away from zero tolerance. The coalitions worked closely with foundation partners at Atlantic and the Open Society Foundations to ensure a unified voice and to leverage the insider access of philanthropy. The interplay of state and local actions, engagement of diverse partners, and a presence in Washington ultimately proved critical. These tactics introduced the problem and viable alternatives to administration and congressional staffers, "softening up" (Kingdon, 1995) federal policy makers to the idea of school discipline reform by building staff familiarity with the issues and understanding of the urgent need for reform.

Illustrating this point, Kristen Harper (personal communication, March 13, 2012), the Department of Education's lead official in the federal initiative, recalled the impact of meeting with AEJ youth in February 2011:

> What got me on board was the Voices in Action summit in Washington DC.[10] I was there to present to young people about what my office was doing to address school climate. I shared with them our framework and how we thought student surveys would help make links to student voice and engagement in schools. And the youth threw it right back in our faces. They said it was not good enough. I remember one student said, "They suspend us for nothing." And another said, "I've been expelled and I don't know what to do." They wanted to know what we were doing to stop schools from suspending and expelling them.
>
> I was devastated, walking away from that meeting. I remember telling my director about it and how we had to do something. So when Justice came to us with [the Supportive School Discipline] plan, we were ready.

The Department of Education already had taken strides to elevate school climate issues, most notably through policy guidance and high-profile summits to reduce bullying in schools. That work, combined with department officials' direct conversations with AEJ youth and Dignity in Schools members, as well as their own prior reform experiences, influenced the agency's perspective on school suspensions. Consequently, when Secretary Duncan saw the Justice Department's proposal for a school discipline initiative in early July, he agreed immediately to the plan (federal agency staff member, personal communication, March 13, 2012).

On the Justice Department side, advocates believe that meetings with senior leadership played a similar role in paving the way for action. The NAACP LDF and lawyers in the DSC had met previously with Justice Department officials to discuss the disparate impact of school discipline policies on students of color. These legal advocates, along with grassroots leaders in the DSC, also conducted substantial work with congressional leaders and staff, trying to line up a legislative bill on school discipline. While that effort eventually stalled, it did ensure that political leaders—both Democrat and Republican—were hearing about school discipline concerns. As a result, when the findings from the Texas study were presented, Attorney General Holder was predisposed to act (civil rights advocate, personal communication, February 13, 2012). Behind-the-scenes meetings among advocates, CSG researchers, and Atlantic staff positioned the foundation to reach out, following Thompson's briefing, to assist Justice Department officials in creating the SSDI plan.

While policy change requires alignment among the problem, policy, and political streams, these streams typically run independent of each other (Kingdon, 1995). Catalyzing events, like the release of the CSG *Breaking Schools' Rules* report, do not always translate into reform. In this case, the framing of zero tolerance and school push-out as a problem undermining educational goals, together with examples of reform, fostered a perception among political leaders of school discipline as a problem that could be resolved. Persistent demands for change by grassroots groups and youth leaders across the country helped federal officials understand the need for action and ultimately set in motion what agency staffers describe as an "unprecedented" and "lightning-speed" collaboration between two cabinet-level secretaries.

THE ROAD AHEAD

As I have shown above, a ten-year effort of grassroots organizing was instrumental in creating a policy window for federal action on the school-to-prison pipeline. That organizing effectively framed the issue, uncovered and legitimated workable policy alternatives, and built a political context of demand and support for action. Federal staff members readily acknowledge the impact of advocates' efforts on their sense of urgency on this issue, as well as on the priorities and rollout of the SSDI initiative. In the months following the SSDI announcement, federal agencies moved to address advocates' concerns by releasing newly expanded civil rights data on school suspensions, expulsions, and arrests, launching communities of practice to assist state-level educators and judicial leaders in developing reform initiatives, and by requiring school district recipients of competitive federal grants programs to address racial disparities in school discipline.

The decentralized nature of the grassroots organizing movement, anchored in states and local school districts, as well as in Washington, DC, has fostered a reinforcing pressure between federal action and state capitols. Fifteen school discipline–related bills were under consideration in state legislatures in 2011, all focused on curbing the excesses of zero tolerance—whether by expanding data collection and reporting or by encouraging nonexclusionary disciplinary alternatives, improving training for school resource officers, reducing school referrals to the juvenile justice system, or creating better reentry procedures for students returning from juvenile detention facilities (Advancement Project, 2011). In the early months of 2012, the state of Colorado passed landmark legislation to roll back the zero tolerance practices of local school districts, and the Maryland State Board of Education took up policy recommendations to implement a similar set of statewide reforms.

Despite these promising steps toward reform, significant challenges lie ahead. Central is the question that young people and advocates in the Alliance for Educational Justice and the Dignity in Schools Campaign are raising about the contradictions between the Obama administration's stated goals for supportive discipline and the larger focus of the Department of Education's primary education reform strategies. In particular, they point out that the current emphasis on charter school expansion, test-based teacher evaluation systems, and acceleration of "alternative route" pathways for new teachers and administrators all intensify the pressure on increasingly inexperienced school staffs to raise test scores, making exclusion of struggling students a tempting resort. In a statement to education officials last May, youth leaders in AEJ expressed grave concern about the impact of these strategies on low-income communities and communities of color around the country.

> We agree with the Obama Administration that education is the "civil rights issue of our generation," but we have significant disagreements with their policy reforms intended to "fix" our schools. Many of their proposals . . . are dominated by a set of misguided ideas that will do further damage to low-income communities and communities of color around the country . . . It is . . . time to stop "getting tough" on so-called failing schools, teachers, and students and instead get smart about using our resources in ways that benefit young people, families and communities over the long term. (AEJ, 2011, pp. 2, 3)

Reflecting on their educational experiences as students, parents, and teachers, AEJ and DSC members have proposed a variety of strategies to reduce the incentive for push-out in schools, including: greater use of performance-based assessments as an alternative to the reliance on standardized tests; systematic inclusion of student input in teacher evaluations to inform classroom practice and improve student-teacher relationships; shifting resources from school police and security hardware to preventative measures such as counselors and early intervention programs; and addressing systemic inequities in educational funding. As advocates have argued, the lack of resources for academic enrichment programs, extracurricular activities, school counselors, and mental health services negatively impact on the climate for learning in schools—reducing the supports teachers have to improve their instructional practice and resolve classroom management issues and limiting the opportunities for students to experience a rich and engaging curriculum or to get help when they need it.

A second challenge arises, paradoxically, from the very framing of the school-to-prison pipeline that has helped propel advocates' success. Advocates have raised the visibility of zero tolerance discipline on the national agenda in part through targeted pressure on sympathetic policy makers. Further advances will require a wider base of public and political support to ensure that legislative bills are passed and appropriately funded and to monitor school-level implementation. The involvement of institutional stakeholders, such as school board members, superintendents, school principals, teachers, and teacher unions, will be particularly important to make sure that policy reforms, when they happen, succeed in changing practice in schools. Yet, recent messaging research indicates that the school-to-prison pipeline language may make it difficult for grassroots groups to partner with these frontline educators successfully (Advancement Project, 2012). Educators say the term unfairly blames them for larger societal failures and that it fails to acknowledge the pressures they face. Nonetheless, even school principals and teachers who use exclusionary discipline acknowledge that suspensions often do little to teach children how to behave appropriately in school. Alliance building between advocates and educators will require a communications frame that acknowledges the challenges that classroom teachers face on a daily basis, as well as their need for greater supports and training in classroom management, adolescent development, and culturally responsive pedagogy.

A third challenge is the need to squarely address the underlying narrative about the limited capacities of young people of color that drives and legitimates punitive and racially biased disciplinary responses in schools. This requires helping school administrators, teachers, and other school staff to acknowledge and confront the unconscious racial and other biases that influence their interpretations of student behavior. Additionally, as young people, parents, and advocates assert, it also requires structural reforms that address the larger patterns of segregation and social isolation in schools and communities that feed racial stereotypes and perpetuate inequality (AEJ, 2011). Importantly, shifting the narrative of young people's capacity requires creating opportunities for them to exercise leadership in their schools and communities and to demonstrate how their conviction, energy, and insights can advance the task of helping students succeed.

I have argued here that the new federal school discipline initiative both responds to and brings much-needed visibility and legitimacy to the long struggle to end the school-to-prison pipeline. Yet the SSDI must compete with innumerable other priorities for federal policy makers' attention and is being implemented in an environment of budget austerity at all levels of government. With the many pressures facing school districts, there is little incentive or capacity to change practice, despite the benefits of doing so. Grassroots groups have been central to bringing this issue to the fore, and their continued engagement will be a vital source of pressure and support in the future. Continued support for their efforts from foundations and partnerships with researchers, legal advocates, and educators will be essential to make sure that the current window of opportunity opens onto lasting and meaningful change.

NOTES

1. The NCES (1998) defines zero tolerance policy "as a school or district policy that mandates predetermined consequences or punishments for specific offences."
2. Data from the U.S. Bureau of Justice indicates that the number of school resource officers increased from 9,446 in 1997 to 13,056 in 2007. Thurau & Wald (2010) estimate that there are currently 17,000 school resource officers and school-based police nationwide.
3. Restorative practices is a community-building technique used in schools and classrooms to help build relationships among students and to provide a mechanism for resolving conflicts when they arise. The concept focuses on repairing harm after an incident, rather than on punishing the offender. For more information on restorative practices, see the International Institute for Restorative Practices, http://www.iirp.edu/what-is-restorative-practices.php
4. Positive Behavior Intervention Supports (PBIS) is a set of tools and strategies that help schools use data to develop procedures and agreements about student behavior, identify student needs, and link students to additional academic, social/emotional, or mental health supports. See http://www.PBIS.org
5. See also Sullivan (2007).
6. Many of these organizations participate in legal strategy conversations through the American Bar Association, a listserv hosted by the ACLU, and a legal strategies roundtable convened by the NAACP LDF.
7. See, for example, Kim, Losen, and Hewitt (2010); Kupchik (2010); and Nolan (2011).
8. Founding members of the Funders Collaborative on Youth Organizing included Edward W. Hazen Foundation, Ford Foundation, Jewish Funds for Justice, Merck Family Fund, Open Society Institute, Rockefeller Brothers Fund, and the Surdna Foundation. See http://www.fcyo.org/missionvisionandhistory
9. See, for example, the *Washington Post* series by Donna St. George (February–June 2011) on a Virginia high school student who committed suicide after being suspended from school.
10. The Voices in Action Summit, led by the Department of Education's then director of community outreach, Alberto Retana, capped a tour of thirteen cities to gather input from young people about the impediments to success in school and college. The summit drew four hundred students from thirty states and featured in-depth conversations among youth and education officials about key youth concerns.

REFERENCES

Advancement Project. (2010). *Test, punish, and push out: How zero tolerance and high stakes testing funnel youth into the school-to-prison pipeline.* Washington, DC: Author.

Advancement Project. (2011). *Impact of increased school-to-prison pipeline funding on media, state legislation, local policymaking and advocacy.* Report prepared for The Atlantic Philanthropies.

Advancement Project. (2012). *School-to-prison pipeline focus groups: Key findings.* Washington, DC: Author.

Advancement Project & Harvard University Civil Rights Project. (2000). *Opportunities suspended: The devastating consequences of zero tolerance and school discipline policies.* Report from a National Summit on Zero Tolerance, Washington, DC: Advancement Project.

Alliance for Educational Justice [AEJ]. (2011, May). *Youth S.U.C.C.E.S.S. Act.* Washington, DC: Author.

American Civil Liberties Union [ACLU] & ACLU of Connecticut. (2008, November). *Hard lessons: School resource officer programs and school-based arrests in three Connecticut towns.* New York: ACLU.

American Psychological Association [APA] Zero Tolerance Task Force. (2008). Are zero tolerance policies effective in the schools? An evidentiary review and recommendations. *American Psychologist, 63*(9), 852–862.

Blumenson, E., & Nilsen, E. S. (2002). One strike and you're out? Constitutional constraints on zero tolerance in public education. *Washington University Law Quarterly, 81*(65), 65–117.

Children's Defense Fund. (1975). *School suspensions: Are they helping?* Washington, DC: Washington Research Project.

Chow, M., Lizardo, R., Olsen, L., & Dowell, C. (2001). *Mapping the field of school reform organizing in California: Los Angeles and the San Francisco Bay Area.* California Tomorrow. Providence, RI: Annenberg Institute for School Reform at Brown University.

Colorado Senate. (2011, May 23). *Governor Hickenlooper in Arvada today signing bill by Senator Hudak to reform discipline in public schools.* Retrieved from http://coloradosenate.org/home/press/governor-hickenlooper-in-arvada-today-signing-bill-by-senator-hudak-to-reform-discipline-in-public-schools

Community Asset Development Re-Defining Education [CADRE]. (n.d.). Accomplishments. Retrieved from http://www.cadre-la.org/core/accomplishments/

Community Asset Development Re-Defining Education [CADRE]. (2010, June). *Redefining dignity in our schools: A shadow report on school-wide implementation of Positive Behavior Support implementation in south Los Angeles, 2007–2010.* Los Angeles: CADRE, Mental Health Advocacy Services, & Public Counsel. Retrieved from http://www.publiccounsel.org/tools/publications/files/RedefiningDignity.pdf

Davenport, S. (2001). *Mapping school reform organizing in Chicago, 1985–2000.* Providence, RI: Annenberg Institute for School Reform at Brown University. Retrieved from http://annenberginstitute.org/cip/publications/2001/case-studies/chicago-rpt.pdf

Dignity in Schools Campaign [DSC]. (2012, March 5). *Member support and capacity building.* New York: Author.

Fabelo, A., Thompson, M. D., Plotkin, M., Carmichael, D., Marchbanks, M. P., & Booth, E. A. (2011). *Breaking schools' rules: A statewide study of how school discipline relates to student achievement and juvenile justice involvement.* New York: Council of State Governments Justice Center & Public Policy Research Institute.

Figlio, D. N. (2006, May). Testing, crime and punishment. *Journal of Public Economics, 90* (4–5), 837–851.

Fowler, D., Lightsey, R., Monger, J., & Aseltine, E. (2010). *Texas' school-to-prison pipeline: Ticketing, arrest and use of force in schools; How the myth of the blackboard jungle reshaped school disciplinary policy.* Austin: Texas Appleseed.

Freeman, J., Neill, M., & Guisbond, L. (2010, April). *Zero tolerance, high stakes testing and the school-to-prison pipeline.* Washington, DC: Advancement Project & Fair Test.

Ginwright, S. (2001, August). Critical resistance: African American youth and U.S. racism. *Youth Development Journal, 3,* 15–24.

Ginwright, S. (2004). *Black in school: Afrocentric reform, urban youth and the promise of hip-hop culture.* New York: Teachers College Press.

Himmelstein, K. E., & Bruckner, H. (2010, December 6). Criminal-justice and school sanctions against nonheterosexual youth: A national longitudinal study. *Pediatrics.* Retrieved from http://pediatrics.aappublications.org/content/early/2010/12/06/peds.2009-2306

HoSang, D. (2003). *Youth and community organizing today.* New York: Funders Collaborative for Youth Organizing.

HoSang, D. (2006). Beyond policy: Ideology, race and the reimagining of youth. In S. Ginwright, P. Noguera, & J. Cammorota (Eds.), *Beyond resistance! Youth activism and community change* (pp. 3–19). New York: Routledge.

Kalstein, M., McCornock, K. A., & Rosenthal, S. A. (1992). Calculating injustice: The fixation on punishment as crime control. *Harvard Civil Rights–Civil Liberties Law Review, 27*(2), 575–655.

Kelly, J. (2011, July 21). Obama administration to fight harsh discipline. *Youth Today.* Retrieved from http://www.youthtoday.org/view_article.cfm?article_id=4928

Kim, C., Losen, D., & Hewitt, D. (2010). *The school-to-prison pipeline: Structuring legal reform.* New York: New York University Press.

Kingdon, J. W. (1995). *Agendas, alternatives and public policies* (2nd ed.). New York: Addison, Wesley, Longman.

Kupchik, A. (2010). *Homeroom security: School discipline in an age of fear.* New York: New York University Press.

L.A.'s truancy trouble—A fresh look [Editorial]. (2012, February 19). *The Los Angeles Times.* Retrieved from http://articles.latimes.com/2012/feb/19/opinion/la-ed-truancy-20120219

Lahoud, J. (2000). *Suspended education: A preliminary report on the impact of zero tolerance on Chicago Public Schools.* Chicago: Generation Y, a Project of the Southwest Youth Collaborative.

Lambright, N. (2001). Mapping school reform organizing in the Mississippi Delta. Providence, RI: Annenberg Institute for School Reform at Brown University.

Landsman, M. (2011). *Books not bars.* Oakland, CA: Ella Baker Center/Witness.

Losen, D. J., & Skiba, R.J. (2010). Suspended education: Urban middle schools in crisis. Montgomery, AL: Southern Poverty Law Center.

Males, M. (1996). *The scapegoat generation: America's war on adolescents.* Monroe, MN: Common Courage Press.

McAdam, D., McCarthy, J. D., & Zald, M. N. (Eds.). (1996). *Comparative perspectives on social movements: Political opportunities, mobilizing structures and cultural framings.* New York: Cambridge University Press.

McMurrer, J. (2007). *Choices, changes, challenges: Curriculum and instruction in the NCLB era.* Washington, DC: Center on Education Policy.

McNeely, C. A., Nonemaker, J. M., & Blum, R. W. (2002). Promoting student connectedness to school: From the National Longitudinal Study of Adolescent Health. *Journal of School Health, 72*(4), 138–147.

Mediratta, K., Cohen, A., & Shah, S. (2007). Leveraging reform: Youth power in a smart education system. In R. Rothman (Ed.), *City schools* (pp. 99–116), Cambridge, MA: Harvard Education Press.

Mediratta, K., & Fruchter, N. (2001). *Mapping the field of organizing for school improvement.* Providence, RI: Annenberg Institute for School Reform at Brown University.

Miller, J., Ofer, U., Artz, A., Bahl, T., Foster, T., Phenix, D., Sheehan, N., & Thomas, H. A. (2011). *Education interrupted: The growing use of suspensions in New York City's public schools.* New York: New York Civil Liberties Union & Student Safety Coalition.

Monroe, C. (2005). Why are bad boys always black? Causes of disproportionality in school discipline and recommendations for change. *The Clearing House: A Journal of Educational Strategies Issues and Ideas, 79*(1), 45–50.

Moreno, I. (2011, October 18). Post Columbine school discipline changes move forward in Colo. *Huffington Post.* Retrieved from http://www.huffingtonpost.com/2011/10/19/school-discipline changes_n_1019337.html

Mukherjee, E. (2007). *Criminalizing the classroom: The over-policing of New York City schools.* New York: New York Civil Liberties Union & American Civil Liberties Union.

National Center for Education Statistics [NCES]. (1998, March 18). *Violence and discipline problems in U.S. public schools: 1996–97.* Statement by Pascal D. Forgione Jr., U.S. Education Commissioner of Statistics. Retrieved from http://nces.ed.gov/pressrelease/violence.asp

National Center for Education Statistics [NCES]. (2009). School discipline, indicator 28. *The Condition of Education.* Washington, DC: U.S. Department of Education.

National Center for Education Statistics [NCES]. (2011). Indicator 20. *The Condition of Education.* Washington, DC: U.S. Department of Education.

New York Civil Liberties Union. (n.d.). *A look at New York City school safety.* Retrieved from http://www.nyclu.org/schooltoprison/lookatsafety

Nolan, K. (2011). *Police in the hallways: Discipline in an urban high school.* Minneapolis: University of Minnesota Press.

Osher, D., Bear, G. G., Sprague, J. R., & Doyle, W. (2010, January/February). How can we improve school discipline? *Educational Researcher, 39*(1), 48–58.

Padres y Jovenes Unidos & Advancement Project. (2005). *Education on lockdown: The schoolhouse to jailhouse track.* Washington, DC: Advancement Project.

Padres y Jovenes Unidos & Advancement Project. (2010). *Victory at last: The struggle to end the schoolhouse to jailhouse track in Denver Public Schools.* Washington, DC: Advancement Project.

Raffaele Mendez, L. M., & Knoff, H. M. (2003). Who gets suspended from school and why: A demographic analysis of schools and disciplinary infractions in a large school district. *Education and Treatment of Children, 26(1),* 30–51.

Rausch, M. K., & Skiba, R. J. (2006). *Discipline, disability, and race: Disproportionality in Indiana schools.* Bloomington, IN: Center for Evaluation & Education.

Schlosser, E. (1998). The prison-industrial complex. *The Atlantic.* Retrieved from http://www.theatlantic.com/magazine/archive/1998/12/the-prison-industrial-complex/4669/

Schmitt, J., Warner, K., & Gupta, S. (2010). *The high budgetary cost of incarceration.* Washington, DC: Center for Economic Policy Research.

Shah, N. (2011, July 21). New initiative targets "school-to-prison pipeline." *Education Week.* Retrieved from http://blogs.edweek.org/edweek/campaign-k12/2011/07/from_guest_blogger_nirvi_shah.html

Skiba, R. J., Michael, R. S., Nardo, A. C., & Peterson, R. L. (2002). The color of discipline: Sources of racial and gender disproportionality in school punishment. *Urban Review, 34*(4), 317–342.

Skiba, R. J., Peterson, R. L., & Williams, T. (1997, August). Office referrals and suspension: Disciplinary intervention in middle schools. *Education and Treatment of Children, 20*(3), 295–315.

Snow, D. (2004). Framing processes, ideology, and discursive fields. In D. A. Snow, S. A. Soule, & H. Kriesi (Eds.), *Blackwell companion to social movements.* Malden, MA: Blackwell.

Sparks, S. (2010, October 6). Spurred by statistics, districts combat absenteeism. *Education Week*. Retrieved from www.edweek.org/ew/articles/2010/10/.../06absenteeism_ep.h30.html

Sprague, J., & Vincent, C. (2011). *LAUSD discipline foundation policy evaluation of the relationship between School-Wide Positive Behavior Interventions and Supports (SW-PBIS) implementation and outcomes*. Retrieved from http://www.scribd.com/doc/72492855/Evaluation-of-the-Discipline-Foundation-Policy-October-24-2011

St. George, D. (2011, February 20). Suicide turns attention to disciplinary policies. *The Washington Post*. Retrieved from http://www.washingtonpost.com/wp-dyn/content/article/2011/02/19/AR2011021904528.html

St. George, D. (2011, February 24). Fairfax County school board to review discipline policies. *The Washington Post*. Retrieved from http://www.washingtonpost.com/wp-dyn/content/article/2011/02/24/AR2011022408513.html

St. George, D. (2011, March 10). Teenager suspended from Fairfax County school over acne drug. *The Washington Post*. Retrieved from http://www.washingtonpost.com/wp-dyn/content/article/2011/03/10/AR2011031006261.html

St. George, D. (2011, March 30). Fairfax schools chief proposed changes to controversial discipline policies. *The Washington Post*. Retrieved from http://www.washingtonpost.com/local/education/dale_proposes_changes_to_fairfax_discipline_process/2011/03/30/AFz2kC4B_story.html

St. George, D. (2011, June 1). More schools rethinking zero-tolerance discipline stand. *The Washington Post*. Retrieved from http://www.washingtonpost.com/local/education/fairfax-to-scale-back-forced-school-transfers/2011/06/09/AGKnB3NH_story.html

St. George, D. (2011, June 9). Fairfax scales back discipline policy. *The Washington Post*. Retrieved from http://www.washingtonpost.com/local/education/fairfax-to-scale-back-forced-school-transfers/2011/06/09/AGKnB3NH_story.html

Sterling, E. E. (2009). The failed policies of sentencing reform: Seriously rethinking federal sentencing policy. Prepared for the Rethinking Federal Sentencing Policy and the 25th anniversary of the Sentencing Reform Act. Washington, DC: Congressional Black Caucus, CBC Community Reinvestment Task Force, and the Charles Hamilton Houston Institute for Race and Justice of Harvard Law School.

Stoudt, B. G., Fine, M., & Fox, M. (2012). Growing up policed in the age of aggressive policing policies. *New York Law School Review, 56*,1293–1333.

Sullivan, E. (2007). *Deprived of dignity: Degrading treatment and abusive discipline in New York City and Los Angeles public schools*. New York: National Economic and Social Rights Initiative.

Sullivan, L., & Morgan, D. (2010). *Pushed out: Harsh discipline in Lousiana's public schools denies the right to education*. New York: Families and Friends of Louisiana's Incarcerated Children & National Economic and Social Rights Initiative.

Tavernise, S. (2010, December 1). The man behind Baltimore schools' transformation. *The New York Times*.

Thurau, L., & Wald, J. (2010). Controlling partners: When law enforcement meets discipline in public schools. *New York Law Review, 54*, 977–1020.

U.S. Department of Education. (2011, July 21). *Secretary Duncan, Attorney General Holder announce effort to respond to school-to-prison pipeline by supporting good discipline practices*. Retrieved from http://www.ed.gov/news/press-releases/secretary-duncan-attorney-general-holder-announce-effort-respond-school-prison-p

U.S. Department of Education. (2012). *New data from U.S. Department of Education highlights educational inequities around teacher experience, discipline and high school rigor*. Retrieved from http://www.ed.gov/news/press-releases/new-data-us-department-education-highlights-educational-inequities-around-teache

U.S. Department of Justice. (2011a, May 21). *Coordinating council on juvenile justice and delinquency prevention meeting summary.* Retrieved from http://www.juvenilecouncil.gov/meetings.html

U.S. Department of Justice. (2011b, July 21). Attorney General and Education Secretary announce joint project to address school disciplinary practices. *OJJDP News at a Glance.* Retrieved from https://www.ncjrs.gov/html/ojjdp/news_at_glance/235188/sf_1.html

Voices of Youth in Chicago Education [VOYCE]. (2011). *Failed policies, broken futures. The true cost of zero tolerance in Chicago.* Chicago: Author.

Wald, J., & Losen, D. (2003, Fall). Deconstructing the school-to-prison pipeline [Special issue]. *New Directions for Youth Development, 99,* 9–15.

Wald, J., & Thurau, L. (2010). *First, do no harm: How educators and police can work together more effectively to preserve school safety and protect vulnerable students* (CHHIRJ Policy Brief). Cambridge, MA: Charles Hamilton Institute for Race & Justice, Harvard Law School.

Wallace, J. M., Goodkind, S., Wallace, C. M., & Bachman J. G. (2008). Racial, ethnic, and gender differences in school discipline among U.S. high school students: 1991–2005. *Negro Educational Review, 59*(1–2), 47–62.

Welch, K., & Payne, A. A. (2010). Racial threat and punitive school discipline. *Social Problems, 57*(1), 25–48.

White House. (2009). *Education.* Retrieved from http://www.whitehouse.gov/issues/education

Youth United for Change & Advancement Project. (2011). *Zero tolerance in Philadelphia. Denying educational opportunities and creating a pathway to prison.* Washington, DC: Advancement Project.

The author gratefully acknowledges the leadership, dedication, and perserverance of the grassroots organizers and leaders, legal advocates, researchers, and foundation partners whose work catalyzed the reforms discussed in this article. A special thank you to Robin Delany-Shabazz, Kristen Harper, Judith Browne-Dianis, and Tanya Coke for reviewing drafts of this essay. Deep appreciation goes to Donna Lawrence at The Atlantic Philanthropies for her guidance and vision in advocating for the foundation's involvement in addressing the school-to-prison pipeline and to Tanya Coke for her wise and thoughtful partnership in co-constructing Atlantic's school discipline grant making strategy.

TROUBLE TO TRIUMPH

FIGHTING FOR EDUCATION EQUALITY
AS AN INCARCERATED YOUTH

■

STARCIA AGUE

At fifteen, I was not anxiously holding my learner's permit and the keys to my parent's car or hoping for the phone to ring. No. At fifteen I was held at gunpoint and arrested on my first and only warrant for a criminal matter. My mother was not around. She was completing her court-ordered, in-patient treatment for an addiction that rendered her mostly absent, even when she was physically around. My father was on the run for his eleven pending felonies. I landed in a Thurston County, Washington, detention center, where I would await a transfer hearing requesting I be tried as an adult I knew I would be waiting for some time because my parents lived as if they were untouchable by the law. The justice system happily served me a slice of its version of justice, setting bail at $10,000. Clearly, making bail was not an option. What I didn't realize at the time was that I was going to discover the value of schooling as a way out of the dead-end future my childhood was directing me toward.

I was raised in the midst of child abuse, poverty, and criminal activities. I lived in homeless shelters, safe places for battered women and children, and even a car at times. From the time I was very young, my parents made crystal clear that I should/could not trust anyone with authority—not the school, not the police, and not child protective services. What happened in our house stayed in our house . . . or else! I consistently had a problem with head lice, but due to her addiction my mother would never take care of it properly. The school's "no nit" policy, my family's distrust of authority, and our transient lifestyle began what was to become an ever-widening gap between my academic standing and that of my age cohort. As a child, the schools failed to reach out and engage me. When I entered the court system, at age fifteen, I was reading at a third-grade level and had fifth-grade math skills.

My personal experience with the social services systems relating to at-risk youth began early. I was frequently removed temporarily from my home and placed in foster care. Each time my foster care ended, I was returned to my mother, whose abuse of me continued unabated. My formal schooling suffered greatly from the frequent out-of-home placements. After numerous foster care placements and many new schools admissions, my interest in school was seriously eroded. But these experiences in the social services systems did give me an important type of informal education; my experience exposed me firsthand to the insidious and diverse injustices that marginalized, disenfranchised youth deal with on a daily basis and to the systems that fail us too often.

While on the run from my final foster care placement, I was arrested with three young adult co-defendants for an armed robbery. I had been known to the court as a "runner" from foster placement because my experience had been that I was repeatedly placed in homes where I was a subject of abuse and neglect. After spending 214 days in detention, I was finally sentenced to "juvenile life"—that is, confinement until age twenty-one. I say "finally" because I went through five judges and three attorneys and nonetheless got the harshest sentence possible as a juvenile. I was never treated like a true client; rather, I was an appointment for a number of attorneys, none of whom ever established an attorney-client relationship in which I could explain the facts as I knew them to be. I am very thankful, however, that the judge decided not to try me as an adult. Upon entering the juvenile justice system, I decided to work on my education. I felt as though education was the only way others would ever see me as "normal"—the only way for me to rise above my disadvantaged circumstances, overcome my criminal past, and get beyond my bad choices.

But when I started seeking information about college courses, facility administrators scoffed at the idea, saying, "It's never going to happen." I quickly realized that there was an unspoken, commonly shared belief that juvenile offenders will never attend college. The prevailing approach to education was "let's push for GEDs and high school diplomas." When I was incarcerated, the policy was that incarcerated youth could not take college classes because access to the Internet was perceived as a security risk. Meanwhile, the funding for secure residential care facilities for juvenile offenders is based on the number of youth residing in a facility on a specified day. There are no additional funding sources, local or federal, to pay for juvenile offenders taking college classes. Currently, incarcerated youth are not eligible for federal student financial aid. It seemed to me that the people who ran the facility did not promote the educational interests of the youth serving time.

These obstacles and words of discouragement motivated me, however, to be increasingly insistent. So at age sixteen, trapped in a juvenile jail, I began a three-year fight for my education. Despite the fact the institutional staff threw up many barriers, I was determined to achieve my educational goals. I did manage to find a handful of people who were willing to go against the system and fight for me to have an opportunity to further my education. Most of those people were not formal educators, teachers, or administrators but, rather, a variety of good people—police detectives, pastors, cooks, and other mentors—who cared enough about my future to help me get through high school and qualify for college admission and to achieve eventual graduation. These were all people who had nothing to gain from my success other than a sense of having served justice and having lent a helping hand to a soul they deemed worthy. Time and again, when I pushed the system to provide greater access to educational opportunity—to online courses, to sources of financial support for college study, to research material and study guides—I found supporters who either helped me make my case or who bent a rule or two to make room for me to accumulate credits.

In my first position working with youth after my release, an internship in the Spokane County Public Defender's office, I became starkly aware of the limitations imposed on ex-offenders due to their criminal history. Although my job required me to interview newly detained youth, my criminal background barred me from entering the juvenile detention facility. While ultimately I was successful in gaining entry into the facility, the fact that our state sells juvenile records to private vendors who charge for criminal history background checks means that continual barriers to employment, housing, and credit purchases are constant features of life for the one-time juvenile offender.

After contacting numerous attorneys and youth-serving agencies, I was told that class-A felonies (serious violent offences, including robbery in the first degree) cannot be vacated and sealed under the juvenile code. In reaction to this discovery, I worked with some state legislators, youth advocate attorneys, and some amazing law students to draft and help pass the first legislation expanding the range of juvenile offenses that can be sealed to include class-A felonies. Shortly thereafter I sought and obtained a pardon from Governor Christine Gregoire. To date, I am the only juvenile ever in the state of Washington to receive a full and unconditional pardon! My work in this area of juvenile justice reform is fueled by my belief that current policies too greatly limit the ability for youth who have records to go on to be productive citizens.

During my five-and-a-half years of incarceration and following my release, I have found the strength and determination to change to a new life course. This change has entailed not only examining and accepting responsibility for the choices that led to my incarceration but also to questioning the systems that were supposedly designed to protect me. My life story is a testament to the strength and resolve of one person who was given a little help at critical times from caring adults and who has positively affected opportunities for many youth to come. Many at-risk and system-involved youth have unrecognized strengths similar to mine. Our systems of care can do more to support, as opposed to discourage, progress and youth goal achievement. However "bad" the youth's behavior might have been, our systems of care must find and build on assets and avoid the thrown-away-youth syndrome far too commonly encountered.

RESTORATIVE JUSTICE IS NOT ENOUGH

SCHOOL-BASED INTERVENTIONS IN THE CARCERAL STATE

■

JANE HERETH, MARIAME KABA, ERICA R. MEINERS, AND LEWIS WALLACE

In the last ten years, a movement advocating and implementing restorative justice alternatives developed in Chicago Public Schools as a direct result of the massive expansion of the carceral state and the growth of zero tolerance and school-to-prison tracking. Working from the authors' Chicago-based practices, research, and activism, this essay assesses the potential of restorative justice practices to interrupt the school-to-prison pipeline. Hereth, Kaba, Meiners, and Wallace conceptually and historically map the progression of restorative justice in Chicago in order to outline strengths of interventions and to detail their concerns about the direction of the restorative justice movement in schools and its ability to intervene in the school-to-prison pipeline. They conclude with an analysis of transformative justice to highlight valuable practices and political frameworks to center in interventions.

"Take her! Take her!"

It's 9:00 A.M. on Monday, and the visibly upset kindergarten teacher screams at me from across the hall. She is holding a six-year-old by her wrist. The little girl, with a dozen pink and white barrettes framing her tear-stained face, yells, "Get off me, let me go!" The teacher pushes the student toward me. I reach out my hand, and the little girl grabs it.

"When should I bring her back?" I ask.

"NEVER," the teacher yells. "I don't want her! Never bring her back!"

Before I make it to the main office at Lockwood Elementary[1]—a K–8 school in a northside Chicago neighborhood—to get the Peace Room key and sign in, two more students are assigned to me.

At noon I am paged over the intercom: "Ms. C, please come to the assistant principal's office immediately." In Mrs. Edwards's office I recognize a fourteen-year-old eighth-grader, Trevon, sitting across from her with his head in his hands.

"You are lucky that Ms. C is here," Mrs. Edwards says. "Otherwise, you would be on your way to jail in handcuffs."

Trevon had lashed out in the lunchroom at one of his peers, repeatedly shouting inappropriate and sexual slurs at a female classmate who had touched his neck while he was waiting in line to eat. Two security guards approached him. He continued to shout and was physically removed from the lunchroom and taken across the hall to the administrative office.

As Mrs. Edwards recounted the incident, Trevon interrupted several times: "She started it!" he yelled. "This is unfair, why isn't she sitting up in here?" When Mrs. Edwards suggested I find a Black male mentor to work with him, he laughed derisively. "A what?" he asked. As she tried to explain, he started to laugh uncontrollably and muttered something as he folded his arms into his chest. "Ha ha ha! In THIS neighborhood? At THIS school? GOOD LUCK WITH THAT! Ha ha ha!"

I ask him if he would like to go for a walk with me to see the Peace Room and talk, and he responds, "Not really."

Mrs. Edwards chimes in from her seat, "Or I can call the police . . ."

At 3:30 p.m., right outside of the middle school building, a nasty fight erupts between two young men. Two students run up to the Peace Room: "Ms. C, Ms. C, please come to the basketball court. Jesse and Chris are fighting and the police are going to arrest them." By the time I get downstairs, both young men are in handcuffs and being put into the back of a squad car. I ask Officer Hernandez to please not take the young men to the station. I promise to intervene. "I will run a peace circle," I say. "Do you both agree to participate in a circle?" I ask both young men. They nod. Officer Hernandez looks skeptical but agrees to release them. He looks over to the boys and says, "You are lucky Ms. C is here vouching for you, but next time, you are going to the station."

This snapshot is from an average day in the work of Project NIA, a Chicago-based community organization that attempts to engage alternative justice practices to halt the movement of young people from our communities into our prisons and jails. Lockwood Elementary and Middle School looks similar to many public schools across Chicago. At Lockwood, 65 percent of the 540 students spread out across two buildings are African American and 26 percent are Latino; the majority (nearly 95%) qualifies for free and reduced lunch (a federal designation signifying low income); and almost 20 percent are classified as having limited English proficiency. Over the past twenty years, students at Lockwood have consistently tested below national norms. And at Lockwood high rates of suspension are the norm.

In Chicago these high rates of suspension in a school with a majority of African American and Latino students are not remarkable. Data from the Department of Education's Office for Civil Rights documents that while African American students represented 45 percent of the Chicago Public School (CPS) enrollment in 2009–2010, 76 percent of students receiving at least one out-of-school suspension that year were Black (Civil Rights Data Collection, 2012). CPS's African American students are five times more likely to be suspended than their White peers. Police officers proliferate in CPS, and in 2010 there were 5,574 school-based arrests of juveniles under eighteen years on school property. Unsurprisingly, Black youth accounted for 74 percent of school-based juvenile arrests in 2010; Latino youth represented 22.5 percent of arrests (Kaba & Edwards, 2012). This data confirms what we know: select Chicago schools actively funnel Black and Brown youth into the prison system.

When members of Project NIA walked through the doors of Lockwood Elementary in August 2009, we were greeted by an enthusiastic and brand-new principal who was determined to improve the culture and morale of teachers, staff, and students. Starting in September, NIA established and ran a Peace Room at Lockwood, staffed by a team of trained volunteers and interns (supervised by a licensed clinical counselor employed by NIA), to serve as an alternative to suspensions and expulsions. Disruptive students would be taken out of class and sent to the Peace Room so that the teachers and other students could continue with their work without further interruption. Parents who believed that CPS wanted their children to fail would be given an opportunity to have their concerns addressed, and strategies could be created to ensure better communication and develop trust among students and among students, staff, and families.

On paper these goals appeared straightforward. While most teachers had no idea that a Peace Room even existed at Lockwood in Room 305—an out-of-use classroom that housed countless boxes of old supplies—community members came to assist in doing peace circles and afterschool activities, and young people dropped by the room to check it out, becoming immediately engaged by art projects, discussions, and snacks. While the afterschool activities were popular, it was a challenge to get teachers to refer students into the Peace Room during school hours. NIA was told that students needed to work on their reading and math skills—not create art projects or that "peace stuff." Many teachers were reticent, if not downright hostile, if a student was referred to the room during the school day. "He needs to be punished—not rewarded!" was a common refrain. In addition, the principal and the assistant principal were new, and their priorities simply did not accommodate helping the space to get established. As NIA pressed for schoolwide announcements or a space to introduce the organization in each classroom, the requests fell by the wayside, and the Peace Room seemed to flounder.

Collaborating with the wider school community was also challenging. Many parents and caregivers did not want anyone at the school to know of the challenges faced in their homes, primarily out of fear that the Department of Children and Family Services or other state agencies would "get in their business." While this sentiment initially expressed itself as resistance or hostility toward the organization's staff and volunteers who attempted to engage parents and families, it did not take long before NIA members built trust with some key stakeholders. Without trust, all of the knowledge, training, funding, good intentions, professional skills, techniques, modalities, and programming would amount to nothing. Toward the end of the first school year, the Peace Room began to feel like a space that was established and recognized within the school community.

In the two years that Project NIA implemented the Peace Room at Lockwood Elementary, staff and volunteers offered peace circles, individual restorative counseling, case management, homework help, referrals and follow-up with other agencies, home visits, a grandmothers' support group, art projects, field trips, and conflict mediation. Often the work was simply listening, offering the students a chance to verbalize their greatest concerns. The Peace Room offered a unique space, a respite from judgment and discipline that combined teaching new communication practices with providing concrete and necessary forms of support for the young people facing dire struggles ranging from daily trauma at home to severe untreated mental health issues.

Yet after two years at Lockwood, Project NIA came to recognize that our model and intervention were unsustainable. Funding from a small community organization was not enough to create a full-time job for an experienced professional while also providing logistical support and the necessary supplies and additional work hours required to keep a Peace Room open full-time in a school. The constant threat of school closure by the district due to low scores on state standardized tests at Lockwood made it difficult to secure clear commitments from administrators to dedicate resources, thought, and time to integrating the work of the Peace Room into the school as a whole. And the wholesale lack of support from the CPS system—despite the system's stated commitment to supporting restorative justice alternatives—meant that Project NIA was essentially fully responsible for providing a service that we believed ought to be integral to the school's operations. We believed that a restorative justice program had the potential to save the school system time and money while also diverting dozens of young people away from suspension, expulsion, and arrest, but we could not sustain this project without critical support from the school district.

Here we assess the potential of restorative justice practices, such as those run by Project NIA, to interrupt the school-to-prison pipeline.[2] Building from our own practice, research, and activism in Chicago, and raising more questions than providing answers, we examine the implementation of restorative justice in our communities and schools. As the vignette above highlights, we have found that this work offers significant promise but also faces deep challenges at the school and district level.

The essay is organized into five parts. First, we began with the above example of restorative justice at Lockwood in order to ground our analysis in praxis. Second, we explain the interdisciplinary theoretical and methodological basis for our analysis. Third, we define *restorative justice* and outline key components of the framework. Fourth, we conceptually and historically map the progression of restorative justice in Chicago to link our current work to historical efforts at juvenile justice reform. Finally, we outline both the promises that these initiatives demonstrate and our concerns about the direction of the restorative justice movement in schools and its ability to intervene in the school-to-prison pipeline, and we provide an analysis of *transformative justice* as a set of practices and frameworks we have found useful.

THEORETICAL CONTEXTS AND METHODOLOGICAL COMMITMENTS

Our analysis is guided by several interdisciplinary theoretical frameworks, including a critical analysis of the carceral state, a commitment to a long-term vision of prison abolition, and an understanding of the importance of intersectional and intermovement analysis.

First, we center our work in an understanding that the United States has the dubious distinction of locking up more people than any other nation. With 5 percent of the world's population and 25 percent of the total prison population, the number of people incarcerated in the United States has increased since the 1970s not because of an increase in violence or crime but because of policies including three strikes legislation, mandatory-minimum sentencing, and the war on drugs (Alexander, 2010; Davis, 2003; Gilmore, 2007a; Mauer, 1999; Pew Center on the States Public Safety Performance Project, 2008). Who is harmed by this expansion of our prison nation is not arbitrary: the more than two million people locked up and warehoused in prisons and jails across the United States are disproportionately poor, mentally ill, under- or uneducated, gender nonconforming, noncitizens, and/or people of color.

Activists, organizers, academics, and those directly impacted have popularized the term *prison-industrial complex* to refer to the creation of prisons and detention centers as a perceived growth economy in an era of deindustrialization and as "a set of symbiotic relationships among correctional communities, transnational corporations, media conglomerates, guards' unions and legislative and court agendas" (Davis, 2003, p. 107). These relationships drive prison expansion and subsequently naturalize prisons as inevitable. We also use the term *carceral state* to highlight the multiple and overlapping state agencies and institutions that have punishing functions and effectively regulate poor communities: child and family services, welfare/workfare agencies, public education, immigration, health and human services, and more (Richie, 2012; Roberts, 1997; Wacquant, 2009).

The expanding carceral state has led many to raise the question of abolition and to ask whether prisons are obsolete (Davis, 2003). Critical Resistance (n.d.), a national antiprison organization, defines prison abolition as "the goal of eliminating prisons, policing, and surveillance and creating lasting alternatives to punishment and imprisonment." Prison abolition doesn't mean that there will be no violence. Rather, it acknowledges that prisons are not a just, efficient, or moral solution to the problems that shape violence in our communities.

This essay also centers an *intersectional* analysis. Legal theorist Kimberlé Crenshaw (1994) developed the term *intersectionality* to refer to the multiple ways that power and privilege intersect. Intersectionality describes how identities—ethnicity, gender, sexuality, ability, race—are mutually constituted. But while we may easily understand our own multiple intersecting identities—for example, as a queer Black man or as a disabled woman—our civil rights and justice movements and our service organizations are not typically organized based on an intersectional analysis. A failure to encompass intersectionality in our analysis of social problems or in our intervention strategies can result in the animation of significant and longer-term structural problems. For example, as antibullying legislation and policies have become more widespread in recent years, these policies aim to address the decades-long failures to provide even a measure of "safety" for lesbian, gay, bisexual, transgendered, queer (LGBTQ), and gender-nonconforming youth in schools. At the same time, all too often these policies heavily sanction and persecute perpetrators. The turn to a criminalization of perpetrators of antigay violence in schools results in more school sanctions, more punishment, and potentially more push-out in an educational context where school disciplinary actions disproportionately harm youth of color. Only through an intersectional analysis of the effects of antigay violence, of racism and classism in school discipline, and of disproportionate punishment and incarceration, can we effectively forge policies that address violence without also furthering injustice.

As educators in formal and informal contexts, social workers, antiprison organizers, and researchers, we write this essay as a form of collaborative movement assessment. Collectively, we share the goals of both ending the school-to-prison pipeline and of building sustainable, vibrant, and just communities. We value theorizing about our practices and stepping away from our overlapping projects to critically assess our work within a wider sociopolitical landscape. Mariame Kaba is the founder and director of Project NIA, an organization dedicated to developing community-based alternatives to youth incarceration. Lewis Wallace coordinates volunteer trainings and programming for Project NIA. Jane Hereth has been trained as a circle keeper through Project NIA and is a social worker. Erica Meiners is one of the founders of the St. Leonard Adult High School, a diploma-granting institution for formerly incarcerated individuals, and a faculty member at a local university. All four authors are members of the Chicago Prison Industrial Complex Teaching Collective, which has created and facilitates introductory workshops and distributes free materials about the prison-industrial complex.[3]

The limitations of this methodological approach must also be foregrounded. Our work centers around analysis and examples that are geographically constrained, making occasional nods or linkages to work outside of Chicago. We, and others, lack longitudinal data on the use of any of the practices we identify. The very terms and practices we chart here—for example, restorative justice and transformative justice—are understood flexibly across the United States and around the world, making it challenging to generalize from the contexts we illustrate in this essay. Also, we are cognizant that when we write about work in progress—particularly work in which we have deep personal and professional investments—objectivity is neither possible nor desired. Many of the organizations we map we have supported, developed, worked with or alongside, and more. We struggle to represent this work reflectively, critically, and also with generosity. While potential criticisms are numerous and daunting, we know that analysis of in-process, praxis-related work is vital, and we offer these limitations at the start in order to contextualize our work.

REFRAMING JUSTICE

In this section, we offer a working definition of restorative justice (RJ) based on the literature and our own experiences as activists. We embed this definition in a brief history of the emergence of the movement for restorative justice in Chicago. We recognize that defining RJ is a part of praxis rather than a finite exercise, and this definition will continue to be adapted and reinterpreted through our activism.

The Restorative Justice Movement

Restorative justice is an approach that attempts to empower communities to respond holistically to violence and harm. As defined by the Chicago organization Community Justice for Youth Institute (CJYI, n.d.), an RJ model is based on "a theory of justice that emphasizes repairing the harm caused by crime and conflict" (para. 1). As such, RJ takes into account the needs of victims, offenders, and others affected by an incident of harm working to rebuild what was lost rather than viewing punishment as a final resolution. In incidents on school grounds, often there is not a clear line between "victim" and "offender," and punishment tends to overlook the underlying causes of the original offense. The overall goals of RJ practices are to try to heal the whole community from an incident in which people were harmed and, ideally, to help prevent the same sort of harm from happening again. RJ practices may include peacemaking circles, mediation, alternative sentencing, and other accountability processes.

The fundamentals of RJ have their basis in indigenous cultures of the Americas and, to some extent, the world. For example, the CJYI (n.d.) mentions that their practices "have come to us by way of Kay Pranis, Gwen Chandler-Rhivers and Sally Wolf, who learned them from the Tlingit Tagish tradition of the Yukon Territories. Our work has also been greatly influenced by the peace and reconciliation work in the townships of South Africa" (para. 3). Some contemporary restorative justice activists also credit South Africa's Truth and Reconciliation Commission as an inspiration. Quaker and Mennonite communities have also long used a circle format as a mode of both prayer and problem solving. In their current iteration, restorative models provide an alternative to the traditional Western model of justice based on penance (what we refer to as "punitive justice").

The contemporary RJ movement emerged in the late twentieth century at a time when zero tolerance policies, gang laws, and stricter drugs laws were justifying and increasing the policing, criminalization, and incarceration of youth of color. Media and political scapegoating of youth of color as dangerous criminals created political support for these draconian laws and policies (Dohrn, 2000). In addition to working to reform these laws to stop the overly punitive treatment of young people, RJ activists began to call for the development of alternative responses to violence and harm, and these movements have impacted the treatment of youth in schools and begun to shift parts of the juvenile justice system in Illinois.

While a more thorough overview of the history of juvenile justice is outside the scope of this essay, we highlight that juvenile justice and criminal reform initiatives have long histories in the city of Chicago; formed in 1899, the Chicago Juvenile Court was the first juvenile court system to be created in a major U.S. city and reflected a desire to protect young people from the cycle of incarceration (Willrich, 2003; Wolcott, 2005). Yet, over one hundred years later, those who are seventeen years old in Chicago are frequently transferred into adult courts at rates that are far higher for African American youth, and those seventeen years of age and under still face incarceration in a juvenile prison and a conviction on their criminal record unless they go through the costly and time-consuming process of expungement.

These ongoing tensions have always motivated communities to resist and to push back on the criminalization of youth. In the early 2000s, Illinois Criminal Justice Information Authority (ICJIA), a state agency, began to advocate for the broad implementation of RJ within Illinois's juvenile legal system (Ashley & Stevenson, n.d.). In 2006, the state formally separated its juvenile incarceration functions from the adult corrections system in an attempt to shift (again) away from a punitive model and toward a model of support and treatment (Illinois Department of Juvenile Justice, 2009).

In addition, movement activists nationwide have popularized the use of RJ in schools as a model that may provide an alternative to engagement with the school-to-prison pipeline. In Chicago, 20 percent of juvenile arrests occur while young people are on school grounds; police presence in elementary and high schools in poor neighborhoods is the norm rather than the exception. While community activists have taken on overpolicing, racial profiling, and criminalization as problems unto themselves, the RJ movement has attempted to provide schools and communities with a viable alternative to policing young people. The hope is that when implemented in a school over time, RJ can have the effect both of establishing a culture of accountability and of interrupting the school-to-prison pipeline by reducing youth arrests, suspensions, and expulsions.

RJ practices in schools can take a number of forms. Peer juries bring together a student who has broken a school rule with trained student jurors.

Together, they discuss what happened, who was harmed, and what the student can do to repair the harm. Peer mediation brings two or more students together to resolve a conflict with the assistance of trained student mediators. Peace circles can be used in a number of settings—to help students get to know one another, celebrate student accomplishments, foster discussion, process a difficult topic, or make collective decisions. Schools call these practices by different names, but the concepts remain the same (Alternatives, Inc., n.d.; Transforming Conflict, n.d.).

Even lacking significant resources and support, the movement for RJ in schools appears to be growing across the United States. Nationally, RJ has been implemented in public school systems in several states, including California, Minnesota, and Wisconsin; in Chicago, RJ organizations and projects continue to emerge every year, driven both by the desire of the school district to reduce violence and increase attendance and by the political goals of community organizations aiming to reduce or end youth expulsion, dropouts, and incarceration while also addressing violence and harm. In 2007, a four-year campaign led by local organizations convinced the Chicago School Board to revise its student code of conduct to include RJ as a required part of schools' responses to student misconduct (Wallace, 2007). The interests of the groups working toward and ultimately approving these policy changes are fascinatingly varied: for some, youth violence is viewed as the primary problem, while for others youth incarceration and policing are the issues at stake.

Preliminary implementation of RJ in schools has yielded promising results toward these varying goals. Community-based organizations such as Chicago's Community Organizing and Family Issues (COFI) have documented positive effects on attendance and behavior as well as reduced suspensions in schools that have implemented community peace rooms staffed by parents and volunteers (POWER-PAC Elementary Justice Committee, 2010). In 2006–2008, one Chicago public high school documented decreases in arrests and misconduct reports of up to 82 percent after one year of implementing RJ programming (Dyett High School Restorative Justice Report, n.d.). At Fenger High School, a Chicago high school that became infamous after the death of student Derrion Albert, the administration has been diligently implementing RJ practices, including victim-offender mediation, conferences, peer juries, and peace circles. At a gathering in March 2012, the principal at Fenger, Elizabeth Dosier, presented data suggesting that "violent and drug related misconducts decreased by 61% from Semester 1 (SY2010) to Semester 1(SY2012)."[4]

WHAT IT TAKES: YOUTH, PARENTS, AND COMMUNITY ORGANIZATIONS

Despite the successful campaign to add RJ to the Code of Conduct in 2007, CPS has never provided citywide support to schools desiring to implement RJ; furthermore, the state of Illinois's RJ mandate has never been accompanied by significant, robust, or consistent funding.[5] However, even in the face of school closures, takeovers, and budget cuts, many Chicago schools have nonetheless been implementing RJ projects, including peer juries, peer mediation, and peacemaking circles. Here we outline some of the individuals and groups whose involvement has been integral to these successes in Chicago.

Youth Leadership

Youth leadership is central to the inner workings of RJ practices. Peer juries and peer mediation programs are intended to be youth driven. Engaged and active youth participation and leadership are central to support a healthy and effective RJ program. Youth are more likely to support educational programs, including RJ work, when practices are introduced by their peers who they know have had similar experiences (Morrell, 2007; Tuck, 2011). And when youth are knowledgeable about the school-to-prison pipeline, they are invested in resolving conflict in ways that can challenge how young people are funneled into the pipeline.

Youth leadership has also been central to educating both youth and adults about the school-to-prison pipeline in Chicago. Blocks Together, based in Humboldt Park, works to educate communities about the school-to-prison pipeline using art and popular education through a training model that taps into participants' personal experience and knowledge to develop an understanding of the world around them and that supports social action. In a similar vein, in 2009, Project NIA and the Young Women's Action Team (YWAT), a group of young women resisting street harassment, launched Suspension Stories, a participatory action research project aimed at collecting young people's stories about being suspended or expelled from school. Young people used this information to create a curriculum, zines, art work, and other educational materials about school suspension and how it funnels students into the school-to-prison pipeline.

Furthermore, in public campaigns to challenge the school-to-prison pipeline and to implement RJ, centering the voices and experiences of those most affected by school violence and the school-to-prison pipeline helps to build support and causes allies and stakeholders to take notice of what is going on. For example, youth working with Blocks Together were involved in the campaign that culminated in successfully adding restorative justice to the CPS student code of conduct in 2007. And youth from two Chicago organizing projects (Southwest Youth Collaborative and Fearless Leading by the Youth) are working to improve conditions in or close the Cook County Juvenile Temporary Detention Center (CCJTDC, also known as the Audy Home). This campaign is led by youth who are directly impacted by juvenile incarceration. In October 2011, county board president Toni Preckwinkle expressed her support for closing the facility and moving young people to community-based programs (Slife & Eldeib, 2011). Hearing from youth who were previously incarcerated at CCTJC about violence and overcrowding makes a strong impact and helps illustrate why change is needed and imperative.

Parent Involvement

In addition to youth leadership, parent involvement is important to the creation and success of RJ programs. Parents are concerned about their children's safety in schools, and they also want to protect their children from unnecessary involvement with the criminal legal system.[6] Parents Organized to Win, Educate and Renew–Policy Action Council (POWER-PAC) was a leader in the 2003–2006 campaign to add RJ to the CPS Student Code of Conduct. Following that success, the group created the Austin Peace Center at Brunson Elementary School on the west side of Chicago, staffed by parent volunteers who assist with talking circles and mediation. This was followed a couple of years later by the opening of a parent-led Peace Room at Wells High School. POWER-PAC continues to work to eliminate unnecessarily punitive elementary school polices to keep children of color out of the school-to-prison pipeline. When parents organize for school policy changes, they are a powerful force, and POWER-PAC's work is an excellent example of this. The continued involvement of those and other parents and committed adults in peace rooms and organizing efforts has great promise for transforming our schools and communities.

Community Involvement and Coalition Building

Community-based organizations were behind the effort to have RJ added to CPS policy and continue to pressure schools to develop and fund restorative practices. Community organizations offer staff with skills and expertise in areas often less well represented in school staff, including youth and parent organizing, RJ practices, fund-raising, and legislative-based mobilizations. Members and staff of groups also can contribute knowledge about the needs and issues within the community that differ from the data school based workers possess. Community groups are often better positioned to push for policy change than CPS staff, so these organizations are needed to continue working for progressive policy changes that incorporate RJ programs into schools while eliminating punitive processes that funnel youth into the school-to-prison pipeline. In the fall of 2010, a coalition of seven organizations citywide came together to form the High HOPES Campaign, which has the stated goal of reducing suspension and expulsion in CPS by 40 percent through the citywide implementation of RJ programs. A 2012 report released by the coalition draws on national and local data to argue that RJ can both dramatically reduce suspension, expulsion, and dropout rates and simultaneously save the school district money (High HOPES Campaign, 2012). They also provide a clear road map for the implementation of RJ throughout CPS via peer juries, peer mediation, peace rooms, and training for all staff. High HOPES proposes that every school should have at least one full-time staff person devoted to RJ programming, a cost that would ultimately be offset by the increase in attendance and the reduction in school security costs, such as cameras, guards, and police.

At the same time, CPS maintains that budget cuts and lack of resources make it difficult to implement wide-scale RJ programs like those recommended by High HOPES. Therefore, despite being hard-hit by the state and city financial crises, community groups are still working to run programs and to offer training and support for school-based RJ programs. Project NIA's program at Lockwood Elementary is one such example and illustrates both the promise and challenge of this model. Several Chicago programs have been providing that support for years. For example, the Community Justice for Youth Institute provides RJ training for students, parents, teachers, and administrators, as well as for community members hoping to implement restorative practices with youth in settings outside of schools. Alternatives, Inc., an organization serving youth on the north side of Chicago, has been training schools and youth across the city in RJ practices for fifteen years. They operate a summer internship program, bringing peer mediators and peer jury members from around the city together for skill sharing, leadership development, and relationship building. Alternatives, Inc., also uses restorative practices to mediate conflict within their afterschool programs for youth. Outside of the work at Lockwood Elementary, Project NIA offers talking circles and other restorative practices for youth. Most of the facilitators doing this work are volunteers. Although it would be beneficial if CPS fully funded and supported RJ programming at all schools in the district, involvement from outside groups is also important.

RJ work offers valuable opportunities for coalition building among different community-based organizations. Coalitions that are built across constituencies are also important because they encourage us to think creatively and broadly about creating solutions that will be beneficial for all. For example, the 2003–2006 campaign that successfully added RJ to the CPS Student Code of Conduct in 2007 involved youth, parents, and community members from around the city and linked groups working on a broad range of issues, including youth empowerment and racial and economic justice, as well as those advocating for safety and equity for LGBTQ youth. The High HOPES Campaign involves many of the same organizations as well as faith-based groups and community development groups. In 2007, Voices of Youth in Chicago Education (VOYCE), a youth organizing collaborative composed of seven local organizations, was established. In 2011, this group of students released a report that again identifies the impact of Chicago harsh disciplinary policies and calls for RJ interventions.

In March 2012, joined by local elected officials, students from VOYCE stood outside the CCJTDC to share their research and their personal experiences with school discipline. A young woman named Davisha, a freshman at Gage Park High School and a leader with the Southwest Organizing Project, spoke about attending multiple elementary schools, where she was suspended and arrested for minor infractions and forced to transfer due to a lack of special education services, and of her dream of going on to become a doctor. "These experiences didn't prepare me for a career in medicine, but instead to end up on the streets or in jail," she said. "Mayor Emanuel, put yourself in my shoes. Listen to my story, and end harsh discipline."[7]

These coalitions provide strong examples of movement building around RJ in Chicago, and these connections build bases of support that can be mobilized to respond to other issues in schools and communities. For example, currently, many of these same groups are also fighting proposed school closures and privatizations.

CHALLENGES

In this section we outline what we perceive to be some of the central challenges facing those using restorative practices to try to interrupt the school-to-prison pipeline. We also view these challenges as sites of opportunity. Our analysis, drawn from our own local work and from our conversations with people across the United States, is not exhaustive. Those working in differing contexts will undoubtedly be able to add based on their experiences. In addition, we do not view the tensions and places for movement that we identify below as discrete; rather, we understand them to be interrelated and overlapping.

What No School Can Do

The first challenge for those working to address the school-to-prison pipeline is, in part, a persistent problem of all school reform movements. It is seductively tempting to think that problems commonly identified with schools can be fixed by simply tinkering with schools. But identifying something as a "school" problem can gloss over important structural factors. *New York Times* education reporter James Traub (2000) describes this seduction in regards to poverty:

> It is hard to think of a more satisfying solution to poverty than education. School reform involves relatively little money and no large-scale initiatives, asks practically nothing of the nonpoor and is accompanied by the ennobling sensation that comes from expressing faith in the capacity of the poor to overcome disadvantage by themselves. Conversely, the idea that schools by themselves can't cure poverty not only sounds like an un-American vote of no confidence in our capacity for self-transformation but also seems to flirt with the racialist theories expressed by Charles Murray and Richard Herrnstein, who argued in "The Bell Curve" that educational inequality is rooted in biological inequality.
>
> An alternative explanation, of course, is that educational inequality is rooted in economic problems and social pathologies too deep to be overcome by school alone. And if that's true, of course, then there's every reason to think about the

limits of school, and to think about the other institutions we might have to mobilize to solve the problem. We might even ask ourselves whether there isn't something disingenuous and self-serving in our professed faith in the omnipotence of school. (para. 8&9)

Traub's observation highlights the ongoing romance between the United States and the idea of public schooling and the challenge that arises when the unit of analysis for the problem is narrowly drawn as the school.[8]

Just as schools cannot alone interrupt or undo poverty, schools cannot alone stem the nation's material and ideological investments in a carceral state. The very concept of the school-to-prison pipeline erases intricate linkages between schools and the carceral state and simultaneously constrains our abilities to create sustainable and long-term responses. If the cause of the pipeline were simply school discipline policies or racist special education classification practices, altering these would block the pipeline. This framing of the school-to-prison pipeline potentially narrows the landscape, erasing the key roles larger economic and political forces continue to play in shaping and justifying the carceral state. Understanding how and why the school-to-prison pipeline is possible necessitates linking the practices inside schools to larger sociopolitical shifts in the United States that have fueled, and naturalized, prison expansion.

While this analysis presents a seemingly intractable challenge—how can the anti-school-to-prison-pipeline work that is rooted in restorative and transformative practices somehow exceed the confines that have constrained previous school reform initiatives—we are energized by current multisector and cross-issue organizing that encompasses and exceeds work to shut down the pipeline. In addition to the Chicago coalitions we have previously highlighted, we are excited by coalitions such as Californians United for a Responsible Budget (CURB) that emerged after that state spent more on corrections than higher education in 2010. CURB has been a statewide force in pushing for political education, policy shifts, and decarceration initiatives and has persistently linked education to incarceration at the macro level.

Co-optation

A second challenge, which arises in almost all justice movements engaged in reform work, is co-optation. We do not offer this point in the conspiracy theory vein or intend to propose that the movement will be infiltrated and taken over. But we do understand that the carceral state is not static, and it continues to accommodate new tools and practices. The most ambitious efforts at social change can and have become arms of the state. In fact, the current youth justice system in Chicago was begun as a progressive attempt to protect children from the adult prison system. Yet, the juvenile court has come to be a broker of incarceration rather than an alternative (Caputo, 2010), suggesting that it was ultimately co-opted by the expanding industry of incarceration. The current steps toward integrating RJ systemwide in CPS put the RJ movement at risk for co-optation by the school system, whose connections to private corporations, police, and youth incarceration will not end overnight (Shipps, 2006). Thus, even slow integration of RJ practices and discourses in a very limited number of places invites us to pause.

We are particularly interested in two sets of questions regarding the potential co-optation of RJ. The first is about the impact on young people of integrating RJ into state functions. Are young people, individually or collectively, made more vulnerable by, for example, the implementation of peace circles within juvenile justice detention centers? Do these practices become soft extensions of the carceral state and actually *extend* and even *mask* the state's ability to punish and harm, presenting a state with a kinder and gentler face to the public? When schools start to offer RJ, and these practices are tied these to juvenile justice systems, there must be assessments about what is won and what is lost with these moves. These should not be investigations that limit us but, rather, challenge and question our work.

These challenges must be addressed systemically but can also be struggled with locally. While at Lockwood, we insisted that student participation in the Peace Room had to be voluntary. In other words, students had to affirmatively choose to participate in restorative practices once they had an opportunity to learn about what they were. Similarly, parents and teachers must come willingly to the work. Our rationale was that mandated participation would mirror the carceral state and become seen as a form of "punishment."[9] This choice must be preserved for students.

The second question centers on the intricate relationships between the organizations that provide RJ services (not-for-profits, local grassroots organizations, and/or religious groups) and the changing face of state-run school systems. Working inside and alongside schools, training teachers in RJ practices, providing services for young people and families, these organizations become state actors despite the fact that they are funded by individuals and foundations rather than by taxes. These organizations essentially fulfill functions that were once identified as the purview of the state. The term *shadow state* describes the constellation of foundations, nonprofit organizations, for-profit entities, and other nongovernmental forces that engage in providing these services (Gilmore, 2007b; Wolch, 1990).

As RJ communities expand, we are reminded that the decentralization key to neoliberal policies does not mean that the state withdraws; rather, the state's relationships and abilities to negotiate power, to "govern" from a distance, shift and potentially expand. This presents potential challenges at the local and structural level. At the local level, if RJ practices in a school are being run by largely un- or underpaid community workers (probably funded by soft money) and these practices are problematic, to whom does the student or parent appeal? Are these public systems? Structurally, as public funding for education shrinks or becomes stagnant and the private sector fills this void, how does the move in local grassroots organizations to implement RJ practices take the responsibility off of schools or public teacher education programs (as two examples) to do this work?

Sustainability

As illustrated by the example of work at Lockwood, the overwhelming majority of work around RJ is done by local nonprofit organizations with few staffers and small, insecure budgets. This is resource-intensive work, and it has been outsourced from schools into community-based organizations and volunteers. This makes the work unsustainable. Shifting paradigms for discipline and justice in schools (as in communities) requires resources to be reallocated and redistributed. For example, in the summer of 2011, CPS proposed purchasing new surveillance cameras for fourteen high schools at a cost of $7 million (Ahmed-Ullah, 2011b)—$7 million that could be spent in other ways to make structural shifts that promote school and community safety.

Sustainability is also an issue at the individual level. Many of the small community-based organizations we identify may not be in operation after this volume is published. Often, organizational work is hugely dependent on an individual who works beyond a forty-hour workweek and sustains the organization: delivering programs, writing grants, organizing volunteers, building relationships, troubleshooting, and more. Generally underfunded or unfunded, organizations vanish if one of the two or three charismatic and dedicated leaders has a health, employment, family, or other crises. We have seen this happen too many times.

Sustainability is also intimately linked to who is being recruited, trained, and supported to participate in building nonpunitive justice responses in schools. In the example of Lockwood School, Trevon responded to his assistant principal's suggestion that the NIA staff person, Ms. C, find him a Black male mentor with surprise and disbelief. In Chicago, the majority of RJ practitioners are female and White. As RJ programs are scaled-up, the gender and racial diversity must be increased, and the staff and nonpaid workers in community organizations and schools must strive to mirror the demographics of the neighborhoods. For Chicago, this means we must involve more men, people of color, and LGBTQ and gender-nonconforming individuals; we should strive toward models, such as COFI's, that directly engage parents and grandparents in RJ work within their own community. In general, we propose that the roles that race, gender, sexual orientation, and class play in the administration and in the reception of restorative practices must be continuously examined and theorized.

School Privatization

Sustainability of programs in and outside of schools is also challenged by shifting urban educational policies and the wider push toward school privatization. In Chicago, and increasingly in other U.S. cities, public schools in some of most racially isolated and economically marginalized neighborhoods are being "reconstituted" (and sometimes privatized). The impact of reconstitution is severe: all teachers in the school are dismissed, students are often separated and relocated to other schools, and relationships between the schools and local organizations are severed. These disruptions make it challenging to build new cultures and paradigms of discipline and to establish trust between and among teachers, students, and community members. Earlier we cited the research from Dyett High School as one of the most promising examples of the impact of RJ in CPS. Dyett was targeted for school turnaround, and the new principal immediately dismantled the highly successful RJ program. Educational privatization and high-stakes accountability almost always impact the schools with the most vulnerable students first.

Assessment

Another challenge for this work is that there are few consistent evaluation methods to gauge the success of RJ work. While we previously summarized some research on RJ, the amount of research available is narrow and the data is sparse. Anecdotally, teachers are collecting data and attempting to measure the effectiveness of their interventions.

Whether concerned with reducing youth violence and misconduct and/or with decreasing youth contact with police and prisons, the growing RJ movement must demonstrate its effectiveness at meeting stated goals. Anecdotal data is important, but it is not enough. As practitioners, educators, and community members, we want rigorous tools to gather helpful information about how these interventions work. We want to know whether young people who participate in peace circles instead of a traditional detention hall are less likely to end up getting pushed out of class. But we also want to collect information that is helpful for us to build new tools and to respond to the new faces of violence and power within our communities. Teachers must be provided the time and resources, in nonpunitive environments, to learn new frameworks and skills to support these paradigms.

One fear is that the traditional metrics of student success—test scores on state standardized tests, and attendance/truancy and graduation rates—will be used against the implementation of alternative and RJ practices in schools. In this era of accountability, there is little room in schools to use precious teacher or student time to engage in any practices that do not immediately impact students' scores on standardized state achievement tests. Schools that work with low-income students, immigrants, English language learners, and/or students with other demands and challenges—generally the most underresourced schools to start with—are often particularly vulnerable.

Pushing the Limits of Restorative Justice with Transformative Justice

While we clearly support and practice restorative justice, our work is also informed by those who work primarily outside school systems to build alternative responses to punitive justice systems. As activists, educators, and research-ers who work to combat the widespread effects of the prison industrial complex within and outside school systems, the limited and cautious use of RJ models in the context of a generally punitive justice system sets up several contradic-tions. Most significantly, while RJ aims to provide a potentially holistic alter-native to punitive justice, youth who participate in RJ often do so under the threat of engagement with the punitive system. For example, in an "alterna-tive sentencing" model, youth may be given the option of either going to court for traditional sentencing or participating in a circle process that could result in a criminal sentence but could also result in actions such as apologizing to the victim(s), returning or repairing stolen or harmed property, or work-ing to rebuild trust with the affected community. Within schools, particularly heavily policed urban schools, the threat of punitive consequences thus places manipulative pressure on youth to participate in a restorative process and lim-its the possibility for RJ to provide a genuine alternative to the school-to-prison pipeline.

The limitations of RJ as a response to harm have led some to identify more closely with the idea of *transformative justice* (TJ). Like RJ, TJ is an approach that has deep roots in the histories of indigenous peoples of color. In a con-temporary context, it has been defined in opposition to the ideological and material functions of punitive justice systems in the United States and Canada. A similar framework is sometimes referred to as "community accountability" (Chen, Dulani, & Piepzna-Samarasinha, 2011; Incite, 2003). According to the group GenerationFIVE, TJ is "liberation from violence through a process that would confront state and systemic violence for individual and social justice (as quoted in TJLP, 2010, para. 4)." The Transformative Justice Law Project of Illi-nois (2010) defines TJ:

> Through community-based movements, Transformative Justice seeks to resist state-run responses to violence (such as the police state and systems of punish-ment, detention, and incarceration) and instead promotes support, compassion, dialogue and community building. In this way, reliance on violent and oppressive State level systems is transformed and replaced with community empowerment. (para. 4)

TJ questions whether harm can ever truly be healed or restored in a con-text where structural inequality is the pervasive norm. It seeks to address vio-lence and harm while also empowering communities to fight injustice. It is an inherently flexible approach, structured less as a single model and more as a political outlook driven by values of prison abolition, harm reduction (the goal of reducing harm caused to an individual or community by an action regardless of whether the action can be completely stopped or prevented), and holistic healing. In a TJ approach, the prison-industrial complex and the school-to-prison pipeline are generally viewed as *sources of,* rather than neces-sary *responses to,* harm (Incite, 2001).

Nationally, the scope of projects that identify themselves with TJ is very difficult to map. Many TJ groups and practices are small, ad hoc, and based in local communities rather than in formal organizations. Other practices may be located sheltered under organizations that do not publicly identify with the framework of transformative justice. Still others have been reticent to identify with the term for fear of co-optation by nonprofit or state systems and simply avoid the use of a formal title.[11] In particular, for organizations that are primarily focused on direct engagement with state systems such as schools or the criminal legal system, the central framework of TJ is in open contradiction with the ideology of these systems. We suspect that this is at least part of the reason why individuals and organizations involved with RJ in schools have rarely publicly identified this work as TJ. To do so might necessitate the admission that they/we oppose some of the basic tenets of the approach to schooling in poor communities of color today, in particular the public schools' connection to and ongoing dependence on incarceration and punishment.

For some organizations and individuals, restorative justice and transformative justice are two distinct frameworks, while other groups use the two terms interchangeably. Use of *restorative* or *transformative* can be an indication of different long-term visions and goals, but, in practice, RJ and TJ could also end up looking quite similar. Several organizations in Chicago identify at least in part with the framework of TJ, including some of the organizations highlighted above, such as Project NIA, Blocks Together, and Transformative Justice Law Project. As an example of TJ practice, we offer examples from the Young Women's Empowerment Project (YWEP), a youth-led organization for young women involved in the sex trade, and from Gender JUST, an LGBTQ youth organizing initiative. According to YWEP (2009), "Transformative Justice is a mode that acknowledges that state systems and social services can and often do create harm in the lives of girls. Transformative Justice supports community-based efforts for social justice beyond the government or other state-sponsored institutions (p. 12)." Using harm reduction, a framework that focuses on empowering people to reduce the potential harm of behaviors rather than encouraging total abstinence from those behaviors, YWEP works to create community-based solutions so young women do not need to rely on harmful systems, like schools, hospitals, or shelters can sometimes be. YWEP conducted a participatory action research project to collect information about young people's "bad encounters" with institutional violence and found that many young people experienced violence and barriers to access within education systems. YWEP developed the Street Youth Bill of Rights in response, demanding the right to an education that respects the dignity and learning styles of youth. In addition to other demands related to policing, health care, and social services, the Street Youth Bill of Rights calls for more accessibility to schooling, including online school, homeschooling, and child care for parenting teens. It states, "We have the right not to be subjected to unnecessary searches in school; discriminatory enforcements of rules, police and metal detectors in school, arrest or violent punishments for missing school, sexual harassment and discipline without a chance to be heard" (YWEP, n.d., para. 9). The transformative work YWEP is doing includes providing information about violence within schools and other systems and advocating for alternatives within and outside those systems. TJ challenges us to not think of programs we can add to the existing school systems but, rather, to think about transforming schools to eradicate violence.

Another organization, Gender JUST, an organization of LGBTQ young people and adult allies working for racial and economic justice, has advocated for RJ while also connecting its advocacy to a longer-term vision of TJ, demonstrating the flexible relationship between the two. RJ frameworks invite us to question if punitive measures truly create safe and secure schools and to consider whether criminalizing youth who harm other youth or adults decreases violence overall. Opponents of RJ sometime suggest that restorative practices can actually undermine the safety of young people who have experienced violence or harassment by not adequately "punishing" offenders or perpetrators. Yet, some of the most marginalized groups in society have countered that restorative practices can provide youth who have been victimized with significant recourse while also working to address the root causes of violence.

A powerful example comes from LGBTQ youth organizers with Gender JUST, many of whom have experienced violence and harassment due to their gender and sexual identity. In 2010, they successfully campaigned to get CPS to adopt a harassment and violence grievance procedure. Rather than advocating a punitive model, however, the young people insisted that the grievance procedure (1) be based in RJ practices, (2) be student-driven, and (3) be governed by a student oversight committee.

Later that year, when bullying of LGBTQ youth became a focus of attention nationwide, Gender JUST (2010) released a statement calling for restorative solutions to violence and reminding us that violence against LGBTQ youth was not increasing but reports and discussions were. The statement pointed out that violence against youth of color is also not new, stating, "As queer and transgender youth of color in public schools, violence is a reality we live daily in our schools, on our streets, in our communities, and in our lives." Instead of creating harsher antibullying laws, as many LGBTQ leaders and concerned adults were calling for, Gender JUST (2010) proposed RJ practices as a solution:

> Our greatest concern is that there is a resounding demand for increased violence as a reaction, in the form of Hate Crime penalties which bolster the Prison-Industrial-Complex and Anti-bullying measures which open the door to zero-tolerance policies and reinforce the school-to-prison pipeline. At Gender JUST, we call for a transformative and restorative response that seeks solutions to the underlying issues, takes into account the circumstances surrounding violence, and works to change the very culture of our schools and communities. (para. 5)

Gender JUST's work provides a clear example of young people affected by violence engaging RJ models while also calling for fundamental systemic change.

TJ creates spaces for promise and inspiration, and it also raises a lot of questions. What would TJ practices within schools look like? In addition to contributing to the elimination of the school-to-prison pipeline, what else might TJ accomplish? What new possibilities for school transformation are possible? What other methods could be used to repair harm that do not rely on punitive justice systems?

Whether a restorative or transformative framework is explicitly named or not, all of the organizations we highlight here are engaged in the challenging work of rethinking what justice, safety, and conflict resolution resemble in schools. The power of a transformative framework is that it creates space to not just *restore* relationships or school conditions to what they were prior to a conflict or incident but to imagine, transform, and build more just communities. TJ encourages us to think creatively about new interventions and builds on the foundations of RJ frameworks.

MOVING FORWARD

Despite our significant concerns outlined in the previous section, our work in schools and communities convinces us that RJ and TJ both have the potential to be radically transformative and are a promising part of the movement to end the school-to-prison pipeline. We need all the tools available to us in this effort. The problem at Lockwood Elementary was not that the Peace Room was not working or that community members, parents, and (some) teachers were not supportive. Instead, the challenges were linked to capacity, sustainability, and the persistent challenges faced by social movements. The school-to-prison pipeline is a part of a larger cultural and state commitment to a "tough-on-crime" carceral framework, and a restorative justice *program* in schools cannot intervene alone. Moving away from a superficial programmatic response, RJ can address conflict in schools and communities, but, more centrally, these practices and philosophical commitments can also build positive community for all stakeholders in the school, from the janitors, school security staff, parents, teachers, and students to the administrators and the surrounding community.

But small grassroots community organizations cannot and should not shoulder the responsibility of doing this work alone. As traced throughout this essay, and as echoed in the numerous reports cited by community-based coalitions, including VOYCE (2011) and the High HOPES Campaign (2012), we advocate for sustainable and robust funding to develop new practices and to support the organizations that have been engaging in restorative and transformative justice practices to be able to collectively analyze and document their work. The state must take on some of the work. The resources are available and must be redistributed. The relationships created through the coalitions outlined in this article will ensure that this struggle will continue in Chicago.

NOTES

We are honored to continue to do our work in community with many of the organizations identified in this article. We also thank Sam Worley for his assistance and appreciate the detailed feedback from the *HER* editors.

1. Lockwood is a pseudonym.
2. Across the United States there has been over a decade of growth in organization, analysis, and scholarship surrounding the school-to-prison pipeline and a corresponding focus on reforming the juvenile justice system (Advancement Project, 2010; Duncan, 2000; Meiners, 2007; Schaffner, 2006; Simmons, 2009; Winn, 2010). While the term *school-to-prison pipeline* aims to highlight a complex network of relations that naturalize the movement of youth of color from our schools and communities into under- or unemployment and permanent detention, the United States has always framed particular populations as superfluous to our democracy yet necessary to fill low-wage jobs or jobs available after full White employment.
3. See the appendix for a complete list of organizations and Web sites identified in this article.
4. This information was shared as part of a PowerPoint presentation at a Chicago Restorative Justice Gathering facilitated by Judge Sophia Hall on March 1, 2012.
5. An exception to this could be the 2010 CPS initiative Culture of Calm, which directed millions of dollars of funding into a year of antiviolence programs across the district, a small percentage of which went to local RJ partners. In 2011, the city renewed the funding in an attempt to extend the positive effects of the program, which appeared to have helped reduce violence and increase attendance. This program was triggered by the high-profile death of Derrion Albert (Ahmed-Ullah, 2011a).
6. We use *parent* as a proxy term to represent the range of adults who function as primary caregivers in communities, including grandparents, aunts, uncles, guardians, and/or older siblings.
7. Anecdote from VOYCE e-newsletter, March 12, 2012.
8. Related to Traub's analysis, schools become sites vulnerable to persistent and often unchecked reform initiatives. As Charles Payne (1997) noted, good ideas can fail in schools where the climate and culture are dysfunctional because some schools have adopted so many reform initiatives over the years that educators find themselves resistant (often with good reasons) to being subjected to the "latest" foolproof program guaranteed to transform their practice.
9. At Lockwood, given a choice, some students chose to go to the traditional detention room and suggested that they would be "left alone" there.
10. Comments from conversations confirmed via e-mails, March 2012.
11. Organizations we have encountered nationwide that are affiliated with transformative justice and community accountability include Philly Stands Up! (http://phillystandsup.wordpress.com), Communities United Against Violence (http://www.cuav.org), Communities Against Rape and Abuse (CARA) Seattle (http://cara-seattle.blogspot.com), Support New York (http://supportny.org), and many others cited in *The Revolution Starts at Home* (Chen et al., 2011). Much of this work is taking place under different titles or in small corners of communities that might not have a Web site, appear in a book, or identify themselves with the terminology used in this article.

REFERENCES

Advancement Project. (2010). *Test, punish, and push out: How "zero tolerance" and high-stakes testing funnel youth into the school-to-prison pipeline.* Washington, DC: Author.

Ahmed-Ullah, N. (2011a, June 9). Programs for at-risk students' safety at risk. *The Chicago Tribune.* Retrieved from http://articles.chicagotribune.com/2011-06-09/news/ct-met-culture-of-calm-0610-20110609_1_cps-fewer-students-programs-for-at-risk-students

Ahmed-Ullah, N. (2011b, July 24). Chicago Public Schools officials eyeing updated security cameras for 14 high schools. *The Chicago Tribune.* Retrieved from http://articles.chicagotribune.com/2011-07-24/news/ct-met-cps-security-cameras-0724-20110724_1_security-cameras-surveillance-cameras-surveillance-network

Alexander, M. (2010). *The New Jim Crow: Mass incarceration in the age of colorblindness.* New York: New Press.

Alternatives, Inc. (n.d.). *What is restorative justice?* Retrieved from http://www.alternativesyouth.org/restorative_justice/what-restorative-justice

Ashley, J., & Burke, K. (n.d.). *Implementing restorative justice: A guide for schools.* Illinois Criminal Justice Information Authority. Retrieved from http://www.icjia.state.il.us/public/pdf/BARJ/SCHOOL%20BARJ%20GUIDEBOOOK.pdf

Ashley, J., & Stevenson, P. (n.d.). *Implementing restorative justice: A guide for law enforcement.* Illinois Criminal Justice Information Authority. Retrieved from http://www.icjia.state.il.us/public/pdf/BARJ/BARJ%20law%20enforcement.pdf

Caputo, A. (2010, August 31). Seventeen. *The Chicago Reporter.* Retrieved from http://www.chicagoreporter.com/news/2010/08/seventeen

Chen, C., Dulani, J., & Piepzna-Samarasinha, L. (2011). Introduction. In C. Chen, J. Dulani, & L. Lakshmi Piepzna-Samarasinha (Eds.), *The revolution starts at home: Confronting intimate violence within activist communities* (pp. xix-xxxvi). Cambridge, MA: South End Press.

Civil Rights Data Collection. (2012). Office of Civil Rights. Retrieved from http://www2.ed.gov/about/offices/list/ocr/data.html

Community Justice for Youth Institute [CJYI]. (n.d.). *CJYI services.* Retrieved from http://cjyi.org/cjyi-services

Crenshaw, K. W. (1994). Mapping the margins: Intersectionality, identity politics, and violence against women of color. In M. A. Fineman & R. Mykituk (Eds.), *The public nature of private violence* (pp. 93–118). New York: Routledge.

Critical Resistance. (n.d.). Not so common language. Retrieved from http://www.critical-resistance.org/

Davis, A. (2003). *Are prisons obsolete?* New York: Seven Stories Press.

Dohrn, B. (2000). "Look out, kid, it's something you did": The criminalization of children. In V. Polakow (Ed.), *The public assault on America's children: Poverty, violence, and juvenile justice* (pp. 157–187). New York: Teachers College Press.

Duncan, G. A. (2000). Urban pedagogies and the celling of adolescents of color. *Social Justice: A Journal of Crime Conflict and World Order, 27*(3), 29–42.

Dyett High School Restorative Justice Report. (2008). *Informal report compiled by high school staff and shared with Mariame Kaba* [Internal document]. Dyett High School, Chicago.

GenderJUST. (2010). GenderJUST statement on recent studies. Retrieved from http://genderjust.org/2012-news/1010statement

Gilmore, R. W. (2007a). *Golden gulag: Prisons, surplus, crisis, and opposition in globalizing California.* Berkeley: University of California Press.

Gilmore, R. W. (2007b). In the shadow of the shadow state. In Incite! Women of Color Against Violence (Ed.), *The revolution will not be funded: Beyond the non-profit industrial complex* (pp. 41–52). Cambridge, MA: South End Press.

High HOPES Campaign. (2012, February). *From policy to standard practice: Restorative justice in Chicago Public Schools*. Community Renewal Society. Retrieved from http://www.box.com/s/86i7djik1i72p47tnlnf

Illinois Department of Juvenile Justice. (2009, February 10). *Illinois Juvenile Justice Commission annual report to the governor and General Assembly for calendar years 2007 and 2008*. Illinois Department of Human Services. Retrieved from http://www.dhs.state.il.us/page.aspx?item=43000

Incite! Women of Color Against Violence. (2001). *Critical resistance statement on gender violence and the prison industrial complex*. Retrieved from http://incite-national.org/index.php?s=92

Incite! Women of Color Against Violence. (2003). *Community accountability working document*. Retrieved from http://www.incite-national.org/index.php?s=93

Kaba, M., & Edwards, F. (2012). Policing Chicago Public Schools: A Gateway to the school-to-prison pipeline. Retrieved from http://policeincps.com/

Mauer, M. (1999). *A race to incarcerate*. New York: New Press.

Meiners, E. (2007). *Right to be hostile: Schools, prisons and the making of public enemies*. New York: Routledge.

Morrell, E. (2007). Youth participatory action research, civic engagement, and educational reform: Lessons from the IDEA Seminar. In J. Cammarota & M. Fine (Eds.), *Revolutionizing education: Youth participatory action research in motion* (pp. 155–185). New York: Routledge.

Parents Organized to Win, Educate and Renew—Policy Action Council [POWER-PAC] Elementary Justice Committee. (2010). *Parent-to-parent guide: Restorative justice in Chicago Public Schools*. Community Organizing and Family Issues. Retrieved from http://cofionline.org/files/parenttoparent.pdf

Payne, C. (1997). "I don't want your nasty pot of gold": Urban school climate and public policy [Working paper]. Evanston, IL: Institute for Policy Research, Northwestern University. Retrieved from http://www.eric.ed.gov/PDFS/ED412313.pdf

Pew Center on the States Public Safety Performance Project. (2008). *One in 100: Behind bars in America 2008*. Retrieved from http://www.pewcenteronthestates.org/uploadedFiles/One%20in%20100.pdf

Richie, B. (2012). *Arrested justice: Black women, male violence and the build-up of a prison nation*. New York: New York University Press.

Roberts, D. (1997). *Killing the black body: Race, reproduction, and the meaning of liberty*. New York: Vintage Books.

Schaffner, L. (2006). *Girls in trouble with the law*. New York: Rutgers University Press.

Slife, E., & Eldeib, D. (2011, December 9). New goal for juvenile center: Clear it out. *The Chicago Tribune*. Retrieved from http://www.chicagotribune.com

Shipps, D. (2006). *Chicago school reform, corporate style: Chicago, 1880–2000*. Lawrence: University of Kansas Press.

Simmons, L. (2009). End of the line: Tracing racial inequality from school to prison. *Race/Ethnicity: Multidisciplinary Global Perspectives, 2*(2), 215–241.

Transformative Justice Law Project of Illinois [TJLP]. (2010). *Who we are*. Retrieved from http://tjlp.org/aboutwho.html

Transforming Conflict. (n.d.). *Restorative approaches and practices*. Retrieved from http://www.transformingconflict.org/Restorative_Approaches_and_Practices.php

Traub, J. (2000, January 16). What no school can do. *The New York Times*. Retrieved from http://www.nytimes.com/2000/01/16/magazine/what-no-school-can-do.html?pagewanted=all&src=pm

Tuck, E. (2011). *Urban youth and school pushout: Gateways, get-aways, and the GED*. New York: Routledge.

Voices of Youth in Chicago Education [VOYCE]. (2011). *Failed policies, broken futures: The true cost of zero tolerance in Chicago.* Retrieved from http://www.voyceproject.org/voyce-demands-end-harsh-discipline-chicago-public-schools

Wacquant, L. (2009). *Punishing the poor: The neoliberal government of social insecurity.* Durham, NC: Duke University Press

Wallace, L. (2007, September 4). Restoring classroom justice. *In These Times.* Retrieved from http://inthesetimes.com/article/3304/restoring_classroom_justice/

Willrich, M. (2003). *City of courts: Socializing justice in progressive era Chicago.* Cambridge: Cambridge University Press.

Winn, M. (2010). *Girl time: Literacy, justice, and the school-to-prison pipeline.* New York: Teacher's College Press.

Wolch, J. R. (1990). *The shadow state: Government and voluntary sector in transition.* New York: The Foundation Center.

Wolcott, D. (2005). *Cops and kids: Policing juvenile delinquency in urban America, 1890–1940.* Columbus: Ohio State University Press.

Young Women's Empowerment Project [YWEP]. (n.d.). Street youth bill of rights. Retrieved from http://ywepchicago.wordpress.com/our-work/our-campaign

Young Women's Empowerment Project [YWEP]. (2009). *Girls do what they have to do to survive: Illuminating methods used by girls in the sex trade and street economy to fight back and heal.* Retrieved from http://ywepchicago.wordpress.com/our-work/our-campaign

APPENDIX: NAMED ORGANIZATIONS

Alternatives, Inc., www.alternativesyouth.org
Blocks Together, www.btchicago.org
Community Justice for Youth Institute, www.cjyi.org
Critical Resistance, www.criticalresistance.org
Gender JUST, www.genderjust.org
Fearless Leading by the Youth, www.stopchicago.org
INCITE! Women of Color Against Violence, www.incite-national.org
Parents Organized to Win Education Rights (POWER-PAC), www.cofionline.org
Prison Industrial Complex Teaching Collective, www.chicagopiccollective.com/
Project NIA, www.project-nia.org
Southwest Youth Collaborative, www.swyc.org
Suspension Stories, www.suspensionstories.com
Voices of Youth in Chicago Education, www.voyceproject.org
Young Women's Empowerment Project, www.youarepriceless.org
Young Women's Action Team, www.rogersparkywat.org

THE BATTLE

■

DEREK R. RUSSEL

Tell me, my love,
have you weathered the exhaustion,
grabbed beauty from all things
distant and near,
shook it between your teeth?

Why, when I think of you,
do I think of your poppy tan feet,
suddenly surrounded,
wrapped in scarlet's and lime?
that place where I stood in the dead of the day,
fiercely transparent in dampness:
muted by the earth.

My dear, if only in imagination,
stop and travel to me.
Go out, and with your precious hands,
grab for the whole earth, grab for the lone sky,
search for the steps of an immense movement,
search out to sea, out to the edge,
out to the merging of two rivers.

Crossing over multitudes,
over years and bells and grapes,
heavy legged
with the same tenacity as the wheel barrow's step,
I shall come to you.
Arriving, I shall gather certain candies and fruits,
and a straw basket
to place your steps in.
And the battle, when it comes,
in strong syllables,
in vanished kisses,
utter to me the color of your love,
and your tiny hands, like two weapons,
carefully knead them around my heart.

265

PART IV

EPILOGUE

EDITOR'S REVIEW

WHAT WE CAN LEARN FROM FIVE RECENT BOOKS
ABOUT THE SCHOOL-TO-PRISON PIPELINE

■

PAUL KUTTNER

HOMEROOM SECURITY: SCHOOL DISCIPLINE IN AN AGE OF FEAR
by Aaron Kupchik
New York: New York University Press, 2010. 288 pp. $35.00.

POLICE IN THE HALLWAYS: DISCIPLINE IN AN URBAN HIGH SCHOOL
by Kathleen Nolan
Minneapolis: University of Minnesota Press, 2011. 224 pp. $22.95.

GIRL TIME: LITERACY, JUSTICE, AND THE SCHOOL-TO-PRISON PIPELINE
by Maisha T. Winn
New York: Teachers College Press, 2011. 192 pp. $27.95.

CHALLENGING THE PRISON-INDUSTRIAL COMPLEX: ACTIVISM, ARTS, AND EDU-
CATIONAL ALTERNATIVES
Edited by Stephen J. Hartnett
Champaign: University of Illinois Press, 2010. 312 pp. $25.00.

THE SCHOOL-TO-PRISON PIPELINE: STRUCTURING LEGAL REFORM
by Catherine Y. Kim, Daniel J. Losen, and Damon T. Hewitt
New York: New York University Press, 2010. 240 pp. $22.00.

My first experience as something of an educator was in a minimum-security prison in Jackson, Michigan. A college student at the time, I co-facilitated a theater workshop with a group of adult men as part of a university class. As I stumbled through my first lessons, making plenty of mistakes and learning far more than I was teaching, the participants were both patient and supportive. It was one of the most rewarding educational experiences I have had, and for the fifteen men in the program, the opportunity to learn something new and to express themselves through writing and performance was a welcome break from a monotonous, dehumanizing daily reality.

The following semester I switched to teaching in a juvenile detention facility. My co-facilitator and I worked with a group of young women to create an original play about an extended family that was gathering, for the first time in years, at a funeral. These youth gave me a much harder time, challenging me in ways the men never did—both pedagogically and emotionally. But by the end, their engagement in, appreciation for, and connection to both the work and each other was richer for it.

After college graduation, I moved to Chicago and began to teach theater in public school programs and in afterschool programs. Raised in a wealthy, largely white suburb of Boston, this was my first introduction to massive comprehensive high schools, security officers, metal detectors, and surveillance.

By making my way from prisons to juvenile detention centers to urban public schools, I had, in a strange way, walked backward down what many are now calling the *school-to-prison pipeline*. This term names a disturbing trend in which young people—particularly certain groups of young people, such as youth of color and youth with disabilities—are effectively pushed out of schools and into the juvenile and adult justice systems. The forces behind this trend are multiple: zero tolerance policies that criminalize noncriminal school misbehavior, racially disparate use of suspensions and expulsions, overrepresentation of racial minority students in special education, media stereotypes that frame youth of color as criminals, and the growth of both public and private prisons (Advancement Project, 2005; Hartnett, 2011; Kim, Losen, & Hewitt, 2010; Rethinking Schools, 2011). While we had never heard of that term at the time, it was not hard for my fellow teachers, my students at the schools and detention centers, and I to see the parallels and connections among these institutions of education and incarceration.

I am an avid reader, with books overflowing from boxes and shelves at home. So when we decided to put out a book on disrupting the school-to-prison pipeline, I took the opportunity to dive into five recently published academic books on the topic. I was seeking not to judge the available literature but to mine it for insights, best practices, and innovative ideas. The purpose of this Editor's Review is not to critique these books but, rather, to draw out valuable lessons from them. No single book can capture the complexity of the school-to-prison pipeline; it is too multifaceted and involves too many interlocking institutions. By drawing on this set of books from teachers, lawyers, artists, academics, and more, we can begin to weave together a web of understanding and a set of strategies for addressing one of the most important justice issues we face today.

SCHOOL DISCIPLINE IN AN ERA OF ZERO TOLERANCE

The most visible face of the school-to-prison pipeline is what Aaron Kupchik (2010) calls "the new homeroom security"—the shift in school discipline toward zero tolerance policies and the increasing use of law enforcement tools and personnel in many public schools. This is also the aspect of the pipeline that has garnered the most widespread concern, due to a series of absurd episodes of school discipline overenforcement that have made headlines, such as a ten-year-old student handcuffed and detained at a police station for bringing a pair of scissors to school that she had been using at home for a school project (cited in Advancement Project, 2005). Given both the literal and symbolic power of police walking school hallways, it is perhaps not surprising that two recent academic books look closely at this new world of school discipline.

The New Homeroom Security

In the first of these books, *Homeroom Security: School Discipline in an Age of Fear*, Aaron Kupchik reports on a thorough, mixed-methods study of school discipline practices at four U.S. high schools that he conducted with the support of a team of research assistants. Situated in an extensive array of theories and philosophies—from theories of social control to debates about the purpose of education—Kupchik makes a concerted effort to be evenhanded by sharing the perspectives of multiple actors. Still, in the end, this book is an indictment of modern school discipline practices as harmful, inequitable, and obstructing the work of educating our youth.

Kupchik's team studied four schools in two regions of the United States, in each region looking at one school that serves largely low-income families of color and one school that serves largely middle-class white students. Thus, Kupchik is uniquely positioned to speak to differences within and across schools. *Homeroom Security* supports the "mountain of prior research" (p. 159) demonstrating that poor youth and youth of color, particularly African Americans, are disproportionately targeted by school discipline practices. For example, Kupchik explains that within each state, the poorer school with more students of color suspended students at a much higher rate. Similarly, within schools, African American students are shown to receive disproportionately harsher disciplinary sanctions. Kupchik offers a nuanced explanation of how this latter process happens, which combines the direct effects of racial stereotypes with the practice of giving out harsher penalties to lower-performing students—who are disproportionately black. This last point is important, because it implies that those students who need the most support and have the lowest test scores are more likely to interface with the justice system and thus to leave school and raise the school's overall test scores.

But though Kupchik finds some significant difference across schools, a perhaps more surprising finding is the overwhelmingly *similar* practices and discourses at these different schools. He takes this as evidence of the rapid spread of harsh discipline across the country, explaining that "practices that were once used primarily for schools hosting poor youth and youth of color are now implemented in white, middle-class schools as well" (p. 161).

Kupchik finds that having a police presence in a school can be helpful to administrators, who can rely on the police in difficult situations, and to police precincts, which can use the school-based officer to extend their ability to monitor and regulate the community. However, though most youth he and his assistants spoke with were either positive or ambivalent about the police presence (perhaps, he suggests, because they have not known any other reality), Kupchik finds that having police in schools on a regular basis is on the whole harmful to students. He charts a number of reasons for this, but at the core he is arguing that officers

> affect the overall school climate. Having an officer can escalate disciplinary situations; increase the likelihood that students are arrested at school; redefine situations as criminal justice problems rather than social, psychological, or academic problems; introduce a criminal orientation to how administrators prevent and respond to problems; and socialize students to expect a police presence in their lives. (p. 115)

Kupchik also finds that all four schools he studied are caught up in what he calls "teaching to the rules." Comparing this phenomenon to the common complaint of schools "teaching to the test" rather than engaging young people in deep critical thinking, Kupchik argues that these schools have come to a point where the goal of school rules becomes merely to follow the rules and to reinforce the school's authority, rather than to actually change behaviors or teach young people how to resolve conflict. This orientation toward discipline leads adults to focus on rules rather than root causes (such as life issues students might be dealing with), to not listen to students, and to discount student resistance to rules even when their complaints might be legitimate. This can lead, he argues, to the alienation, and potential dropping out, of students who see the school as illegitimate in its use of power or, conversely, to students being socialized to simply obey rules uncritically.

The alternatives offered in *Homeroom Security* include better classroom management, more listening to students, eliminating zero tolerance policies, and full-time police only in schools with serious crime problems. These are important, though rather moderate, responses given some of the deep critiques offered earlier in the book. One of the more exciting and potentially paradigm-shifting recommendations is the authentic involvement of students in the crafting of discipline policies. After all, "students know best what goes on in the school . . . they have more at stake in a safe school than anyone else" (p. 195). It is this kind of practice that has great potential to move schools closer to the vision Kupchik offers of schools as developers of active citizens.

Reproduction in an Age of Zero Tolerance

In *Police in the Hallways: Discipline in an Urban High School,* researcher and former teacher Kathleen Nolan offers a deep ethnography of one school in the Bronx, New York. Documenting one year in the life of the school, *Police in the Hallways* draws out the diverse perspectives of students, educators, and police officers and gives an up-close-and-personal look at the "culture of control" documented by both Nolan and Kupchik.

Nolan situates her discussion in previous scholarly work on social reproduction, specifically Paul Willis's classic *Learning to Labor* (1981), in which he
argues that the rejection of middle-class schooling by working-class youth in
his study (the "lads") contains an implicit, rational critique of social inequality. At the same time, Willis argues, through this rejection the lads take part
in their own reproduction as working-class adults. Nolan seeks to update this
understanding in a different context and era—modern urban public schooling in the United States among youth of color. She shows how, in a deindustri-
alized age and an era of mass incarceration, this new school discipline works
not toward the "reproduction of a *working* class but the *production of a whole
population of criminalized, excluded youth*" (p. 157).

Nolan's work serves to complicate our discussion of the school-to-prison
pipeline. While noting the usefulness of the metaphor of the "pipeline," Nolan
puts aside the metaphor to focus on a "nuanced description of daily life" (p.
72). In the tradition of good ethnography, she challenges deterministic discourses that place all the blame on systems, leaving youth and educators no
agency. Nolan pushes us to see students as agents, interacting in complex ways
with systems, and often taking part in their own construction as a "criminalized class" through their oppositional behavior in schools. Nevertheless, she
does not blame students for the results of this interaction, arguing successfully
that oppositional behavior is both a legitimate critique and a rational response
to the oppressive situation—often offering very real benefits for youth.

Nolan offers a vivid understanding of the way that, under this system of discipline and control, involvement in the criminal justice system often begins
with rule infractions that break no law. Once confronted by security personnel, often in a disrespectful way that challenges students' dignity, minor infractions escalate. Maybe a police officer grabs the student, who then pushes the
officer's arm away. This is then seen as "disorderly conduct" and ends up in
a court summons. If security had not been present, no law breaking would
have taken place, and the situation could have been dealt with in a productive, educative manner. One particularly powerful story points to this dynamic
very clearly:

> I remember asking one day in the deans' office, "What was that student arrested
> for?" The answer I received was resisting arrest. I persisted. "But why was he
> arrested in the first place?" The dean with whom I was conversing gave me a
> confused look and after a moment conceded, "Oh, I don't know. I wasn't there."
> (p. 59)

Though the book starts with the image of police in the hallways, it ranges
far beyond this most visible piece of the story. Nolan draws a link back to the
classroom, arguing that the trajectory of a student from school to court begins
there. The process starts with an alienating and boring curriculum, shaped
heavily by high-stakes testing, which pushes students away from learning and

makes them far more likely to skip classes. It is in the hallways where tiny disciplinary infractions like wearing a hat or simply being in the hall during class escalate into summonses to court. In this way, Nolan supports Linda Christensen's (2011) argument that the school-to-prison pipeline "begins when we fail to create a curriculum and a pedagogy that connects with students, that takes them seriously as intellectuals, that lets students know we care about them, that gives them the chance to channel their pain and defiance in productive ways" (pp. 24–25).

Nolan is sympathetic to educators who, she argues, seek to maintain their identity as educators by stepping in to deal with disciplinary issues or avoiding calling in the police. She notes how the teachers who work as disciplinarians in the school use what she calls "culturally relevant disciplinary practices," in which community context and student background are taken into account, and how they try to "reach" students. But even these educators become inured to and seem to buy into the overall logic of the criminal justice system, which pervades the school through "discourses of control." These include the discourse of "he got what he deserved," which lays blame on the youth who should have known better than to break the rule—even if the rule is unjust. They also include the discourse of "better five days now than five years later on," which frames this heavy-handed discipline as a deterrent despite the lack of evidence that it works.

With *Police in the Hallways*, Nolan paints a nuanced and respectful portrait of school discipline, which nevertheless urgently points readers toward the conclusion that modern school discipline is working against the very socioemotional and educational purposes we expect from our nation's schools.

JUVENILE JUSTICE AND PRISON: THE OTHER END OF THE PIPELINE

Kupchik and Nolan both show how zero tolerance policies, school policing, criminalizing discourses, and non–culturally relevant curriculum combine to push students out of schools, putting them at risk of falling into the juvenile justice system—or, at times, sending them directly there. Nolan's story follows some of the youth out of the school and right to the courthouse. These next two books pick up where Kupchik's and Nolan's books leave off, taking us into juvenile detention centers and exposing us to the broader prison system in which the pipeline is embedded.

Challenging the "Single Story"

In *Girl Time: Literacy, Justice, and the School-to-Prison Pipeline*, Maisha T. Winn offers a close look at an arts-based initiative that works to challenge the school-to-prison pipeline. The program, Girl Time, runs playwriting and theater workshops with incarcerated girls and works with formerly incarcerated girls to write plays that are then performed in detention centers for other youth and staff. Based on interviews and extended participant observation, in which

Winn was trained to lead the theater workshops, Winn shares the pedagogy of the Girl Time program, the stories of the facilitators and participants, and her own thoughts on how girls in the program "use this permissive space to create, question, and imagine something different—a life on their terms as contributors to the world" (p. 120).

Through what she calls "performance ethnography," Winn teases out the pedagogical and learning processes that make up the Girl Time model. Each piece of the program—from where the teachers sit on the first day of the workshop to the facilitation of discussions with the audience after the performances—is carefully crafted to create a space in which writing becomes a form of power and theater becomes a performance of possibilities.

Girl Time focuses our attention on how gender intersects with the pipeline, noting that conversations around school discipline, crime, and juvenile punishment often revolve around boys of color while sidelining the stories of girls. Arrests of girls have been increasing, and as of the most recent data, girls "account for one in four juvenile arrests in the United States" (p. 113). While the forces that lead girls toward juvenile detention and prison are in some ways similar to those that affect boys, girls also face their own particular challenges. For instance, girls have to deal with gender-based expectations from teachers that marginalize them for talking back and expectations from peers to stand by young men even through criminal activities. And once girls end up in juvenile detention, institutions are not well prepared to address their particular needs.

Like Nolan, who drew out the discourses of control that drive school discipline, Winn alerts us to another of the narrative, or discursive, faces of the school-to-prison pipeline. The trajectories of the girls in *Girl Time* are shaped not only by the institutions around them but also by the stories that are told about them. Young women become trapped in "the single story of incarcerated and formerly incarcerated girls as dangerous, unworthy, and undeserving of an audience" (p. 143), often internalizing this story and telling it themselves. In response to this single, confining narrative, Winn offers the artistic space of Girl Time as one way to support girls in retelling their own stories, "inviting them to revisit, and in some cases rewrite, scenes from their lives, as well as the lives of their peers . . . an opportunity to reintroduce themselves through the medium of playwriting and performance" (p. 3). Winn structures the book itself to challenge the single story, refusing to supplant it with a singular alternative. Instead, she presents a mosaic of individual stories from participants and facilitators, each utterly unique while still connecting to one another.

The Prison-Industrial Complex and the School-to-Prison Pipeline

To fully understand the school-to-prison pipeline and integrate the multiple individual stories such as those called out in Winn's book, we must at times take a step back and view the larger context within which it functions. *Challeng-*

ing the Prison-Industrial Complex: Activism, Arts, and Educational Alternatives does just that. It is an edited volume that gathers together scholars and educators—along with incarcerated poets and visual artists—to illuminate the workings of the prison-industrial complex (PIC) and share strategies for confronting it.

The first half of the book, "Diagnosing the Crisis," is dedicated to understanding the PIC: the web of government and for-profit institutions that monitor, control, discipline, and incarcerate millions of U.S. residents. The book argues that in the United States, "punishment has become a driving force in contemporary American life" (p. 6), and thus the country has become a "punishing democracy." The chapters span an impressively wide range, illuminating multiple facets of the PIC. Erica Meiners uncovers the economic underpinnings of the PIC and the ways that surveillance and control are privatizing public space; Julilly Kohler-Hausmann offers a compelling and disturbing account of how our domestic police force has been increasingly drawing on military tools, strategies, and metaphors since the Vietnam War; while other pieces look at stereotypes in the media and the "war on drugs."

Rose Braz and Myesha Williams present a chapter titled "Diagnosing the Schools-to-Prisons Pipeline: Maximum Security, Minimum Learning." Looking largely at California, the authors offer an overview of the harm that zero tolerance policies and school policing practices such as drug testing and surveillance have on learning. Like the books outlined in the first section of this review, these authors point to the ways that these practices lead away from a focus on root issues and quality pedagogy and toward creating a culture of fear and control. Braz and Williams also connect this conversation to larger processes, including the huge imbalance between state funding of prisons versus education and the perverse incentives from No Child Left Behind that encourage schools to push out low-performing students.

By situating this discussion within a larger conversation about the PIC, the book as a whole pushes us to understand the effort to disrupt the school-to-prison pipeline as part of a larger effort to reform or dismantle the prison industrial complex. As Meiners and colleagues argue in this volume, we cannot solve the problem of the school-to-prison pipeline without addressing the larger issues of control and punishment in our society, any more than we can truly improve learning in schools without addressing issues of inequality, health, and housing as well. Programs working only within the school walls, while important, will never be sufficient on their own.

The second half of the book, "Practical Solutions, Visionary Alternatives," offers a series of stories about on-the-ground work being done to engage with, shift, and challenge the PIC. I would hesitate to call them "solutions," given the daunting task they take on, but they offer practical actions that real people are taking to begin to move our society from a "punishing democracy" to an "abolition democracy." Drawing on writing by Angela Davis, Hartnett argues for the abolition of the PIC, stating that prison abolition is not a negative effort of simply shutting down prisons but a proactive process of creation. He says that "shutting down the prison-industrial complex will require nothing less than a revolution—the question is not only how to abolish prisons, but how to reimagine a democracy that does not need such institutions" (p. 4).

It is perhaps because of the centrality of "reimagining" to the prison abolition movement that the arts play a central role in this section of the book. Readers are treated to narratives by arts education practitioners who run three different programs with incarcerated adults and youth. It begins with Buzz Alexander, writing about the Prison Creative Arts Project (PCAP) at the University of Michigan, the same program that introduced me to this work back in college. Alexander gives a bold yet humble account of PCAP's theater and writing workshops in prisons, juvenile detention centers, and public schools, as well as their annual visual art show, highlighting both the messiness and the promise of this work. Robin Sohnen shares the work of the Each One Reach One program, which runs playwriting and tutoring in prisons, and Jonathan Shailor recounts his experiences directing Shakespeare in prisons. While each of these programs has a different focus, pedagogy, and theory of change, together they demonstrate the potential of artistic programming to build humanizing relationships between those inside and outside of the prison system; to help individuals develop and grow; to spread awareness of the oppressions of the system and of the humanity of the incarcerated; and to begin much-needed dialogue about the future of our democracy.

Situated in a discussion of the history of "race-making" in the United States is Garrett Albert Duncan's chapter "Fostering Cultures of Achievement in Urban Schools: How to Work toward the Abolition of the Schools-to-Prisons Pipeline." Duncan points to a set of promising educational reforms: the Kalamazoo Promise Fund—which offers four years of tuition to state schools to all students who graduate from Kalamazoo, Michigan, public schools—and similar efforts across the country. While noting that this effort was not created with the school-to-prison pipeline in mind, it nonetheless holds promise to "stem the flow of black and Latino youth into America's jails and penitentiaries" (p. 215).

Throughout the book, readers encounter pieces of poetry from incarcerated men and women and a stunning set of images from the PCAP Annual Exhibition of Art by Michigan Prisoners. These pieces bring some concreteness to the stories told by the authors and connect a reader with not just the idea of prisoners but incarcerated humans in the particular. As this book clearly demonstrates, both art and education can serve as access points for addressing the school-to-prison pipeline—but they are not the only avenues for seeking change.

LEGAL STRATEGIES FOR DISRUPTING THE PIPELINE

The final book in this review addresses one promising avenue for disrupting the pipeline: the courts. In *The School-to-Prison Pipeline: Structuring Legal Reform*

(2010), Catherine Y. Kim, Daniel J. Losen, and Damon T. Hewitt offer a thorough map of this avenue as a starting point for advocates of all stripes looking to challenge the pipeline in the legal arena. The book emerges from a partnership between the Racial Justice Program of the American Civil Liberties Union Foundation, the NAACP Legal Defense and Education Fund, and the Civil Rights Project at UCLA and fills an important gap in the pipeline literature.

The authors start with a more narrow definition of the pipeline than some of the other books in this review, arguing that it is, at its foundation, a failure of both the educational system and the juvenile justice system to meet the needs of large swaths of the population. The mechanisms that lead to this failure include inadequate resources, intentional and unintentional discrimination, and the criminalization of school-based misconduct. Importantly, like Braz and Williams in *Challenging the Prison-Industrial Complex*, these authors situate these pipeline mechanisms within the current climate of test-based accountability, which is creating perverse incentives for schools to push out students who are performing poorly on high-stakes tests.

The book is broken up into chapters based on particular points at which policies and their implementation push students into the pipeline, from widespread school resource deficiencies to racial discrimination, from special education to schooling in juvenile detention centers. Each point in the pipeline is then used as an access point for advocates. The authors offer a well-researched argument for the importance of each access point and discuss the relevant laws, regulations, or constitutional provisions. Then they lay out the legal theories underpinning potential challenges and what can be learned from past or extant cases about the potential and challenges to each strategy.

While the authors state that this book is not an exhaustive resource, no one could claim it is not thorough and well researched. Thus, the book can serve as an invaluable resource for any organizing groups, advocates, or others seriously considering legal remedies.

Overall, *The School-to-Prison Pipeline: Structuring Legal Reform* offers a vision of advocates across the country using a multiplicity of strategies to chip away at the pipeline while facing significant barriers to success. Underlying much of the struggle is the fact that the U.S. Constitution does not guarantee a fundamental right to education. However, the authors are quick to point out that legal remedies will never be the answer on their own. Such remedies must be in conjunction with grassroots organizing, advocacy, and lobbying efforts. While they do not mention it, this argument supports the need for efforts like the current campaign, led by civil rights veteran and educator Bob Moses, for a constitutional right to quality education (Perry, Moses, Wynne, Cortés, & Delpit, 2010)—an effort that, if successful, would open up many new legal avenues for cases like those laid out in this book.

CONCLUSION

Each of the books reviewed offers its own well-formulated lessons about the school-to-prison pipeline and suggestions for reform. Taken together, we begin to see a more comprehensive picture, which can offer overarching lessons for activists, organizers, students, artists, educators, and others who seek to understand and disrupt it. We see that the school-to-prison pipeline has multiple faces, each of which is too often understood in isolation from the others:

The Pedagogical Face. The pipeline begins with curriculum and pedagogy that fails to engage young people from where they are and is exacerbated when pedagogical and socioemotional goals become subservient to systems of punishment and control. In response, educators and administrators need to develop educational spaces in which culturally relevant pedagogy, caring relationships, and high expectations are the norm.

The Discursive Face. The pipeline is driven by societal narratives that shape how poor youth, youth of color, LGBTQ youth, girls, and others are understood—and even at times how they understand themselves. In response, artists and activists of all ages can offer new counterstories that challenge and, ultimately, replace these narratives with others that are more authentic and empowering.

The Disciplinary Face. The systems of punishment and control that pervade our school and justice systems are increasingly criminalizing noncriminal behavior and overshadowing teaching and learning. There is a role for those involved—from school and district administrators to police and corrections officials—to challenge both the ethics and the effectiveness of these techniques and to implement alternatives that promote healing and restoration over punishment and marginalization.

The Legal Face. The pipeline includes both intentional and unconscious discrimination against several subgroups of students, leading to a set of disturbing disparities in discipline, punishment, and incarceration. These disparities can be understood as an issue of civil and human rights. A response to these rights violations from lawyers and advocates can use current laws to challenge these disparities, alongside organizing efforts to strengthen our civil rights apparatus.

The Policy Face. Some educational policies, such as high-stakes testing and accountability systems, which are designed to be color-blind or even to specifically improve the education of youth in marginalized communities, have had adverse effects such as incentivizing schools to encourage low-testing youth to leave schools. At the same time, local and national policy work holds promise for advocates addressing many points in the pipeline.

The Relational Face. The pipeline is sustained by a lack of authentic, humanizing relationships between students and teachers, between youth and adults, and between those inside and outside the justice system. This issue calls people to build humanizing spaces through art, education, political activity, etc., where people can connect and dispel for themselves the "single stories" that are told about us all.

These books do not encompass a full look at the school-to-prison pipeline field, but they do suggest which areas are receiving the most focus and what pieces of the conversation may need more attention. For one, books on the school-to-prison pipeline look most commonly at high school–age students, and sometimes at middle or elementary school students. But the pipeline actually begins much earlier; a 2005 report found that preK students were 2.5 times more likely to be expelled from school than their K–12 counterparts (Gilliam, 2005). Similarly, attention to much younger children could uncover some of the ways that the school-to-prison pipeline becomes a circle, looping back around through the additional strains and challenges of young people whose parents are incarcerated (Haniyah, 2011; Sokolower, 2011). Furthermore, while boys are often the focus of study around discipline, Winn argues convincingly that the experiences of girls need to be attended to much more thoroughly. In addition, the particular forces affecting LGBTQ youth have not been as well connected to the school-to-prison pipeline literature. Finally, though both the problems and some of the possible alternatives to school discipline have been getting attention (specifically PBIS and restorative justice), little is being written, it seems, about how to organize to create the political will to implement these reforms in systemic, sustainable ways (Dzurinko, McCants, & Stith, 2011).

Together, these books point to the need for a multiplicity of voices in discussion if we are to fully understand and challenge the school-to-prison pipeline. They offer visions of the many roles people can play based on their particular passions, interests, and skills. We need the voices of civil rights lawyers and youth artists, educators and police, researchers and social workers who are open to sharing their piece of the puzzle and collaborating with others. As Winn explains so eloquently in *Girl Time*, we must resist prescriptive and singular solutions to the problems of the school-to-prison pipeline: "There is no single answer, just as there is no single story . . . The first step in this work is to bring everyone to the table" (p. 124). This Editor's Review, and the volume it is a part of, seeks to begin just such conversations, and to serve as a symbol of the kind of collaborative work we must do to truly disrupt the pipeline.

REFERENCES

Advancement Project. (2005). *Education on lockdown: The schoolhouse to jailhouse track.* Washington, DC: Author.

Christensen, L. (2011). The classroom-to-prison pipeline. *Rethinking Schools, 26*(2), 24–27.

Dzurinko, N., McCants, J., & Stith, J. (2011, Spring). The campaign for nonviolent schools: Students flip the script on violence in Philadelphia. *Voices in Urban Education, 30,* 22–30.

Gilliam, W. S. (2005). *Prekindergartners left behind: Expulsion rates in state prekindergarten programs* [FDC Policy Brief Series No. 3]. New York: Foundation for Child Development.

Haniyah.(2011). Haniyah's story. *Rethinking Schools, 26*(2), 28–32.

Hartnett, S. J. (Ed.). (2011). *Challenging the prison-industrial complex: Activism, arts, and educational alternatives.* Urbana-Champaign: University of Illinois Press.

Kim, C., Losen, D. J., & Hewitt, D. (2010). *The school to prison pipeline: Structuring legal reform.* New York: New York University Press.

Kupchik, A. (2010). *Homeroom security: School discipline in an age of fear.* New York: New York University Press.

Perry, T., Moses, R. P., Wynne, J. T., Cortés Jr., E., & Delpit, L. (2010). *Quality education as a constitutional right: Creating a grassrooots movement to transform public schools.* Boston: Beacon Press.

Rethinking Schools. (2011). Stop the school to prison pipeline [Special Issue]. *Rethinking Schools, 26*(2).

Sokolower, J. (2011). Teaching Haniyah. *Rethinking Schools, 26*(2), 29–32.

Willis, P. E. (1981). *Learning to labor: How working class kids get working class jobs.* New York: Columbia University Press.

ABOUT THE EDITORS

Sofía Bahena is a doctoral student in the culture, communities, and education program at the Harvard Graduate School of Education. A daughter of immigrants, Bahena's research interests have been informed by her parents' resilience and her own academic and personal journey. Her research focuses on Latino identity development using a historic and dynamic lens. Informed by psychological, sociological, and immigration studies, she is exploring the role of hope in the success and well-being of Latino students in the United States. Previously, Bahena was a policy and research assistant at the Alliance for Excellent Education, where she worked on various projects informing federal secondary school policy and authored an issue brief on teacher attrition. She has also served as a school partnership coordinator in Baltimore and currently works with a Washington, DC-based national organization, the Hispanic College Fund, in evaluating its precollege summer programs. She holds a BA in sociology and business from Trinity University, San Antonio, TX.

North Cooc is a doctoral candidate in quantitative policy analysis in education at the Harvard Graduate School of Education. His research explores the home and school factors that contribute to the disproportionate enrollment of minorities in special education, particularly the underrepresentation of Asian American students. His immigrant upbringing continues to inform a personal interest in the barriers to educational success and mobility for immigrant children and their families. Prior to his doctoral studies, Cooc worked in educational research in Washington, DC, where he conducted evaluations and studies of out-of-school time programs, early literacy initiatives, and youth development programs. He also spent two years teaching junior high school English in rural Japan through the JET Programme. Cooc holds an EdM in international education policy from the Harvard Graduate School of Education and a BA in history and Japanese from the University of California, Berkeley.

Rachel Currie-Rubin completed her doctoral degree in human development and education from the Harvard Graduate School of Education in May 2012. Her research focused on ill-structured problem solving, specifically about how novice reading specialists and expert assessment specialists weigh and understand assessment data about challenging cases of students with reading difficulties. Her research has looked at vowel perception of children with and without reading difficulties and at vocabulary and comprehension in Calca, Peru. Currie-Rubin currently works at CAST, a research and development organization, but she has also worked as a reading teacher for children and adults and as an educational specialist at Children's Hospital Boston. She holds an EdM in language and literacy from the Harvard Graduate School of Education and a BA in speech and hearing education from Ithaca College.

Paul Kuttner is a doctoral candidate at the Harvard Graduate School of Education studying community and youth organizing, community-school partnerships, and arts education. His work is founded on a conviction that the arts create powerful spaces where youth and adults can discuss, imagine, and work collectively toward individual and community transformation. As a theater educator in Chicago, Kuttner co-founded Communities Creating Change, a community-based arts project. His dissertation research looks at cultural organizing with young people—the intersection of youth organizing and arts. He is also a graphic designer and cartoonist, exploring ways to integrate comic book art into social science research. Kuttner holds an EdM from the Harvard Graduate School of Education and a BA from the University of Michigan, Ann Arbor.

Monica Ng is a doctoral student in education policy, leadership, and instructional practice at the Harvard Graduate School of Education. Her research interests include teacher leadership, inclusive education, and community and parental involvement in schools. She is interested in teacher collaboration and school-based educational reform. Ng is a research assistant for the Project on the Next Generation of Teachers, studying teachers' working conditions in high-poverty schools. Prior to Harvard, Monica taught third grade, kindergarten, and preschool in the San Francisco Bay Area. She also worked as a program coordinator for an AmeriCorps literacy project in Oakland, California, and with the Early Academic Outreach Program and the Student Learning Center at the University of California. Monica holds a BA in literature/writing from University of California, San Diego and an EdM in school leadership from Harvard Graduate School of Education.

ABOUT THE CONTRIBUTORS

Starcia Ague holds a BA in criminal justice from Washington State University. She currently works as a research coordinator in the Division of Public Behavioral Health and Justice Policy at the University of Washington. She is actively involved in advocating for reforms in the juvenile justice system in the Washington state legislature and in working directly with at-risk and delinquent youth in King County, WA. Ague was a contributor to the John D. and Catherine T. MacArthur Foundation's Models for Change juvenile justice reform initiatives in Washington state and continues to be involved in outcomes resulting from that work. In 2009 she was the recipient of Washington state's Spirit of Youth Award, presented annually to youth involved with the Juvenile Rehabilitation Authority. Ague currently serves on the Governor's Washington State Partnership Council on Juvenile Justice as a co-chair, and she continues to work on enhancing educational opportunities in the state's juvenile justice system and building a stronger youth voice in the system.

"Curtis Banner" is a graduate of the Social Justice Academy in Boston, MA. He is currently studying to become a medical technologist.

Laurent Bennett is a graduate of Charlestown High School in Charlestown, MA. He attends conferences on restorative justice and has also helped train preservice teachers about how to use circles as a disciplinary practice.

Kathy Boudin is the director of the Criminal Justice Initiative: Supporting Children, Families and Communities, an interdisciplinary project located in the Columbia University School of Social Work. During her twenty-two years of incarceration, Boudin was involved in issues surrounding adult literacy, the AIDS epidemic, mother-child relationships, and higher education in prison. She has maintained those commitments, publishing in each of these areas, and additionally works in restorative justice and parole reform with "long-termers" in prison. She received her doctoral degree in education from Columbia University Teachers College, her work focusing on adolescents with incarcerated mothers.

Kathleen B. Boundy is an attorney for and co-director (1990–present) of the Center for Law and Education (CLE). She has an extensive background in federal education policy, analysis, and advocacy and has participated in the reauthorizations of both the Individuals with Disabilities Education Act and Title I of the Elementary and Secondary Education Act. She has testified before the U.S. Senate and the U.S. Civil Rights Commission on the exclusion of students with disabilities and poor and racial minority students from educational opportunities. For five years she directed CLE's participation through the PACER Center in the U.S. Department of Education's FAPE Project, with its focus on including students with disabilities in education reform and promoting high academic standards and achievement for all students. In the courts she has represented economically disadvantaged students on a range of issues, such as high-stakes testing; the denial of special education and related services for incarcerated youth; disproportionate identification of racial minorities by disability category; disciplinary exclusion of students; and failure to provide students with disabilities an education consistent with state standards. She holds an AB from Manhattanville College, an MAT from the Boston College Graduate School of Arts and Sciences, and a JD from Northeastern University School of Law.

Joseph Cambone is an associate professor and senior associate dean in the Graduate School of Education at Lesley University, where he is developing initiatives that provide deep, guided clinical practice for early-career teachers. Prior to Lesley, he was the associate executive director of Walker Home and School, a comprehensive education and treatment center for troubled children. He also directed the Institute for Equity in Schools, a multidisciplinary consulting group that assisted public school superintendents and central office personnel in reducing the overrepresentation of minority children in special education classes and increasing student performance through the reorganization of existing programs and management, new program development, resource reallocation, curriculum realignment, and staff development.

Janet Connors is a long-time community and social justice activist who has lived and worked in and around Dorchester, MA, all her life. A single mother who raised three children, Ma, or Mama J, as she is known to many young people, has more than forty years of experience working with youth and families in community-based organizations. She is currently a Community Fellow with the Center for Restorative Justice. Connors works as an independent restorative justice consultant and as a trainer and practitioner with the JUST Circles team. Her work encourages restorative discipline practices, seeks restorative resolutions to conflict, and promotes healing through the use of circles in schools and in community settings. She is on the leadership team of the Family Advisory Committee for the Department of Children and Families and is a survivor-to-survivor support consultant with the Beth Israel Deaconess Violence Prevention and Recovery Center. She is on the faculty of the MOVA (Massachusetts Office of Victim Assistance) New Advocate Academy. Connors received the 2011 Leadership in Community and Restorative Justice Award from the National Conference on Restorative Justice.

Seth G. Cooper is twenty-four and serving a fourteen-year prison term. Prior to his incarceration in 2006, he was a lifelong resident of Cape May County, NJ. Cooper is an inmate paralegal at Garden State Youth Correctional Facility. He is eligible for parole in 2014.

Christopher Dankovich has been incarcerated since he was fifteen years old. He is originally from Oakland County, MI, where he was an honor roll student. During his incarceration, he began to educate himself simply out of a desire to learn but then wanted to use his education to help others. He has tutored and taught his fellow inmates since 2007 while also continuing his self-education and working toward his bachelor's degree.

Bobby Dean Evans, Jr. was born on January 20, 1965, in Pontiac, MI, to Thelma Jean and Bobby Dean. He has three siblings, "all girls and the better part of me"; six children, "my Baby Girl, who inspires me greatly, and her three brothers and two nephews"; and a beautiful grandson. "The amazing part of this Mystory is my Pop suffered the same public educational experience 60 years ago . . . One day I will write his Mystory."

Jane Hereth, an educator, organizer, and social worker, has been a volunteer with Project NIA since 2009 and is a trained circle keeper. As a volunteer with Project NIA's Chain Reaction, she works with youth at a center for LGBTQ youth to collect and disseminate stories about young people's interactions with the police. Her interest in restorative and transformative justice grew out of her advocacy work with survivors of sexual assault, and she continues to promote community-based responses to harm and violence. Hereth coordinates a behavioral research study on HIV prevention among transgender youth. She received an MSW from the Jane Addams College of Social Work at the University of Illinois at Chicago and a BA in sociology from Grinnell College.

Mariame Kaba is an organizer, educator, and writer who lives in Chicago. Her work focuses on ending violence, dismantling the prison-industrial complex, and supporting youth leadership development. She is the founder and director of Project NIA, a grassroots organization with a mission to end youth incarceration. A published author and a teacher, Kaba has co-founded several organizations and groups including the Chicago Freedom School, the Chicago Taskforce on Violence Against Girls and Young Women, and the Rogers Park Young Women's Action Team.

Joanne Karger is a 2011–2012 postdoctoral fellow in Universal Design for Learning at CAST and Boston College Lynch School of Education. Prior to her fellowship, she worked as an attorney at the Center for Law and Education, where she wrote analyses of key federal education legislation. She also represented low-income families and provided technical assistance to legal services and pro bono attorneys in a variety of education-related matters, including the rights of students with disabilities. Karger is a member of the professional advisory board of the National Center for Learning Disabilities and has served as a consultant for the National Center on Accessible Instructional Materials. Previously, she served on a team of consultants that evaluated the special education programs of New York City, the District of Columbia, and several low-income school districts in Massachusetts. Karger is the author of numerous publications focusing on the educational rights of children and youth. She has a law degree from Boston College Law School and a doctorate in education from the Harvard Graduate School of Education in administration, planning, and social policy.

Daniel J. Losen is the director of the Center for Civil Rights Remedies at the University of California, Los Angeles Civil Rights Project/Proyecto Derechos Civiles and a former lecturer at Harvard Law School. His work at the Civil Rights Project concerns the impact of federal, state, and local education law and policy on students of color. His most recent efforts have focused on addressing the school-to-prison pipeline and on implementation concerns about the No Child Left Behind Act.

Kavitha Mediratta is a program executive at The Atlantic Philanthropies and is responsible for the foundation's grant making to reform school discipline policies nationally. She was previously director of youth organizing and community organizing research at the Annenberg Institute for School Reform at Brown University. Her work in community organizing began in 1995 when she joined the staff of the Institute for Education and Social Policy at New York University. She developed and served as co-director of the institute's Community Involvement Program, overseeing policy analyses and technical assistance to education advocacy groups in New York City. Mediratta is the author of numerous publications, including *Community Organizing for Stronger Schools: Strategies and Successes* (Harvard Education Press, 2009). She has received several awards for her work, including the prestigious Warren Weaver fellowship at the Rockefeller Foundation and the Aspen Institute's nonprofit research fellowship. She has taught in elementary and middle public and private schools in New Jersey, Chicago, and India. She has a BA from Amherst College and a MEd from Columbia University's Teachers College and is currently working toward a PhD in education at New York University.

Erica R. Meiners is involved with a number of initiatives linked to justice, specifically antimilitarization campaigns, prison abolition movements, and queer and immigrant rights organizing. She is the author of *Right to Be Hostile: Schools, Prisons, and the Making of Public Enemies* (Routledge, 2007), *Flaunt It! Queers in the Struggle for Public Education and Justice* (Peter Lang, 2009), and articles in a range of publications, including *AREA Chicago, Radical Teacher, Meridians, Urban Review, Academe,* and *Women's Studies Quarterly.* A 2011–2012 visiting research faculty at the Institute for Research on Race and Public Policy at the University of Illinois at Chicago, Meiners is a member of the labor union and University Professionals of Illinois Local 4100 and is also a professor of education and gender and women's studies at Northeastern Illinois University.

Pedro A. Noguera is the Peter L. Agnew Professor of Education at New York University, where he holds tenured faculty appointments in the Departments of Teaching and Learning and Humanities and Social Sciences at the Steinhardt School of Culture, Education and Development. He is also the executive director of the Metropolitan Center for Urban Education and the codirector of the Institute for the Study of Globalization and Education in Metropolitan Settings. Noguera is the author of seven books and more than 150 articles and monographs. His most recent books are *Creating the Opportunity to Learn* (with A. Wade Boykin, ASCD, 2011) and *Invisible No More: Understanding and Responding to the Disenfranchisement of Latino Males* (with A. Hurtado and E. Fergus, Routledge, 2011). Noguera appears as a regular commentator on educational issues on CNN, NPR, and other national news outlets. He serves on the boards of numerous national and local organizations, including the Economic Policy Institute and *The Nation.* In 2009 he was appointed by the governor of New York to serve as a trustee for the State University of New York.

Sung-Joon Pai is in his thirteenth year working in the Boston Public Schools. He was a founding faculty member of the Boston Arts Academy, teaching science there for seven years. He then was the founding principal of the Media Communications Technology High School at the West Roxbury Educational Complex for four years. In 2010, Pai joined the administration at Charlestown High School as the director of ELL and Alternative Programs, where he is working to implement restorative disciplinary practices in the Diploma Plus program, an in-house alternative education option for students who have previous academic struggles.

Douglas W. Price has, for more than three decades, worked in education as a teacher and administrator in public and private schools as well as developed and presented classroom programs for the private sector. He is impressed every day with the respect, cooperation, and strong desire to learn and succeed that he sees in his students in his English classes at the Gordon Bernell Charter School in Albuquerque, NM. He tells his students that they have hard-earned wisdom and wonderful potential. His students prove to themselves that they are writers—a wonderful discovery that effectively supports the school's motto: Changing Lives from the Inside Out.

Elizabeth A. Reid is a student at Green River Community College and a former Guest Scholar at the University of Washington, where she was the recipient of the 2012 Martin Achievement Scholarship. She is currently preparing to transfer to the University of Washington, where she will major in English. After completing her undergraduate degree, she plans to attend law school. Her goal is to become an attorney specializing in social justice/public policy practice. Currently, she is an associate of the Post-Prison Education Program (PPEP) in Seattle, where the focus is placed on creating a "prison-to-school pipeline." PPEP works at outreach events in prisons to recruit future college students on release. Reid speaks at these events and other community forums in support of higher education in an attempt to reduce the cycle of recidivism. She also works with community groups reaching out to at-risk youth to help break the intergenerational cycle of imprisonment. She is one of the founding members of the Post-Prison Community Collaboration Project, in conjunction with the Honors Program at the University of Washington, which works in the community to educate citizens about the problems of mass incarceration, racial injustice, homelessness, mental illness, and the stereotypes held about those formerly incarcerated.

David H. Rose is a developmental neuropsychologist and educator whose primary focus is on the development of new technologies for learning. In 1984 he co-founded CAST, a not-for-profit research and development organization whose mission is to improve education for all learners through innovative uses of modern multimedia technology and contemporary research in the cognitive neurosciences. That work has grown into a new field called Universal Design for Learning, which now influences educational policy and practice throughout the United States and beyond. Rose also teaches at the Harvard Graduate School of Education, where he has been on the faculty for more than twenty-five years. He is the author of several scholarly books, numerous award-winning educational technologies, and dozens of chapters and research journal articles. He has been the principal investigator on grants and contracts from the National Science Foundation, the U.S. Department of Education, and many private foundations. Rose holds a BA in psychology from Harvard College, a master's in teaching from Reed College, and a doctorate from the Harvard Graduate School of Education.

Derek R. Russel says that "poetry all started with Lorca for me back in 2009. Since, I've dawdled from one cultural seaport to another—reading everything from Harfiz to Montale."

Michael Satterfield was born in Fayetteville, NC, but has lived in Germany, Georgia, and New Jersey. He has been incarcerated since April 2006 for two counts of armed robbery and is currently an inmate at the Garden State Youth Correctional Facility. He has worked as an apprentice cabinet installer, a bindery assistant at a print shop, a roofing apprentice, and at various odd jobs and, presently, as a teacher's assistant. Satterfield is currently working on an associate degree in liberal arts.

Hilary Shanahan, a native of Cambridge, MA, has been an urban public school teacher for the past eleven years, eight in the Boston Public School system. She came to restorative justice and circle practices by way of her school's commitment to finding a different way to solve conflict and lower the suspension rate of students in its building. Her most recent and most powerful connection to circle practices was teaching a class called Law and Justice, in which her students were trained in circle facilitation and ran a peer justice system solving schoolwide disciplinary problems in circles.

Peter Sipe teaches English at Boston Collegiate Charter School, having previously taught at elementary and middle schools in Brooklyn, Albany, and Seattle. Prior to becoming a teacher, he worked as a public health consultant in West Africa and as a refugee monitor in Rwanda.

Sabina E. Vaught is an associate professor of urban education at Tufts University, where she teaches courses on critical race theory, pedagogy, and the sociology of schooling in the Department of Education and the American Studies Program. Her scholarship examines the institutional contexts and dynamics of race, schooling, and power. Specifically, she has conducted institutional ethnographic studies in a large urban school district and in a state division of juvenile affairs and its prison schools. She is the author of *Racism, Public Schooling, and the Entrenchment of White Supremacy: A Critical Race Ethnography* (SUNY Press, 2011).

Alejandro G. Vera was born in Mexico City and brought to the United States at the age of two. "I grew up my whole life in San Anto, and as the oldest of six children born to first generation immigrants I learned everything through hard knocks at home and in school—but mostly on the streets. Nobody in my family has ever been to college or graduated and I hope to prove a lot of people wrong and be the first one. I feel my poetry is an extension of my beliefs and emotions harmonizing in an art form. Every poem is a peek of what goes on inside a revolutionary mind."

Anita Wadhwa is a doctoral student and instructor at the Harvard Graduate School of Education, where she studies restorative justice, zero tolerance discipline policies, and the school-to-prison pipeline. She is a former high school teacher from Houston, TX.

Lewis Wallace, a freelance writer and activist based in Chicago, began his activism in the late 1990s as a youth rabble-rouser and part of the Gay-Straight Alliance movement, cofounding a queer youth leadership program called Riot Youth in southeast Michigan. He has since worked as a sex educator, coffee slinger, freelance writer, anti-oppression trainer, child care provider, and curriculum developer on topics ranging from transphobia to the prison-industrial complex to medieval European history. His interest in restorative and transformative justice stems from a personal history of confronting issues of sexual assault and interpersonal violence within queer communities. Wallace began working with Project NIA in its early stages, helping to coordinate NIA's peacemaking circle trainings and volunteering in its peace room. In line with Project NIA's mission, he believes in working to end incarceration while also developing community-based forms of accountability and responses to harm. Wallace graduated from Northwestern University in 2010 with honors in religious studies. He is currently pursuing an ongoing study of the medieval bearded woman saint known as Wilgefortis, who was a patron saint of prisoners, unmarried women, and abuse survivors.

Robert Wilson, homeless at age sixteen, earned a GED from the Hispanic Education Program in Albuquerque, NM, while living in abandoned houses. During this time he discovered writers whose styles challenged him to seek out his own creative voice. Traveling and working numerous jobs, he never gave up on the idea of self-education. The Gordon Bernell Charter School helped transform Wilson's writing from a solitary endeavor to a gift he wishes to share with others. For the first time, he sees his situation as one of hope and his life as one of purpose; he feels he must redeem himself with worthwhile effort to eclipse his criminal history. Wilson is the proud father of Malcolm Aulbach-Wilson, a fifteen-year-old who attends the high school his father dropped out of. They read all of the same books. He plans to pursue an English degree and begin a career in grant writing. In the meantime, in jail, he has written over two million words. He has experienced the school-to-prison pipeline as a student and as a parent and hopes that this, his first published piece, will allow him to enter the conversation.

INDEX